Design and Analysis of Single-Case Research

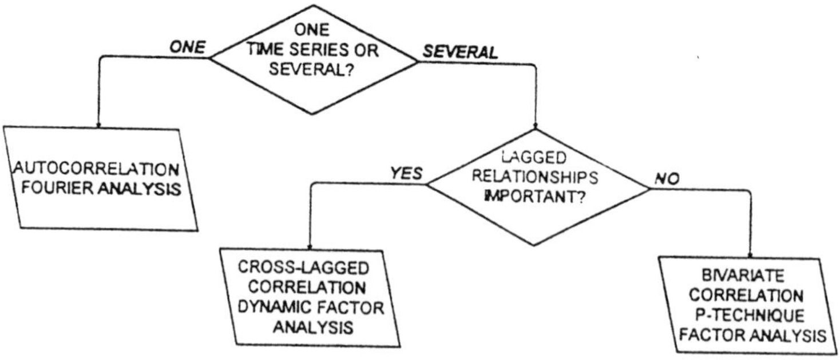

Correlational strategies.

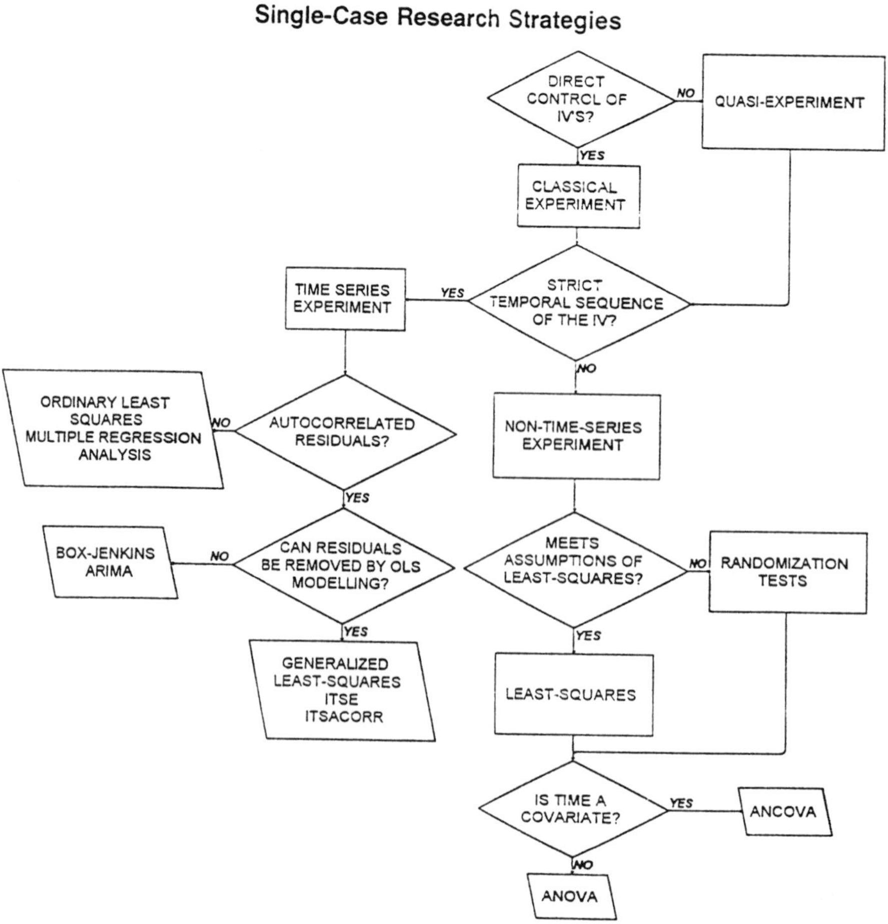

Experimental strategies.

Design and Analysis of Single-Case Research

Edited by

Ronald D. Franklin
The Child Development Center, St. Mary's Hospital

David B. Allison
New York Obesity Research Center, Columbia University College of Physicians and Surgeons

Bernard S. Gorman
Nassau Community College/SUNY and Hofstra University

LEA LAWRENCE ERLBAUM ASSOCIATES, PUBLISHERS
1997 Mahwah, New Jersey

Lawrence Erlbaum Associates, Inc.
10 Industrial Avenue
Mahwah, New Jersey 07430-2262

Cover design by Jessica LaPlaca

Library of Congress Cataloging-in-Publication-Data

Design and analysis of single-case research / edited by Ronald D. Franklin, David B. Allison, and Bernard S. Gorman.
p. cm.
Includes bibliographical references and index.
ISBN 0-8058-1618-6 (cloth : alk. paper). — ISBN 0-8058-1619-4 (pbk. : alk. paper)
1. Psychology—Research—Methodology. 2. Case Method. 3. Psychometrics. I. Franklin, Ronald D. II. Allison, David B. III. Gorman, Bernard S.
BF76.5.D38 1996
150'722—dc20 96-5883
CIP

Books published by Lawrence Erlbaum Associates are printed on acid-free paper, and their bindings are chosen for strength and durability.

Printed in the United States of America
10 9 8 7 6 5 4 3 2 1

Contents

Preface

A few years ago, at a meeting of the *American Psychological Association* (August, 1993), I was asked to be the discussant for a series of papers on new research designs for the analysis of single subject data. Some of these papers now appear as chapters in this book. For me, this was an unusual request for two reasons. First, I am a terrible discussant, often drifting far afield from the main topic of the papers at hand. Second, most of my previous research has centered on latent variable structural equation modeling of cognitive abilities using large population based sample (McArdle, 1994). However, as these presenters soon found out, I also advocate the use of more basic models using single subjects. This apparent contradiction on my part requires some further explanation.

The statistical features of the "law of large numbers" are well-known to the contemporary psychologists. In my first college level stats class (circa 1969), I learned the dictum, "odd things happen more often in small samples." Even though this principle is often misunderstood (see Nisbett, 1983), I was sure psychologists were mainly concerned with finding reliable and replicable results, so this was essential knowledge. In later classes on experimental design I learned that the surest way to achieve *significant* results was to have a very large sample (*N*); I think this early training accounts for much of my behavior today.

But then I went to graduate school (circa 1973), and things became more complicated. In my very first class I learned that some people had actually written papers on the benefits of what they called N = 1 designs. I was outspoken at this statistical heresy and I paid the price: I was forced (by Dr. Harold Yuker) to read and write about papers by Dukes (1965) and Shapiro (1964), a really difficult article by Rozeboom (1971), and something fairly new by Gottman (1973). I became aware of the importance of the "idiographic versus nomothetic" approaches to construct validation, and I began to understand the central concerns of "generalization" (Cronbach et al., 1972). Although I was respectful of clinical practice, I thought that people were so different from one another that no scientifically useful fact could be found using only one person. I scoffed at this research, took the vows of a different psychologist, and I denied my prior training in experimental psychology. But to be honest, I was pretty young and confused by all this methodological epistemology talk. Secretly, I vowed never to be so cocky about statistics again.

Like all good resolutions, this one passed quickly. In my postgraduate years (1977–1980) I learned to accept my internal conflicts by studying multivariate time series analysis. This was a decidedly eclectic combination of Cattell (1952), Anderson (1963), Lilly (1975), Hibbs (1977), and Huber (1977). After reading about Haldane's (1929) personal breathing experiments, I, like many before me, rushed to start making a statistical analysis of my own behaviors. I tried to take my own cognitive and mood measurements on a daily basis, using my new Apple and a program (PSYLOG) made expressly for me by a computer wiz friend of mine (Boker & McArdle, 1995). This proved to be way too time consuming for me, although I did try to make daily measurements on my wife and child (this lasted for only one weekend before they both stopped speaking to me).

My personal attempts to search for meaning in measurement were not a complete loss because they did alert me to what I now view as a critical statistical misunderstanding—the N in statistical data analysis is not the number of persons but the *density of observations*. The N we use can refer to the number of variables, the number of occasions, or any set of replicate samples from the larger data box (see Cattell, 1966). The law of large numbers suggests we collect a large number of data points, and especially some kind of replicates, but this does not always refer to subjects. Of course, as in any good experimental design, many levels of replication are important here, including the measurement of multiple occasions, multiple variables, and multiple experimental interventions (Nesselroade & Jones, 1991). I was hooked on this "radical" way of thinking and, as I confess here, I even carried out a multivariate structural modeling analysis of a single subject (McArdle, 1982; reported in Nesselroade & McArdle, 1985).

But enough about me, let me turn briefly to the good work of this book.

This book is about one important aspect of psychological research—the intensive study of people measured one (or more) at a time. Some important historical material is detailed in several chapters here, and this makes a strong connection to previous works in psychology. The authors of several chapters here present important details on classical and novel methods to study behavior over time, and they do so in the context of appropriate statistical methods. This appropriately reflects the growing interest in examining *dynamic* behaviors by objective behaviors by objective measurement. Key experimental design principles are expertly stated by these authors. This reflects the growing interest in studying the individual course of development for *invariants* in behaviors, including some unusual constructs (e.g., cycles, punctuated equilibria, etc.). This book also deals with practical contemporary problems in psychology. The increased possibility of using clinical research tools is well documented here. As you read this book I am sure you will be tempted to try some of these procedures out for yourself. In sum, this book is filled with interesting historical points, informative mathematical and statistical analyses, and practical methods.

These single-case designs can also be used in scientific work in psychology to help us better understand a critical data analysis assumption—often termed *homogeneity of variance* or, more generally, *homoskedasticity*. In data analyses with large numbers of subjects we routinely assume that the structural (regression) parameters are precisely equivalent or invariant across all our subjects; but we know this is not necessarily true. We use many well-known models in an attempt to test these assumptions: in regression, we examine subgroups or model interactions (Aitken & West, 1991); in factor analysis, we test hypotheses about factorial invariance (McArdle & Cattell, 1994); in multilevel analysis, we examine hypotheses about the impacts of the group variables on the changing regressions within the group (Longford, 1993). From this structural modeling perspective, then, single-case studies represent the natural extension of the mathematical and statistical study of heterogeneity.

Every science is defined to some degree by the objects of its study and the devices used to measure these objects. When we think about astronomy, we think about the planets and the stars viewed through telescopes. When we think about biology, we think about cells and virus viewed through microscopes. When we think about chemistry, we think about the elements and molecules viewed through test tubes. When we think about physics, we think about the traces of quarks and atoms viewed through cyclotrons. When we think about psychology, we think about people and persons viewed through objective measurement. If we do this with enough density of observations and replications, who knows—we might learn a great deal about some people, and we might even help create a science of psychology!

John J. McArdle
Charlottesville, Virginia
July, 1995

ACKNOWLEDGMENTS

The editors gratefully acknowledge software grants from the following:

Statistica/W
StatSoft
2325 E. 13th Street
Tulsa, OK 74104

STATA
Computing Resources Center
1640 5th Street
Santa Monica, CA 90401

Number Cruncher Statistical System
Pacific Ease Co.
601 Pacific Street
Santa Monica, CA 90405

STATlab
SciTech
2231 N. Clybourne Ave.
Chicago, IL 60614-3011

The editors initially planned an extensive software review, comparing packages and programs of interest to single subject and small N researchers. So many software revisions occurred during our editing process that we soon realized our analysis would be out-of-date before coming into print. Therefore, we opted to describe methods, rather than programs, in the text. Our hope is that readers can then use analysis methods available in these (and other) fine statistical packages to address their individual needs.

We appreciate the encouragement of Jack McArdle, Judith Amsel, and Kathleen Dolan, as well as the patience of our contributors.

Much of the data presented in chapter 5, "Graphics Analysis and Visual Display," and the practical clinical considerations presented therein, were gleaned from the work of behavior specialist supervisees of the senior author at South Florida State Hospital.

The authors of chapter 6, "Statistical Alternatives," wish to thank Myles Faith, Philip Good, Jack McArdle, David Rindskopf, and Richard Ittenbach for their ongoing commentary and support as the chapter emerged.

REFERENCES

Aiken, L. S., & West, S. G. (1991). *Multiple regression: Testing and interpreting interactions.* Newbury Park, CA: Sage.

Anderson, T.W. (1963). The use of factor analysis in the statistical analysis of multiple time series. *Psychometrika, 28*(1), 1–25.

Boker, S. M., & McArdle, J. J. (1995). *A psychotelemetry experiment in fluid intelligence.* (paper under review)

Cattell, R. B. (1952). P-technique factorization and the determination of individual dynamic structure. *Journal of Clinical Psychology, 8*(1), 5–10.

Cattell, R. B. (1966). *The handbook of multivariate experimental psychology.* Chicago: Rand McNally.

Cronbach, L. J., Gleser, G. C., Nanda, H., & Rajaratnam, N. (1972). *The dependability of behavioral measurements: Theory of generalizability for scores and profiles.* New York: Wiley.

Dukes, W. F. (1965). N = 1. *Psychological Bulletin, 64*(1), 74–79.
Gottman, J. M. (1973). N-of-one and N-of-two research in psychotherapy. *Psychological Bulletin, 80*, 93–105.
Haldane, J. S. (1929). Nonexperimental analysis from the general point of view of scientific method. *Bulletin of the International Statistical Institute, 42*(1), 391–424. (as reported by H. A. O. Wold, 1969).
Hibbs, D. A. (1977). On analyzing the effects of policy interventions. Box-Jenkins and box-Tiao vs. structural equation models. In D. R. Heise (Ed.), *Sociological Methodology*, 1976. San Francisco, CA: Jossey-Bass.
Huber, H. P. (1977). Single case analysis. *Behavioral analysis and modifications, 1*, 1–15.
Lilly, J. C. (1975). *Simulations of God: The science of belief.* New York: Simon & Schuster.
Longford, N. (1993). *Random coefficeint models.* Oxford: Clarendon Press.
McArdle, J. J. (1982). *Structural equation modeling applied to a case study of alcoholism.* National Institute on Alcohol Abuse and Alcoholism. (NIAAA No. AA05743)
McArdle, J. J. (1994). Structural factor analysis experiments with incomplete data. *Multivariate Behavioral Research, 29*(4), 409–454.
McArdle, J. J., & Cattell, R. B. (1994). Structural equation models of factorial invariance in parallel proportional profiles and oblique confactor problems. *Multivariate Behavioral Research, 29*(1), 63–113.
Nesselroade, J. R., & Jones, C. J. (1991). Multi-model selection effects in the study of adult development: A perspective on multivariate, replicated, single-subject, repeated measures designs. *Experimental Aging Research, 17*(1), 21–27.
Nesselroade, J. R., & McArdle, J. J. (1986). Multivariable causal modeling in alcohol use research. *Social Biology, 33*(4), 272–296.
Nisbett, R. (1983). Use of statistical heuristics in everyday inductive reasoning. *Psychological Review, 90*, 339–363.
Rozeboom, W. W. (1971). Scientific inference: The myth and the reality. In S. R. Brown & D. J. Brenner (Eds.), *Science, psychology and communication: Essays honoring William Stephenson.* New York: Academic Press.
Shapiro, M. B. (1964). The single case in fundamental psychological research. *Journal of Psychosomatic Research, 8*, 283–291.

Contributors

Vincent C. Alfonso holds an appointment as assistant professor at Fordham University Graduate School of Education where his research interests include psychoeducational assessment, preschool issues, and professional training. Concomitantly, he is a staff psychologist at the Crossroads School for Child Development. Dr. Alfonso has also held academic positions with St. Johns and Hofstra Universities. Additional applied appointments have included Milestone School for Child Development, Nassau Center for the Developmentally Disabled, and Adults and Children With Learning and Developmental Disabilities. His publications have appeared in *Behavior Genetics, School Psychology International, The Journal of Psychoeducational Assessment, School Psychology Review,* and *Psychology in the Schools.* Dr. Alfonso's presentations have appeared at The American Psychological Association, The American Psychological Society, The National Association of School Psychologists, and The American Association of Applied and Preventative Psychology. He has served as president of the School Division of the New York State Psychological Association and is a nominee for president of the School Psychologists Educators Council of New York State. Dr. Alfonso earned his PhD in clinical and school psychology from Hofstra University in 1990.

David B. Allison received an undergraduate degree from Vassar College and earned his PhD degree from the School of Psychology of Hofstra University, Hempstead, New York. He completed a postdoctoral fellowship in Behavioral Pediatrics at the Johns Hopkins School of Medicine and the Kennedy Institute. Dr. Allison completed a second postdoctoral fellowship at the New York Obesity Research Center at St. Luke's Roosevelt Hospital Center. He is currently the assistant professor of psychology in psychiatry at the New York Obesity Research Center in Columbia University College of Physicians and Surgeons. Dr. Allison has received several awards including those from the American Society for Clinical Nutrition and the Society for Behavioral Medicine. He is currently funded by the National Institute of Health to conduct research regarding the genetics of human obesity. He has published over fifty peer review articles in areas including obesity, behavior management, and statistics and research design.

T. Mark Beasley joined the faculty of St. John's University in 1993 after earning a PhD in statistics and measurement from Southern Illinois University. He also holds BA and MA degrees in psychology and clinical psychology from Middle Tennessee State University. Dr. Beasley was awarded membership in honor societies for psychology, sociology, and foreign language. He was nominated as outstanding graduate student in psychology at Middle Tennessee State University and for the outstanding dissertation award at Southern Illinois University. Educational Testing Service selected Dr. Beasley as a predoctoral intern where he formulated research hypotheses and analyzed data for the Advanced Placement examinations. He teaches program evaluation, advanced research design, statistics, and computer technology in education. Dr. Beasley's publications have appeared in *The Journal of Experimental Education, Multiple Regression Viewpoints, Journal of Clinical Psychology, Journal of Adolescence, Journal of Educational Research, Applied Psychological Measurement*, and others.

Miles S. Faith earned a BA in psychology from Rutgers University and his MA and PhD degrees from Hofstra University. He currently is an NIH fellow in the Department of Medicine and Columbia University's Obesity Research Center. He has published several articles and book chapters relating to body image, emotional caring, and psychological functioning among obese people. NATO awarded him a Young Investigator Award in 1993 and he received a Dissertation Award from the American Psychological Association in 1994. Dr. Faith completed an internship at the Institute for Rational Emotive Therapy and has served as a statistical and programming consultant for Consulnet Inc. He has authored many technical reports, presentations, and clinical workshops.

Ronald D. Franklin is president of The Center for Forensic and Neuropsychology. He also serves as neuropsychological consultant to Saint Mary's Hospital and Good Samaritan Hospital in West Palm Beach, Florida where he coordinates Behavioral Medicine. Other appointments have included senior psychologist at South Florida State Hospital and Mental Health Program Manager for the North Carolina Department of Correction. He has held adjunct academic appointments at Florida International University, Barry University, Florida Atlantic University, and Nova University. His undergraduate studies were concluded at East Carolina University and his PhD at North Carolina State University. Dr. Franklin completed a postdoctoral fellowship at The Johns Hopkins School of Medicine and The Kennedy Institute. He has published more than fifty articles and presentations. Dr. Franklin is a member of the American Psychological Association, The International Neuropsychological Society, and The National Academy of Neuropsychology. He is licensed in North Carolina and Florida where he is in full-time private practice.

Bernard S. Gorman received his PhD (1971) in Personality and Social Psychology from the City University of New York, and completed postdoctoral studies in psychotherapy at the Institute for Rational Emotive Therapy. He has written numerous articles and presented many convention papers in the areas of personality assessment, multivariate analysis, and relationships between cognition and affect. He co-authored the textbook *Developmental Psychology* (Van Nostrand, 1980) with Theron Alexander and Paul Roodin, and co-edited the research monograph, *The Personal Experience of Time* (Plenum, 1977) with Alden Wessman. He is the author of several instructional computer packages. He is professor of psychology and State University of New York Faculty Exchange Scholar at Nassau Community College/SUNY, where he teaches courses in clinical and developmental psychology. He also holds an adjunct professorship in Hofstra University's graduate psychology programs, where he teaches courses in multivariate statistical analysis, computer applications in psychology, and psychometrics. He combines his interests in measurement research, clinical issues, and teaching at Queens Children's Psychiatric Center, where he is a psychologist in the Quality Assurance and Program Evaluation Department. He's currently vice president of the Metropolitan New York Chapter of the American Statistical Association.

Kenneth M. Greenwood earned BB Sc. and PhD degrees in behavioral science from La Trobe University, Australia, along with a graduate diploma in computer sciences. He is registered as a psychologist in the state of Victoria and maintains membership in the Australian Psychological Society. Dr. Greenwood's publications address important issues of autocorrelation in time-series designs, psychometric properties in composite scaling, interpretation of interrupted time-series designs, and the effects of serial dependence on visual judgement. His papers have appeared in *Ergonomics, Behavioral Assessment, American Journal of Occupational Therapy, Journal of Applied Behavior Analysis, Australian Psychologist*, and others. Presently, he holds appointment as senior lecturer in the Department of Behavioural Health Sciences at La Trobe University, Bundoora, Australia.

Frank M. Gresham is a professor in the School of Education at the University of California in Riverside. His PhD comes from the Department of Psychology at the University of South Carolina. Professor

Greshamteaches quantative courses that include Methodology and Research Design, Advanced Psychometrics, and Applied Multivariate Statistics. Professional recognitions include election as a fellow in APA (divisions 16 and 5) and The American Psychological Society. He has directed more than 20 dissertations, published 28 books (including chapters, monographs, or tests), 75 refereed journal articles, and 11 review articles. Dr. Gresham serves on the editorial boards of *School Psychology Review, Journal of Learning Disabilities, Journal of School Psychology, School Psychology Quarterly, Learning Disability Quarterly, Journal of Emotional and Behavioral Disorders,* and others.

Richard F. Ittenbach is assistant professor of educational psychology at the University of Mississippi where he teaches statistics and research design. He received a BS degree in biology from Butler University, MEd in counseling from Auburn, and the PhD in educational psychology from The University of Alabama. Dr. Ittenbach completed postdoctoral study at the University of Minnesota where he taught psychoeducational assessment and coordinated computer and statistical support services in the University Affiliated Program for Persons with Developmental Disabilities. He is a member of many professional associations including the American Association for the Advancement of Science, American Association on Mental Retardation, American Statistical Association, and The American Psychological Association. He has co-authored two textbooks on mental retardation. He has written numerous articles on measurement and mental retardation, which appear in journals such as *School Psychology Review, Research in Developmental Disabilities, American Journal on Mental Retardation, Measurement and Evaluation in Counseling and Development, Educational and Psychological Measurement, Journal of School Psychology,* and *Journal of Counseling Psychology.*

William F. Lawhead is assistant professor of philosophy at The University of Mississippi, where he was recognized as Outstanding Teacher of the Year in 1988. He received his BA from Wheaton College and The University of Texas at Austin where he was awarded a PhD in philosophy in 1977. Dr. Lawhead has a strong academic publishing background, with his works appearing in *Teaching Philosophy, Religious Studies, Journal of Religion,* and *Ready Reference: Ethics.* He is also author of *The Voyage of Discovery: A History of Western Philosophy.* His nonacademic writings include a syndicated series for newspapers addressing medical ethics, "Hospitals and Value Decisions." Dr. Lawhead's work has been presented to the Mississippi Philosophy Association, Mid-South Philosophy Conference, and Mississippi's Department of Health Care Administration. He is past president of The Mississippi Philosophical Association.

Thomas A. Matyas received a BA with honors from the University of New South Whales and the PhD from Macquarie University, Australia. He is a member of the Australian Psychological Society. Dr. Matyas has published extensively on the topics of statistical conclusion validity, autocorrelation in statistical time-series, and the analysis of single case time series. He has also used single-case methodology in research on restoration of sensory and motor functions after brain damage. He has been repeatedly published in journals which have shown a concern for single case methodology or its application to physical medicine and rehabilitation, such as *Journal of Applied Behavior Analysis, Archives of Physical Medicine and Rehabilitation, Behavioral Assessment, American Journal of Physical Medicine, Physical Therapy,* and the *Australian Journal of Physiotherapy.* He has been selected to review manuscripts on single case methodology or employing single case methodology for several journals including the *Psychological Bulletin.* He currently holds the appointment of Reader in the School of Behavioural Health Sciences, Faculty of Health Sciences, at La Trobe University in Melbourne, Australia.

Louis H. Primavera became a professor at St. John's University in 1987 where he teaches univariate and miltivariate statistics, psychometrics, scaling, and experimental design. He is currently Associate Dean of the Graduate School of Arts and Sciences. Dr. Primavera obtained his doctorate from the City University of New York and Masters from Queens College. Professor Primavera has taught at Hofstra University, St. Francis College, Long Island University, Malloy College, Nassau Community College, Queens College, and St. Albert's College in addition to St. Johns. Moreover, Dr. Primavera recently served as Director of Research at the Derner Institute of Adelphi University, Coordinator of Research at the St. John's Psychological Services Center, and as a Research and Statistical Consultant to Marketing Analysts, Inc. Earlier experiences include consultantships to many agencies and organizations such as The Hay Group, Inc., Long Island Research Institute, Creedmoor Psychiatric Center, RCA Service Company, College Careers Program, Continental Can Company, and the New York City Board of Education. He is licensed in New York and a member of many professional organizations including the American Psychological Association and the Psychometric Society.

Professor Primavera has published 2 books of readings, 2 book chapters, and more than 90 articles, presentations, and workshops. His works appear in *Evaluation and Psychological Measurement, Psychological Reports, The Journal of Psychology, Psychology in the Schools, Journal of Consulting and Clinical Psychology, Behavioral Psychiatry, Professional Psychology,* and *Journal of Clinical Psychology.* Professor Primavera is qualified as an expert witness in statistics by the New York Supreme Court and has served as a reviewer for The American Psychological Association, Academic Press, Random House, Mayfield Publishing Company, and McGraw Hill.

Jay M. Silverstein is a licensed psychologist and clinical director of the Crossroads School for Child Development. He holds appointments as adjunct professor of graduate psychology at Fordham, Pace, and St. John's Universities. Dr. Silverstein is the author of numerous presentations, peer review journal articles, and workshops. He has worked for over 5 years with young children, adolescents, and families, and supervises psychologists, social workers, and graduate interns.

List of Equations

1

Introduction

Ronald D. Franklin, PhD
Center for Forensic and Neuropsychology, Boca Raton FL
Saint Mary's Hospital, West Palm Beach FL

David B. Allison, PhD
Obesity Research Center
St. Luke's/Roosevelt Hospital Center
Columbia University College of Physicians and Surgeons

Bernard S. Gorman, PhD
Nassau Community College
Hofstra University

INTRODUCTION

Scientific knowledge includes two paths, *deductive reasoning* and *inductive reasoning*. The former involves logical proofs and deductions and is not the subject of this volume. The latter involves drawing inferences from experiences and empirical data. Within the empirical method, there are both observational (sometimes called *correlational*) studies and experimental studies. Although both kinds of studies are essential to scientific progress, experimental studies generally play a greater role in the evaluation of interventions and therefore are the primary (although not exclusive) focus of this book.

Some authors reserve the term *experiment* for those studies in which experimenters assign observations *randomly* to different levels of the treatment (independent variable). Here, we use the term in a more liberal sense by defining an *experiment* as any study in which the experimenter manipulates the independent variable, even if assignment is not random.

Virtually all scientists and most clinicians have had at least one course in research methods and in that course have learned a bit about experimental design. The overwhelming majority of time spent on design probably involved discussion of "group designs" in which researchers group *n* subjects within *k* different conditions or "treatments." Sometimes scientists include a "within-subjects" component, allowing subjects to receive more than one treatment, perhaps in differing orders (e.g., crossover designs; for a review of group-based experimental designs, see Winer et al., 1991).

Fewer scientists and clinicians receive exposure to an alternative paradigm of experimental design—single-case research. Single-case designs (also known as "single-subject designs" and "*N*-of-1 trials") appear most prevalently in research conducted by psychologists and educators and are the primary means of inference in applied behavior analysis. The use of these designs has a long history (see Ittenbach & Lawhead, chap. 2, this volume) but have their recent origins in the writings of Skinner (1953) and Sidman (1960).

Although single-case designs have strong roots in psychology, the fields of education, rehabilitation, sport and athletic performance, and medicine also find them useful (Estrada & Young, 1993; Kearns et al., 1992; Williams, 1992). Their use aids in the analysis of treatments ranging from visual feedback to improve balance in stroke patients (de Weerdt, Crossley, Lincoln, & Harrison, 1989) to pharmacological agents (Jones, Ghannan, Nigg, & Dyer, 1993) and dependent variables ranging from self-injury (Iwata, Dorsey, Slifer, Bauman, & Richman, 1994) to written and oral reading (Sugishita, Seki, Kobe, & Yunoki, 1993).

WHY SINGLE-CASE DESIGNS?

Both single-case and group-based designs have their advantages and disadvantages, with neither being universally better than the other. Throughout this book we highlight contexts in which single-case designs may be preferable. Single-case designs present advantages in three situations.

First, research funds are scarce, especially for people working in private practice or small clinical settings. Nevertheless, many clinicians pursue a scientist–practitioner model. Single-case designs offer individual clinicians, working alone or in small groups with individual patients, the opportunity to contribute important findings to the scientific knowledge base. Their work can provide important benefits to their patients at a much lower cost than most group designs. Because of their generally lower costs, single-case designs can also be useful in the early stages of group research as a means of generating pilot data.

Second, single-case designs are helpful when one wishes to intensely study the *process* of change. By taking many measurements over time, the single-case researcher can observe dynamic aspects of change over time.

Finally, in much clinical work the crucial question is "Does the treatment work for *this* patient," not "Does the treatment work for the *average* patient?" Group designs, well suited to answering the latter question, ignore the former. Only single-case designs allow rigorous objective experimental assessment of the efficacy of treatment for the individual.

THE NEED FOR THE PRESENT VOLUME

For most researchers who wish to conduct single-case studies, their first exposure to scientific training probably consisted of undergraduate and graduate courses that emphasized controlled laboratory experimentation. Students were typically introduced to the canons of research design through classic texts like Campbell and Stanley (1966), Underwood (1986), or Stevens (1986). Each of these books discussed threats to the validity of experimental findings, and advocated manipulation of independent variables, tight control for unwanted variation, and random assignment of subjects to treatment conditions. Students were shown how to analyze experimental results by analysis of variance through textbooks like Keppel (1982), Kirk (1968), Maxwell and Delaney (1993), and Winer et al. (1991). Teachers likely introduced psychometric theory and measurement issues through books like Cronbach et al. (1972). In all, traditional education prepared students to conduct research in controlled laboratory studies with large samples, or to carry out large-scale correlational studies using standardized, normed, reliable tests.

Although they had classical experimental training, most neophyte clinical researchers soon faced the realization that the world of meaningful clinical research often was far from the ideals of classical experimentation. In fact, single-case literature, especially work that came from behavior modification approaches, seemed to lead a life of its own!

Authors like Barlow and Hersen (1984), Kazdin (1982), and Johnston and Pennypacker (1980) preserved many of the traditional canons of good research design but downplayed many other aspects of traditional research. For example, following the leads of Skinner (1953) and Sidman (1960) there were strong preferences on visual graphic inspection of results and skepticism about the value of rigorous quantitative techniques (e.g., Parsonson & Baer, 1978). For many, the topic of measurement reliability often referred to percentages of rater agreement—an approach that modern psychometric research and theories demonstrates is fraught with problems.

In some ways, the present volume is both conservative and innovative. It is conservative because we aim to incorporate traditional issues of solid experimental design, psychometrically sound measurement procedures, adequate sample sizes, and statistical analysis methods that are appropriate to the questions posed. It is innovative to the degree that the book presents readers with state-of-the-art developments in measurement, statistical power analysis, treatment integrity, visual inspection, the effects of confounds like cyclicity and autocorrelation, and the use of meta-analytic approaches to synthesize single-case findings.

Although the book addresses research design issues, it is not a design monograph per se. In fact, we encourage readers to use Barlow and Hersen (1984) and Kazdin (1982) for that purpose. Rather, here we intend to provide a bridge between the world of scientific research and the pragmatic, "hands-on" world of single-case clinical research and practice. We have taken care in writing this book at a level that should be accessible to advanced undergraduates, graduate students, practitioners, and researchers.

A BRIEF REVIEW

Historical and Philosophical Foundations

In chapter 2, Ittenbach and Lawhead provide an historical overview of social science research, including single-case research, that represents a subspecialty of the broader field of scientific research. As such, single-case methods may be considered a synthesis of contributions from personalities spanning as many disciplines of thought as the 50 centuries of its documentation. Beginning with the emergence of scientific thought, Ittenbach and Lawhead present developmental milestones leading into the current era of experimental methods, dividing the development into four ages: Early Scrutiny, Protected Learning, Enlightened Spirit, and Foundations for a New Science.

Measurement of Dependent Variables

In chapter 3, Primavera, Allison, and Alfonso address one of the few clear commonalities between traditional practitioners of single-case and group research—the concern with dependent variable measurement. However, the measurement approaches adopted by practitioners of these two methods are often very different. For example, in applied behavioral analysis (ABA), there is an exceptionally strong concern with reliability, but ABA advocates implicitly assume that validity is a necessary consequence of reliability. Behavioral observations are the common stuff of dependent variables in ABA and "reliability" usually (although not always) has some form of interrater agreement. Authors keep the quantitative level simple, percentages are common, and data are often treated as though they were on a ratio scale (in actuality, they may not be).

In contrast, scientists trained in the psychometric tradition generally consider reliability a necessary but insufficient condition for validity. They often express reliability and validity in correlation-based metrics under the assumption that variables are measured on interval or ordinal scales, and that relative position is more important than absolute position. By distinguishing between the *construct* and the *measurement* taken, they employ a latent variable model so popular among psychometricians today.

Primavera et al. show how many concepts and metrics developed by psychometricians can be applied to data from single-case designs. In assessing reliability they consider interobservor agreement, reproducibility, and internal consistency independently, offering instructions for the computation of each. Also, Primavera et al. discuss the nature and control of observer drift and other forms of bias. Additionally, they discuss methods for forming composites of dependent variables, a topic traditionally neglected by single-case methodologies. Finally, Primavera, Allison, and Alfonso provide an enlightening review of time sampling. The authors review extant methods, providing definitions, advantages, disadvantages, and implementation of each.

Treatment Integrity in Single-Subject Research

In chapter 4, Frank Gresham explains that despite behavioral scientists' longstanding concern with the reliability and validity of their dependent variables, until recently researchers gave little attention to the "validity" of independent variables. The term *treatment integrity* refers to the actual occurrence of the treatment (independent variable) as designed and intended (Yeaton & Sechrest, 1991). For example, if an experimenter intends to study the effects of reinforcement delivered on a fixed ratio schedule, but the experimenter's staff deliver the reinforcer inconsistently, there is little treatment integrity and the results of the study will say little about the effects of fixed ratio reinforcement. Gresham's chapter presents the major topical concerns in four sections.

First, Gresham explains the importance of treatment integrity. In practical terms, he discloses relationships between treatment integrity and the classes of variables under study. Second, he presents recent findings on the prevalence (or lack of it) of treatment integrity assessments. From these findings he describes factors that relate to the integrity of treatment. Third, Gresham considers methods for conceptualizing and assessing treatment integrity. Specification and definition of treatment components, interpretation of treatment integrity data, and psychometric issues in assessing treatment integrity receive thorough discussion. Finally, Gresham offers recommendations for promoting treatment integrity.

Graphical Display and Visual Analysis

We must communicate our research findings with others if they are to benefit from our work. Graphic presentation of data has a long and strong history in single-case research. With the evolution of desktop publishing, our capacity for visual presentation has mushroomed. In chapter 5, Franklin, Gorman, Beasley, and Allison review basic tenets of visual display and discuss important ideas that remain the mainstay of graphics in single-case research. They also present newer techniques, advanced by creative explorations with graphics computer displays. Included are basic time series graphs, smoothing, autocorrelation graphs, and fourier analysis and spectral density graphs.

Franklin et al. also challenge traditional views of inferential error associated with evaluation of the single case via visual inspection. The chapter reviews empirical findings of Type I error rates appearing in published literature that show that Type I errors may be much greater than generally believed. The authors review data on the reliability of visual inspection and discuss the highly subjective nature of visual inspection as an analytic strategy. On these bases, the authors recommend using visual inspection as an adjunct to statistical analysis and not a replacement.

Statistical Alternatives for Single-Case Designs

Visual analysis can often provide researchers and their readers with snapshot views of the treatment course. Still, reliance on visual analysis alone is insufficient because it does not permit researchers to establish whether interventions have produced change at greater than chance levels. Also, visual analyses provide no indices of the strengths of effects in forms suitable for evaluation with meta-analytic techniques.

In chapter 6, Gorman and Allison acquaint readers with a variety of quantitative time series approaches that have appeared in the psychometrics, business forecasting, and industrial quality control literature. Most psychological researchers will have some familiarity with the ordinary least-squares regression (OLS) techniques. This chapter shows the conditions under which OLS is feasible, but it also emphasizes the possibility that OLS techniques can produce seriously misleading results when researchers violate the assumptions behind OLS. The chapter progresses from least-squares approaches to modified least-squares approaches and then to statistical models that fall outside the boundaries of the least-square formulation.

Their goal is to help readers become sophisticated consumers of time series techniques. To do this, the level of presentation focuses on rationales for quantitative methods. Gorman and Allison present many brief examples about strengths and weaknesses of each approach discussed. Although the level of mathematical reasoning is high, formulas are few and readers with minimal undergraduate psychology or education statistics preparation should have no difficulty with this chapter. The authors refer readers to specialized textbooks, articles, and computer software should they wish to explore these techniques in greater depth.

The techniques presented in this chapter include ordinary least-squares regression-discontinuity approaches, modified least-squares methods, Box-Jenkins ARIMA models, models borrowed from statistical quality control, sequential analysis methods, randomization models, and P-technique factor analysis. Each technique includes examples suitable for single-case analysis.

Serial Dependency in Single-Case Time Series

Controversy surrounds the presence and the effects of autocorrelation and serial dependency in single-case designs. Huitema (1985) argued that autocorrelation is a "myth" in behavioral data, a claim that provoked many counterarguments (e.g., Suen & Ary, 1989). In chapter 7, Matyas and Greenwood review the findings and criticisms of earlier studies on autocorrelation. From original research, they show that serial dependency in published literature is common and can have profound effects on inferences gleaned from single-case designs. They observe that much work lies ahead because the debate to date has centered on whether a null hypothesis could be sustained in the presence of lag 1 autocorrelation. The effects of other levels of autocorrelation (i.e., lag 2, 3, etc.) remain for consideration.

Meta-Analysis of Single-Case Research

Until recently, meta-analyses excluded single-case studies. Drawing on recent literature, in chapter 8 Faith, Allison, and Gorman present an overview of meta-analytic techniques, providing emphasis on problems unique to single-subject research. They discuss methods and limitations of calculating effect size with the single subject, advantages and disadvantages of proposed strategies, and potential solutions to problems of evaluation.

From a general review of the use of meta-analysis, Faith et al. provide a discussion of the limitations of traditional meta-analytic formula for single-case designs. They highlight the importance of effect size, and give formulae for its computation. Percentage of nonoverlapping data, percent zero data, trend analysis, and regression models constitute the core of single-case methods reviewed. The authors present new formulae that overcome some limitations inherent in earlier models but argue that much work remains to be done in this area.

Faith et al. describe methods for obtaining and preparing single-case data for meta-analysis. They describe methods for overcoming common deficiencies of statistical reporting in published research and methods for extracting raw data from graphs in single-case studies.

The Potentially Confounding Effects of Cyclicity: Identification, Prevention, and Control

In chapter 9, Beasley, Allison, and Gorman consider how cyclicity may confound the evaluation of treatment effects in single-case designs. They argue that the probability of confounding is related to the phase change criteria used. The authors present three heuristics for making phase change decisions: (a) "predetermination" of the order and length of phases, (b) determination of phase changes based on the data as they are collected, and (c) randomization.

Using published single-case designs as examples, Beasley et al. show how cyclicity can confound experimenter interpretation. They present the presence of biological rhythms, cyclically chained responses, and institutional schedules affecting reinforcement as influential patterns that may produce cyclical variation in studies of human subjects. They present methods for uncovering cyclicity and evaluating data when cyclicity is present.

Power, Sample Size Estimation, and Early Stopping Rules

In chapter 10, Allison, Silverstein, and Gorman argue that either excessive or insufficient data collection creates an unethical waste of time and other resources. They present power analysis as a mechanism for minimizing such waste. Jacob Cohen, who began writing about power analysis approximately 30 years ago (Cohen, 1965), popularized its importance in research design. Then, Cohen showed that most psychological researchers obtained very low power. Since then, theoreticians elaborated methodologies for conducting power analyses. Several excellent texts exist (e.g., Cohen, 1988; Kraemer & Thieman, 1987; Lipsey, 1990), and useful software has become available.

However, the key question in power analysis is often erroneously construed to be "How many subjects?" More aptly, the question should be "How many observations?" Thus, the issue of power analysis has been almost completely ignored in single-case research. Chapter 10 presents a simple and concise description of power analysis for single-case designs. The authors also describe how to conduct power analyses for a variety of situations and provide tables and software options to simplify the computation.

In clinical trials, it is desirable to end the trial as soon as possible. Not only do trials consume resources, but it is important to provide the client access to the best treatment (and freedom from inferior treatments) as soon as possible. A traditional strength of ABA has been the practitioner's capacity for systematically and quantitatively evaluating treatment in progress. Practitioners' use of response-guided experimentation has allowed them the flexibility to end or change trials as necessary as the data were collected. Still, response-guided experimentation produces inferential problems. Authors advance the early stopping rule as a formalization of response-guided experimentation that maintains control of the Type I error rate.

FUTURE DIRECTIONS

We hope that the information and ideas compiled in this volume help investigators make valid, sophisticated, and informative use of single-case research. Yet, areas needing further development remain. Of primary importance, stressed in most of the presented chapters, is the need for practitioners of single-case research to collect greater numbers of observations. From the perspectives of power analysis, statistical testing, cyclicity assessment, providing effect sizes for meta-analysis, and even producing more reliable inferences from visual inspection, the need for more observations is clear. Second, practitioners need more effective means for dealing with autocorrelation. As several chapters point out, autocorrelation remains a problem for most statistical and meta-analytic techniques and even stymies visual inspection. Our understanding of autocorrelation beyond lag one remains largely speculative. Third, the validity of visually interpreted data remains unproven. Fourth, computer software programs (Statistica/W, SYSTAT, etc.) are beginning to merge visual and statistical methods, but practitioners need more intuitive user interfaces. Finally, practitioners need more flexible statistical methods that are easier to understand and use when observations must be limited.

The common connection between these five basic needs is the schism that has developed between proponents of visual and statistical analysis models. The advancement of science is more likely when persons holding opposing views of reality drink from the pierian[1] spring together. We hope this book is a step in that direction, but success will depend on the creativity and industriousness of future investigators.

REFERENCES

Barlow, D. H., & Hersen, M. (1984). *Single case experimental designs* (2nd ed.). New York: Pergammon Press.

Campbell, D. T., & Stanley, J. C. (1966). *Experimental and quasi-experimental designs for research.* Skokie, IL: Rand McNally.

Cohen, J. (1965). Some statistical issues in psychological research. In B. B. Wolman (Ed.), *Handbook of clinical psychology* (p. 95). New York: McGraw-Hill.

Cohen, J. (1988). *Statistical power analysis for the behavioral sciences.* Hillsdale, NJ: Lawrence Erlbaum Associates.

Cronbach, L. J., Gleser, G. C., Nanda, H., & Rajaratnam, N. (1972). *The dependability of behavioral measurements: Theory of generalizability for scores and profiles.* New York: Wiley.

de Weerdt, W., Crossley, S. M., Lincoln, N. B., & Harrison, M. A. (1989). Restoration of balance in strokes patients: A single case design study. *Clinical Rehabilitation,* 3(2), 139–147.

Estrada, C. A., & Young, M. J. (1993). Patient preferences for novel therapy: An *N*-of-1 trial of garlic in the treatment of hypertension. *Journal of General Internal Medicine, 8*(11), 619–621.

Huitema, B. E. (1985). Autocorrelation in applied behavior analysis: A myth. *Behavioral Assessment, 7,* 107–118.

Iwata, B. A., Dorsey, M. F., Slifer, K. J., Bauman, K. E., & Richman, G. S. (1994). Toward a functional analysis of self-injury. *Journal of Applied Behavior Analysis, 27*(2), 197–210.

Johnston, J. M., & Pennypacker, H. S. (1980). *Strategies and tactics of human behavioral research.* Hillsdale, NJ: Lawrence Erlbaum Associates.

Jones, E. E., Ghannam, J., Nigg, J. T., & Dyer, J. F. (1993). A paradigm for single-case research: The time series study of a long-term psychotherapy for depression. Special section: Single-case research in Psychotherapy. *Journal of Clinical & Consulting Psychology, 61*(3), 381–394.

Kazdin, A. E. (1982). *Single case research designs. Methods for clinical and applied settings.* New York: Oxford University Press.

Keppel, G. (1982). *Design and analysis: A researcher's handbook* (2nd ed.). Englewood Cliffs, NJ: Prentice-Hall.

Kirk, R. E. (1968). *Experimental design: Procedures for the behavioral sciences.* Belmont, CA: Brooks/Cole.

---

[1]Representing the fount of knowledge, from Alexander Pope's *An Essay on Criticism,* circa 1715.

Kraemer, H. C., & Thieman, S. (1987). *How many subjects? Statistical power analysis in research*. Newbury Park, CA: Sage.

Lipsey, M. W. (1990). *Design sensitivity. Statistical power for experimental research*. Newbury Park, CA: Sage.

Maxwell, S. E., & Delaney, H. D. (1993). Bivariate median splits and spurious statistical significance. *Psychological Bulletin, 113*, 181–190.

Parsonson, B. S., & Baer, D. M. (1978). The analysis and presentation of graphic data. In T. R. Kratochwill (Ed.), *Single subject research* (pp. 101–163). New York: Academic Press.

Sidman, S. M. (1960). *Tactics of scientific research: Evaluating experimental data in psychology*. New York: Basic Books.

Skinner, B. F. (1953). *Science and human behavior*. New York: Free Press.

Stevens, J. (1986). *Applied multivariate statistics for the social sciences*. Hillsdale, NJ: Lawrence Erlbaum Associates.

Suen, H. K., & Ary, D. (1989). *Analyzing quantitative behavioral observation data*. Hillsdale, NJ: Lawrence Erlbaum Associates.

Sugishita, M., Seki, K., Kabe, S., & Yunoki, K. (1993). A material control single-case study of the efficacy of treatment for written oral naming difficulties. *Neuropsychologia, 31*(6) 559–569.

Underwood, B. A. (1986). Evaluating the nutritional status of individuals: A critique of approaches. *Nutrition Reviews Supplement*, 213–224.

Winer, B. J., Brown, D. R., & Michels, K. M. (1991). *Statistical principles in experimental design* (3rd ed.). New York: McGraw-Hill.

Yeaton, W., & Sechrest, L. (1991). Critical dimensions in the choice and maintenance of successful treatments: Strength, integrity, and effectiveness. *Journal of Consulting and Clinical Psychology, 49*, 156–167.

2

Historical and Philosophical Foundations of Single-Case Research

Richard F. Ittenbach
William F. Lawhead
Educational Psychology Program
and Department of Philosophy and Religion
The University of Mississippi

Scientific research consists of a vast number of contributions throughout history. Each contribution to the broader fabric of science represents a blend of personalities and perspectives over time. Additionally, many individuals and movements are responsible for the principles and practices of what have now come to be known as *research design*. Two factors stand out as particularly important in the evolution of the design and analysis of all types of research: better methods for controlling the performance of variables of interest and improved mathematical modelling of behavioral phenomena. Yet, large-group research designs, designs for which most developments and issues have emanated, actually originated in the study of the individual.

Single-subject research, a subcategory of social science research, may well be the point of origin for all scientific research. As early as 2500 BC, politicians and mercantilists struggled with the notion of dividing human labor based on people's skills and abilities. More recently, single-subject research, in union with new developments in statistical methodology and computer technology, has been used to better understand the patterns of individuals' behaviors well beyond what was thought possible only a few decades ago.

The purpose of the present chapter is to lay the foundation for a more complete discussion of research designs in general and single-subject research designs in particular by tracing the evolution of scientific thought from the earliest of times to the design-related issues of today. To achieve this end, the material in this chapter has been organized into five subsections: age of early scrutiny, age of protected learning, an enlightened spirit, foundation for a new science, and essentials of experimentation.

AGE OF EARLY SCRUTINY

Foundations of Measurement

A discussion of research design should not begin without brief discussions of the history of science and the origins of measurement. Before behaviors can be analyzed, observationally or mathematically, the values of those behaviors must first be measured with a known degree of accuracy. Measurement is the process by which numerical values are applied to the characteristics of people, places, or conditions according to a logically agreed-on rule. In short, blue eyes have been labeled as blue and poor people as poor based on socially and scientifically agreed-on rules of observation.

Very early in recorded history, approximately 3000 BC, life was exceptionally demanding. People looked to science, magic, and religion in an attempt to understand how nature and the universe operated. In this era, fixed units of measurement, however modest, were standardized and used to better understand the world around them. For the Babylonians, the standard unit of length was the finger, with a foot equal to 20 fingers and a cubit equal to 30 fingers. Multiplication tables complete with squared and cubed values have been identified on Babylonian tablets dating to 2500 BC. Although the concepts of day and month were in place by 4000 BC, it was not until nearly 2000 BC that a year was believed to consist of 12 months and 360 days (Dampier, 1948). As primitive as these measures appear, one might quickly conclude that profound scientific principles were still several millennia away. However, this was not the case. With the development of formal measurement came signs that formal science was already emerging.

By 2200 BC, measurement applications extended beyond the units of time, length, and space to the classification of goods and services based on the skills and abilities of people. According to Wainer (1990), formalized testing procedures began in China during the Chan Dynasty (c. 1115 BC) to determine who was best suited for public service, similar in many ways to the notion of a civil service exam today. There is even evidence in the Old Testament of standardized methods of assessment. Two examples stand out as most relevant here. In the first, Jephthah, leader of the Gileadites, suspected the presence of Ephraimite infiltrators and asked that all soldiers be presented with the same request—to say the word *Shibboleth*. Those who could say the *sh* sound were considered to be Gileadites. Those who could not say the *sh* sound (and, instead, mispronounced the word as *Sibolleth*) were executed—some 42,000 in all (Judges 12:1–7). In the second example, Gideon was instructed by God to thin the ranks of his army prior to battle with the Midianites. Consequently, Gideon first asked anyone who was afraid of battle to leave their ranks. Gideon then tested those who remained by asking them to drink from the Jordan river. Approximately 300 soldiers raised the water to their mouths with their hands, their heads up and their eyes open. Those who placed their heads over the water and "lapped up the water like a dog" were dismissed (Judges 7:1–8). Even at this very early time in recorded history, it was understood that observations made about performances under controlled conditions could be generalized to performances occurring in less formal settings (H. Wainer, personal communication, December 17, 1993).

Reality and Reason

There is little evidence of either scientific or philosophical attempts to theorize rationally about reality before the 6th century BC. The early Greeks explained natural events as either the product of random, inexplicable forces or as the equally unpredictable will of the gods. According to their mythical accounts, the gods' actions were often impulsive, making it useless to search for a rational explanation of natural events. In 585 BC, a Greek thinker by the name of Thales predicted a solar eclipse after making careful observations of the heavens. Thales realized that such events were the product of a consistent, natural order that could be studied and made the basis of generalizations and predictions. His scientific successes gave him the philosophical courage to speculate on the very essence of reality.

Thales represents a significant turning point in Western intellectual history, because he did not appeal to tradition or the stories of the gods to support his theories. Instead, he offered his opinions to public scrutiny, allowing his ideas to stand or fall on their own merits. Consequently, his successors critiqued his ideas and offered competing accounts of their own. In this way, the early Greek thinkers began to wrestle with the foundational concepts of truth and reality (Ittenbach & Swindell, 1993). From the womb of this spirit of inquiry and argument, both science and philosophy were conceived. Of all these early theories, it is the work of Pythagoras (c. 515 BC) and the Pythagoreans that is most relevant for students of research today. For the Pythagoreans, numbers constituted the basis of all things. Although their mathematical research was motivated by religious mysticism, they introduced the notion that reality is best understood through quantification. The Pythagorean Theorem is one example of their lasting influence.

What the early Greeks lacked in technical sophistication they made up for in their efforts to explain observable events in nature using general laws. For example, Anaximenes (c. 545 BC) is credited with the first scientific experiment of recorded history (Lawhead, 1996). He found that changing the shape of one's mouth produced changes in the temperature of the air one exhaled. In short, he found that quantitative changes in performance produced qualitative changes in an event. It was nearly a century later when Empedocles (c. 450 BC) began unraveling the complexities of causality. In his efforts to explain change in both form and movement, Empedocles believed that two offsetting forces, love and hate, were responsible for causing change. That is, love provided the forces necessary to draw such elements as earth, air, fire, and water together, whereas hate provided the negative forces necessary to move these elements apart.

Origins of Western Thought

Few people in the history of the Western world hold the prominence of Socrates, Plato, and Aristotle. Although their direct influence on those around them spanned only approximately 125 years, their indirect influence has been so profound as to influence many of the principles and practices of modern life. Whether one is interested in the mechanics of everyday living or the principles of scientific scrutiny, these early Greek thinkers established the ground rules for contemporary scientific inquiry.

Socrates (c. 470–399 BC) was a marketplace philosopher who left no written records of his ideas. What is known about Socrates comes through others' writings, such as those of Plato and Aristotle. In contrast to the Sophists (Socrates' immediate philosophical predecessors, who believed it was impossible for people to know anything), Socrates believed in fixed and stable truths. For Socrates, pursuing truth meant pursuing knowledge, a knowledge that was synonymous with virtue and that, if found, would provide the foundation for a good life.

Pursuit of knowledge was not to be taken lightly, however, and was possible only through thoughtful and disciplined inquiry. Knowledge was discovered within the soul and made explicit through discussion and rigorous questioning. This method is known today as the Socratic (or Dialectic) method. The Socratic method consists of a series of repetitions in which an initial opinion is subjected to criticism, modified, and then subjected to criticism again, ultimately leading to a stable truth or knowledge—much like the process of modern day scientific inquiry. Inherent in this process is the necessity of fixed points of convergence for those engaged in the discussion. Modern day investigators who casually define their variables and conditions would not have an ally in Socrates.

Plato (c. 428–348 BC) was the most well known of Socrates' students. Foremost among Plato's contributions was a unified system of reasoning that joined many previously disparate areas of thought (e.g., ethics, epistemology, metaphysics, physics, politics, and religion). Plato's belief in the benefits of formalized instruction and the pursuit of scientific truths manifested itself in the founding of his Academy, Western Europe's first university. With math at the center of the curriculum, Plato's protegees were able to extend the work of the early Pythagoreans. Like the Pythagoreans, Plato believed that mathematical reasoning allowed one to look beyond appearances to timeless ideas and ultimate reality.

Plato argued that people do not have genuine knowledge if they merely have isolated observations and opinions. Instead, he insisted, genuine knowledge consists of a systematic, coherent account of reality in which each conclusion is rationally justified. Furthermore, he taught that what is particular, observable, and concrete must be understood in terms of higher-level principles that are comprehensive, theoretical, and abstract. This ideal of knowledge persists within the halls of science today. Plato's disdain for the changing, uncertain world of experience and his preference for the world of ideal, eternal realities led him to favor mathematics over the empirical sciences. It was one of his students, Aristotle, who showed that it was possible to have a rigorous science of the changing world of nature. Nevertheless, Plato's conviction that mathematics can lead one to the heart of reality would bear scientific fruit in the work of later scientists such as Copernicus, Kepler, and Galileo.

In addition to his contributions to epistemology, Plato was also interested in the makeup of the human personality. To account for the war of conflicting desires within all people, Plato divided the psyche into three parts: reason, spirit, and appetites. Although everyone has all three faculties, one will be dominant in a particular person. In this way, Plato provided a simple classification of personality types. Although there is no hard evidence that Freud derived his tripartite division of the psyche from Plato, a number of similarities between the two theories can be drawn (Price, 1990). For example, there are multiple references to Plato's account of the way illicit desires express themselves in dreams, his theory that insight comes from recalling unconscious memories, and his theory of eros and sexuality (Price, 1990).

Socrates' and Plato's ideas were seized and modified by Aristotle (384–322 BC). Influential as both a scientist and logician, Aristotle contributed to science on many fronts. His division of knowledge into separate sciences, although different from today's taxonomy, was influential in partitioning the sciences into key disciplines, each with its own methodology. One example is Aristotle's distinction between the theoretical and the practical sciences (see Fig. 2.1). The former represented the pursuit of knowledge for its own sake, whereas the latter consisted of knowledge that could be used to influence a particular course of events (Taylor, 1919/1955). One can easily see this division as the forerunner of the distinction between basic and applied research.

Aristotle's second major contribution was formal logic. He believed that logic served as the bridge between language, thought, and reality. In his logic, Aristotle developed the first system for representing reasoning in terms of symbolic notation. Aristotle's discoveries in logic were so insightful that it was not until the late 19th century that modification of his system became desirable. His theory that scientific knowledge should take the form of an axiomatic, deductive system still plays an important role in many of the sciences today. The taxonomy of the natural sciences and the scientific method are two examples of his enduring influence in this area.

Aristotle was much more empirical in his orientation than was Plato. For Aristotle, attempting to understand leadership by simply analyzing the concept was useless. Instead, one should make a study of successful leaders and inductively discover the general properties found common to all. Because he thought nature could be the subject of science, the study of change and causality played a prominent role in his philosophy.

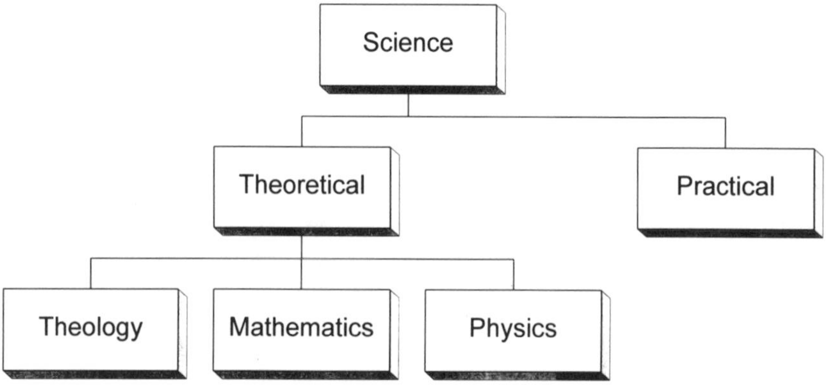

FIG. 2.1. Aristotle's classification of science. Adapted from Taylor (1919/1955).

In fact, Aristotle's theory of causality influenced the study of nature for the next 1,000 years. He believed that there were four types of causes necessary to understand any entity. First, the material cause is the matter from which it is formed. Second, the efficient cause is the motion or agency that produced it. Third, the formal cause is the internal principle of development—the essence that makes it a certain type of entity. Fourth is the final cause—its end or purpose. For the Greeks and the medievals, it was the formal and final causes that were most important. Why do objects fall? For Aristotle and the medievals, heavy objects had an innate tendency (formal cause) to seek the earth as their natural resting place (final cause). Why does an acorn grow? It strives to achieve its natural end of becoming an oak, they might say. Very little attention was paid to the material constituents and forces that lead to change. Early scientists of the modern period abandoned explanations in terms of final ends and focused on the material and efficient causes of events. Consequently, the rise of modern science followed the decline of the Aristotelian model.

AGE OF PROTECTED LEARNING

Struggle for Influence

Prior to this time the center of political, cultural, and civil life in the West was Greece. With the development of trade and transportation, communities migrated throughout Western Europe. During the next several hundred years the center of Greek life shifted to what is now Rome. If the thinkers of antiquity influenced the way humans thought, the generals and emperors of the Roman Empire shaped the conditions under which people thought.

What began as a series of small, unrelated communities spaced along the coast of Italy soon turned into an amalgamation of political and religious colonies. The Romans demonstrated an extraordinary ability to negotiate agreements with friends and foes alike. Whether on the battlefield or at the negotiating table, the Romans succeeded in unifying Italy under one political, economic, and religious system. From the Latins came a beautiful, albeit cumbersome, language; Etruscans contributed the benefits of mercantilism and trade; and the Greeks contributed science, art, and literature (Grant, 1991). The hallmark of the Roman period, however, was its system of laws and organization. Ironically, its organization ultimately became so cumbersome as to be unworkable—and Rome fell under the weight of its own bureaucracy.

The period of Roman domination did not bring an end to Greek contributions. It did, however, require that the Greek way of life submit to the influence of the Roman dictum in a multitude of ways. The size of the empire produced depersonalization; individuals did not find a sense of personal fulfillment in their relationship with society. Whereas early Greek thinkers meshed the needs of the individual and society into one, the Epicureans, Stoics, and Skeptics debated the issues of personal freedom and moral philosophy within an individualistic perspective. The philosophical orientations of the time represented disparate perspectives. That is, whereas the Stoics believed that reason and cosmic law were synonymous, the Epicureans believed that the workings of the universe were random, leaving the Skeptics (who inherited Plato's Academy), to question everything. The latter believed that absolute knowledge was, at best, probable, but usually futile; their search for truth and knowledge was a never-ending process. Many academics of the 20th century continue to hold a similar view.

Roman deficits in theoretical knowledge were compensated for by adroit practical applications. Except for a few key developments in medicine and algebra, the end of the classical period of philosophy (c. 200 AD) brought with it a marked decline in the spirit of early scientific thought and innovation.

> The Romans seem to have cared for science only as a means of accomplishing practical work in medicine, agriculture, architecture or engineering. They used the stream of knowledge without replenishing its source—the font of learning loved for its own sake—and in a few generations the source, and with it the stream, ran dry. (Dampier, 1948, pp. 52–53)

Many historical topics exist in which theological matters and secular matters share few commonalities. Although research design today seems reserved for issues far removed from theology, it is precisely because of the efforts of major theologians that research methods have advanced as they have. Most of the major philosophical figures of the Middle Ages, and the very ones on whom the philosophers of the Renaissance depended, were clergymen. Catholic, Jewish, and Moslem writers, among others, served as the conduit through which Greek ideas and literature remained available to the West.

For many individuals, true wisdom represented an intermixing of faith and reason. St. Augustine (354–430 AD) believed that there was a spiritual world separate from the material world and that skeptical doubts could be overcome through sound arguments. Augustine believed that there was an order to the world and that it was indeed knowable. This conviction would provide fertile soil for later scientific endeavors. However, his otherworldliness turned attention away from nature. It would take both the intellectual genius and religious piety of St. Thomas Aquinas some 800 years later to make Christian intellectuals comfortable with earthly concerns.

If the Romans valued science and insight only as a means to an end, the Franco, Anglo, and Germanic tribes who overran the Romans in the early 5th century valued it even less. The next 1,000 years constituted a barren time for exploratory thought. The fall of the Roman Empire left in its wake three distinct civilizations: Byzantine, European, and Islamic. Among the few bright spots in Western Europe was the founding of abbey schools by Charlemagne in the latter part of the 8th century. In these schools, and local church-based communities, the organizational structure of the Roman culture was transmitted. In the later half of the Middle Ages, most of the great universities of Europe would rise from the institutions that Charlemagne founded.

As the Roman Empire was declining in the West, the Arab empire was ascending in the East. Critical to the Eastern drive for new learning was the integration of rediscovered Greek thought with Islamic culture. Within the mathematical sciences, algebra, geometry, and trigonometry received renewed attention and development. In fact, Arabic numbers used by Western cultures today were not exclusively developed by the Arabs. Rather, they were developed in Greece, refined in India, and then modified by the Arabs into a form similar to those of today (Dampier, 1948). By 1100 AD the baton of scientific progress was again passed from Islam to Europe. The few centuries of Islamic science leave their mark each time an Arabic numeral is written in the name of scientific research.

Scholastic Thought

It was not until the latter part of the Middle Ages that Western thinkers caught up with the philosophical and scientific developments of those in the East. Before then, that portion of the Middle Ages known as the Dark Ages (500–1000 AD) was a time of turmoil and unrest. With Roman domination no longer present, personal and civil allegiances changed with great frequency. Little time and energy was available for speculation and deep thought. Just staying alive was a challenge.

The perseverance of scientific thought through the Dark Ages was made possible principally by scholasticism and St. Thomas Aquinas (c. 1225–1274 AD). Aquinas was a philosopher as well as a theologian who wrote in excess of 25 volumes of dense, scholarly arguments. Aquinas christianized Aristotle's philosophy in such a way as to reconcile theology with science and philosophy. His system was the culmination of the ideals of scholasticism.

Scholasticism represents an integration of faith and reason. In its broadest sense, Scholasticism implies the use of deductive logic to explain religious dogma. Although there are many different types of scholastic thought (e.g. Christian, Islamic, Judaic), the most common form of scholasticism found in the West was that developed by Roman Catholic thinkers during the 12th and 13th centuries. The contribution of scholasticism as a major philosophical force in Western philosophy stems from the intellectual pursuits of instructors of the most protected seats of learning in Europe, the monasteries. A number of rituals in higher education today are holdovers from monastic times (e.g., graduation robes, academic degrees, defense of theses).

More important for today's researchers, Aristotle's logic was inextricably woven into the fabric of the sciences through Aquinas and his mentor, Albertus Magnus, a Dominican monk and one of the premier scientists of the Middle Ages. Through Magnus' work, Aquinas saw that Aristotle's conceptions of the external world could be used to better understand Christian doctrines. Consequently, all facets of Aquinas' philosophy were framed in the context of Aristotelian logic and science (Stumpf, 1989).

As influential as Aquinas' work was to medieval thought, it only raised the stakes for others to challenge with equal vigor. One such challenger was Roger Bacon (c. 1210–1292), a Franciscan monk who agreed with Aquinas on the importance of integrating faith and reason but differed on the means by which this should be achieved. Evermore the analyst and empiricist, Bacon sought to pursue truth through observation and experimentation rather than through rational speculation. Fundamental to his training as a scientist and consistent with early Greek thought was Bacon's belief in experimental evaluation as a foundation for scientific inquiry. Dampier (1948) considered Bacon to be an experimentalist, first and foremost, and described his perspective on this topic in the following way:

> There is one science, he says, more perfect than others, which is needed to verify the others, the science of experiment, surpassing the sciences dependent on argument, since these sciences do not bring certainty, however strong the reasoning, unless experiment be added to test their conclusions. *Experimental science alone is able to ascertain what can be effected by nature, what by art, what by fraud.* (p. 93, italics added)

The growing schism between faith and reason widened further with the work of William of Occam (c. 1280–1349). Although he was a Franciscan monk, Occam was a rigorous empiricist. Consistent with his brand of empiricism, Occam was also a nominalist, someone for whom there was no such thing as real essences or universals inherent in the nature of reality (cf. Aristotle). According to him, labels assigned to objects were only names and did not represent underlying qualities. One of the legacies of this position may be found in today's nominal level of measurement, the lowest, least sensitive level in which objects are classified into groups based on observable characteristics.

Although theological considerations played a large role in the formation of Occam's ideas, his thought was crucial in shifting the basis of science from an Aristotelian–medieval foundation to one that was more conducive to the growth of modern science. For example, Occam emphasized that God was sovereign and free in the way He created the world; hence, creation did not have to conform to any a priori structure of rational essences. Contrary to what Aristotle and the medievals taught, this meant that one could not understand the world by simply contemplating that which was logically necessary. Occam introduced the notion that the structure and contents of the world are radically contingent; only observations and experiments will reveal how things actually are.

Students of multivariate statistics will recognize immediately one of Occam's better known tenets, the methodological principle now known as Occam's Razor. Occam's principle states: That which can be explained by fewer principles (or variables) should not be explained by more. Occam's philosophy contained the seeds of qualitative inquiry; he believed that science's value to humanity lay in its descriptive qualities, not in theory or speculation. Science should be practiced by first gathering, then describing and reporting data. Then, only when the data are in hand, can the most economical explanation be sought, thereby avoiding any flights of speculation. Occam asserted that one type of truth was available through science, another through revelation. By isolating theology from science and assigning them to separate domains of inquiry, Occam hoped to protect theology from the critical questioning intrinsic to science. Instead, he made it possible for science and philosophy to become secular, autonomous disciplines, freed from their subservience to theology. Although the early scholastics had sought to bring science, philosophy, and theology together, these disciplines began moving apart at the close of the Middle Ages.

AN ENLIGHTENED SPIRIT

Return to Secular Learning

During the 300-year period (c. 1300–1600) following the Middle Ages, Europeans rediscovered the classical culture. Vestiges of Rome's tradition and authority were giving way to a renewed spirit of optimism absent since the time of the early Greeks. The new spirit was one of excitement, anticipation, and a glorification of the individual—a spirit of humanism. Just as Christopher Columbus discovered a new geographic world, Renaissance thinkers sought to discover new worlds of thought.

The renewed interest in learning created fertile ground for the development of science. As the need for knowledge grew, so grew a need for new centers of higher learning. But where would persons go for formal education in the sciences if they were not interested in a monastic life? To meet this need, universities were built throughout western Europe (e.g., Bologna, Cambridge, Oxford, Paris). By the year 1500 the number of universities exceeded 80, many of which are still in existence today.

Concomitant with the development of new centers of learning was the co-evolution of new methods of learning. From the 15th through the 17th centuries, scientists acquired a new appreciation for the importance of mathematical reasoning and experimental observation. The mathematical harmony of the world was extolled by Nicholas Copernicus (1473–1543). Copernicus, a Polish priest well versed in neo-Platonism, reasoned that there was a mathematical simplicity to the heavens that the Ptolemaic scheme had been missing. The Copernican model supposed that the planets and the earth revolved around the sun. Because he had no original data to offer, the support for his model rested only on his philosophical preferences for a mathematically elegant order. Similarly, Johannes Kepler's (1571–1630) search for geometrical perfection was the driving force behind his science. Even though Galileo (1564–1642) was primarily guided by his mathematical conception of the universe, he did not neglect the importance of experimentation. Although many of Galileo's experiments were "thought experiments" only and were never carried out in practice, he did give momentum to the experimental side of science.

With the influence of scholasticism diminishing and the spirit of scientific optimism increasing, it seemed to many thinkers that the method of inquiry was the key to all knowledge. One such person was Francis Bacon (1561–1626). Bacon, a persistent critic of Aristotle, believed that the ways of the medieval philosophers were mistaken and that the slate of the mind should be cleaned of all former theories so that the search for knowledge could begin anew. To Bacon, humankind had obfuscated nature's innocence and beauty with faulty reasoning. Consequently, Bacon formulated the logic of inductive reasoning to guide scientists in their work. The first stage of his inductive investigation was methodical observation. Methodical observation requires the investigator to make three kinds of lists.

> First, the researcher creates a diverse list of all the positive instances of the phenomenon in question.

Second, the researcher finds situations similar to those on the first list, but where the phenomenon is absent.

Finally, the researcher generates a list of degrees where the instances are ordered according to the quantity and intensity of the phenomena.

In the second stage of a scientific investigation, one inductively generalizes from the data by finding substantive correlations. This is done by seeking a conjunction of properties such that it "is always present or absent with the given nature, and always increases and decreases with it" (Bacon, 1620/1939, p. 110). Bacon assumed that a set of properties meeting these conditions caused the phenomena. His confidence in this method was so great that he claimed "the discovery of all causes and sciences would be but the work of a few years" (Bacon, 1620/1939, p. 75). Even though his optimism proved to be naive, Bacon's method became the leading model for the new science.

Another early promoter of the scientific method was Thomas Hobbes (1588–1679), a contemporary of Bacon. Hobbes viewed human nature, thought, and society as bodies in motion. Hobbes believed that human thought and behavior followed the laws of the physical world, and he saw these phenomena through the eyes of a physicist and geometrician. He developed one of the first mechanistic accounts of human cognitive processes. Hobbes was also history's first political scientist in the sense that he attempted to find empirical laws that would provide a rational explanation of the origins of society and government. He theorized that humans had a natural drive for survival. Accordingly, Hobbes argued that society is neither intrinsic to human nature nor divinely ordained, but is a survival mechanism invented by people in order to achieve a stable environment.

Competing Philosophies

Francis Bacon wrote about a new method for studying nature. Hobbes applied the principles of the new science to the study of human behavior, but neither was as radical nor as influential as René Descartes (1596–1650) in thrusting philosophy in a new direction. Descartes rejected any idea that could not be proven with certainty. He believed that if philosophy could possess the exactness and certitude of mathematics, then its followers would no longer wander in the forest of uncertain opinions. As he expressed it: "We reject all such merely probable knowledge and make it a rule to trust only what is completely known and incapable of being doubted" (Descartes, 1628/1970, p. 3).

Convinced of the importance of methodology, Descartes set down rules for guiding the mind in its endeavors. The foundation of his method was rationalism. Rationalists believe that knowledge is a function of reason alone, that everything is explainable through one overarching system of reasoning, and that reasoning is deductive in nature (Flew, 1979). This position stands in sharp contrast to the position of Bacon and Hobbes, who considered experiences to be the foundation of all knowledge. Descartes modeled his philosophy after his mathematics, because he believed that the mind could be trained to produce clear and consistent truths just as one can deduce theorems from axioms through proofs. Although he made important contributions in optics and analytic geometry, his methodological rules were too severe for broader scientific applications. Scientists needed a greater appreciation of the role of experience as the source of ideas and concepts as well as a greater tolerance for probable knowledge.

British empiricism rose in response to the apparent deficiencies of rationalism. John Locke (1632–1704) rejected Descartes' rationalism because of what he considered to be the logical limits of the human mind. The mind has no innate ideas from which to draw conclusions, Locke argued. Locke further believed that the mind was a blank slate (*tabula rasa*) upon which experiences left their marks. Locke's theory of knowledge paved the way for scientific psychology, because he attempted to analyze the mechanisms of the mind. For example, he proposed that all complex, abstract ideas were constructed from simple, concrete ideas produced through one's experience.

The 18th-century philosophers cannot be appreciated without considering the impact of Issac Newton. Newton united all known laws of physics into a single theory. The Greek and medieval scientists had followed Aristotle in assuming that the laws governing earthly phenomena were different from those governing celestial events. Newton showed how all physical events, earthly or heavenly, followed the same laws. Through his work, the universe became less mysterious and more open to human understanding, prediction, and control. Newton's mathematical laws provided substance to the 18th-century image that the universe was like a giant, mechanical clock in which every event was determined and predictable.

Although Newton's influences on the philosophy of science are many, two have permeated scientific thought with greatest impact. First, the great synthesizing mind of Newton recognized the importance of both the deductive, mathematical approach favored by scientists and philosophers such as Galileo and Descartes, as well as the inductive, experimental approach favored by empiricists such as Francis Bacon and Robert Boyle. Second, Newton's successes in the physical sciences encouraged philosophers to seek similar successes in the human sciences. Consequently, the philosophers of the 18th century were consciously trying to be the "Newton" of the human mind.

The model of Newtonian physics haunted the psychology of this era. Corresponding to the physical particles whose laws of motion Newton unveiled, the contents of the mind were thought to be mental particles (ideas) that could be analyzed into fundamental, atomic units whose behaviors were governed by psychological laws. Although Locke originated this model, it was further refined by David Hume (1711–1776), who developed it into a theory of associationistic psychology. For Hume, "The laws of the association of ideas were the mental counterpart of the law of gravity in physics, that they were the universal principles for the operation of the mind" (Schultz & Schultz, 1992, pp. 45–46).

Later philosophers would combine elements of both rationalism and empiricism in their quest to gain clarity about the nature and grounds of knowledge, particularly in regard to the sciences. One such example is that of Immanuel Kant's (1724–1804) critical idealism. For Kant, all knowledge arose out of experience. Yet, bare experience would be chaotic. Hence, when experiencing the world, Kant said, the mind is continually at work in the background, organizing the sense data by means of the categories of reason. Although Kant identified knowledge with science, he found it necessary to postulate a reality that transcended the world of sensation, a reality that was not amenable to the scientific approach but that could be glimpsed in moral, religious, and aesthetic experience. This latter point was unsatisfactory to the positivists, such as Auguste Comte (1798–1857). Comte said that if one could not know something scientifically, then it could not be talked about at all. Positivism represents the most optimistic, albeit extreme, view of the empiricist movement. Its followers claim that science alone, when executed flawlessly, is capable of providing all truth and knowledge. Comte's empiricism was so extreme that he thought science could only describe the phenomena and could not make use of unobservable forces, entities, and causes in an effort to explain what is behind the observed events. Later positivists such as Jeremy Bentham (1748–1832) and John Stuart Mill (1806–1873) welcomed the emphasis on positive, empirical knowledge, but distanced themselves from the more extreme aspects of this orientation.

Method of Science

Four issues concerning the method of science emerge from this brief overview of the historical interaction between philosophy and science. The first issue concerns the role of reason and experience. The rationalists stressed the primacy of reason and, therefore, placed greater emphasis on mathematics. Among the philosophers who have been mentioned, those who took this approach were Pythagoras, Plato, Augustine, and Descartes. Among the scientists, Copernicus and Galileo favored this position. The empiricists stressed the primacy of experience and, thereby, favored the role of observation and experimentation. These would include: Aristotle, Aquinas, Occam, Roger Bacon, Francis Bacon, and Hobbes. However, influenced by the work of Newton, philosophers of later generations recognized that science requires a combination of mathematical reasoning and experimental observation.

The second issue concerns the completeness of science. Is science capable of investigating all areas of reality? The classic example of the negative response was offered by Descartes. Although Descartes was an enthusiastic promoter and practitioner of science, he believed that the domain of science was limited. Insofar as human beings are physical entities, the methods of physics and physiology can explain human reality. However, he believed that humans are divided beings, who have not only bodies but minds as well. According to Descartes' dualism, the mind is a nonphysical entity that forever eludes the natural sciences. Thoughts cannot be weighed and measured as can bones and ligaments. In this way, Descartes gave science its due while preserving the dignity and freedom of human beings. People are more than matter in motion, controlled by deterministic laws, he insisted. His contemporary, Hobbes, took the affirmative position. According to Hobbes, anything real can be explained by the laws of motion, and that includes all human thought and behavior. Although his position was controversial in its day, it eventually became the majority opinion within the human sciences.

The third issue concerns the ultimacy of science. Even if all reality falls within the domain of science, does science provide the final truth about reality? Kant said "No." Although he believed that everything within experience can be interpreted through the grid of the physical sciences and mathematics, he also believed that this grid only provided a limited perspective on reality. The cognitive categories used by science (which Kant thought were intrinsic to the mind) are like tinted lenses. They reveal the world but also add their own coloring to it. According to Kant, the scientist can give a complete account of human behavior from the outside in terms of deterministic, empirical laws. Yet, the perspective of science is not ultimate. That is, the inner experiences of free, moral agents reveal an aspect of the self that is not captured by the categories of empirical science. The Kantian position was accepted in psychology by those that stress the subjective standpoint of the agent, such as existentialist, phenomenological, and humanistic personality theories. On the other hand, the positivists insisted that what could not be known by empirical science could not be known at all. Most advocates of behaviorism in psychology agree with the positivists that the scientific perspective is most descriptive of reality.

The fourth issue is causality. As was mentioned previously, the Aristotelians and medievals explained natural phenomena in terms of final ends or purposes. The rise of modern science occurred when scientists began studying events in terms of the mechanistic processes that produced them and left questions about their purposes to the theologians and poets. As scientists were enjoying the fruits of this new approach, David Hume's radical empiricism shook the foundations of 18th-century science. He wondered whether causal judgments could be rationally justified or whether they were simply a matter of psychological habit. According to Hume, a judgment that event X causes event Y is based on several observations: the spatial proximity of X and Y, the temporal priority of X to Y, and the constant conjunction of X and Y (the fact that they invariably occur together). From these facts, Hume said, we can assume that there is a necessary connection such that X will always produce Y. This causal judgment is merely the result of a psychological habit (much like Pavlov's dogs). The problem that Hume raised can be put in two ways: (a) we never experience something called a "necessary connection" and (b) we have no rational guarantee that what has been true in the past will remain true in the future without arguing tautologically. In responding to Hume's arguments, Cook and Campbell (1979) acknowledged that all causal relationships in the social sciences will be fallible and probabilistic. Furthermore, they determined that scientific theories and causal relationships cannot, strictly speaking, be proven. For Cook and Campbell, best practice simply eliminates untenable, rival hypotheses. Their approach, although not completely satisfactory, does enable one to discover workable hypotheses that allow researchers to control their experimental world and, at the same time, permits them to make predictions that have not been proven false. Others have merely been content to settle with "what works."

FOUNDATIONS FOR A NEW SCIENCE

Convergence of the Sciences

In spite of numerous, unresolved conceptual problems, early scientists' dreams of a unified science have come closer to realization in the last two centuries. As the sciences of the mid-19th century began developing, it became apparent that methods used to pursue truths in one discipline were markedly similar to methods used in other disciplines. For example, biology was borrowing from anthropology, physics was borrowing from astronomy, and medicine was borrowing from chemistry. Science was becoming synergistic. Although the spectrum of science remained constrained, it was becoming evident that there was a method to this madness, a method that was common and to some degree responsible for the many breakthroughs throughout the sciences. Soon it would become known as *the* method. The glimmerings of a methodological unity to the sciences would spark a transformation of the philosophy of the mind into the science of psychology.

Scientific psychology owes much of its success to its early union with physics, today referred to as *psychophysics.* Leahey (1991) referred to the spirit of the late 19th century as one of "physics envy." Physicists were, for the first time, capable of measuring such things as the speed of light, strength of magnetic fields, and rate of molecular movement. If such elusive variables could be measured and manipulated, why not the mental activities of the human being?

William Wundt (1832–1920) is generally cited as the founder of scientific psychology. He is credited with two major turning points in the evolution of the new discipline, the first psychological laboratory and the first professional journal, *Psychological Studies.* Were it not for the work of several early 19th-century psychophysicists as Fechner, Muller, and von Helmholtz, Wundt would not have had the material with which to work. Fechner, for example, provided the logarithmic statement, $S_{(\text{STIMULUS})} = k_{(\text{CONSTANT})} \times \log R$, where R = the magnitude of the stimulus. To counter errors of observation, Fechner and A. S. Volkmann (a physiology professor at the University of Halle) developed the notion of "average error." Modifying Bernoulli's Law of Large Numbers, Fechner and Volkman believed that the more observations a psychophysicist made of an individual's sensory data, the more likely the psychophysicist was to identify the true measure of a performance (Schultz & Schultz, 1992).

Origins of Experimental Design

Prior to the 18th century, measurement techniques were based largely on the laws of the physical world. Throughout the 18th and 19th centuries, a foundation was laid for the application of measurement principles to phenomena that were social. It was not long before others from the fields of biology, psychology, sociology, math, medicine, and statistics would join forces to develop more effective descriptive and inferential (viz., statistical) techniques. Once the techniques were in place, statisticians began incorporating inferential methods in their empirical research.

From Anaximenes' modest experiments with the rarefaction of air in 545 BC to the large, clinical drug trials of today, the design and analysis of single-case research have indeed changed over the years. Reviews of the early case histories of such prominent figures as Freud, Jung, Adler, and others document very successfully the impact major theorists have had on psychology proper. On the analytical side, researchers such as Broca, Fechner, and Ebbinghaus have demonstrated that there was more to science than naturalistic case studies. Through the in-depth and repeated investigations into the physiological functioning of the individual, these early psychophysicists were able to quantify the sensory thresholds and functioning of individuals, one at a time.

Graunt (1662) was the first to gather, report, and analyze data in aggregate form. He reported mortality data in 17th-century London. Findings such as that women live longer than men, more boys are born per capita than girls, and stable death rates across years are a few of the many widely held notions today traceable to John Graunt (Hellemans & Bunch, 1988). Although Graunt laid the foundation for the new field of statistics, it was Sir Francis Galton (1822–1911) and his student Karl Pearson (1857–1936) who provided the field with its sophistication. Galton, the first cousin of biologist Charles Darwin, was interested in the transference of hereditary traits through generations. Galton had the ideas, but Karl Pearson had the mathematical acumen to sell it to the world. Emanating from Galton and Pearson's work was the correlation of physical and mental traits that later became known as *regression.*

Although the budding subdiscipline of experimental psychology began as a science of the individual (viz., psychophysics), it wasn't long before the lure of both the marketplace and large numbers changed the course of development for the new science. Galton found that by setting up a booth at the 1884 International Exposition in London he could gather sensory data from large numbers of persons (Anastasi, 1988). Different from today's researchers, however, the subjects paid Galton to measure their characteristics and abilities. But Galton's studies, and the statistical tests that emanated, were designed to identify measures of association about factors that covaried in nature. Galton's contributions to certain subdisciplines of psychology (e.g., testing, differential psychology, experimental psychology) were so profound as to influence many young researchers to see the world in descriptive, covariate terms.

Cowles (1989) reported that by the mid-20th century, psychologists had grown skeptical of Galton's approach and were in need of a more broadly based, truly experimental set of procedures with which to analyze their data. Sir Ronald Fisher's classical approach to the study of group differences offered them an option. Fisher offered the analyst designs with varying levels of complexity and a means by which multiple variables could be manipulated within the context of a single study.[1] Using Fisher's principles, a researcher could build into the design vary-

[1]The reader is referred to Meehl (1978) for an interesting discussion of the ways in which variables are incorporated into experimental studies.

ing levels of a factor, including the absence of a factor (control). The analytical design that makes this all possible is referred to as a *factorial design* and was first analyzed using a technique called *Analysis of Variance (ANOVA)*. Using a set of techniques that demanded both logical and statistical integrity, Fisher brought statistical analysis and experimental design together under one well-organized plan. The two have remained inseparable ever since. Lost among many students of statistics is the realization that the *F*-test so closely identified with ANOVA is actually named in honor of Fisher (Cowles, 1989).

Ronald Fisher, a biometrician by training, questioned the manner in which tests of association should be calculated, in particular the error term. In an effort to better understand Pearson's chi-square technique, Fisher derived mathematically the sampling distribution of the correlation coefficient and, for the first time, the standard normal *z*-distribution. Estimating errors of measurement for correlated data using small samples was the task of W. S. Gossett. Together, Fisher and Gossett derived and refined the *t*- and *z*-distributions still used by statisticians today. Had the brewery Gossett worked for in the early 1900s had a policy encouraging independent research, the *t*-tables in statistics books may now carry his name rather than that of his pseudonym, Student's *t*.

ESSENTIALS OF EXPERIMENTAL DESIGN

Controlled Variation

For the physical scientist working in a lab, the standard normal distribution is one of many factors held constant. For the social scientist working in a field setting, the referent distribution may be the only fixed entity. According to Cowles (1989), "Social scientists, biologists, and agricultural researchers have to contend with the fact that their experimental material (e.g., people, animals, plants) is subject to irregular variation that arises as a result of complex interactions of genetic factors and environmental conditions" (p. 148). Social scientists, then, must take active control over factors that are within their control, those factors that reduce the amount of irregular, unaccounted-for variation and, at the same time, increase the sensitivity of their analyses.

Few factors characterize experimental designs more than the ability to control key facets of an investigation, an ability that Sidman (1960) believed is absolutely essential to the success of the experiment. The major benefit of this is to let the examiners see through the fog of uncontrolled variability. For the novice experimenter, experimental control likely means holding firm one or more levels of a single variable expected to influence a particular outcome. For the experienced investigator, it likely means attempting to control *all* aspects of a given study—the variables of interest as well as the extraneous and confounding variables that may pose a threat to the integrity of the study. The researcher whose life is invested in a given problem and its potential solutions soon realizes that the factors of interest in a well-designed, highly controlled study are limitless. According to Johnston and Pennypacker (1993), the researcher doesn't just control factors but is often controlled by them as well. If science is the ability to predict and control behavior, then it can be said that one's scientific ability increases as a function of one's ability to control the relevant variables.

The notion that science proceeds through the manipulation of variables in a systematic fashion was put forth very convincingly by three well-known philosophers and scientists of the Middle Ages and Renaissance. As evidenced by information presented previously, Roger Bacon believed that the only way to true knowledge was through experimentation. Although Bacon did not experiment much himself, he was a scholar and writer of the first order and would very likely have written much more had he not been censored and imprisoned by his religious superiors. Francis Bacon, Roger Bacon's namesake, offered later scientists the concepts of inductive reasoning and hypothesis testing. Francis Bacon believed that hypotheses should be "framed in accordance with fact," tested through observation or experimentation, and then reframed in such a way as to move the experimenter increasingly closer to a given fact (Dampier, 1948, p. 126)—the experimental equivalent of the Dialectic Method.

The philosopher who gets most credit for codifying both Bacons' beliefs about experimentation is John Stuart Mill. Different from Hume, who thought that causal relationships are a function of the human mind, Mill believed that causal inferences correspond to reality and that all inductive reasoning must, necessarily, end in a search for causes. Within the area of clinical psychology, George Kelly stands out as someone who considered people to hypothesize constantly about causal factors that would allow them to predict and control key aspects of their environment. However, it was another humanist, Carl Rogers, who adopted many of Mill's premises in the context of therapy, particularly Mill's Law of Causality:

> Research is the experience in which I can stand off and try to view this rich subjective experience with objectivity, applying all the elegant methods of science to determine whether I have been deceiving myself. The conviction grows in me that we shall discover laws of personality and behavior

> which are as significant for human progress or human relationships as the law of gravity or the law of thermodynamics. (Rogers, 1961, p. 14)

Thus far, only the issue of experimental control has been presented. Two other types of control often used within the context of experimental designs are also worth mentioning. The first is referred to as *statistical control*, the uniform distribution of the effects of extraneous variables across all treatment groups. The notion is consistent with Fisher's logic of experimental design in that if you can't build an influence into the study, then at least spread its effect out over all groups and, where possible, systematically remove it from the error term, thereby increasing the informational yield of the experiment (Kennedy & Bush, 1985). Classical analysts have several methods at their disposal. Three routinely used within the context of standard parametric analyses are as follows: crossing (all levels of one variable appear with all levels of every other variable), blocking (concomitant classification variable with maximally homogeneous subgroups), and nesting (every level of one factor appears in only level of the second factor). Other investigators, in a far less defensible approach to statistical control, sometimes employ higher-order statistical techniques for nonexperimental treatment conditions in the hopes of overriding the limitations of violating important assumptions. This method is often employed by investigators who are unfamiliar with the conditions under which the tests were developed and the belief that the power of their analysis resides in the test statistic and not in the quality of the experiment.

A second type of control affecting experimental designs is that imposed by limited resources. For example, an investigator may know what should be done, or how things should be done, but not have the resources necessary to conduct a study the way it should be. The earnest investigator will likely try to compensate for any shortcomings in time, energy, or finances by cutting back in other areas. The less-than-earnest investigator may not even try to compensate for recognized (or unrecognized) shortcomings and settle for simply "getting the job done." Although this is clearly not a perfect world and the perfect study has yet to be conducted, all efforts to compensate for shortcomings generally bring their own costs to bear on an investigation. Simply stated, a limited number of resources must, out of necessity, control (or limit) the extent to which research progresses.

The notion of a control group originated from Fisher's agricultural work in the early 1920s (Cowles, 1989; cf. Fisher, 1926). In an effort to rule out chance factors that might also be responsible for differences in crop yields, and as a result of his dissatisfaction with the designs of previously collected studies, Fisher found it necessary to construct "control" plots that had no treatment at all. That way Fisher could know with certainty what would happen if the status quo had been allowed to run its course. It must be kept in mind, however, that control plots were only a few of many plots that existed within the context of a carefully thought-out sequence of treatment conditions, such as fertilizers, minerals, and administration times, taken together and in union with one another. The sequence of plots allowed Fisher to identify differences attributable to main effects, interactions of treatments, and the status quo. The critical discovery in all this was Fisher's ability to combine mathematical induction with sound experimental design principles using inferential statistical techniques.

Randomization

Few have argued against the nobility of the early years of statistics, yet beneath the commitment, dedication, and persistence of its early investigators is a less than noble origin—games of chance. The potential for winning sizable sums of money at the gaming tables provided many of the discipline's earliest stalwarts with the motivation necessary for calculating their odds for success. For other members of the scientific community, probabilities for success took on another term, *odds ratios*, and had applications well beyond the gaming tables. But according to Stigler (1986), what seems today like a very logical set of circumstances, aggregating data to aid in one's predictions, was not always viewed as logical. Early astronomers, for instance, viewed aggregating data as illogical. Unless observations were made under exactly the same conditions, it was believed that the variability in conditions would accentuate errors inherent in the different measurements and thus contaminate the data. The position of the early astronomers on this issue is not far removed from positions held today by many measurement theorists.

Predicting phenomena based on known events represents one level of understanding. Refining those predictions based on known characteristics of the errors in one's measurements represents another. Two individuals stand out as historically significant persons in this regard. From his writings on inverse probabilities to his founding of the Central Limit Theorem, Laplace's contributions to mathematics and statistics are considered foundational. For Pierre de Laplace (1749–1827), choosing the mean of discordant measures meant estimating a value that minimized the amount of error on both sides of a distribution (Stigler, 1986). For statisticians, today as then, that means using the least squares method. A contemporary of Laplace's, and a colleague on whom Laplace counted to further explain the errors associated with the normal curve, was Karl Gauss (1777–1855). Gauss is best known for the development of the normal curve that bears his name, the Gaussian (Normal) Curve.

The link between Laplace and Gauss' important work in generating a referent distribution lies in Adolphe J. Quetelet's application of the Gauss–Laplace synthesis to human characteristics and abilities. For Quetelet, even large data sets that consist of widely disparate values can yield reliable information if the influencing forces are strong enough. In addition, if subgroups of a distribution demonstrate instability through different means, one has evidence for different causes (Stigler, 1986). Quetelet had his share of critics. Many present-day practitioners of statistics subscribe to these same positions. Although Quetelet used the Normal Curve to demonstrate how *similar* segments of a population were, Galton used the same curve and the same principles of statistics to show how *different* segments of the same population were. In this regard, Galton's model has been most influential.

Another of Fisher's major contributions to statistics extends randomization beyond that historically associated with probability to that of randomized experimental units. The purpose of the assumption of random selection and assignment of subjects to all parametric tests lies in its ability to distribute random errors equally across all experimental groups. Although Fisher does and should receive much credit for incorporating mathematically rigorous randomization procedures into experimental designs, he was not the first to do so. That honor should go to C. S. Peirce and J. Jastrow (1885) for their extension of Fechner's earlier work with repetitious lifting of weights. Not only did Peirce and Jastrow improve on Fechner's methodology by having a group who lifted without the extra weights (control), but they did so with the benefit of blind trials, the first of recorded history (cited in Stigler, 1986).

For Fisher, a statistical test was only as good as its error term. Much of Fisher's tests were concerned with estimating and minimizing the amount of unexplained error in an analysis. Fixed and random variables constitute another major consideration of classical designs. Fixed variables are those chosen specifically for their use in the experiment. Random variables, on the other hand, are those variables in which certain levels are selected randomly from among a host of other levels. Choosing 4th graders and 6th graders, exclusively, to participate in a study because of an interest in studying only 4th graders and 6th graders would represent levels of the fixed variable grade. However, if one were to randomly select, say 3rd and 6th graders from among 1st through 8th grades, grade level would be a random variable. In the first case, inferences about the results could extend only to 4th and 6th graders because of the fixed nature of the sampling. In the second example, inferences could be made to all grade levels because of the random nature of the variable. The error term determines how this information is actually tested.

For Fisher, refinement of one's design depended on one's ability to identify, estimate, and remove factors contributing more to error than to the task at hand. Fisher's theoretical work generating the random sampling distributions against which most statistical tests are compared was so complete and detailed that Fisher is given credit for many major methodological breakthroughs in sampling methodology as well. Given Fisher's contributions to statistics and research design, it is not surprising that by the 1940s, his work had led to a division within the field of experimental psychology. Analysis of Variance (ANOVA) had become the test of choice for experimental psychologists in the second half of the 20th century.

Emergence of Single-Subject Methodology

If one were to sit down and list all of the sciences known today, it would be a most challenging task, even with the aid of taxonomies and reference materials. It has taken the field of science several thousand years to implement and expand upon Aristotle's notion of different branches of science alluded to previously. Interestingly, it has taken the field of psychology less than 100 years to identify a plethora of subspecialties, one of which is known as *applied behavior analysis*. Whether psychology is defined as the science of the mind, the science of behavior, or something in between, it is fair to say that the paths leading to the formal analysis of the individual are multiply determined. Uniting the many competing factions is a common continuum that traces back to the thinkers of antiquity. Ironically, much of what is known about the day-to-day functioning of individuals has come from data based not on the individual but, rather, from data generated from tens, hundreds, thousands, or tens of thousands of individuals, in aggregate form.

Interest in the structure and function of single-subject research combined the efforts of countless investigators who struggled to unlock the mysteries of science, life, and human behavior. Before psychology emerged, the focus of science was on the laws of nature and the tools needed to understand nature's various codes. Psychology introduced a new awareness of the importance and complexity of the individual, an organism subject to the physical laws of the universe yet fully capable of behaving in ways that seem to deviate markedly from others of the species. No other discipline had faced such a task. So the case study was born.

The case study, introduced by Fechner in the mid-19th century, has been an accepted part of psychological methodology for over a century. However, it has been received with mixed success outside of the discipline of psychology. Poor empirical support, a general lack of methodological techniques, and a shortage of investigators versed in both theories and methods have all limited the case study's acceptance. For the new discipline of psychology to qualify as a science in the 20th century, it had to evidence characteristics of the sciences—the natural sciences. But psychology was not quite there yet. Psychology's new investigators had not yet brought its tools and its theories close enough together to do what it was trying to do: understand, predict, and control human behavior.

For many years, the clinical case study seemed to be the only means of investigating intrapsychic phenomena. That is not to say, however, that there weren't earlier efforts to study individuals. As for the experimental sciences, early physiologists such as Fechner, Helmholtz, Muller, and Wundt were pursuing laws of mental functioning in the areas of sensation and perception, and they were indeed interested in the abilities of individuals. But Freud's departure from the traditional laboratory methods of physiology to his very applied psychoanalytic techniques took the practice of psychology to such a conceptual depth that it was decades before the clinical part of the discipline could reestablish itself with the experimental part. Even Allport, a well-respected analyst who believed that individuals possessed preferred neurological pathways responsible for a person's tendencies toward one psychological disposition as opposed to another, tended toward nomothetic comparisons in his research and idiographic comparisons in his clinical practice.

By 1940, psychologists began dissenting from the clinical model. B. F. Skinner believed that psychology was best suited for the laboratory and that if psychologists were to truly understand human behavior, it must be done one person at a time, in a laboratory, and under highly controlled settings. For Skinner, it was impossible to study all of the conditions affecting people's behaviors. Skinner and his followers, hereafter referred to as *behavior analysts*, believed that statistical techniques offered the analyst no discernable advantage in understanding the behavior of individuals. From 1939 until 1963, a total of 246 single-subject studies had appeared in the published literature, enough to make their presence felt as a formidable research design for both the present and the future (Dukes, 1965). This trend continues now. Today, social scientists have an armada of tools that were not available even a decade ago. Many such tools are presented in the chapters that follow.

REFERENCES

Anastasi, A. (1988). *Psychological testing* (6th ed.). New York: Prentice-Hall.

Bacon, F. (1939). Novum organum. In E. A. Burtt (Ed.), *The English philosophers from Bacon to Mill* (pp. 24–123). New York: Random House, The Modern Library. (Original work published in 1620)

Cook, T. D., & Campbell, D. T. (1979). *Quasi-experimentation: Design & analysis issues for field settings*. Boston: Houghton Mifflin.

Cowles, M. (1989). *Statistics in psychology: An historical perspective*. Hillsdale, NJ: Lawrence Erlbaum Associates.

Dampier, W. C. (1948). *A history of science: And its relation with philosophy & religion*. New York: Cambridge University Press.

Descartes, R. (1970). Rules for the direction of the mind. In E. Haldane & G. Ross (Eds.), *The philosophical works of Descartes* (Vol. 1, pp. 1–77). New York: Cambridge University Press. (Original work published in 1628)

Dukes, W. F. (1965). N = 1. *Psychological Bulletin, 64*(1), 74–79.

Fisher, R. A. (1926). The arrangement of field experiments. *Journal of the Ministry of Agriculture, 33*, 505–513.

Flew, A. (1979). *A dictionary of philosophy* (rev. 2nd ed.). New York: St. Martin's Press.

Grant, M. (1991). *The founders of the western world: A history of Greece and Rome*. New York: Scribners.

Graunt, J. (1662). *Observations upon bills of mortality*. London: Martyn & Allestry.

Hellemans, A., & Bunch, B. (1988). *The timetables of science: A chronology of the most important people and events in the history of science*. New York: Simon & Schuster.

Johnston, J. M., & Pennypacker, H. S. (1993). *Strategies and tactics of behavioral research* (2nd ed.). Hillsdale, NJ: Lawrence Erlbaum Associates.

Ittenbach, R. F., & Swindell, L. K. (1993, December). Empiricism and early scientific thought. *Teaching Statistics in the Health Sciences*, pp. 1–4.

Kennedy, J. J., & Bush, A. J. (1985). *An introduction to the design and analysis of experiments in behavioral research*. Lanham, MD: University Press of America.

Lawhead, W. F. (1996). *The voyage of discovery: A history of western philosophy*. Belmont, CA: Wadsworth.

Leahey, T. H. (1991). *A history of modern psychology*. Englewood Cliffs, NJ: Prentice-Hall.

Meehl, P. (1978). Theoretical risks and tabular asterisks: Sir Karl, Sir Ronald, and the slow progress of soft psychology. *Journal of Consulting and Clinical Psychology, 46*(4), 806–834.

Peirce, C. S., & Jastrow, J. (1885). On small differences in sensation. *Memoirs of the National Academy of Sciences for 1884, 3*, 75–83.

Price, A. W. (1990). Plato and Freud. In C. Gill (Ed.), *The person and the human mind* (pp. 247–270). Oxford, England: Clarendon Press.

Rogers, C. R. (1961). *On becoming a person*. Boston: Houghton Mifflin.

Schultz, D. P., & Schultz, S. E. (1992). *A history of modern psychology* (5th ed.). Fort Worth, TX: Harcourt Brace Jovanovich.

Sidman, M. (1960). *Tactics of scientific research: Evaluating experimental data in psychology*. New York: Basic Books.

Stigler, S. (1986). *The history of statistics: The measurement of uncertainty before 1900*. Cambridge, MA: Harvard University, Belknap Press.

Stumpf, S. E. (1989). *Philosophy: History and problems* (4th ed.). New York: McGraw-Hill.

Taylor, A. E. (1955). *Aristotle* (rev. ed.). New York: Dover. (Original work published in 1919)

Wainer, H. (1990). Introduction and history. In H. Wainer (Ed.), *Computerized adaptive testing: A primer* (pp. 1–22). Hillsdale, NJ: Lawrence Erlbaum Associates.

3

Measurement of Dependent Variables

Louis H. Primavera
Department of Psychology
St. John's University

David B. Allison
Obesity Research Center
St. Luke's/Roosevelt Hospital Center
Columbia University College of Physicians and Surgeons

Vincent C. Alfonso
Graduate School of Education
Fordham University and
Crossroads School for Child Development

This chapter considers theoretical and applied issues in the measurement of dependent variables. It is divided into three broad sections. The first is primarily conceptual in nature and discusses the meanings of and distinction among constructs, operations, and measures. The second section concerns the assessment of dependent variable reliability or agreement. Finally, the third concerns practical issues in obtaining the actual data.

CONSTRUCTS, OPERATIONS, AND MEASURES

In using single-subject designs it is necessary to decide on an outcome measure or measures. It is common for researchers to choose behaviors that reflect some salient behavioral problem and that can be measured easily. In choosing measures, careful thought needs to be given to the constructs these measures represent. Cronbach and Meehl (1955) defined a construct as "some postulated attribute of people, assumed to be reflected in test performance" (p. 283). If *measure of behavior* is substituted for *test performance* in this definition it becomes clear that a construct can be defined as a concept that is reflected in behavior. Some familiar constructs include intelligence, anxiety, depression, self-injury behavior, and so on. It is important to recognize that constructs are never measured directly but rather are inferred from measurements of behavior. This idea involves the important scientific concept of "operational definitions." Operational definitions define constructs in terms of observable and measurable operations. That is, constructs and the phenomena that they are intended to represent are defined by the way they are measured. Although operational definitions have been credited to the physicist Percey Bridgeman (1927/1960), Sigmund Koch (1992) demonstrated that what Bridgeman intended was incorrectly transformed by psychologists of that era who wanted to enhance psychology's scientific rigor and credibility and use the authority that Bridgeman's reputation carried. Whoever is credited with introducing the concept of operational definition into psychology, it has taken a firm place in the science of psychology and is important in any discussion of measurement.

Constructs, by their nature, are often difficult to describe and define completely. The problem is partly due to the complexity of constructs, but mainly due to the inability of words to totally encompass and unambiguously communicate meaning. Imagine trying to describe everything that is meant by the construct of anxiety. We do not believe that anyone would be willing to say that we could describe everything that is meant by either this or any other construct. Even if researchers read everything that was written about a construct, they would not necessarily conclude that they knew everything there was to know about that construct. Now think of the task that one is attempting to accomplish when trying to define a construct in terms of observable and measurable operations. The task seems overwhelming. Trying to define operationally a construct is like trying to take a picture of a very large elephant while standing in a very small room. It is not possible to stand back far enough and take a single picture of the elephant, because the room is too small. The only choice you have is to take a series of pictures in a systematic way and then try to put these pictures together so that you'd have as complete a composite as possible. If you were very careful and systematic, the final picture would look something like the elephant but would never be totally accurate. Operational definitions are similar to one of these pictures because they represent only one or more aspects of the construct.

This conception of operational definitions leads to two important principles concerning the relationship between operational definitions and constructs. The first principle is that a construct cannot be thought of as the sum of its operations. The second is that no one operation or set of operations can fully describe a construct. This last principle is particularly important for researchers who choose one or two measures of a construct in an experiment and then discuss their results in construct terms. Suppose an investigator was studying the effect of a behavioral treatment on depression and used the Beck Depression Inventory (BDI) as a measure of depression (Beck, Ward, Mendelson, Mock, & Erbaugh, 1961). It would not be correct for the investigator to discuss the results in terms of how this treatment affected the construct of depression in general. It would be correct to discuss the results in terms of how this treatment affected the aspect of depression that is measured by the BDI. This indicates the need to have as many different kinds of measures for the same construct as is feasible. This strategy has been referred to as *multi-operationalism* (Cook & Campbell, 1979).

Although operations appear to be more concrete and less ambiguous than constructs, they also have a natural ambiguity because they are also expressed in language, and words cannot totally and unambiguously communicate meaning. It is important to underscore this point. Researchers should not work under the delusion that using operational definitions clears up all ambiguity in scientific investigation. Operational definitions help us to be more concrete and less ambiguous, but they do not remove all ambiguity. Also, the price we pay for the concreteness is the loss of generality. To demonstrate what we are saying, do a little demonstration for yourself. Try writing an operational definition of any construct and ask several colleagues to do the same. Have all of them read all of the definitions, and ask them to see if they can, as a group, arrive at one definition. Observe what happens. We suspect that you will see the points we are trying to make.

Constructs are not independent of each other. They exist in a system of constructs generally conceptualized as a theory. This further adds to the difficulty in defining constructs, because the same operation may be indicative of two related but not completely overlapping constructs. For instance, stomach pains can indicate anxiety, excitement, or indigestion, and perfuse perspiration can indicate anxiety, excitement, or a myocardial infarction.

Another point to be made is that all constructs are defined in reference to a theory, and therefore all operations or measures also reflect a theory. Theories differ in terms of which aspects of a concept they postulate as being most important and which constructs they include and exclude. Two of the most widely used measures of depression are the

BDI and the Hamilton Depression Scale (Hamilton, 1967). In reading each of these measures it is easy to see that the BDI reflects a cognitive conception of depression, whereas the Hamilton reflects a more general psychodynamic view of depression. These two measures have been shown to have a very modest intercorrelation (Polaino & Senra, 1991). The lack of high correlation indicates that, although the two measures have something in common, some aspect of what each is measuring is different. It is tempting to say that the aspect they have in common is depression and the aspects they do not have in common represent other constructs. It could be argued that both tests are measuring different aspects of the construct of depression. The reason they do not correlate very highly is due in large part to the fact that the behaviors they measure are manifestations of different aspects or parts of this construct. An important implication of this point is that it is best to be explicit about the theoretical construct one intends the measure to represent. If researchers are not explicit about the theory, measures will not be clearly defined. We believe that those measures that have the best psychometric properties (reliability and validity) are frequently those that are constructed to reflect a clearly defined theory.

WHAT TO DO IN PRACTICE

The preceding presentation was not meant to discourage efforts in conducting single-subject research, but it was meant to raise awareness of the important issues in measurement that are present in all empirical research. An important goal in research is to choose measures (operations) that reflect as many aspects of a construct as is feasible in each study, and to be as precise as language will allow. This is a difficult task, and it requires vigilance and careful attention. In order to choose the appropriate measures, we suggest the following steps.

Step 1

Decide on the constructs to be measured. The idea here is to make sure that the measures chosen have some general theoretical meaning. If this is done, the results of the research will be interpretable in theoretical terms and can be related to the relevant literature. It is important to ensure that the measures chosen are described in both theoretical and operational terms. It is better to try to study the behavior of pulling hairs out of the scalp as an indicator of some general construct like self-mutilation or self-directed anger than not to specify what construct and theory the behavior is intended to reflect.

Step 2

Review the pertinent theoretical and empirical literature concerning the constructs to be measured. This allows an understanding of what theories have been proposed to understand and explain the phenomena under study. Although it is not necessary to pick one theoretical approach for understanding a phenomenon and those constructs involved in it, it greatly simplifies many of the issues in doing the research.

Reviewing the pertinent theoretical and empirical literature allows a researcher to identify how other researchers have attempted to measure aspects of the constructs that are to be studied. This permits the researcher to evaluate the proposed measures in terms of the evidence presented about the measures' reliability and validity as well as the adequacy and appropriateness of the norms for these measures. It is crucial in choosing measures that involve a subject's understanding of language that an investigator carefully examine the language in terms of its appropriateness for the subjects that will be tested. This includes both the test items and the instructions. It would be unwise to choose a measure for studying depression in older adolescents that was constructed for measuring depression in young children because the language of the items may not have the same meaning and/or be appropriate for both groups.

It is not uncommon in both single-subject and group research for investigators to choose measures that are easy to obtain. This applies to both standardized tests as well as behavioral observations. Researchers sometimes do this in spite of the fact that the measures chosen may not appropriately operationalize the constructs of interest. This tendency is particularly likely when measures are contained in an archive or a part of the regular information-gathering function of some organization. Schools often keep exhaustive records on students, which may include standardized test scores, IQ measures, number and pattern of days absent from school, and number of discipline referrals. Although it may be tempting to take advantage of this archival data, none of these measures may reflect the constructs of interest. Additionally, when archival data are used there is no assurance about the reliability and validity of the data, because these issues are rarely a matter of concern for the record keepers. Also, reporting criteria may change over time or across reporters.

Although counting some easily observed behavior is common in single-subject design, ease of data collection may lead a researcher to choose measures that do not accurately reflect the constructs of interest. Forcing a measure and construct fit is as problematic as trying to put a size 6 shoe on a size 12 foot.

Step 3

For each construct, draw a blueprint. A *blueprint* is an outline of the construct to be measured. A good blueprint is drawn from the theory on which the measure is based. It is best to have the blueprint in outline form so that it contains an organized list of the basic behaviors that can be observed and reported. The blueprint is meant to be a well-defined plan for choosing items, measures and/or behaviors. It is important for the blueprint to include a complete breakdown of the construct, including a statement of the hypothesized factorial complexity and structure of the construct. It is also important that it is made clear as to how the behaviors that will be measured fit together and are related to each other (factorial structure). Suppose a researcher was interested in measuring anxiety as a dependent measure in a single-subject experiment. After reading the literature on anxiety, the researcher decided that anxiety could be defined as a subject's response to an aversive or fear-producing stimulus, and that response would have cognitive, physiological, and behavioral components. Using these three major categories the researcher could begin to make a detailed list for each of these three categories of the behaviors that he or she might expect would evidence the presence of anxiety. This detailed list would be the blueprint for the construct of anxiety. In making the blueprint the researcher would have to specify how each behavior would be measured, because different measuring procedures might produce different results. For example, if the researcher thought that increased heart rate was a behavior that indicated the presence of anxiety, different results might be obtained if heart rate changes were measured using self report, EKG recordings, or pulse taken by an experimenter.

Once the researcher has drawn up a proposed blueprint, it would be necessary for the researcher to hypothesize how the various aspects of the blueprint fit together (factorial structure). If the researcher believed that anxiety is a unitary construct, then it would be expected that all of the behaviors would correlate highly and indicate the presence of a single factor. If the investigator thought that the behaviors within each category would correlate highly, but that the major categories of anxiety would not be correlated, then it would be expected that anxiety was a higher-order construct and was composed of three factors. The reason why one is interested in determining factorial structure is that it indicates the number of scores that can be used as dependent measures. If anxiety is a single factor, then one score (a total) would reflect it adequately. If anxiety is thought to be three factors, then three scores would be needed to represent it. A number of factorial structures could be postulated for the measure of any construct. We believe that it is necessary for researchers to hypothesize a factorial structure for their measures. The analysis of the data will provide the ultimate test as to the factorial structure of a measure, but it is necessary, as in all scientific investigations, to be guided by a theoretically derived hypothesis.

After the blueprint is made for each construct, draw a schematic plan that outlines the construct to be measured and shows how each construct is related to the other constructs in the theory. The schematic plan should be drawn from the theory that is used to explain the phenomena under consideration. The schematic plan should be in outline form and contain the basic behaviors that can be observed and reported (operationalized). A path diagram is a good example of a schematic plan showing relationship among constructs and measures.

It is probably a good idea to show the blueprint(s) and schematic plan to other researchers in the field to get feedback on the ideas. This provides independent verification of one's own translation.

Step 4

Once Steps 1, 2, and 3 are completed, measures can be chosen for the study. It is best to use measures that have established evidence for their reliability and validity. Many investigators are aware of this principle and apply it to measures that are used in group studies of constructs, such as intelligence, anxiety, and depression. Investigators who conduct single-subject and group behaviorally oriented research often assume that there is no need to consider the concepts of reliability and validity of their measures. The implication seems to be that if what is measured is easily observable, then there is no need to consider these concepts. Moreover, if a measure has been shown to be reliable, then it will also be valid. Shoe size, as measure of intelligence, will very likely be reliable, but we doubt that many people would be willing to attest to its validity. We hope that this exposition dispels the previously stated misconceptions because, in all cases, measures or operations are maximally useful and informative when they reflect constructs that are imbedded in a theoretical system and have been shown to have evidence for both validity and reliability.

VALIDITY

Validity can be thought of as the scientific utility of a measuring instrument broadly defined as the degree to which a measuring instrument measures what it purports to measure (Nunnally & Bernstein, 1994). There are three types of validity: construct validity, predictive validity, and content validity. Each one corresponds to the type of information necessary to demonstrate the utility of a given measuring instrument. See Nunnally and Bernstein (1994) for a detailed description of the methods and issues in validity.

Construct validity refers to a series of procedures that demonstrate the degree to which a measuring instrument measures a given construct. Predictive validity refers to the establishment of a statistical relationship between a measuring instrument and a clearly definable criterion. Content validity refers to the degree to which a measuring instrument reflects a clearly defined content area. Nunnally and Bernstein (1994) indicated that some psychometricians have suggested that because all of these procedures involve scientific generalization, they all can be considered to be part of construct validity. They stated that, although this point is well taken, each of these types of validity involve a different aspect of scientific generalization and, therefore, should be kept separate.

Validity is a matter of degree and not an all-or-none characteristic of a measuring instrument. Nunnally and Bernstein (1994) pointed out that all validation requires the gathering of empirical data. Content validity involves the determination of the degree to which a measuring instrument accurately reflects a content domain. The methods for establishing content validity include the development and evaluation of a detailed blueprint, as outlined earlier. The empirical data gathered here consists of ratings of the appropriateness of the blueprint by the experts. These ratings can be used as the quantitative evidence for content validity.

Predictive validity involves the establishment of a functional relationship between a measure and a criterion. A criterion is an independent measure of the construct that is being assessed. Criteria must have strong evidence for their own reliability and validity in order to be useful in the validation process. There are a number of problems in establishing the predictive validity of a measuring instrument, the most important of which is finding an appropriate criterion.

Construct validation involves determining the relationship between a measuring instrument and other measuring instruments to determine what aspects of the construct the measuring instrument reflects (convergent validity) and what constructs it does not reflect (discriminant validity). Construct validity involves gathering many sets of data to determine just what the measuring instrument is and is not measuring. For example, if one were to construct a measure of test anxiety, it would be expected that it would correlate moderately with a measure of general anxiety, negatively with various measures of well-being and positive adjustment, and very low with measures of social desirability and intelligence. It would also be expected that the scores of subjects scoring high on this measure would decrease with standard treatments for anxiety. If any of these expected relationships were not obtained with many samples and different types of measuring instruments (self-report, peer ratings, etc.), then one might revise the measuring instrument so that the expected relationships would result. Alternatively, one might redefine what it was this measuring instrument was actually measuring. It might be pointed out that if the measures of test anxiety and general anxiety were very highly correlated (e.g., .80 or .90) there would be no basis for claiming that the measure of test anxiety measured something uniquely different from anxiety in general. Campbell and Fiske (1959) clarified the importance of separating method variance and attribute variance in gathering data for construct validity. This is why it is important to include measuring instruments that use different methods (self-report, expert ratings, peer ratings, etc.) in a validity study. Campbell and Fiske's (1959) multitrait-multimethod matrix is considered to be a major advancement in the study of validity.

Validity involves the use of empirical data to define a construct and, therefore, validity studies help the researcher define in operational terms what his or her measuring instruments are measuring. Validity is best thought of in terms of the use of a measure. Measures that are valid for one use may not be valid for another. A ruler might be an excellent measure of length but a poor measure of weight. It is important in choosing a measure that sufficient evidence be available for the validity of the use of that measure.

Although validation procedures and evidence for validity are an essential part of the construction and evaluation of standardized measuring devices in a number of areas of psychological, educational, and sociological work, they have not received much attention in observation and single-subject research (e.g., Barlow & Hersen, 1993). Barlow and Hersen pointed out that behavioral observations have been considered by some to have an inherent validity because they are based on a direct sampling of behavior and require minimal inference on the part of the observer. Therefore, one might argue that it is not necessary to validate the observation of a head bang as a dependent measure in a research study. All that needs to be done is to ensure that the raters observing this behavior are doing so reliably because what constitutes a head bang is obvious. The assumption of inherent validity is an epistemological error (Haynes, 1978). Data obtained by human observers may not be veridical descriptions of behavior. Validity studies are necessary because of this lack of veridicality, which can be due to a number of factors including various sources of unreliability, contamination by reactivity effects, and other sources of measurement bias (Barlow & Hersen, 1993).

The need for validation is argued on logical and practical grounds. Is it true that what constitutes a head bang is obvious? Are all movements of the head toward a solid surface head bangs? Are all head bangs exactly the same? Are all head bangs so obvious that they will be recorded as such by all or most observers? Is there any cranial contact with a solid surface that would not be classified as a head bang? It may be obvious to the reader that what is needed here is a definition of exactly what constitutes a head bang. The process of definition is exactly what validation is all about. Validity can be thought of as gathering empirical information for determining exactly what a measuring instrument does and does not measure. We begin with a set of rules which constitute the measuring instrument. These rules are then tested by gathering data (predictive, construct, or content) that support or help us modify these rules. This is the process of validation. It should be pointed out that it is not possible to do a reliability study unless some validity has been established and that the source of unreliability in many observational measures is the lack of clear definition and rules (validity).

RELIABILITY

Reliability refers to the repeatability and/or consistency of measurement. It is considered by many to be a fundamental characteristic of measurement (eg., Ghiselli, Campbell, & Zedeck, 1981). Reliability can be defined as the proportion of a measurement that reflects true score, that is, it is the part of obtained score that reflects the actual characteristic or construct that is being measured. For example, if you used a ruler and made several independent measures of the length of an object, it is highly unlikely that all of the resulting measurements would be the same. Because it is reasonable to believe that the actual length of object (true score) did not change from time to time, how would one explain the fact that the measurements were not all exactly the same? The variability among the measurements could be explained by assuming that each time the length of the object was measured there were a number of random factors that affected the resulting measurement. These random factors might include slight variations in where the end of the ruler was placed, variations in how evenly the ruler was held, differences in the angle at which the measurements were read, and a large, perhaps infinite, number of other possible factors. These factors that collectively are called sources of *measurement error* are random in that they vary from measurement to measurement in an unsystematic way. If there is a factor that affects measurement in a consistent way, then it is called a *bias*. Biases affect agreement indices but have no effect on association indices.

There are a number of possible sources of measurement error that can be identified for any measurement procedure (see Stanley, 1971, for details). It is the job of those who construct measuring procedures to be aware of these sources of measurement error and construct the procedures to control for as many of these as possible. Sources of measurement error for observational instruments usually center around the degree to which the rules for observation unambiguously represent the construct of interest, the degree to which observers' biases affect the observations and measurements that they make, and the degree to which observers understand and follow the directions for observation. Given this, it is necessary to spend a good deal of time constructing the directions and rules for observation. It is essential to determine the degree to which the tasks that the observers are to perform are specified in an unambiguous manner and conform to the constructs under consideration. In order to do this, it is a good idea to construct the observational tasks using a systematic, theory-based procedure like the one previously outlined in detail in Step 3.

Once the directions and tasks for observation are clearly specified and reflect that construct under consideration, it is necessary to specify clearly what prior experience, education, or training observers need to have to do an effective job. Once this is done, it is important to lay out how observers will be trained to ensure that they will follow the procedures for observation consistently. The training needs to involve not only the understanding of what is to be done, but also the identification of possible observer biases and ways that observers can be aware of and counteract these biases. It cannot be overly stressed how important it is to plan time for training observers. This training should involve empirical trial measurements in which assessments of reliability and biases are made, evaluated, and feedback given to the trainees. It is often necessary to have a number of training trials before one can be confident that observers will be reliable and be able to identify and counteract their own biases. If observers learn on the job it will never be clear what they are learning or doing. The impact of this is likely to be undefinable sources of unreliability and bias that will unduly affect measurements.

There are essentially two classes of methods for determining the reliability of observational measurement procedures. The first method involves having a number of observers make observations and measurements of the same set of subjects on one occasion, and quantifying the degree to which observers agree. This method has been referred to as the method of *interrater reliability* and is analogous to the method of parallel forms used to estimate the reliability of many psychometric instruments. The advantage of this method is that it can be done efficiently and repeatedly as part of a training procedure. Its disadvantage is that it does not allow for the estimation of the temporal stability of the measurement procedure.

The second method for estimating the reliability of observational measurement procedures involves having a number of observers make observations and measurements on a number of subjects on more than one occasion. The degree to which observers agree with themselves across time is then quantified. This method is referred to as the method of *intrarater reliability* and is analogous to the method of retest reliability, which has also been used to estimate the reliability of some psychometric instruments. This method also allows for the estimation of *interrater reliability* at each time period, and therefore provides a great deal of information about the reliability of the procedure under consideration. The advantage of this method is that it allows for the estimation of the temporal stability of the measurement procedure because measurements are taken with some meaningful time in between them. A major disadvantage is that estimates of reliability using this method can be contaminated by practice and memory effects and therefore rendered inappropriate. This is especially likely if the repeated measurements are done in close proximity. It is also very time and resource consuming. It is interesting to note that the method of interrater reliability is the most widely used method for assessing the reliability of observational measurements.

There are a number of methods for quantifying the reliability of observational measurements procedures. The next section presents many of these methods in detail.

QUANTIFYING RELIABILITY

Reliability indices can appraise either or both of two different things: the extent to which alternative ratings are similar in *relative* position (i.e., association indices), or the extent to which alternative ratings are similar in *absolute* position (i.e., agreement indices; Stine, 1989). A brief illustration may be helpful. Table 3.1 shows data on six hypothetical observations evaluated by five hypothetical raters. Raters 1 and 2 have perfect association (the correlation among their responses would be 1.0) but zero agreement, that is, they never agree. Raters 3 and 4 exhibit some agreement (they agree half of the time) but zero association, that is, their responses are uncorrelated. Finally, Raters 1 and 5 have perfect agreement and association.

Later in the chapter we present reliability indices in categories of those that measure association, agreement, or both. The reader should

TABLE 3.1
Six Hypothetical Observation Units Evaluated by Five Hypothetical Raters

	Rater				
ID #	*1*	*2*	*3*	*4*	*5*
1	2	4	1	0	2
2	3	6	0	0	3
3	4	8	1	1	4
4	5	10	0	1	5
5	6	12	1	0	6
6	7	14	0	0	7

note that our listing of possible reliability indices is not exhaustive. A bewildering variety of indices has been proposed over the years, and many are minor variations on one another or have rarely been used. These are not presented here. More comprehensive listings can be found in Hartmann (1982), Page and Iwata (1986), Suen and Ary (1989), Tinsley and Weiss (1975), and the references cited therein. The reliability indices we review and some of their important characteristics are given in Table 3.2. For the case of two raters and a dichotomous response variable, Suen and Ary (1986) provided formulae to convert one index to another. After reviewing reliability indices, we briefly consider some related issues such as the appropriate unit of analysis for reliability calculations, ways to promote reliability, the current "state of the art," and useful software.

In the presentation to follow, we frequently refer to *raters* and *interrater reliability*. However, the reader should note that we use the term *rater* in a very generic sense to mean a thing that collects and records data, so that where we have *interrater reliability* the reader could equally appropriately read *interactometer reliability*, *intercaliper reliability*, *interobserver reliability*, and so on. This points out that raters are but one facet of reliability. Reliability might also be assessed over time, instruments, settings, and so forth. In fact, the most sophisticated approach to reliability might be to assess ratings over several of these facets or factors simultaneously in an ANOVA framework. If one continued on this path, one would reinvent *generalizability theory*. Generalizability theory is a very general approach to reliability that can consider multiple sources of error variance (e.g., raters, instruments, etc.) simultaneously. In fact, the intraclass reliability approach, which we advocate later in this chapter, can be seen as a one-facet (i.e., one-factor) generalizability study. The

TABLE 3.2
Summary of Some Common Reliability Indices

Index	*Type of Data Suitable for*	*Usable With > 2 raters*	*Standard Error Known*	*Takes Chance Agreement Into Account*	*Assesses Association or Agreement*
1. PPMC	Dichotomous, ordinal, interval, ratio	No	Yes	N/A	Association
2. ICCs	Ordinal, interval, ratio	Yes	Yes	N/A	Association or both depending on the ICC
3. Proportion agreement	Dichotomous, nominal	No	Yes	No	Agreement
4. Occurrence & nonocurrence agreement	Dichotomous	No	No	No	Agreement
5. Total agreement	Ratio	No	No	N/A	Agreement
6. Exact agreement	All	No	Yes	No	Agreement
7. Kappa	Dichotomous, nominal	Yes	Yes	Yes	Agreement
8. r_{wg}	Ordinal, interval, ratio (w/finite range)	Yes	No	N/A	Agreement
9. Lin's Index	Ordinal, interval, ratio	No	Yes	N/A	Both

reader interested in pursuing the generalizability approach further is referred to Cronbach, Gleser, Nanda, and Rajarartnam (1972). Mitchell (1979) discussed the possibility of conducting single-case generalizability studies.

INDICES OF ASSOCIATION OR SIMILARITY IN RELATIVE POSITION

Pearson Product Moment Correlation

The Pearson product moment correlation (PPMC) coefficient is one of the most widely used reliability indices. Because virtually all statistics texts (e.g., Hays, 1988) cover this statistic extensively, we do not delve into methods for its computation in detail here. Succinctly, if both raters' scores are expressed as standardized deviations from their respective means (i.e., *z*-scores), the PPMC can be calculated as the average of the cross-product of ratings. In the case of dichotomous data, the PPMC is algebraically equivalent to the phi coefficient.

Advantages. The PPMC has numerous advantages. On the human factors side, it is well known, easy to calculate, and easy to interpret because the metric is so familiar. From a statistical viewpoint, its properties are well known (including its standard error), confidence intervals are easily constructed, and significance tests can be performed on single PPMCs or on the difference between two or more independent or dependent PPMCs. Finally, the statistic is tied to a large body of measurement theory and method, allowing its integration into many other useful formulae, such as the correction for attenuation due to unreliability or range restriction. See Allen and Yen (1979) for an exposition on these topics.

Disadvantages. Like all measures of similarity in relative position, the PPMC ignores systematic differences in absolute position. In addition, the PPMC cannot be used when there are more than two raters.

The Intraclass Correlation Coefficients (ICCs)

Many reports refer to *the* intraclass correlation coefficient. However, Shrout and Fleiss' (1979) excellent article pointed out that there are actually many different ICCs. ICCs are typically calculated from the summary table of a two-way (session by observer) analysis of variance (MacLennan, 1993). ICCs are essentially ratios of "true" variance to "error" variance. We describe two ICCs in this subsection and two more in the subsection on indices of both agreement and association. Others are described by Shrout and Fleiss (1979).

Following Shrout and Fleiss' (1979) notation, the two ICCs we discuss here are ICC(3,1) and ICC(3,k). These ICCs treat the judges (observers) as "fixed effects," and therefore, variance due to judges is not included in the error term of the ICC. This has the effect of ignoring differences among judges in terms of mean level and making ICC(3,1) and ICC(3,k) indices of association rather than agreement. ICC(3,1) is an appropriate index when *all* of the actual data to be analyzed will be collected by one and only one person, and is essentially equivalent to a Pearson correlation. ICC(3,k) is an appropriate index when *each datum* to be analyzed will be the average of the same k judges. In other words, if the same k judges observe behavior or provide ratings at every session (trial, day, etc.) and the average of these k judges is used as the dependent variable, then ICC(3,k) is the appropriate index. In both of these two cases, variability among judges (that is systematic differences in level) is never allowed to influence the dependent variable, and it is therefore not necessary to include it in the error term.

ICC(3,1) is calculated as:

$$ICC(3,1) = \frac{BMS - EMS}{BMS + (k - 1)EMS} \tag{3.1}$$

where BMS is the between-session (day, interval, etc.) mean square, EMS is the error mean square, and k is the number of raters. ICC(3,k) is calculated as:

$$ICC(3,k) = \frac{BMS - EMS}{BMS} \tag{3.2}$$

ICC(3,k) will virtually always be higher than ICC(3,1), which illustrates the advantage of averaging multiple ratings. In this context, it is instructive to note that ICC (3,k) is equivalent to Cronbach's coefficient α if raters are considered items.

Confidence Limits. Methods for placing confidence limits around ICCs are presented in the Appendix.

Advantages. The ICCs are excellent choices for reliability coefficients for several reasons. First, they can be used when more than two raters are available. Alternate forms are available to suit the appropriate situation. Like PPMCs, their statistical properties are well worked out, allowing one to estimate confidence intervals (Shrout & Fleiss, 1979), to test for differences between coefficients (Alsawalmeh & Feldt, 1992), and generally incorporate them into other measurement procedures.

Disadvantages. The primary disadvantage of the ICCs is their relative computation complexity, but this is easily solved by available software (see software section later in this chapter). A second minor disadvantage is that ICCs can occasionally attain values < 0 or > 1 (Lahey, Downey, & Saal, 1983), but in our experience this is quite rare.

INDICES OF AGREEMENT OR SIMILARITY IN ABSOLUTE POSITION

To aid our exposition of agreement indices, we introduce Table 3.3 and some notation. Table 3.3 is a 2×2 cross-tabulation of two judges' dichotomous scoring of a series of stimuli.[1] In the context of single-case research, these stimuli are usually discrete time intervals within an observation period. For example, each judge could be recording whether or not an autistic child head-banged in each 30-second interval of a 30-minute observation session. In Table 3.3, a, b, c, and d are frequencies; $p_1 = (a + b)/(a + b + c + d)$; $p_2 = (a + c)/(a + b + c + d)$; $q_1 = 1 - p_1$; and $q_2 = 1 - p_2$.

Proportion Agreement

Proportion agreement (also called "interval agreement," "overall agreement," "combined agreement," and "Type II reliability"; Page & Iwata, 1986) is probably the most commonly reported measure of interobserver agreement (Kelly, 1977). Proportion agreement is calculated as $((a + d)/(a + b + c + d))$; where a, b, c, and d are defined as in Table 3.3. Frequently, proportion agreement is multiplied by 100 and expressed as a percent agreement. The standard error of proportion agreement is given by:

$$SE_{P_a} = \sqrt{(P_a(1-P_a))/N} \tag{3.3}$$

where $N = a + b + c + d$. This is a large sample approximation that we believe will be quite satisfactory when $N \geq 50$. For more exact standard

[1]Two-by-two tables such as Table 3.3 are tied to many important statistics (e.g., relative risk, odds ratio, etc.) including the concepts of *sensitivity* and *specificity*, terms frequently used to describe the accuracy of diagnostic tests. Specifically, a/c can be thought of as sensitivity and b/d as specificity.

TABLE 3.3
Cross-Tabulation of Two Judges' Dichotomous Scoring of a Series of Stimuli

		Rater 1: 1 (Yes; Occurred; Present)	Rater 1: 0 (No; Did Not Occur; Absent)	
Rater 2	1	a	b	p_2
	0	c	d	q_2
		p_1	q_1	

errors and methods for constructing asymmetric confidence intervals, see Stuart and Ord (1991).

Advantages. The main advantage of proportion agreement is its simplicity.

Disadvantages. Proportion agreement is only suitable when data are discrete (i.e., not continuous) and only two raters are involved. An additional major problem with many indices of agreement is that they fail to account for "chance agreement" and proportion agreement is no exception (Hawkins & Dotson, 1975). This is especially problematic when responses have markedly unequal frequencies or "asymmetric marginal distributions." Consider the following example: $p_1 = p_2 = .9$. Therefore, $q_1 = q_2 = .1$. Even if Rater 1's judgments are completely unconnected to Rater 2's judgments, on the average both raters will report an occurrence 81% of the time (i.e., $.9^2$) and a nonoccurrence 1% of the time (i.e., $.1^2$). Thus, proportion agreement will be .82, which seems quite respectable even if the raters are responding completely at random! For this reason, we generally do not consider proportion agreement an adequate reliability index, especially when the marginal distributions are markedly asymmetric (i.e., with very high or low frequency behaviors).

Occurrence and Nonoccurrence Agreement

Occurrence and nonoccurrence agreement indices were developed to overcome the chance agreement problem (Hawkins and Dotson, 1975) and are suitable when the response variable is measured on a dichotomous scale. Given Table 3.3, occurrence agreement is defined as $a/(a + b + c)$, and nonoccurrence agreement is defined as $d/(b + c + d)$. Variations on these indices and suggestions for combining them can be found in Harris and Lahey (1978) and Page and Iwata (1986).

Advantages. The greatest advantage of the occurrence and nonoccurrence agreement indices is that they are not completely distorted by chance agreement.

Disadvantages. There are several major disadvantages of the occurrence and nonoccurrence agreement indices. The first is that one ends up with two separate, and potentially quite disparate, indices. *It is therefore essential that any investigator using these indices report both.* Second, occurrence and nonoccurrence agreement do not completely control for chance agreement (Hopkins & Hermann, 1977). Rather, they merely ensure that, under chance agreement, at least one of the two indices will be fairly low. Specifically, if the two raters are responding completely at chance, one of the two indices can be no greater than .33. However, the value of the other index can still approach 1.0 under completely chance responding. Third, to our knowledge, their standard errors are unknown. Finally, occurrence and nonoccurrence agreement are only suitable when data are dichotomous and only two raters are involved.

Total Agreement

Total agreement, also called "smaller/larger index" "Type I reliability," and "marginal agreement index" (Page & Iwata, 1986; Suen & Ary, 1989), is very simple to calculate. One obtains the rating (frequency count, number of intervals containing the behavior, etc.) from each of two raters. The smaller rating is divided by the larger rating and the result is multiplied by 100. This yields an index of reliability that can range from 0 to 100%, where 100% presumably indicates "perfect" reliability.

Advantages. Total agreement is extremely simple to calculate. In addition, it can be calculated given even a single score for each rater and, therefore, does not require the amount of data that many other indices (e.g., PPMC, ICCs) do.

Disadvantages. Total agreement cannot be used when more than two raters provide ratings. In addition, there are far more serious problems with the total agreement index (see Suen, Lee, & Prochnow-LaGrow, 1985, for a thorough critique). Not the least of the problems with the total agreement index is that its expected value approaches 100 as the coefficient of variation[2] of the ratings decreases even if there is complete stochastic independence[3] among the raters. In other words, even if raters pick numbers at random, total agreement indices will be high if the standard deviation of ratings is small relative to mean ratings. Because the mean and standard deviation have such a large impact on the index, it is completely inappropriate for use with interval and ordinal data where the mean and standard deviation are arbitrary. Finally, the standard error of the statistic is not known, which makes its interpretation somewhat difficult. For these and other reasons, we concur with Suen and Ary (1989) and do *not* recommend use of the total agreement index.

Exact Agreement

Exact agreement is calculable when data exist in the form of frequency counts during numerous intervals. In this case, exact agreement (E_a) = (N_a/N_t), where N_a is the number of intervals during which the two raters agreed *exactly* on the number of responses emitted and N_t is the total number of intervals during which observations took place. As with proportion agreement, the standard error of the exact agreement is given by:

$$SE_{E_a} = \sqrt{(E_a(1-E_a))/N_t} \tag{3.4}$$

Again, this is a large sample approximation that we believe works quite well when $N_t \geq 50$. For more exact standard errors and methods for constructing asymmetric confidence intervals, see Stuart and Ord (1991).

Advantages. Again, the main advantage of exact agreement is that it is simple.

Disadvantages. First, exact agreement is only suitable for use with two raters. Second, it is frequently stated that exact agreement is very conservative or stringent because raters do not get credit for an agree-

[2]The coefficient of variation is defined as the standard deviation divided by the mean.

[3]By "complete stochastic independence" we mean that there is *no* relationship (as opposed to simply no linear relationship).

ment during an interval unless they agree perfectly. However, we believe that the terms *conservative* or *stringent* have unjustifiably positive connotations in this context. Instead, we would call exact agreement an "ignorant" index because it "ignores" important differences among differences; that is, it treats large and small differences as though they were the same. For example, it treats an interval in which Rater 1 records a frequency of 0 and Rater 2 records a frequency of 100 the same as an interval in which Rater 1 records a frequency of 99 and Rater 2 records a frequency of 100. Ignoring the differences among these differences is equivalent to discarding a great deal of information (Mitchell, 1979; Tinsley & Weiss, 1975). For this reason, we do not recommend the use of exact agreement.

Kappa

Kappa was developed by Cohen (1960) to provide an index of agreement that accounted for the base rate problem (i.e., chance agreement). Kappa is suitable when responses are measured on a nominal scale including dichotomous (yes–no) data. When multiple raters are involved, multiple kappa (Fleiss, 1971) may be used. *Kappa* is defined as the observed proportion agreement minus the expected agreement all over 1 minus the expected agreement; i.e., $K = (p_o - p_e)/(1 - p_e)$, where p_o is the proportion agreement; p_e is the agreement expected by chance and calculated, in the case of a dichotomous variable, as $(p_1p_2 + q_1q_2)$; and p_1, p_2, q_1, and q_2 are defined as in Table 3.3. In the two rater and two response class situation, kappa can be reexpressed as a function only of p_o, p_1, and p_2:

$$\kappa = \left[\frac{(p_o - 1)}{p_1 + (1 - 2p_1)p_2} \right] + 1 \tag{3.5}$$

The more general expression for kappa is:

$$\kappa = \frac{\sum_{i=1}^{N} \sum_{j=1}^{k} n_{ij}^2 - Nn\left[1 + (n - 1) \sum_{j=1}^{k} p_j^2 \right]}{Nn(n - 1)\left(1 - \sum_{j=1}^{k} p_j^2 \right)} \tag{3.6}$$

where N is the total number of stimuli (e.g., intervals) being rated, n is the number of ratings per stimulus, k is the number of categories into which stimuli can be assigned (usually two in single-case research, i.e., occurred and not occurred), the subscripts i and j represent the subjects and categories respectively, n_{ij} is the number of raters who assigned the ith subject to the jth category, and p_j is the proportion of all assignments that were in the jth category (Fleiss, 1975).

The standard error of kappa (Fleiss, 1971) is:

$$SE(\kappa) = \sqrt{\left(\frac{2}{Nn(n-1)}\right)\left(\frac{\sum_j p_j^2 - (2n-3)\left(\sum_j p_j^2\right)^2 + 2(n-2)\sum_j p_j^3}{\left(1-\sum_j p_j^2\right)^2}\right)} \quad (3.7)$$

This formula is a large sample approximation. For those interested in exact standard errors for small samples and building asymmetric confidence intervals, see Everitt (1968) and Hale and Fleiss (1993). If this formula seems daunting, one might use simple nomograms for estimating approximate standard errors that were provided by Hanley (1987). We reproduce the nomogram for the 2 × 2 case here (see Fig. 3.1).

Frequently, a published paper only reports percent agreement and p_1. Yet, the reader may wish to estimate kappa. In this case, Lee and Suen (1984) provided useful formulae. They showed that if one can calculate the maximum and minimum possible values of p_2, one can estimate the maximum and minimum possible values of kappa. To estimate the maximum value of p_2, Lee and Suen (1984) provided the following inequalities:

$$p_2 \leq 1 - p_o + p_1$$
$$p_2 \leq 1 - p_1 + p_o$$
$$p_2 \leq 1$$

To estimate the minimum value of p_2, Lee and Suen (1984) provided the following inequalities:

$$p_2 \geq 1 - p_o - p_1$$
$$p_2 \geq p_1 + p_o - 1$$
$$p_2 \geq 0$$

Having found the minimum and maximum values of p_2, they can be substituted into Equation 3.3 to find the minimum and maximum values of kappa, respectively.

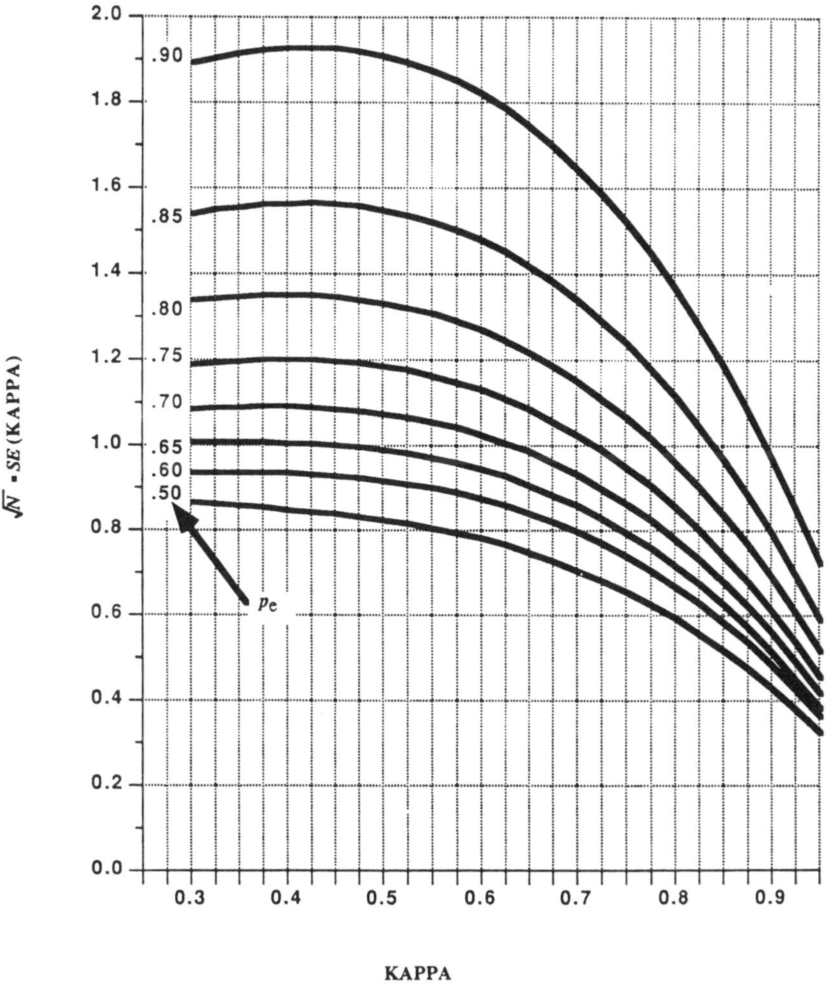

FIG. 3.1. An approximation to $\sqrt{N} \cdot SE(\kappa)$ when κ is calculated from a 2 × 2 table. Each curve is derived from 14 data points, corresponding to $\kappa = 0.3(0.05)0.95$; each data point was obtained by averaging the *SE*s from 20 different tables yielding the same value of κ and p_e; the error of approximation in using this nomogram instead of Equation 1 to calculate $SE(\kappa)$ is generally on the order of $1/\sqrt{N}$ to $3/\sqrt{N}$ percent. Reprinted with permission.

Kappa often surprises investigators by appearing overly stringent in the face of *seemingly* higher reliability. Although kappa can theoretically reach a value of 1.0, it can only do so when the marginal distributions are equal for the two (or more) raters. For this reason, some investigators (e.g., Soeken & Prescott, 1986) suggest that kappa be expressed as a ratio of the obtained kappa over the maximum possible kappa given the observed marginal asymmetry. However, we are in agreement with Cohen (1960) that this is not a logical procedure because unequal marginal distributions can only arise from disagreements and therefore should not be "corrected away."

Advantages. Kappa has at least three major advantages to recommend its use. First, it takes chance agreement into account. Second, its standard error is well known and, therefore, confidence intervals can be constructed and significance tests conducted. Third, when multiple raters are used, multiple kappa is available.

Disadvantages. Other than computational complexity, which is minimal in the common 2 × 2 case and easily relegated to a computer in more complex cases, we know of no major disadvantages of kappa. For these reasons, we highly recommend the use of kappa when data are dichotomous or nominal.

The Within-Group Interrater Agreement Index r_{wg}

James, Demaree, and Wolf (1993) proposed a rather interesting index of rater agreement. Just as Yarnold (1988; see Gorman & Allison, chap. 6, this volume for a description) derived data analytic techniques for the limiting situation in which, for example, scores are available on two or more variables for one subject at one point, James et al. derived a method for calculating an agreement index when scores are available from two or more raters for one subject at one point in time. Theoretically, r_{wg} can range from 0, meaning no agreement, to 1, meaning perfect agreement (although values outside this range could occur in practice). One can calculate r_{wg} as: $r_{wg} = (\sigma_e^2 - S_x^2)/\sigma_e^2$, where S_x^2 is the variance of observed scores and σ_e^2 is the variance of scores that would be obtained if each rater were responding at random. One can calculate S_x^2 from the observed data, but σ_e^2 must be estimated from some assumed random distribution and this is the tricky part. James et al. recommended that the distribution be considered to be a uniform (i.e., rectangular) distribution with a range over the entire theoretical response range (e.g., with a 1 to 5 rating scale, the range is 4). In a uniform distribution, the variance is equal to half the range and this is the estimate of σ_e^2 used. Finn (cited in Tinsley & Weiss, 1975) advocated a very similar index.

Although this is an interesting notion, r_{wg} has been heavily criticized (Schmidt & Hunter, 1989). Probably the greatest problem is the rather arbitrary choice of distribution on which to base σ_e^2. For these reasons, we urge researchers to obtain reliability data on far more than one time point on one individual whenever possible. At this point r_{wg} can only be considered a last resort index.

INDICES OF SIMILARITY IN RELATIVE AND ABSOLUTE POSITION

Lin's ρ_c

Lin (1989) proposed a very interesting index of reliability which he referred to as the *concordance correlation coefficient*, or ρ_c. To our knowledge, ρ_c has not yet been applied in single-case designs. This coefficient was specifically designed to simultaneously account the extent to which alternative ratings are similar in relative position *and* the extent to which alternative ratings are similar in absolute position. The calculation of ρ_c is:

$$\rho_c = \frac{\frac{2}{n}\sum (X_{i1} - \overline{X}_1)(X_{i2} - \overline{X}_2)}{S_1^2 + S_2^2 + (\overline{X}_1 - \overline{X}_2)^2} \tag{3.8}$$

where n is the number of observations, $\bar{X}_1$ is the mean for Rater 1, $\bar{X}_2$ is the mean for Rater 2, S_2^1 is the variance for Rater 1, and S_2^2 is the variance for Rater 2. The standard error of ρ_c is:

$$SE_{PC} = \sqrt{\frac{1}{n-2}[(1-r^2)\rho_c^2(1-\rho_c^2)/r^2 + 4\rho_c^3(1-\rho_c)u^2/r - 2\rho_c^4u^4/r^2]} \tag{3.9}$$

where r is the Pearson correlation between Raters 1 and 2, and u is $(\bar{X}_1 - \bar{X}_2)/(S_1^2S_2^2)^{.5}$. This can be used for placing confidence intervals around the obtained coefficient or testing its statistical significance. If desired, Lin (1989) described procedures for obtaining more precise asymmetric confidence intervals using the Fisher r-to-z transformation.

Advantages. Lin's index has much to recommend it. Specifically, it takes into account both random and systematic inconsistencies among observers, it is bounded by −1 and 1, and its standard error has been worked out. (Note the close conceptual similarity between Lin's index and the ICCs presented next.)

Disadvantages. Lin's index is not viable when more than two raters are involved, and is not well known.

Intraclass Correlation Coefficients

Apart from the ICCs described previously, two other ICCs[4] are likely to be useful in single case research. These ICCs all take level into account and therefore measure both association and agreement. Suppose that *k* judges (observers, raters, etc.) provide reliability data. All of the data points in the study will come from one of the *k* judges, but there will not be the same judge every time. In this case, among-judge variance will contribute to the variance of the dependent variable and, therefore, should be included in the error term of the ICC. In this case, the appropriate index is ICC(2,1), which is calculated as:

$$ICC(2,1) = \frac{BMS - EMS}{BMS + (k - 1)EMS + k(JMS - \mathrm{EMS})/n} \tag{3.10}$$

where BMS is the between-session (day, interval, etc.) mean square, EMS is the error mean square, JMS is the between-judges mean square, and k is the number of raters.

Consider a second situation. Each datum is rated by *k* raters but it is *not* the same *k* raters every time. In this case, the appropriate index is ICC(2, k), which is calculated as:

$$ICC(2,k) = \frac{BMS - EMS}{BMS + (JMS - \mathrm{EMS})/n} \tag{3.11}$$

Confidence Limits. Methods for placing confidence limits around ICCs are somewhat complex and are, therefore, presented in the Appendix.

Confidence Intervals and Standard Errors

Throughout this section on reliability indices, we have made a point of providing formulae for estimating standard errors of the coefficients whenever possible. The standard error of a statistic gives an indication of how much the statistic is likely to vary from one sample to the next.[5] Thus, the standard error of a reliability coefficient essentially indicates the reliability of the reliability index. Standard errors can be used to construct confidence intervals around reliability coefficients and evalu-

---

[4]ICCs other than those mentioned here are possible. Moreover, other situations besides the four we have described are possible where various ICCs would be appropriate. Given space limitations, we refer the reader to Shrout and Fleiss (1979).

[5]More precisely, the standard error of a statistic is the standard deviation of the sampling distribution of that statistic.

ate the statistical significance of obtained coefficients. We emphasize the former use here.

How to Construct Confidence Intervals. Commonly, one wishes to construct 90% or 95% confidence intervals. For a 90% confidence interval, the lower limit is calculated as the observed coefficient minus 1.645 times the standard error, and the upper limit is calculated as the observed coefficient plus 1.645 times the standard error. For a 95% confidence interval, the lower limit is calculated as the observed coefficient minus 1.96 times the standard error, and the upper limit is calculated as the observed coefficient plus 1.96 times the standard error. More generally, when constructing the α% confidence interval, find the standard normal deviate (i.e., z-score) above which $(1 - \alpha)/2$% of the normal distribution lies. This can be obtained from any table of the normal distribution. Call this value Z. The lower limit of the confidence is calculated as the observed coefficient minus Z times the standard error, and the upper limit is calculated as the observed coefficient plus Z times the standard error.

If the upper or lower limits exceed 0 or 1, respectively, then they should be set at 0 or 1 respectively. An α% confidence interval can be interpreted in the following manner. If an infinite number of random samples of size n were repeatedly taken and the reliability coefficient calculated each time, then α% of the time this coefficient would fall between the upper and lower limits of the confidence interval.

It is important to note that this method of constructing confidence intervals is approximate. However, it is asymptotically accurate; that is, it approaches perfect accuracy as n approaches infinity. Our experience suggests that it yields very reasonable answers when $n \geq 50$. When reliability coefficients are based on smaller numbers of observations or exact confidence intervals are desired, see the previously cited sources for the specific reliability index.

Why Should One Report Confidence Intervals? Suppose one is conducting a study and reliability is estimated on a subsample of the observations and the obtained reliability estimate is .80. One might interpret this very differently if the 95% confidence interval was .78 to .82 versus .60 to 1.00. One would probably have much greater confidence in the reliability of the remainder of the data in the former case than in the latter.

Other Issues in the Calculation of Confidence Intervals. We have already discussed the approximate nature of the confidence interval construction method we described earlier and the need for asymmetric confidence intervals if greater accuracy is desired. There is a second factor that can render the standard errors we provide less than exact. Hartmann and Gardner (1982) described how autocorrelation among the data on which reliability is estimated can introduce bias into the calculated standard errors. They suggested methods for circumventing this problem.

We are in agreement with Hartmann and Gardner's (1982) point and applaud any energetic researchers who employ their methods. However, our opinion is that, for many purposes, such precise procedures are unnecessary. When constructing a confidence interval, one generally simply wishes to know what "neighborhood" the reliability index is in, and approximate standard errors and confidence intervals will suffice.

Finally, a note about significance tests of reliability coefficients is in order. Some authors have described the use of significance tests for indices of reliability (e.g., Ary & Suen, 1985; Harris & Pearlman, 1977). Although standard errors and confidence intervals can be used to test the statistical significance of obtained reliability coefficients, we have not stressed that use here. This is because statistical significance is such a minimal criterion for adequate reliability that we feel it has little import. Given a moderate to large n, an obtained reliability coefficient can be statistically significant despite being unacceptably low. For example, with an n of 100, a correlation of .30 will be statistically significant but it is hardly an impressive reliability coefficient.

The Unit of Analysis

There appears to be some confusion about the appropriate unit of analysis for the estimation of reliability. Let us consider an example. Suppose that, during a study, an individual is observed for 30 minutes per day. Each 30-minute observation session is broken down into 60 30-second intervals. During each 30-second interval, the data collector observes for the first 25 seconds and records for last 5 seconds. The response being recorded is the frequency of head-bangs during the first 25 seconds. Now, when it comes time to analyze the data, numerous alternatives are possible in terms of the level of aggregation chosen (cf. Johnston & Pennypacker, 1980, chap. 12), but let us suppose the researcher chooses to analyze the data at the level of the day. In other words, frequency counts are summed over the 60 intervals from each day's observation session. Thus, the session total (not the interval frequency) is the unit of analysis.

In the opinion of the present authors and many others (e.g., Johnson & Bolstad, 1973; Mitchell, 1979; Stine, 1989), the appropriate level at which to estimate reliability is the same level at which one will analyze the data. Thus, in our example, it would be appropriate to estimate and report the reliability of session totals. In contrast, our experience is that many investigators would mistakenly estimate and report reliability on the level of the 30-second interval. This is not surprising, because many pedagogical presentations of reliability assessment in the literature (e.g., Haynes, 1978; Page & Iwata, 1986) have emphasized the calculation of reliability at the interval or most "molecular" level possible, seemingly attaching nobility to conservative (but incorrect) procedures. Estimating and reporting the reliability of single 30-second intervals when the unit of analysis is a 30-minute total is akin to estimating and reporting the reliability of individual items on a test when using the whole test score as the unit of analysis. If reliability is estimated at a more "micro" level than the unit of analysis, it will probably (although not necessarily) be underestimated (Mitchell, 1979). If reliability is estimated at a more "macro" level than the unit of analysis, it will probably (although not necessarily) be overestimated.

Promoting Reliability

Assessing reliability is well and good. However, steps can also be taken to *promote* reliability.

Clear Instructions. Whenever raters provide data, they do so by following instructions, whether it be in filling out a rating scale or recording direct observations. The data so provided will tend to be most reliable when the rating, observing, and recording instructions are clearly and unambiguously understandable. Although this point may seem obvious, we have frequently had the experience of collecting data that were later found to be uninterpretable. Following these data back to the original protocol often revealed some ambiguity in the data collection and/or recording instructions. In our experience, *there is no substitute for pilot testing one's data collection procedures,* however brief and informal this pilot testing is.

Training. With training, like the provision of clear instructions, we risk belaboring the obvious. However, there are undoubtedly many instances in which clear instructions are provided but data are collected unreliably because the data collectors are not adequately trained. This is especially true when the recording of the dependent variable requires some skill and experience (e.g., recording blood pressure with a sphygmomanometer and stethoscope).

Spot Checking. Several researchers have shown that reliability tends to be higher when observers know they are being assessed for interrater reliability (Haynes, 1978). In response, Haynes (1978) suggested that rater reliability should be assessed at every recording session. If that is not possible, he suggested that "Assessment of observer accuracy should be carried out as frequently as possible while minimizing the cues differentiating sessions in which agreement is and is not assessed. . . . If an observer expects to be monitored but is unsure of the schedule of monitoring, it is likely that a higher level of accuracy will be maintained across sessions in which interobserver agreement is not assessed" (p. 154). We agree with Haynes' suggestions, but offer two caveats. First, if reliability checks are done sporadically but not unobtrusively, the obtained reliability index should probably be considered an upwardly biased estimate of the reliability across *all* sessions. Second, as Haynes pointed out, Romanczyk, Kent, Diament, and O'Leary (1973) found that reliability was higher when observers knew the identity of the second observer than when they did not. This raises the concern that when knowledge of reliability checks improves reliability of ratings, it may do so as much by creating a dependency among errors as by increasing true variance; that is, observers may increase their attention to what other observers do rather than to the target behaviors. Again, if such a process were operative, reliability estimates obtained when raters are aware of reliability checks being conducted would overestimate reliability (see Johnson & Bolstad, 1973, for a review on this issue).

Averaging. One way to increase reliability is to take the average of several raters. In this way, both idiosyncratic tendencies of individual raters to rate high or low and random errors tend to average out. Assuming that all raters are each about equally reliable, the more ratings one averages, the more reliable the obtained average will be. Allison, Silverstein, and Gorman (chap. 10, this volume) discussed a method for determining the optimal number of ratings to average when cost is a factor. Rosenthal and Rosnow (1991) discussed the use of the Spearman-Brown prophesy formula in this context. If reliability is measured with some correlational statistic, and $\bar{r}$ is the average between rater reliability, then the reliability of the average of k raters' ratings is:

$$R_k = \frac{k\bar{r}}{1 + (k - 1)\bar{r}} \qquad (3.12)$$

Thus, suppose one desires the reliability of his or her dependent variable to be R_k but the average reliability of a single rater is only $\bar{r}$, where $\bar{r} < R_k$. The question is how many raters need to be averaged to obtain the desired reliability. Rearranging equation 4 yields the following answer[6]:

[6]The reader may be interested to note the connection between this formula and ICC(3,k).

$$k = \frac{R_k(\bar{r} - 1)}{\bar{r}(R_k - 1)} \tag{3.13}$$

Thus, given an obtained reliability coefficient ($\bar{r}$), one can estimate the number of raters (k) whose' ratings one needs to average in order to obtained the desired reliability (R_k). The obtained k should be rounded up to the nearest integer.

What Is The State of The Art?

Many practitioners (or at least publishers) of single-case research recognize the need for assessing reliability. For example, Ittenbach, Larson, and Swindell (1992) surveyed reports published in the *American Journal on Mental Retardation* between 1980 and 1989 and found that 67% of single-case research reports provided estimates of interrater reliability. Earlier, Susman et al. (cited in Hollenbeck, 1978) conducted a 16-year survey of 15 journals in child development, clinical child psychology, or child education, and found that 68% reported some estimate of reliability. Unfortunately, the most frequently reported index was the overly simplistic percent agreement. Moreover, Susman et al. found that the use of more sophisticated measures of reliability did not increase over the 16-year period. Similar conclusions were reached by Kelly (1977) and Mitchell (1979).

To see whether things might be different in the 1990s, we examined all research articles using single-case designs in a recent and arbitrarily chosen issue (1992, Vol. 25, #1) of the *Journal of Applied Behavior Analysis* (JABA). We chose JABA because it regularly publishes many single-case studies and is considered by many to be the premier journal in the field of applied behavior analysis. An impressive 10 of 10 articles (100%) calculated and presented some form of interobserver reliability. Unfortunately, 6 of 10 presented only percent agreement, which, as many others have argued and we argued above, is a substandard reliability index. The remaining 4 articles reported some form of *occurrence* or *nonoccurrence* agreement, which, although superior to percent agreement, are also severely limited compared to alternatives as we argued above. Finally, 9 of the 10 articles reported reliability on a level of data that was different from the level of data subsequently analyzed. As Mitchell (1979) pointed out, reliability estimates "should be based on the same scores that are used in the substantive analysis of the study. If a composite score (such as a total of several categories or time units) is to be used for analysis, it is this composite—and not its component individual categories or time units—that should be examined for agreement, reliability, or generalizability" (p. 387).

Thus, we can conclude that there appears to be fairly widespread recognition of the need to estimate reliability. Unfortunately, most investigators use substandard indices of reliability and calculate reliability at an inappropriate level of their data. We hope that the present exposition helps investigators choose the best methods for calculating and reporting reliability estimates.

Software

With respect to interrater reliability indices, many are so computationally simple that little if any software is needed. However, a few tools are useful. Virtually every statistical package and spreadsheet will calculate PPMCs and will provide cross-tabulations of data, as in Table 3.3. Most major packages also have procedures for calculating internal consistency reliability coefficients. Conger (1990) reviewed a program for calculating Kappa, and another was offered by Boushka, Marinez, Prihoda, Dunford, and Barnwell (1990). With respect to the ICCs and other reliability indices, detailed instructions for deriving them from SPSS output were provided by MacLennan (1993). Other software (often available free or at a nominal price) that calculates reliability coefficients can be found in Stoloff and Couch (1988). Finally, Gorman wrote software that implements Shrout and Fleiss' (1979) ICC formulae, kappa and multiple kappa, and other reliability indices, which can be obtained by sending him a blank formatted diskette.

GETTING THE MEASUREMENTS

Introduction

Once the investigator has decided what behaviors, behavioral categories, or behavioral taxonomies to study, and the coding system has been chosen, additional decisions must be made with respect to obtaining data (Sackett, 1978). At the very least, these include (a) what sampling plan (recording technique) should be employed, (b) which source of data to use (e.g., direct observation versus rating scales), and (c) what data aggregation method is best for the investigation (Hartmann & Wood, 1990; Sackett, Ruppenthal, & Gluck, 1978). The present section discusses these three characteristics. However, the reader is directed to several excellent sources regarding these and other important characteristics involved in observational research (e.g., Hartmann & Wood, 1990; Hollenbeck, 1978; Kazdin, 1978; Kerlinger, 1986; Kidder & Judd, 1986; Martin & Bateson, 1993; Reid, Baldwin, Patterson, & Dishion, 1988; Rosenblum, 1978; Sackett, 1978; Wright, 1960).

Behavior Sampling

Although several methods of obtaining observational data have been identified in the literature, including ad lib sampling, diary description, specimen description, time sampling, event sampling, and trait rating (Hartmann & Wood, 1990; Lonner & Berry, 1986; Phinney, 1982; Weick, 1968; Wright, 1960), only time and event sampling are expanded on here, with particular emphasis on time sampling. These methods of behavior sampling have received the most attention in the applied behavior analysis literature (e.g., Arrington, 1943; Cooper, 1981; Kerlinger, 1986; Longabaugh, 1980; Mann, Have, Plunkett, & Meisels, 1991), and usually focus on specific phenomena (Wright, 1960).

Some clarification of terms is required before proceeding, because different researchers have used various names when describing the same methods. For example, partial interval time sampling has also been called *interval recording*, the *interval method*, or *one zero sampling* (Ary & Suen, 1983; Jackson, Della-Piana, & Sloane, 1975; Powell, Martindale, & Kulp, 1975; Repp, Roberts, Slack, Repp, & Berkler, 1976). Momentary time sampling is sometimes referred to simply as *time sampling* or *instantaneous time sampling* (Jackson et al., 1975; Powell et al., 1975; Repp et al., 1976). However, partial and momentary sampling methods are usually subsumed under the umbrella term *time sampling* (Repp et al., 1976; Sackett, 1978) and are presented as such in this chapter.

Event sampling has sometimes been called *event recording, frequency recording, tally method, continuous sampling, focal sampling,* or *actual sampling* (e.g., Mann et al., 1991; Reid et al., 1988). Event sampling, however, as is discussed later, is treated differently here. The former terms usually pertain to continuous real time measurement or continuous observation when actual response frequency of a specific behavior is of primary interest to the investigator (Hartmann & Wood, 1990; Lonner & Berry, 1986; Sackett, 1978).

The continuous real time method has been called the most rigorous and powerful procedure, because every frequency (or duration) of behavior is scored in the noninterrupted observation session (Hartmann & Wood, 1990). Therefore, actual frequencies or duration of behavioral occurrences are obtained instead of estimates (Mann et al., 1991). This procedure also allows for calculation of various derivatives of frequency and duration of response (Hartmann & Wood, 1990).

A consideration that investigators should bear in mind before choosing a sampling plan involves the aspects of behavior that are important to the particular study. The usual characteristics of a behavior include frequency (i.e., number of occurrences of the behavior exhibited by the organism) and duration (i.e., how much time has the organism spent exhibiting the behavior; Ary & Suen, 1983). Related characteristics include probability or relative frequency, relative duration, rate of occurrence, and average duration per occurrence (Reid et al., 1988; Sackett, 1978; Sackett & Landesman-Dwyer, 1982).

Relative frequency and relative duration pertain to the frequency and duration of a behavior relative to the total observation period; specifically, frequency or duration of behavior in an interval (i.e., individual frequency or duration) divided by the total frequency or total observation time, respectively (Reid et al., 1988). Rate and average duration of occurrence are calculated by dividing the frequency or duration of a behavior, respectively, by the interval length (Sackett, 1978). Some researchers have noted that frequency and duration of the behavior should be recorded when feasible, because the derived characteristics can be calculated easily when frequency and duration data have been obtained (Sackett, 1978).

Time Sampling

According to Arrington (1943), time sampling involves observations of an organism's behavior conducted in short time intervals that allows the researcher to *estimate* either the frequency or duration of the particular behavior under investigation. The observer, method of recording, and choice of behavior to be observed are controlled, as opposed to the environment in which the observations are made. In time sampling procedures the observer determines whether or not a particular behavior has occurred within brief, regular intervals (e.g., 10 seconds, 1 minute). The actual total frequencies or durations of behaviors are not recorded; only the single occurrence. That is, either it happened or it did not.

Several advantages and disadvantages of time sampling have been reported in the literature. The primary advantage of this general procedure is ease of use, because equipment and training of observers is limited (Mann et al., 1991). Additional advantages include high interrater reliability, the provision of systematic control through the selection of behavior to be investigated, high probability of obtaining representative samples of behavior, and the use of coding systems that minimize subjectivity and allow for precise ways of quantifying behavior (Kerlinger, 1986; Wright, 1960).

Time sampling procedures, however, have their limitations, which may preclude their use when investigators require actual measures of frequency and duration of behaviors, in which case continuous real time measurement is recommended (Altmann, 1974; Mann et al., 1991). For example, time sampling is useful only when the behavior under study occurs frequently and one is not interested in the antecedents or consequences of a behavior (as is the case with event sampling). In addition, time sampling may lack continuity and naturalness, because it divides the stream of behavior into short time units (Wright, 1960). Consequently, time sampling limits the kinds of behaviors that can be observed, because simultaneous behaviors or sequences of interactions are not recorded. Finally, the comparison of various time sampling studies or continuous sampling studies is limited because they often use different time intervals, which may lead to different conclusions (Mann et al., 1991; Reid et al., 1988; Sackett, 1978; Wright, 1960).

Despite its problems, time sampling has been one of the most frequently used methods of sampling child behavior (Arrington, 1943; Mann et al., 1991; Wright, 1960). Mann et al. (1991) reviewed 10 years of research in *Child Development* and found that 34% of child observational studies used time sampling procedures. Therefore, a more specific description of the advantages and disadvantages of the two most frequently used time sampling procedures follows.

Momentary Time Sampling Versus Partial Interval Recording. In momentary time sampling, a response is scored if it occurs exactly at a predetermined moment (Saudargas & Lentz, 1986). It has been used to estimate duration of time in which a particular behavior occurs by the subject, such as schoolwork or out-of-seat behavior (e.g., Saudargas & Zanolli, 1990). Partial interval recording involves scoring a response if it occurs during any part of the interval. A variation of partial interval recording called whole interval recording was discussed by Powell, Martindale, and Kulp (1975). This type of interval recording involves scoring a behavior only when it occurs throughout the "whole" observation interval (Ary & Suen, 1983; Hartmann & Wood, 1990; Saudargas & Lentz, 1986). Partial and whole interval recording have been used to estimate frequency and duration of behavior (Powell, Martindale, Kulp, Martindale, & Bauman, 1977; Rhine & Linville, 1980; Wright, 1960).

Several studies have examined the accuracy of these time sampling procedures in their estimation of frequency and duration of responses or the derivatives of these behavior dimensions. For example, Repp et al., (1976) used electromechanical equipment (e.g., probability gate and event recorder) to produce records of simulated behavior (i.e., pulses) that occurred at various rates and patterns to compare momentary and partial time sampling methods to an actual frequency method. In essence, they were investigating the accuracy of these methods in assessing rate of responding. They concluded that momentary time sampling was an inaccurate method of estimating all rates (low, moderate, and high) of occurrence. Partial interval time sampling was accurate for low and medium rates of occurrence, but underestimated high rates of occurrence.

Powell et al. (1977) were interested in the accuracy of momentary and partial interval time sampling methods as estimates of duration of responding for in-seat behavior. That is, they compared the estimates from time sampling methods to the actual percentage of time that the behavior occurred, which varied from 20% to 80% of the time period. They determined that momentary time sampling was superior to partial interval recording when assessing the duration of occurrence and that partial interval recording overestimated duration. Harrop and Daniels (1986) also compared the accuracy of momentary and partial interval time sampling methods in estimating various durations and rates of behavior. They concluded that momentary time sampling was more accurate than partial interval recording in estimating absolute duration, and that both methods were inaccurate for estimating absolute rates of responding. These results are consistent with those of Powell et al. (1977), and somewhat different from those of Repp et al. (1976).

In general, then, momentary time sampling is preferred over partial interval time sampling when duration of responding is of interest, and the reverse is true when rate of response is to be estimated (Altmann, 1974; Harrop & Daniels, 1986; Powell et al., 1977; Repp et al., 1976; Saudargas & Zanolli, 1990). The selection of duration or rate of response depends on the research question. However, there are researchers who recommend momentary time sampling over partial and whole interval for estimating frequency or duration of occurrence, because it produces an average that more closely approximates the actual frequencies and durations of a set of behaviors (e.g., Mann et al., 1991; Powell, 1984; Repp, Nieminen, Olinger, & Brusca, 1988; Saudargas & Lentz, 1986). Ary and Suen (1983) delineated a seven step procedure for the use of momentary time sampling to estimate frequency and duration.

In addition, the smaller the observation interval is, the more accurate the estimation of frequency or duration of behavior is, especially with partial or whole interval time sampling techniques (Ary & Suen, 1983; Repp et al., 1988). This is true with respect to frequency because with long time intervals more than one occurrence of a response may be observed, but only a single response is recorded as per the definition of time sampling procedures (Ary & Suen, 1983). One must be careful, however, not to make the interval too short, because a single response may extend into the next time interval and therefore be scored twice (Hartmann & Wood, 1990). Likewise, duration of response may not be estimated accurately when responses are scored if they only occur for a brief period during the observation interval (Ary & Suen, 1983).

Event Sampling

Event sampling usually involves the observation of the whole event (e.g., arguments, temper tantrums) in which a behavior takes place, rather than only a specific behavior of interest as in time sampling or continuous real-time measurement. Therefore, event sampling does not divide the stream of behavior into short time units (as with time sampling), but is concerned with the time span of the event in question (Wright, 1960). These differences may be understood in terms of molar versus molecular levels of behavior. For example, a temper tantrum may be viewed as a behavioral event (molar level), whereas head banging may be viewed as a specific variable (molecular level) that occurs during a temper tantrum. Events inherently include the organisms, environmental setting, behavior, duration of observation, and the intervals between observation (Longabaugh; 1980; Lonner & Berry, 1986). All of these characteristics are observed and recorded.

Event sampling may be viewed as a compromise between the lengthy specimen record and the briefer time sampling procedures (Phinney, 1982). That is, event sampling provides information regarding the dynamics of classes of behavior (e.g., antecedents, duration, and consequences), which is more than a time sampling procedure provides and less information than a specimen record, which requires the recording of all ongoing behavior and is difficult to summarize (Phinney, 1982; Wright, 1960). Although this recording method and focus differ from continuous real time measurement, the data obtained are similar and may yield more accurate estimations of frequency and duration than time sampling. For example, Dawe (1934) used event sampling to study children's arguments by recording 200 incidents and then summarized frequencies of various behaviors exhibited by younger and older boys and girls.

According to Kerlinger (1986) and Wright (1960), event sampling has several positive aspects that contrast with time sampling. The events are natural, lifelike situations that may be inherently valid, represent continuity of behavior, and can be sampled even when the behavior of interest occurs infrequently or rarely. Wright (1960) discussed event sampling in more detail with examples from the literature, and Longabaugh (1980) devoted several pages to this topic. Event and time sampling methods are not mutually exclusive techniques and can be used together to ensure more accurate estimates of occurrence and duration of behaviors (Kerlinger, 1986; Lonner & Berry, 1986; Wright, 1960).

SOURCES OF DATA

Direct Observation

Characteristics of observations include observer inference and bias, reactivity, drift, reliability and validity, categories, units of behavior, generality or applicability, and sampling of behavior (Kerlinger, 1986; Repp et al., 1988; Sackett, 1978; Weick, 1968). These usually pertain to direct observation, in which a sampling plan such as those discussed previously is employed. Although some of these characteristics are discussed here, more detailed discussion of these characteristics are presented throughout this text as well as others (e.g., Hartmann & Wood, 1990; Kidder & Judd, 1986). In addition, Repp et al., (1988) provided a useful table that contains common threats to accurate data collection and recommendations for improving observer accuracy.

The major task of the observer is to record information with as limited inference and bias as possible. That is, objectivity and accuracy are to be maximized, whereas subjective judgment is minimized. This is often easier said than done. Indeed, Salvia and Meisel (1980) surveyed research published in four special education journals and judged that 50% were susceptible to biased observation. Moreover, 75% did not attempt to control for observer inference or bias in any manner (Salvia & Meisel, 1980). Observer inference and bias depend, in part, on the level of behavior observed (Kerlinger, 1986). That is, a molar versus molecular level of behavior observation (Sackett et al., 1978). Observers are more likely to infer or exhibit bias when complex behavioral data are sought (Hartmann & Wood, 1990; Weick, 1968).

The selection of level of behavior or behavioral complexity to observe will also have an effect on observer and subject reactivity, which may affect the reliability and/or validity of the conclusions drawn from the study (Repp et al., 1988). Subject reactivity has been discussed more often than observer reactivity in the literature and is affected by the social desirability of the behavior, subject and observer characteristics, obtrusiveness of observation, and the rationale for observation (Hartmann & Wood, 1990; House, 1978; Repp et al., 1988). Subject reactivity can usually be limited by unobtrusive observation (e.g., Hartmann & Wood, 1990; Weick, 1968).

As we have discussed at several other points, an important factor related to the validity of behavioral observations is the training of observers. Moreover, the use of exact, low-inference operational definitions of behavior delineated in an observational training manual is strongly suggested (Hartmann & Wood, 1990; Weick, 1968). This is one way of limiting observer bias, which is perhaps the most serious problem of direct observational research (Kerlinger, 1986; Repp et al., 1988; Spool, 1978). It also can prevent confrontations among observers, who may become frustrated and defensive if they make frequent errors in scoring (Weick, 1968).

When observers are selected and trained well, many threats to observer accuracy can be avoided (Reid et al., 1988; Repp et al., 1988). Hartmann and Wood (1990) delineated a seven-step system for training observers that includes orientation, learning the observational manual, criterion checks, analogue observations, in situ practice, retraining, and postinvestigation debriefing. For more information regarding observer training, the reader is directed to Johnson and Bolstad (1973), Spool 1978), and Hartmann and Wood (1990).

Observer training also involves attempting to control for observer drift. This refers to the decrement in reliability and/or validity of observations due to observer fatigue, boredom, or habituation (Hartmann & Wood, 1990; Kidder & Judd, 1986; Reid et al., 1988; Repp et al., 1988). Observer drift occurs, for example, when behavior is inconsistently recorded during baseline and treatment phases and the inaccurate recording persists across several evaluators (Repp et al., 1988). That is, two observers may "drift together," which has been called *consensual observer drift* (Johnson & Bolstad, 1973).

Use of Automated Recording of Behavior and Data Collection

Videotaped or other recorded data facilitate the use of multiple coders for each behavior and can therefore increase the reliability of measurement (Kidder & Judd, 1986). The main advantage of taping behavior, however, is also its disadvantage. That is, it can be observed again and again but may increase the complexity of data recording and the time needed to score an interval of behavior (Hartmann & Wood, 1990; Reid et al., 1988). Permanent products of behavior such as videotapes and audiocassettes can control for observer inference/bias, drift, and reactivity and enhance reliability, especially when behavior occurs quickly and is complex (Hartmann & Wood, 1990; Repp et al., 1988). In addition, other behaviors that were not part of the original investigation can be recorded from the preserved videotape (Eisler, Hersen, & Agras, 1973), and multihandicapped populations (e.g., deaf-blind) may be assessed more accurately (Tweedie, 1975).

The use of technological aids includes not only video- or audiotaping the subject for later data recording, but instruments that assist in recording the frequency or duration of behavior such as written records, checklists, event recorders, clocks, and counters (Hartmann & Wood, 1990;

Reid et al., 1988). Electromechanical instruments such as handheld computers and digital keyboards have greater data collection capabilities, are more adaptable to automated analysis of data, and can be less obtrusive than paper-and-pencil records (Hartmann & Wood, 1990; Reid et al., 1988; Saudargas & Zanolli, 1990). Limitations include possible equipment failure and loss of data, data overload, expense, and limited generalizability across investigations (Hartmann & Wood, 1990). A list of technological aids used by applied behavior analysts with references was provided by Hartmann and Wood (1990).

Rating Scales

Another source of data involves the use of rating scales. The data obtained from rating scales are often based on remembered or perceived behavior, as opposed to direct observation. The subject under study need not be present, and the observer makes judgments based on past observations or the perceptions of what the subject will do (Kerlinger, 1986). There are several disadvantages of rating scales. Perhaps the most crucial one is that because they are easy to construct, users may not be aware of their other limitations. Another limitation is susceptibility to constant or biased error, which can be a problem for direct observation as well. These biases include the halo effect, error of leniency, error of central tendency, logical error, contrast error, and proximity error (Guilford, 1954; Kidder & Judd, 1986; Rosenthal & Rosnow, 1991).

The halo effect refers to the influence that previous information about an individual has on the person who is rating another characteristic of the individual. That is, the rater's overall judgment of the individual will influence judgments of specific characteristics (Rosenthal & Rosnow, 1991). The error of leniency pertains to "lenient judgments" made by a rater because the individual is familiar to the judge (Guilford, 1954). Thus, the individual is judged in an overly positive manner. An error of central tendency occurs when raters tend to rate an individual toward the mean of the group; therefore, extreme ratings are rarely recorded (Rosenthal & Rosnow, 1991).

A logical error occurs when judges similarly rate traits that are "logically" related in their minds, but are not related for the individual who is being rated (Guilford, 1954; Rosenthal & Rosnow, 1991). A contrast error refers the rating of an individual on a trait that is opposite that of the judge. For example, a judge who regards himself or herself as honest may judge another individual to be less honest. Guilford (1954) cautioned, however, that raters may also make the converse error and rate individuals to be similar to the judge on that trait. That is, a judge who is honest will rate others as honest. Finally, a proximity error involves rating traits similarly for an individual simply because they are in close "proximity" on the scale (Guilford, 1954).

However, when used correctly, rating scales are valuable because they require less time than other methods, are easy to use, have a wide range of application, impose structure on responses, and can be used with a large number of characteristics (Barkley, 1988; Kerlinger, 1986; Rosenthal & Rosnow, 1991). There are several broad categories or basic formats of rating scales, including checklists (rating by cumulated points), forced choice, numerical, and graphic (Guilford, 1954; Rosenthal & Rosnow, 1991).

Checklists. Checklists usually involve a list of behaviors that the researcher wants to investigate. The observer is simply required to "check off" whether the behavior applies to the subject under study, and the individual's score represents the sum or average of points. This rating scale is one of the simplest to use, because it requires minimum discrimination for raters. Checklists, however, are susceptible to many types of biases, which should be considered before using them (Guilford, 1954).

Forced Choice. Forced choice usually requires the observer to choose among alternatives that appear similar in terms of favorability (see Travers, 1951). It was developed to control for the halo effect by presenting the rater with two competing favorable or unfavorable responses so as to "force" the rater to choose between them (Rosenthal & Rosnow, 1991). For example, a rater may be asked to choose between "assertive" and "motivated."

Zavala (1965) found that the best forced-choice format used four favorable items, and that this type of rating scale was less susceptible to the effects of bias in the forms of response set and social desirability. Problems with this type of rating scale include confounding of ipsative with normative measurement, complexity of devising a scale, resistance on the part of observers, and lack of greater validity than with single-stimulus forms (Guilford, 1954; Rosenthal & Rosnow, 1991; Scott, 1968). Steps to construct a forced-choice instrument were provided by Guilford (1954).

Numerical Scale. Numerical or itemized rating scales apply numbers to each choice in a category (Nunnally, 1978). The numbers may be explicit or implicit, and may be positive or negative. Guilford (1954) suggested that negative numbers should be avoided, because they may suggest a break in continuity of the scale that was not intended. Numerical scales are easy to construct, use, and score. However, as with checklists, they are vulnerable to many biases, and other methods have been constructed to guard against the improper use of these scales (Guilford, 1954; Rosenthal & Rosnow, 1991). Despite their shortcomings, numerical scales are employed often and, if used properly, can provide information for many research questions.

Graphic Scale. Graphic rating scales employ the use of a graph that may or may not be associated with numbers. If the scale is segmented with an odd number of segments, it may denote a neutral rating in the middle segment. However, when an even number of segments is used, either a positive or negative rating is applied to the individual on that characteristic (Rosenthal & Rosnow, 1991). Anchor words that are placed at the ends of the graph should be simple, clear, precise, unidimensional, and relevant to the characteristic that is rated.

This type of scale is preferable to numerical scales without graphs, because a graph provides raters with a visual continuum and decreases errors in making and deciphering ratings (Nunnally, 1978). In addition, they are easy to use, interesting, and allow for fine discriminations (Guilford, 1954). The disadvantages of graphic scales are similar to those of other rating formats (e.g., rater bias) with the addition of more labor involved with construction and scoring. Issues regarding graphic scale construction were provided by Guilford (1954).

METHODS OF DATA AGGREGATION

Essentially, the question here is what to do with the raw data once they have been collected. For example, one may have several behaviors of interest across several time intervals. Each behavior can be a dependent variable or a composite variable could be calculated by combining the dependent variables. "Combining related measures eliminates redundancy and reduces the number of categories used in the final analysis and presentation of results" (Martin & Bateson, 1993, p. 123).

Various methods of constructing a behavior composite are available including metric (e.g., factor analysis) and nonmetric techniques (e.g., cluster analysis; Fralicx & Raju, 1982), even though behavior composites frequently are based on intuition or other sources of knowledge (Berven & Scofield, 1982; Martin & Bateson, 1993). The metric techniques are discussed here and include unweighted and unit-weighted additive methods, and the least squares weighted method. Each has its statistical and practical strengths and limitations.

The unweighted additive method involves calculating the arithmetic mean or sum of the component variables that make up the behavior composite (Fralicx & Raju, 1982). This method is the easiest to perform and is the most frequently used method of behavior analysts. The unweighted additive method is most useful and mathematically sound when the variances of each component variable are approximately equal. That is, each variable contributes the same amount of variance to the behavior composite and the standard deviation of the r^2s (squared correlations of each component variable with the behavior composite) approaches zero. This method also performs well when the component variables are highly correlated.

Conversely, when variances are unequal or correlations among the component variables are less than or equal to .50, each component variable does not contribute equal variance to the behavior composite and/or there is more than one factor being assessed. Therefore, one may be combining apples and oranges to create some type of "hybrid" variable that has little to do with the original variables and distorts the results of the investigation.

The unit-weighted method also involves the arithmetic mean of the component variables, but one converts each component variable to standard form (e.g., *z*-scores) such that each variable has the same mean and standard deviation (Fralicx & Raju, 1982; Martin & Bateson, 1993). When the component variables are standardized, each variable contributes the same amount of variance to the behavior composite. This method appears to be an excellent choice, but is not without its limitations. For example, the standardization of variables may not be understood by some practitioners of behavior research, and the computation of means and standard deviations cannot be done until all the data have been collected, which precludes its use with response-guided experimentation.

A method of least squares weighted estimates is principal components analysis or factor analysis (Gorsuch, 1983; Gottman, 1978; Loehlin, 1992). This is one of the most-often-cited data reduction techniques (e.g., Longabaugh, 1980; Martin & Bateson, 1993). When the component variables represent a single construct (i.e., the behavior composite), a principal components analysis can be used to obtain a single factor. The results of a principal components analysis may also suggest more than one factor that is important information for the investigator to know (Gottman, 1978). It may be unwise for the investigator to combine the component variables to form one behavior composite when more than one factor exists.

Principal components analysis is an excellent means of forming behavior composites, but is one of the most sophisticated methods from a mathematical perspective and requires more training than an introductory statistics course (Comrey, 1988). Therefore, an investigator may not be able to proceed with his or her study as initially planned. Finally, principal components analysis works best with a large number of observations, which may not be possible in many investigations (Short & Horn, 1984).

Each method has its advantages and disadvantages that must be weighed by an investigator according to the parameters of a particular study. Many of the methods discussed previously require calculations (e.g., means, standard deviations, correlations) *after* the data have been collected. This may have serious implications for the researcher and preclude the use of response-guided experimentation. Response-guided experimentation involves inspection of data as they are collected in order to allow the data to guide the experiment. Some researchers espouse this procedure (Sidman, 1960), whereas others find it less favorable (e.g., Allison, Franklin, & Heshka, 1992; Edgington, 1984). For example, Allison et al. (1992) reported that "When visual inspection is combined with response guided experimentation, Type 1 error rates could easily be high as 25%" (p. 45).

The formation of a behavior composite is conditional upon two criteria. First, the component variables should correlate substantially. Second, the component variables should have close to equal variances and covariances. When these two criteria are met, investigators can be reasonably confident that a behavior composite should be formed. When these two criteria are not met, investigators should be inclined to separately analyze each component variable.

CONCLUSION

Science and practice are both at their best when built on a strong foundation of measurement. We can only communicate with each other about "such-and-such" when we can say *exactly* what we mean by "such-and-such." One of the best ways to do this is to specify how we measure "such-and-such." Measurement provides precision to our ideas, theories, and constructs, and we hope that this chapter assists investigators in providing precision in their measurements.

REFERENCES

Allen, M. J., & Yen, W. M. (1979). *Introduction to measurement theory*. Monterey, CA: Brooks/Cole.

Allison, D. B., Franklin, R., & Heshka, S. (1992). Reflections on visual inspection, response guided experimentation, and Type 1 error rate in single-case designs. *Journal of Experimental Education, 61*, 45–51.

Alsawalmeh, Y. M , & Feldt, L. S. (1992). Test of hypothesis that the intraclass reliability coefficient is the same for two measurement procedures. *Applied Psychological Measurement, 16,* 195–205.
Altmann, J. (1974). Observational study of behavior sampling methods. *Behavior, 49,* 227–267.
Arrington, R. (1943). Time sampling in studies of social behavior: A critical review of techniques and results with research suggestions. *Psychological Bulletin, 40,* 81–124.
Ary, D., & Suen, H. K. (1983). The use of momentary time sampling to assess both frequency and duration of behavior. *Journal of Behavioral Assessment, 5,* 143–150.
Ary, D., & Suen, H. K. (1985). Statistical significance of percent interobserver agreement reliability. *Midwestern Educational Researcher, 6,* 31–33.
Barkley, R. A. (1988). Child behavior rating scales and checklists. In M. Rutter, A. H. Tuma, and I. S. Lann (Eds.), *Assessment and diagnosis in child psychopathology* (pp. 113–155). New York: Guilford.
Barlow, D., & Hersen, M. (1993). *Single case experimental designs.* New York: Pergamon.
Beck, A. T., Ward, C. M., Mendelson, M., Mock, J., & Erbaugh, J. (1961). An inventory for measuring depression. *Archives of General Psychiatry, 4,* 561–571.
Berven, N. L., & Scofield, M. E. (1982). Nonmetric data-reduction techniques in rehabilitation research. *Rehabilitation Counseling Bulletin, 25*(5), 297–311.
Boushka, W. M., Marinez, Y. N., Prihoda, T. J., Dunford, R., & Barnwell, G. M. (1990). A computer program for calculating kappa: Application to interexaminer agreement in periodontal research. *Computer Methods and Programs in Biomedicine, 33,* 35–41.
Bridgman, P. W. (1927/60). *The logic of modern physics.* New York: Macmillan.
Bryan, L., Coleman, M., & Ganong, L. (1981). Geometric mean as a continuous measure of androgyny. *Psychological Reports, 48,* 691–694.
Campbell, D. T., & Fiske, D. W. (1959). Convergent and discriminant validation by the multitrait-multimethod matrix. *Psychological Bulletin, 56,* 81–105.
Cohen, J. A. (1960). A coefficient of agreement for nominal scales. *Educational and Psychological Measurement, 20,* 37–46.
Comrey, A. L. (1988). Factor-analytic methods of scale development in personality and clinical psychology. *Journal of Consulting and Clinical Psychology, 56,* 754–761.
Conger, A. J. (1990). A review of Dynastat's kappa program. *Behavioral Assessment, 12,* 379–385.
Cook, D. T., & Campbell, D. T. (1979). *Quasi experimentation: Design and analysis for field experiments.* Boston: Houghton Mifflin.
Cooper, J. O. (1981). *Measuring behavior* (2nd ed.). Columbus, OH: Merrill.
Cronbach, L. J., Gleser, G. C., Nanda, H., & Rajarartnam, N. (1972). *The dependability of behavioral measurements: Theory of generalizability of scores and profiles.* New York: Wiley.
Cronbach, L. J., & Meehl, P. E. (1955). Construct validity in psychological. *Psychological Bulletin, 52,* 281–302.
Dawe, H. C. (1934). An analysis of two hundred quarrels of preschool children. *Child Development, 5,* 139–157.
Edgington, E. S. (1984). Statistics and single-case designs. *Progress in Behavior Modification, 16,* 83–119.
Eisler, R. M., Hersen, M., & Agras, W. S. (1973). Videotape: A method for the controlled observation of nonverbal interpersonal behavior. *Behavior Therapy, 4,* 420–425.
Everitt, B. S. (1968). Moments of the statistics kappa and weighted kappa. *British Journal of Mathematical and Statistical Psychology, 21,* 97–103.
Fleiss, J. L. (1971). Measuring nominal scale agreement among many raters. *Psychological Bulletin, 76,* 378–382.
Fleiss, J. L. (1975). Measuring agreement between two judges on the presence or absence of a trait. *Biometrics, 31,* 651–659.

Fralicx, R. D., & Raju, N. S. (1982). A comparison of five methods for combining multiple criteria into a single composite. *Educational and Psychological Measurement, 42*, 823–827.

Ghiselli, E. E., Campbell, J. P., & Zedeck, S. (1981). *Measurement theory for the behavioral sciences*. San Francisco, CA: Freeman.

Gorsuch, R. L. (1983). *Factor analysis* (2nd ed.). Hillsdale, NJ: Lawrence Erlbaum Associates.

Gottman, J. M. (1978). Nonsequential data analysis techniques in observational research. In G. P. Sackett (Ed.), *Observing behavior: Volume II: Data collection and analysis methods* (pp. 1–14). Baltimore, MD: University Park Press.

Guilford, J. (1954). *Psychometric methods* (2nd ed.). New York: McGraw-Hill.

Hale, C. A., & Fleiss, J. L. (1993). Interval estimation under two study designs for kappa with binary classifications. *Biometrics, 49*, 523–534.

Hamilton, M. (1967). Development of a rating scale for primary depression illness. *British Journal of Social and Clinical Psychology, 6*, 278–295.

Hanley, J. A. (1987). Standard error of the kappa statistic. *Psychological Bulletin, 102*, 315–321.

Harris, C. W., & Pearlman, A. P. (1977). Conventional significance tests and indices of agreement or association. In C. W. Harris, A. P. Pearlman, & R. R. Wilcox (Ed.), *Achievement test items—methods of study* (pp. 17–44). Los Angeles: UCLA Center for the Study of Education.

Harris, F. C., & Lahey, B. B. (1978). A method for combining occurrence and nonoccurrence interobserver agreement scores. *Journal of Applied Behavior Analysis, 11*, 523–527.

Harrop, A., & Daniels, M. (1986). Methods of time sampling: A reappraisal of momentary time sampling and partial interval recording. *Journal of Applied Behavior Analysis, 19*, 73–77.

Hartmann, D. P. (1982). Assessing the dependability of observational data. In D. P. Hartmann (Ed.), *Using observers to study behavior*. San Francisco, CA: Jossey-Bass.

Hartmann, D. P., & Gardner, W. (1982). A cautionary note on the use of probability values to evaluate interobserver agreement. *Journal of Applied Behavior Analysis, 15*, 189–190.

Hartmann, D. P., & Wood, D. D. (1990). Observational methods. In A. S. Bellack, M. Hersen, & A. E. Kazdin (Eds.), *International handbook of behavior modification and therapy* (2nd ed., pp. 107–138). New York: Plenum.

Hawkins, R. P., & Dotson, V. A. (1975). Reliability scores that delude: An Alice in Wonderland trip through the misleading characteristics of interobserver agreement scores in interval recording. In E. Ramp & G. Semb (Eds.), *Behavior analysis: Areas of research and application* (pp. 359–376). Englewood Cliffs, NJ: Prentice-Hall.

Haynes, S. N. (1978). Reliability and interobserver agreement in behavioral observation. In S. N. Haynes (Ed.), *Principles of behavioral assessment* (pp. 137–165). New York: Gardner.

Hays, W. L. (1988). *Statistics* (4th ed.). Philadelphia: Holt, Rinehart & Winston.

Hollenbeck, A. R. (1978). Problems of reliability in observational research. In G. P. Sakett (Ed.) *Observing behavior. Volume II. Data collection and analysis methods*. Baltimore, MD: University Park Press.

Hopkins, B. L., & Hermann, J. A. (1977). Evaluating interobserver reliability of interval data. *Journal of Applied Behavior Analysis, 10*, 121–126.

House, A. E. (1978). Naturalistic observation: Formal and informal difficulties. *Child Study Journal, 8*, 17–28.

Ittenbach, R. F., Larson, S. A., & Swindell, L. K. (1992, May). *Quasi-experimental methods in AJMD/AJMR published research between 1980 and 1989*. Paper presented at the Annual Meeting of The American Association on Mental Retardation.

Jackson, D. A., Della-Piana, G. M., & Sloane, H. N. Jr. (1975). *How to establish a behavior observation system*. Englewood Cliffs, NJ: Educational Technology.

James, L. R., Demaree, R. G., & Wolf, G. (1993). r_{wg}: An assessment of within-group interrater agreement. *Journal of Applied Psychology, 78*, 306–309.
Johnson, S. M., & Bolstad, O. D. (1973). Methodological issues in naturalistic observation: Some problems and solutions for field research. In L. A. Hamerlynck, L. C. Hardy, & E. J. Mash (Eds.), *Behavior change: Methodology, concepts, and practice* (pp. 7–67). Champaign, IL: Research Press.
Johnston, J. M., & Pennypacker, H. S. (1980). *Strategies and tactics of human behavioral research*. Hillsdale, NJ: Lawrence Erlbaum Associates.
Kazdin, A. E. (1978). Methodological and interpretive problems of single-case experimental designs. *Journal of Consulting and Clinical Psychology, 46*, 629–642.
Kelly, M. B. A. (1977). A review of the observational data collection and reliability procedures reported in the *Journal of Applied Behavior Analysis. Journal of Applied Behavior Analysis, 10*, 97–101.
Kerlinger, F. N. (1986). *Foundations of behavioral research* (3rd ed.). New York: CBS College Publishing.
Kidder, L. H., & Judd, C. M. (1986). *Research methods in social relations* (5th ed). New York: Holt, Rinehart & Winston.
Koch, S. (1992). Psychology's Bridgeman vs Bridgeman's Bridgeman. *Theory & Psychology, 2*, 261–290.
Lahey, M. A., Downey, R. G., & Saal, F. E. (1983). Intraclass correlations: There's more there than meets the eye. *Psychological Bulletin*, 586–595.
Lee, P. S. C., & Suen, H. K. (1984). The estimation of kappa from percentage agreement interobserver reliability. *Behavioral Assessment, 6*, 375–378.
Lin, L. I. (1989). A concordance correlation coefficient to evaluate reproducability. *Biometrics, 45*, 255–268.
Loehlin, J. C. (1992). *Latent variable models: An introduction to factor, path, and structural analysis* (2nd ed.). Hillsdale, NJ: Lawrence Erlbaum Associates.
Longabaugh, R. (1980). The systematic observation of behavior in naturalistic settings. In H. C. Triandis & J. W. Berry (Eds.), *Handbook of cross-cultural psychology: Vol. 2. Methodology* (pp. 57–126). Boston: Allyn and Bacon.
Lonner, W. J., & Berry, J. W. (1986). Sampling and surveying. In W. J. Lonner and J. W. Berry (Eds.), *Field methods in cross-cultural research: Vol. 8. Cross-cultural research and methodology series* (pp. 85–110). Beverly Hills, CA: Sage.
MacLennan, R. N. (1993). Interrrater reliability with SPSS for Windows 5.0. *American Statistician, 47*, 292–296.
Mann, J., Have, T. T., Plunkett, J. W., & Meisels, S. J. (1991). Time sampling: A methodological critique. *Child Development, 62*, 227–241.
Martin, P., & Bateson, P. (1993). *Measuring behaviour: An introductory guide* (2nd ed.). New York: Cambridge University Press.
Mitchell, S. K. (1979). Interobserver agreement, reliability, and generalizability of data collected in observational studies. *Psychological Bulletin, 86*, 376–390.
Nunnally, J. C. (1978). *Psychometric theory* (2nd ed.). New York: McGraw-Hill.
Nunnally, J. C., & Bernstein, I. A. (1994). *Psychometric methods* (3rd ed.). New York: McGraw-Hill.
Page, T. J., & Iwata, B. A. (1986). Interobserver agreement: History, theory, and current methods. In A. Poling and R. W. Fuqua (Eds.), *Research methods in applied behavior analysis: Issues and advances* (pp. 99–126). New York: Plenum.
Phinney, J. S. (1982). Observing children: Ideas for teachers. *Young Children, 37*, 16–24.
Polaino, A., & Senra, C. (1991). Measurement of depression: Comparison between self-reports and clinical assessments of depressed outpatients. *Journal of Psychopathology and Behavioral Assessment, 13*, 313–324.

Powell, J. (1984). On the misrepresentation of behavioral realities by a widely practiced direct observation procedure: Partial interval (one-zero) sampling. *Behavioral Assessment, 6,* 209–219.

Powell, J., Martindale, B., & Kulp, S. (1975). An evaluation of time-sample measures of behavior. *Journal of Applied Behavior Analysis, 8,* 463–464.

Powell, J., Martindale, B., Kulp, S., Martindale, A., & Bauman, R. (1977). Taking a closer look: Time sampling and measurement error. *Journal of Applied Behavior Analysis, 10,* 325–332.

Reid, J. B., Baldwin, D. V., Patterson, G. R., & Dishion, T. J. (1988). Observations in the assessmaent of childhood disorders. In M. Rutter, A. H. Tuma, and I. S. Lann (Eds.), *Assessment and diagnosis in child psychopathology* (pp. 156–195). New York: Guilford.

Repp, A. C., Nieminen, G. S., Olinger, E., & Brusca, R. (1988). Direct observation: Factors affecting the accuracy of observers. *Exceptional Children, 55,* 29–36.

Repp, A. C., Roberts, D. M., Slack, D. J., Repp, C. F., & Berkler, M. S. (1976). A comparison of frequency, interval, and time-sampling methods of data collection. *Journal of Applied Behavior Analysis, 9,* 501–508.

Rhine, R., & Linville, A. (1980). Properties of one zero scores in observational studies of primate social behavior: The effect of assumptions on empirical analysis. *Primates, 21,* 111–122.

Romanczyk, R. G., Kent, R. D., Diament, C., & O'Leary, K. D. (1973). Measuring the reliability of observational data: A reactive process. *Journal of Applied Behavior Analysis, 6,* 175–184.

Rosenblum, L. A. (1978). The creation of a behavioral taxonomy. In G. P. Sackett (Ed.), *Observing behavior: Volume II: Data collection and analysis methods* (pp. 15–24). Baltimore, MD: University Park Press.

Rosenthal, R., & Rosnow, R. L. (1991). *Essentials of behavioral research: Methods and data analysis.* New York: McGraw-Hill.

Sackett, G. P. (1978). Measurement in observational research. In G. P. Sackett (Ed.), *Observing behavior: Volume II: Data collection and analysis methods* (pp. 25–43). Baltimore, MD: University Park Press.

Sackett, G. P., & Landesman-Dwyer, S. (1982). Data analysis: Methods and problems. In D. P. Hartmann (Ed.). *Using observers to study behavior: New directions for methodology of social and behavioral science* (No. 14, pp. 81–99). San Francisco, CA: Jossey-Bass.

Sackett, G. P., Ruppenthal, G. C., & Gluck, J. (1978). An overview of methodological and statistical problems in observational research. In G. P. Sackett (Ed.), *Observing behavior: Volume II: Data collection and analysis methods* (pp. 1–14). Baltimore, MD: University Park Press.

Salvia, J. A., & Meisel, C. J. (1980). Observer bias: A methodological consideration in special education research. *Journal of Special Education, 14,* 261–270.

Saudargas, R. A., & Lentz, F. E. (1986). Estimating percent of time and rate via direct observation: A suggested observational procedure and format. *School Psychology, 15,* 36–48.

Saudargas, R. A., & Zanolli, K. (1990). Momentary time sampling as an estimate of percentage time: A field validation. *Journal of Applied Behavior Analysis, 23,* 533–537.

Schmidt, F. L., & Hunter, J. E. (1989). Interrater reliability coefficients when only one stimulus is rated. *Journal of Applied Psychology, 86,* 376–390.

Scott, W. (1968). Comparative validities of forced-choice and single-stimulus tests. *Psychological Bulletin, 70,* 231–244.

Short, R., & Horn, J. (1984). Some notes on factor analysis of behavioral data. *Behaviour, 90,* 203–214.

Shrout, P. E, & Fleiss, J. L. (1979). Intraclass correlations: Uses in assessing rater reliability. *Psychological Bulletin, 86*, 420–428.

Sidman, M. (1960). *The tactics of scientific research: Evaluating experimental data in psychology.* New York: Basic Books.

Soeken, K. L., & Prescott, P. A. (1986). Issues in the use of kappa to estimate reliability. *Medical Care, 24*, 733–741.

Spool, M. D. (1978). Training programs for observers of behavior: A review. *Personnel Psychology, 31*, 853–888.

Stanley, J. C. (1971). Reliability. In R. L. Thorndike (Ed.), *Educational measurement* (2nd ed., pp. 359–442). Washington, DC: American Council on Education.

Stine, W. W. (1989). Interobserver relational agreement. *Psychological Bulletin, 106*, 341–347.

Stoloff, M. L., & Couch, J. V. (1988). *Computer use in psychology: A directory of software* (2nd ed.). Washington, DC: American Psychological Association.

Stuart, A., & Ord, J. K. (1991). *Kendall's advanced theory of statistics, Volume 2. Classical inference and relationship* (5th ed.). New York: Oxford University Press.

Suen, H. K., & Ary, D. (1989). *Analyzing quantitative behavioral observation data*. Hillsdale, NJ: Lawrence Erlbaum Associates.

Tinsley, H. E. A., & Weiss, D. J. (1975). Interrater reliability and agreement of subjective judgements. *Journal of Counseling Psychology, 22*, 358–376.

Travers, R. M. W. (1951). A critical review of the validity and rationale of the forced-choice technique. *Psychological Bulletin, 48*, 25–29.

Tweedie, D. (1975). Videoaudiometry: A possible procedure for "difficult-to-test" populations. *Volta Review, 77*(2), 129–134.

Weick, K. E. (1968). Systematic observational methods. In G. Lindzey & E. Aronson (Eds.), *The handbook of social psychology: Vol. 2. Research Methods* (pp. 357–451). Reading, MA: Addison-Wesley.

Wright, H. (1960). Observational child study. In P. Mussen (Ed.), *Handbook of research methods in child development* (pp. 71–139). New York: Wiley.

Yarnold, P. R. (1988). Classical test theory methods for repeated-measures N = 1 research design. *Educational and Psychological Measurement, 48*, 913–919.

Zavala, A. (1965). Development of the forced-choice rating scale technique. *Psychological Bulletin, 63*, 117–124.

APPENDIX: CONSTRUCTING CONFIDENCE INTERVALS FOR ICCS (FROM SHROUT & FLEISS, 1979)

ICC(2,1)

Let

$$\nu = \frac{(k-1)(n-1)(k\hat{\rho}F_j + n[1 + (k-1)\hat{\rho}] - k\hat{\rho})^2}{(n-1)k^2\hat{\rho}^2F_j^2 + (n(1 + (k-1)\hat{\rho}) - k\hat{\rho})^2} \quad (3.14)$$

where F_j = JMS/EMS and $\hat{\rho}$ = ICC(2,1).
Let

$$F^* = F_{1-\frac{1}{2}\alpha}[(n-1), \nu] \quad (3.15)$$

and

$$F_* = F_{1-\frac{1}{2}\alpha}[\nu, (n-1)] \quad (3.16)$$

where $F_{1-\alpha}(i, j)$ signifies the $(1-\alpha)100^{th}$ percentile of the F distribution with degrees of freedom i and j.

Then, the lower limit of the $(1-\alpha)100\%$ confidence interval is given by:

$$LoLim(2,1) = \frac{n(BMS - F^*EMS)}{F^*[kJMS + (kn-k-n)EMS] + nBMS} \quad (3.17)$$

and the upper limit of the $(1-\alpha)100\%$ confidence interval is given by:

$$UpLim(2,1) = \frac{n(F_*BMS - EMS)}{kJMS + (kn-k-n)EMS + nF_*BMS} \quad (3.18)$$

ICC(3,1)

Let F_o = BMS/EMS.
Let $F_L = F_o/F_{1-1/2\alpha}[(n-1), (n-1)(k-1)]$.
Let $F_U = F_o/F_{1-1/2\alpha}[(n-1)(k-1), (n-1)]$.

Then the lower limit of the $(1-\alpha)100\%$ confidence interval is given by:

$$LoLim(3,1) = \frac{F_L - 1}{F_L + (k-1)} \quad (3.19)$$

And the upper limit of the $(1-\alpha)100\%$ confidence interval is given by:

$$UpLim(3,1) = \frac{F_U - 1}{F_U + (k-1)} \quad (3.20)$$

ICC(2,k)

The lower limit of the $(1 - \alpha)100\%$ confidence interval is given by:

$$LoLim(2,k) = \frac{k(LoLim(2,1))}{1 + (k - 1)LoLim(2,1)} \tag{3.21}$$

and the upper limit of the $(1 - \alpha)100\%$ confidence interval is given by:

$$UpLim(2,k) = \frac{k(UpLim(2,1))}{1 + (k - 1)UpLim(2,1)} \tag{3.22}$$

where LoLim(2,1) and UpLim(2,1) are defined in equations 3.17 and 3.18, respectively.

ICC(3,k)

Let F_o = BMS/EMS.
Let $F_L = F_o/F_{1-1/2\alpha}[(n - 1), (n - 1)(k - 1)]$.
Let $F_U = F_o/F_{1-1/2\alpha}[(n - 1)(k - 1), (n - 1)]$.

Then the lower limit of the $(1 - \alpha)100\%$ confidence interval is given by:

$$LoLim(3, k) = 1 - \frac{1}{F_L} \tag{3.23}$$

And the upper limit of the $(1 - \alpha)100\%$ confidence interval is given by:

$$UpLim(3, k) = 1 - \frac{1}{F_U} \tag{3.24}$$

4

Treatment Integrity in Single-Subject Research

Frank M. Gresham
University of California—Riverside

The empirical demonstration that changes in behavior are functionally related to manipulated changes in the environment is a fundamental principle of behavior analytic research (Baer, Wolf, & Risley, 1968). In other words, researchers must demonstrate that changes in a dependent variable are functionally related to systematic, controlled, and measurable changes in an independent variable. This demonstration requires the representation of the independent variable by known physical parameters of an environmental event. Without clear and unambiguous specification of the independent variable, there can be no definitive conclusions regarding a functional analysis of behavior (Johnston & Pennypacker, 1980; Sidman, 1960).

Recently, researchers and practitioners have demonstrated a heightened interest in what is known as *treatment integrity* (Gresham, Gansle, & Noell, 1993; Gresham, Gansle, Noell, Cohen, & Rosenblum, 1993; Moncher & Prinz, 1991; Peterson, Homer, & Wonderlich, 1982). Treatment integrity (sometimes referred to as *treatment fidelity*) refers to the degree to which treatments are implemented as intended (Peterson et al., 1982; Yeaton & Sechrest, 1981). A subset of treatment integrity is *treatment differentiation,* which refers to the degree to which treatments or treatment conditions differ from one another (Kazdin, 1986).

Treatment integrity is concerned with the *accuracy* and *consistency* with which independent variables are implemented. Treatment integrity is necessary, but not sufficient, for the demonstration of functional relationships between experimenter-manipulated independent variables and dependent variables. That is, some independent variables may be implemented with perfect integrity yet show no functional relationship with a dependent variable. Other independent variables may be functionally related to a dependent variable; however, this functional relationship may be unknown or may be weak because of the poor integrity with which the independent variable was applied.

Practically speaking, researchers expect that treatment agents will implement a treatment as planned. This is particularly acute in treatments that must be implemented by third parties such as teachers, parents, or research assistants. When significant behavior changes occur, the researcher often assumes that these changes were due to the intervention. However, it may well be the case that the treatment agent changed the intervention in ways unknown to the researcher and these changes were responsible for behavior change.

In contrast, if significant behavior changes do not occur, then the researcher may assume falsely that the lack of change is due to an ineffective or inappropriate intervention. In this case, potentially effective treatments that would change behavior substantially if they were implemented properly may be discounted and eliminated from future consideration for similar problems. The cause of weak or nonexistent treatment effects in many cases is due to the poor integrity of potentially effective treatments (Yeaton & Sechrest, 1981).

Some researchers may argue that the imprecise application of independent variables poses no threats to functional statements that can be made between independent and dependent variables. Some researchers may maintain that steady-state responding in a dependent variable implies the stable and accurate application of the independent variable. However, stability in a dependent variable does not necessarily imply the stable application of the indpendent variable. For example, increases in on-task behavior and decreases in motor activity might be incorrectly attributed to a classroom behavior management program (e.g., Differential reinforcement of other behavior {DRO} + response cost) when, in fact, the "real" independent variable unknown to the researcher was a hefty dose of methylphenidate combined with some unknown and unmeasured setting events that were functionally related to the target behaviors.

Other researchers might argue that explicit assessment and demonstration of integrity is not a necessary condition for functional analysis assessment because errors in experimental control are protected by replication within and across subjects in behavior analytic research. However, unless a researcher knows precisely what was done, how it was done, and how long it was done, then replication is impossible. If replicate means to duplicate, copy, or repeat what was done, then this replication depends entirely on a complete and unambiguous specification of experimental procedures and an assessment of whether or not they were implemented as planned.

Peterson et al. (1982) argued that a "curious double standard" has evolved in the behavioral literature, in which operational definitions and measures of reliability are almost always presented when the behaviors serve as dependent variables and are infrequently presented when these same behaviors serve as independent variables. For example, it would not seem credible if a researcher claimed that sharing behavior increased as a function of peer praise when no operational definition of sharing or its reliable measurement were reported. In contrast, probably few consumers of the behavioral literature would have difficulty in accepting the reverse: Sharing behavior (not operationally defined nor measured) was used to increase the frequencies of an operationally defined and reliably measured index of peer praise. Obviously, one should be equally suspicious of either statement in the absence of an operational definition and reliable estimate of both the independent variable and the dependent variable.

Purpose of the Present Chapter

The purpose of this chapter is to discuss the importance of treatment integrity in single-subject research and explain how poor integrity and/or failure to monitor the integrity of treatments poses numerous threats to valid inference making. Reviews of the literature regarding treatment integrity are described and discussed. Factors that are related to the integrity of treatments are reviewed, as are measurement issues involved in monitoring the integrity of treatments. The chapter concludes with specific recommendations for conceptualizing, measuring, and monitoring implementation of independent variables in single-subject research.

TREATMENT INTEGRITY AND THREATS TO VALID INFERENCE MAKING

Failure to ensure the integrity of treatments poses numerous threats to valid inference in behavioral research (Moncher & Prinz, 1991). Experimentation seeks to isolate and measure the effects of independent variables on dependent variables. Without control of extraneous factors operating in the experimental situation, no definitive conclusions can be drawn regarding the effect(s) of independent variables on dependent variables.

Cook and Campbell (1979) identified four types of experimental validity that allow researchers to draw reasonable conclusions from experiments: (a) internal validity, (b) external validity, (c) construct validity, and (d) statistical conclusion validity. Failure to either assess or ensure treatment integrity poses serious threats to inferences that can be drawn in treatment outcome research. Three of these threats are discussed briefly in the following sections. Statistical conclusion validity is not discussed because it deals with inferential statistical analyses, violation of assumptions of statistical tests, and Type I and Type II errors. These issues are discussed by Gorman and Allison (this volume).

Internal validity refers to the extent that changes in the dependent variable can be attributed to the independent variable. Internally valid experiments allow the researcher to rule out alternative explanations of the results (Kazdin, 1992).

If significant behavior change occurs and if there are no data concerning the implementation of the independent variable, then the internal validity of the experiment may be compromised. Similarly, if significant behavior change does not occur and if the integrity of the treatment is not monitored, then one has difficulty in distinguishing between an ineffective treatment and an effective treatment implemented with poor integrity (Gresham, 1989; Wodarski, Feldman, & Pedi, 1974).

In terms of external validity, poorly defined, inadequately described, and idiosyncratically implemented treatments make replication and evaluation of treatments difficult (Johnston & Pennypacker, 1980; Moncher & Prinz, 1991). The absence of information concerning treatment definition and integrity limits the generalizability of treatments across settings, situations, and treatment implementors (Kazdin, 1986).

Johnston and Pennypacker (1980) defined a replication as the degree to which *equivalent environmental manipulations* (i.e., independent variables) associated with earlier observations are duplicated. Replications provide information regarding the generality of a functional relationship over a range of conditions (e.g., subjects, settings, and experimenters). Failure to assess the degree to which treatments are implemented as planned compromises the science of building a replicative history.

Construct validity refers to the explanations of the causal relation between independent variables and dependent variables (Kazdin, 1992). Whereas internal validity involves the demonstration that the independent variable was responsible for changes in the dependent variable, construct validity involves ruling out potential confounds that may compromise the interpretation of results. For example, teacher praise may be used to increase math work completion from a baseline average of 50% to a posttreatment average of 100%. However, the *way* in which the praise was delivered (i.e., warm, sincere, voice inflection, public recognition, etc.) may be the valid explanation of the results. That is, the reinforcement value of the praise for the student is the "construct" explaining the results.

Peterson et al. (1982) described a phenomenon known as *therapist drift* that refers to treatment implementors "drifting" away from the original protocol of treatment procedures. This obviously can change the construct validity of the independent variable. For instance, if a treatment for self-injurious behavior is based on a negative reinforcement functional analysis, and, over time, the treatment implementor drifts toward a positive reinforcement-based treatment (e.g., extinction and/or DRO), then the entire theoretical basis of the intervention is compromised.

Failure to monitor the integrity of treatments does not allow the researcher to identify and/or rule out confounds in an experiment. Using the teacher praise example, a teacher may praise on a variable ratio 2 (VR 2) schedule of reinforcement for the first five days and shift to a VR 20 schedule for the second five days. Obviously, larger treatment effects will occur in the VR 2 condition than in the VR 20 condition. A graphical depiction of these data would show an immediate treatment effect from baseline continuing for five days and a partial extinction effect for the second five days of treatment. If the experimenter did not monitor the implementation of treatment, explanation of these findings would be difficult. In other words, the teacher's thinning of the reinforcement schedule represents a confound in the experiment and a threat to construct validity.

REVIEWS OF THE TREATMENT INTEGRITY LITERATURE

The interest in treatment integrity is a relatively recent phenomenon. Yeaton and Sechrest's (1981) influential paper provided a useful conceptualization of integrity and outlined several key issues involved in its definition, measurement, and evaluation. These authors hypothesized reciprocal relationships among the *strength, integrity,* and *effectiveness* of treatments. In this view, treatments with poor integrity decrease the strength of treatments (i.e., dilute active treatment ingredients) and thereby reduce the effectiveness of those treatments. Thus, treatment integrity is important for evaluating the strength and effectiveness of treatments for different behaviors in different settings, for different individuals, and across different treatment implementors.

Given that treatment integrity represents an important aspect of treatment outcome research, to what degree does this research attend to the integrity of treatments? Four major reviews of the treatment integrity literature have been conducted in recent years (Gresham et al., 1993a, 1993b; Moncher & Prinz, 1991; Peterson et al., 1982). Each of these reviews tap somewhat different areas of the treatment outcome literature and offer varying conceptions of what constitutes treatment integrity. Each of these reviews is briefly discussed in the following sections.

Peterson et al.'s (1982) Review

These researchers conducted one of the most influential reviews of the treatment integrity literature. They reviewed all empirical studies published in the *Journal of Applied Behavior Analysis* (*JABA*) between 1968 and 1980 ($N = 539$). Three categories of independent variable (integrity) assessment were used: (a) yes, which could involve interobserver agreement on application of the independent variable or calibration checks by the experimenter, (b) no, but the risk for inaccurate application was low (e.g., mechanical delivery of tokens), and (c) no, integrity was not assessed and it was necessary. Operational definitions of the independent variable also consisted of three categories: (a) yes, (b) no but unnecessary (e.g., writing on board, modeling a response, etc.), and (c) no but necessary.

Peterson et al. (1982) found that only 20% of the 539 studies reported data on the integrity of treatments. In addition, over 16% of studies did not provide an operational definition of the independent variable. There were no trends suggesting an improvement in integrity assessment and operational definitions of independent variables from 1968 through 1980. These data suggest that the authors of the applied behavior analysis literature as published in its flagship journal (*JABA*) were not overly concerned with the accurate measurement and facilitation of treatment integrity.

Moncher and Prinz's (1991) Review

These authors provided a broad overview of treatment integrity in treatment outcome research, reviewing 359 studies published in eight journals representing clinical psychology (*Journal of Consulting and Clinical Psychology*), behavior therapy (*Behavior Therapy*), psychiatry (*Psychiatry, American Journal of Psychiatry,* and *American Journal of Orthopsychiatry*), and marital/family therapy (*Journal of Marital and Family Therapy, American Journal of Family Therapy,* and *Journal of Sex and Marital Therapy*). Whereas Peterson et al. (1982) only reviewed studies published in *JABA* between 1968 and 1980, Moncher and Prinz (1991) reviewed a more representative sample of treatment modalities and theoretical orientations published between 1980 and 1988.

Five categories of methods used to facilitate treatment integrity were coded: treatment manual to promote compliance with specified treatment procedures, supervision of treatment implementors to enhance adherence to the treatment protocol, monitoring adherence to treatment protocol by examining events occurring in treatment, studies using all three methods, and studies not addressing treatment integrity at all.

Results of the Moncher and Prinz (1991) review showed that approximately 55% of the 359 studies reviewed ignored the issue of treatment integrity all together. Approximately 31% of the studies used manualized treatments (with and without other procedures), 21% employed supervision (with and without other procedures), 18% checked adherence to the treatment protocol (with and without other procedures), and about 6% used all three procedures. These authors concluded that there were significant increases between 1980 and 1988 in the proportion of studies monitoring integrity and utilizing supervision to increase treatment integrity. However, methods and sources used to conduct integrity checks as well as the representativeness of integrity assessments were seen as problematic.

Gresham et al. 1993a, 1993b Reviews

Gresham et al. (1993b) provided an update of the Peterson et al. (1982) review by examining all studies (N = 158) published in *JABA* between 1980 and 1990 that were child studies (i.e., subjects under 19 years of age). Studies were coded according to the four variables of age level, type of dependent variable, operational definition of the independent variable, and assessment of integrity.

Contrary to the Peterson et al. (1982) review, Gresham et al. (1993a, 1993b) used a more stringent criterion for determining whether or not an independent variable was operationally defined. Studies were coded *yes or no* with respect to operational definition. The criterion for an operational definition was stated to raters as follows: "If you could replicate this treatment with the information provided, the intervention is to be considered operationally defined." The independent variable was considered operationally defined only if its specific verbal, physical, temporal, and spatial parameters were described. Integrity assessment consisted of three categories: (a) yes (assessment of integrity and a reported index of integrity expressed as a percentage), (b) no, and (c) monitored (mention of integrity or monitoring but no data presented).

Of the 158 child studies published in *JABA* between 1980 and 1990, only 32.4% (54 studies) provided an operational definition of the independent variable. Only 15.8% of the 158 studies systematically measured and reported levels of treatment integrity, with about half of these studies reporting integrity of 100% (M = 93.8%, SD = 11.63%). Another 8.9% of the 158 studies monitored integrity, with the remaining 75.3%

(N = 119 studies) not bothering to either measure or monitor treatment integrity.

Gresham et al. (1993a) reviewed the integrity of *behaviorally based* treatment outcome studies conducted in school settings between 1980 and 1990 published in seven journals (N = 181). These journals included: *Behavior Modification, Behavior Therapy, Journal of Applied Behavior Analysis, Journal of Abnormal Child Psychology, Journal of Consulting and Clinical Psychology, Journal of Behaviour Therapy and Experimental Psychiatry,* and *Behavioral Disorders.* The criteria for operational definition of the independent variable and evaluation of treatment integrity used by Gresham et al. (1993b) were used in this review.

Overall, only 35% (64 studies) provided an operational definition of the intervention, with approximately 15% of the studies systematically measuring and reporting integrity. Another 10% of the studies monitored integrity and 75% (N = 136) did not address the issue of treatment integrity. Using an index of effect size (Cohen's D), there was a moderate correlation between percent reported integrity and effect size (r = .51).

Summary

It is clear that the majority of treatment outcome studies published in major journals in clinical psychology, behavior therapy, applied behavior analysis, psychiatry, and family/marital therapy do not measure or monitor treatment integrity. On average, only 17.2% of the studies reviewed actually *measured* treatment integrity. In addition, only 28% of these studies provided an operational definition of the independent variable(s) to be implemented.

Failure to gather data on the integrity of independent variable implementation, no matter how inconvenient, compromises the science of intervention efforts. This lack of treatment integrity assessment or monitoring compromises our knowledge of functional relationships between independent variables and dependent variables. If there is no reliable measurement of *both* the independent and dependent variable, then the accuracy of any functional analysis can be questioned. The following section reviews several factors related to the integrity of treatments in behavioral research.

FACTORS RELATED TO TREATMENT INTEGRITY

Several factors appear to be related to the integrity of treatments. These include: complexity of treatments, time required to implement treatments, materials/resources required for treatments, number of treatment agents, perceived and actual effectiveness of treatments, and motivation of treatment agents.

Complexity of Treatments. The complexity of a treatment is directly related to the degree of treatment integrity (Yeaton & Sechrest, 1981). For example, Wolf (1978) suggested that the failure to replicate the effects of the Achievement Place model was due to the lack of treatment integrity. The Achievement Place model is a highly complex token economy system of behavior change requiring the consistent and systematic application of numerous behavioral principles. Similarly, the correct application of the Direct Instruction model (Becker & Carnine, 1980) requires the implementation of a number of interrelated treatment components (e.g., rapid pacing of instruction, frequent questioning, etc.). Becker and Carnine (1980) noted difficulties with maintaining high levels of treatment integrity using the Direct Instruction model.

A general principle of behavior change is that the more complex the treatment is, the lower the integrity of that treatment is. This is particularly problematic in treatments that must be implemented by third parties (e.g., parents and teachers). Without checks on the integrity of treatments implemented by third parties, one must tenuously assume that the treatment was implemented as planned.

Time Required. Time is a universally valued commodity, particularly among teachers.

Happe (1982) found that 87% of respondents in his survey reported lack of time as the most frequent reason given by teachers for not implementing treatment plans.

There is an interaction between the complexity of a treatment and the amount of time required for its implementation. Complex treatments usually require more time to implement than do simple treatments. For instance, a researcher who designs a treatment consisting of token reinforcement, school–home notes, frequent monitoring of behavior, and time-out is asking teachers to invest a great deal of time that they probably do not have or are not willing to invest. The likely result of such a plan is poor treatment integrity and subsequent ineffectiveness in changing behavior.

Materials/Resources Required. Treatments that require additional materials and resources beyond those commonly found in school, home, or community environments are likely to be implemented with poorer integrity than are treatments requiring no special resources. Many treatments require equipment and resources that are either expensive or difficult to access. For example, biofeedback has been used successfully to treat a variety of disorders including headaches, asthma, bladder incontinence, and cerebral palsy (Williamson, McKenzie, & Goreczny, 1988). Biofeedback equipment, however, is expensive, not commonly available, and requires highly trained personnel to operate and interpret.

Researchers designing treatments requiring specialized resources and materials are likely to experience problems in establishing and maintaining adequate levels of treatment integrity. The use of expensive back-up reinforcers, substantial changes in environmental ecologies, technical equipment, and unusual privileges not readily available in most environments is likely to result in low levels of treatment integrity. At the same time, however, this same equipment and supplies may be required to produce treatments of sufficient strength to change certain problem behaviors.

Number of Treatment Agents. Treatments requiring more than one treatment agent may be implemented with poorer integrity than may treatments requiring one agent. In general, treatments requiring multiple treatment agents are likely to be more complex than are single treatment agent interventions. A school–home note system requires cooperation between both teachers and parents. Poor integrity can occur when parents provide inconsistent contingencies at home based on the note, when teachers fail to complete the note consistently or fail to send the note home to parents, or when the child does not take the note home.

A number of treatments depend to some extent on multiple treatment agents. Although these interventions may be effective, they can be rendered ineffective because of failures on the part of treatment agents to follow established treatment protocols. On the other hand, the strength and generality of many treatments depend on the incorporation of multiple treatment agents across multiple settings. Research efforts should investigate the effects of multiple treatment agents on the integrity of those treatments and the subsequent effectiveness of those treatments.

Perceived and Actual Effectiveness. Treatments that are perceived by treatment consumers or treatment agents to be effective may be implemented with greater integrity that treatments perceived to be ineffective. Some authors have suggested that treatment integrity is the central element linking the acceptability and use of treatments (Witt & Elliott, 1985; Yeaton & Sechrest, 1981). That is, acceptable treatments are more likely to be used with greater integrity than less acceptable treatments. In turn, these treatments are more likely to be effective in changing behavior. Perceived effectiveness or the degree to which treatment agents are presented with positive outcome information on treatments has been shown to influence treatment acceptability ratings by teachers (Clark & Elliott, 1988; Von Brock & Elliott, 1987). Moreover, treatments that produce rapid behavior change may be continued with even greater integrity than slower acting treatments. In other words, treatment integrity may be reinforced and maintained by the reinforcer of immediate behavior change.

There is little empirical research, however, addressing the relationship between treatment effectiveness (perceived or actual) and treatment integrity. Practitioners currently lack knowledge of which treatments are most effective with what behaviors and how effectiveness data influence subsequent integrity of treatments. This represents a fruitful avenue for future research.

Motivation of Treatment Agent. The motivation of treatment agents to invest their efforts into a behavior change treatment impacts the integrity with which that treatment will be implemented. Teachers, for example, may request consultation in designing an intervention plan to change problem behavior. Their real motivation, however, may be to have the child tested and removed from the classroom rather than implement an intervention plan with integrity to change the problem behavior. Parents may verbally commit to an intervention plan complete with parent training sessions and implementation of behavioral techniques to decrease noncompliant behavior. In many cases, there may be little correspondence between what parents say they will do and what actually gets done. Thus, the lack of motivation on the part of parents may cause serious deficits in the integrity of parent training interventions (Forehand & McMahon, 1981).

TECHNICAL ISSUES IN TREATMENT INTEGRITY

Several technical issues are involved in the conceptualization and measurement of treatment integrity. These include: specification and definition of treatment components, interpreting treatment integrity data, and psychometric issues in assessing treatment integrity. Each of these issues is discussed in the following sections, along with suggestions for resolving conceptual and empirical problems.

Specification of Treatment Components

The measurement of treatment integrity requires the definition of the treatment and its components. Each treatment component must be defined in specific, behavioral terms so that it can be measured. Johnston and Pennypacker (1980) argued:

> There may be a distinction between what the experimenter thinks or says is the independent variable and the actual controlling variables in the experiment. Ideally, this discrepancy is minimal because the independent variable has been defined in terms that refer to real events in the environment. . . . Such a clear description of the independent variable is essential if any factually accurate statement is to issue from the experimental effort. (p. 40)

Based on the Gresham et al. (1993a, 1993b) and Peterson et al. (1982) reviews, an average of only 28% of the studies provided an operational definition of treatments. One reason for the lack of attention to treatment integrity is the failure of some researchers to provide adequate operational definitions of the treatment and its components. As mentioned earlier, operational definitions of the dependent variable are almost always provided in published treatment outcome studies but are provided less often when the same behaviors serve as independent variables.

Independent variables can be defined along four dimensions: verbal, physical, spatial, and temporal. An example of an adequate operational definition of the components of the independent variable can be found in an investigation by Mace, Page, Ivancic, and O'Brien (1986) that compared time-out with and without contingent delay to decrease disruptive behavior. Mace et al. defined the time-out procedure as follows: (a) Immediately following the occurrence of a target behavior (temporal dimension), (b) the therapist said "No, go to time-out" (verbal dimension), (c) led the child by the arm to a prepositioned time-out chair (physical dimension), and (d) seated the child facing the corner (spatial dimension). (e) If the child's buttocks were raised from the time-out chair or if the child's head was turned more than 45 degrees (spatial dimension), the therapist used the least amount of force necessary to guide compliance with the time-out procedure (physical dimension). (f) At the end of two minutes (temporal dimension), the therapist turned the time-out chair 45 degrees from the corner (physical and spatial dimension), and walked away (physical dimension).

The operational definition of treatment procedures used by Mace et al. (1986) would make replications and external validation of this procedure relatively easy. Contrast the Mace et al. treatment definition with the definition of part of a treatment recently published in *JABA* (Stark et al., 1993): "Specifically, parents were initially taught to use differential attention (praising and ignoring) and were gradually introduced to the use of contingent privileges (loss of a privilege contingent on not meeting a meal goal)" (p. 439). Clearly, the parent training component of the Stark et al. study would be more difficult to replicate than would the time-out study by Mace et al. (1986), based on the operational definition of treatment components. However, can there be too much specificity in defining the independent variable?

One unresolved question in component specification is the level of specificity required. Do we use global, intermediate, or molecular levels of specification? On one hand, it makes sense to define components in very specific terms to ensure clarity of treatment components. On the other hand, a detailed task analysis may be overwhelming to treatment agents, thereby risking consumer rejection of treatments. Additionally, the complexity of the treatment increases as a function of the components specified. Paradoxically, treatments with a large number of well-defined components may be implemented with less integrity than treatments with fewer and more nebulously defined components because of the complexity of the former.

Global levels of treatment specification would involve stating simple principles of behavior change, such as: catch them being good, reward appropriate behavior, use planned ignoring, and so forth. Intermediate levels of specification involve writing the major steps of an intervention program, such as: construct a reinforcement menu for all students, write classroom rules on poster board in four-inch letters with colored markers, review classroom rules daily with the class, remove points contingent on rule violations, and so forth. A molecular level of specification involves a detailed task analysis of every event in an intervention plan. For example, there may be 5 to 10 substeps in one step of an intermediate level specification (e.g., remove points immediately upon rule violation, restate rule to offending student, stand in close physical proximity to student, establish eye contact, etc.).

Another issue in specification of treatment components is the *weighting* of each component. Some components of a treatment are more crucial (i.e., functional) to treatment success than are others. It might be more crucial to treatment success to contingently deliver a positive reinforcer than it is to provide a rationale to students for an intervention program. Given that some treatment components are more important than others, the weighting of components must be taken into consideration when evaluating integrity.

As yet, there is no empirical support for selecting and weighting various treatment components. The decision of how to weight treatment components should be based on an idiographic, functional analysis criterion. That is, treatment components showing functional relationships to target behaviors should be retained and given more weight in intervention plans.

Interpreting Treatment Integrity Data

Researchers must consider the degree of deviation from a treatment protocol and the degree of behavior change. In other words, how far can treatment delivery deviate from a treatment protocol and still produce desired effects on behavior? Peterson et al. (1982) described a phenomenon called "therapist drift" in which a treatment agent gradually alters a treatment plan.

Therapist drift may produce positive effects, negative effects, or no effects at all. In some cases, deviation from a treatment protocol can produce greater changes than what might have been realized by the original treatment (e.g., drifting to thicker reinforcement schedules than specified). In other cases, deviations may produce behavior changes in the opposite direction (e.g., drifting from an extinction schedule to a partial reinforcement schedule). In still other cases, deviations can have the effect of neutralizing treatment strength and still producing no changes in behavior (e.g., drifting too quickly from thicker to thinner schedules).

Kazdin (1992) specified several interpretive problems that might be presented when researchers check or fail to check the manipulation of the independent variable and the subsequent effects on the dependent variable. This same logic can be applied to measurement of treatment integrity. Fig. 4.1 shows four possible scenarios regarding the assessment of treatment integrity and its effects on the dependent variable. Although treatment integrity falls on a continuum (as do dependent variables), Fig. 4.1 uses a dichotomy to capture whether or not treatments were implemented with integrity and whether or not there were changes in the dependent variable.

Cell A creates no particular interpretive difficulty. This cell indicates

	Dependent Variable Change	
Integrity Status	Yes	No
High integrity	Cell A Treatment implemented as planned and changes in dependent variable.	Cell B Treatment implemented as planned but little or no changes in dependent variable.
Low or no integrity	Cell C Little or no integrity but changes in dependent variable.	Cell D Little or no integrity and little or no changes in dependent variable.

FIG. 4.1. Relationships between treatment integrity and changes in the dependent variable.

that treatment procedures were implemented as intended and the dependent variable changed as predicted. An example might be that a response cost procedure was implemented with 100% integrity after baseline, and the frequency of disruptive behavior decreased throughout the treatment phase of the experiment. Increased confidence in this functional relationship is gained by return to a second baseline and subsequent reintroduction of the response cost procedure.

Cell B shows that the treatment was implemented as planned, but had no effect on the dependent variable. Assessment of the independent variable in this case may provide insights into the failure of the treatment to produce desired effects. It should be noted that one will probably not encounter this situation in the published literature, given the bias against publishing negative results. In practice or pilot work, however, this may be a likely occurrence.

For instance, there simply may be no functional relationship between the independent variable and the dependent variable. This faulty functional analysis could explain the results. Alternatively, the integrity may be high, but the manner or quality in which the treatment was delivered did not impact on the dependent variable (e.g., verbal praise delivered in monotone without enthusiasm). Finally, although the treatment was delivered with perfect integrity, it may have been too weak to impact on the dependent variable (e.g., using a thin variable schedule to establish behavior rather than a continuous schedule).

Cell C reflects what happens in the majority of published behavioral research. That is, there is no check on the integrity with which independent variables are implemented, but there are significant changes in the dependent variable. The assumption is that the independent variable was responsible for changes in the dependent variable. As discussed extensively in the beginning of this chapter, this is a tenuous assumption. Interpretation of this effect is clouded by the failure to demonstrate that the independent variable was responsible for behavior change.

Cell D shows that the integrity of the independent variable was not checked and there was no effect on the dependent variable. Again, it is unlikely that this situation will be encountered in the published literature. There are numerous reasons for the failure of treatments to produce changes in behavior. However, many of these reasons can be ruled out by the accurate measurement of treatment integrity.

Psychometric Issues in Measuring Treatment Integrity

Assessment of treatment integrity requires that treatment components be accurately measured. Measurement issues in treatment integrity can be conceptualized in terms of classical test theory (reliability and validity [for more details see Primivera et al., this volume]), Generalizability Theory, or the behavioral notion of accuracy.

Classical Test Theory. From a classical test theory perspective, components that make up a treatment can be viewed much like items on a test or scale. The degree to which each component of the treatment is implemented can be thought of as the reliability (integrity) of that component of the intervention, much like an item-total correlation. Stability would reflect how consistently a treatment or treatment component is implemented over time. Classical reliability theory, however, would assume that these treatment components would be stable and any error in implementation would be completely random.

An applied behavior analytic perspective on reliability would refer to the agreement among observers (or some measuring instrument) viewing the implementation of each component at the same time (Baer, 1977; Johnston & Pennypacker, 1980). Unlike classical reliability theory, a behavioral analytic approach is primarily interested in the degree of homogeneity among observers of behavior rather than in the homogeneity of the components of a treatment. Thus, reliability in behavior analysis is closer to the classical notion of *equivalent forms reliability* in that it reflects the degree to which two observers are behaving as equivalent measuring instruments (Strosahl & Linehan, 1986).

The validity of treatment integrity measurements can be viewed from the traditional perspectives of content, construct, and criterion-related validity. The content validity of treatment integrity is concerned with specifying components comprising a treatment, and how well the measured implementation of these components in a particular situation at a given point in time by a particular observer represents the implementation measured in other situations at other times and by different observers. Clearly, content validity of treatment integrity rests not only on the specification of treatment components making up a treatment, but also on the representative sampling and measurement of treatment implementation.

The construct validity of treatment integrity is primarily concerned with two issues: treatment differentiation and convergent and discriminant validity. *Treatment differentiation* refers to the degree to which treatments differ. Some treatments are more easily differentiated than others. For example, it is not difficult to differentiate drug treatment from contingent reinforcement to change disruptive behavior. In contrast, it is more difficult to differentiate effective teaching strategies found in the educational psychology literature (e.g., overlapping of instruction, frequent questioning, incidental teaching, etc.) from stimulus control techniques found in the applied behavior analysis literature. Although these techniques emanate from two entirely different theoretical literatures, many of these techniques may share the same basic active treatment ingredients.

Convergent and discriminant validity is concerned with the agreement between two or more methods in measuring the degree of treatment integrity. Behavioral assessment assumes and expects low correlations between different methods of measuring the same behavioral construct. Cone (1979) suggested that many behavioral assessment studies fail to control for *content-method confounds*. That is, the lack of correlation between different methods of measuring the same behavior may be due to method differences (direct observation versus self-report) as well as differences in the content of what is being measured (e.g., verbal versus overt-motoric).

There is one significant question regarding construct validity in measuring treatment integrity: How well does the measurement of treatment integrity by one method agree with the measurement of integrity by other methods? For example, how well does direct observation of treatment implementation agree with self-monitoring of the implementation of that same treatment?

Criterion-related validity of treatment integrity is concerned with the relationship between the independent and dependent variables. In other words, does the level of treatment integrity predict the degree of change on the dependent variable? Gresham et al.'s (1993a) finding of a moderate correlation ($r = .51$) between the level of integrity and effect size attests to the criterion-related validity of integrity measurement.

Generalizability Theory. Establishing the reliability and validity of treatment integrity can be conceptualized from the perspective of Generalizability Theory (G Theory) (Cronbach, Gleser, Nanda, & Rajaratnam, 1972). Unlike classical test theory, G Theory combines notions of reliability and validity into domains or universes of generalizability. G Theory identifies and separates a number of sources of systematic variation in test scores, thereby accounting for what might have been considered random error in classical test theory.

Universes of generalizability include scorer, item, time, setting, method, and dimension (Cone, 1977; Cronbach et al., 1972). For instance, *scorer generalizability* is concerned with how representative a scorer or observer of behavior is of all scorers or observers that might have been used. *Time generalizability* refers to the extent to which scores obtained at one point in time are representative of scores taken at other times. In terms of treatment integrity, time generalizability would reflect the representativeness of integrity measured at one point in time (e.g., Monday) to other points in time (Tuesday through Friday). This same logic would hold for item, setting, method, and dimension.

Suen (1990) pointed out some difficulties in using G Theory with observational data. Because of the relatively small number of subjects being observed, the variance across subjects is unstable. In single-case research designs there is no between-subject variance; therefore, true variance cannot be subject variance. Suen suggested that the object of measurement in single-case research is not subjects themselves, but a subject's behavior in *time*. In effect, the variance across observation sessions is the variance of interest.

A criterion-referenced interpretation of generalizability data is most appropriate for single-case research data. This is because criterion-referenced data typically have restricted variances compared to norm-referenced data. As such, traditional generalizability coefficients based on normal distribution assumptions cannot be used with criterion-referenced data (Suen, 1990). Using Brennan and Kane's (1977) dependability index rather than a generalizability coefficient is most appropriate for estimating reliability and validity in idiographic research (Suen, 1990).

Accuracy. Perhaps the most relevant measurement principle in evaluating treatment integrity is accuracy. *Accuracy* refers to the correspondence between measured behavior and the true value of behavior (Cone, 1981; Johnston & Pennypacker, 1980). The requirement for establishing accuracy is the existence of an incontrovertible index or standard against which measures of behavior can be compared. If the "true" value of behavior is known, then different methods of measuring that behavior can be compared.

The accuracy of any assessment method can be established by specifying treatment components in standard and absolute terms and computing a percent accuracy. Peterson et al. (1982) suggested that knowing the true value of a dependent variable in nature is not possible because some portion of the variability in a dependent variable may be influenced by fluctuations in functional relationships between unmeasured and unknown environmental events. Thus, the true value of a dependent variable cannot be specified *a priori*.

In contrast, the "true" value of an independent variable in nature can be operationally defined as the value specified by the experimenter. The extent to which implementation of the independent variable matches or approximates this prespecified value corresponds to its accuracy of implementation. Accuracy can be computed across different scorers over time, using different methods in research and practical applications of treatment integrity assessments.

Summary

Based on the previous discussion, several conclusions can be drawn about the relationship among reliability, validity, and accuracy. First, it is entirely possible for treatment components to be stable, but not internally consistent. That is, a treatment implementor may consistently implement only one or two components of an eight-component treatment package. The unimplemented components in this case may well be the most functional components in changing the dependent variable.

Second, treatments can be internally consistent, but not stable. Treatment agents may implement the entire treatment with high integrity only one or two days per week. This would most likely decrease treatment strength and render the treatment ineffective.

Third, it is possible for treatments to be stable, but not accurate. That is, although treatments may be consistently implemented over time, their specifics may be inaccurately implemented. Likewise, treatments can have high session integrity, but may not be representative of actual or typical implementation of the treatment.

Fourth, treatments can be stable, internally consistent, and accurate, yet may not be valid. That is, some treatments may have little or no effect on behavior. This state of affairs obviously describes the wrong treatment for the target behavior and a faulty functional analysis of behavior.

Fifth, it is possible for treatments to have high integrity by one method of assessment but not by other assessment methods. For example, a treatment may have high integrity when measured by self-monitoring but low integrity measured by direct observation. Interpretation for this lack of correspondence may be clouded by issues of representative sampling of treatment sessions, errors of measurement, and method-content confounds.

ASSESSMENT OF TREATMENT INTEGRITY

Treatment integrity can be assessed using either direct or indirect methods. There are advantages and disadvantages to using both direct and indirect methods of assessing treatment integrity.

Direct Assessment

Direct assessment of treatment integrity is identical to the systematic observation of behavior in applied settings. Foster and Cone (1986) specified several factors to be considered in selection and design of direct observation assessment systems, such as the purpose of making the observations, the subject matter of the observations, the amount of behavior to be observed, and the quality of data produced. These same factors should guide the design of direct observation systems for treatment integrity assessment.

There are three steps in designing a direct observation system to assess treatment integrity. First, the various components of treatment must be clearly specified in operational terms. Key elements of the intervention must be made explicit to minimize the amount of inference required in recording. The assessment of treatment integrity begins with a task analysis of the treatment to be implemented, in which subtasks are defined clearly. These subtasks should be defined in terms of specific verbal, physical, temporal, and/or spatial aspects of the independent variable.

Second, the occurrence and nonoccurrence of each treatment component should be assessed. These measurements will yield the degree of integrity of each treatment component over observation sessions.

Third, the level of treatment integrity can be obtained by calculating the percentage of treatment components implemented by treatment agents. Observers can calculate percentages over time and relate the degree of integrity to rates of the target behavior. These data can be graphed by plotting the percent integrity against behavior rates over time. This amounts to showing functional relationships between treatment component integrities and target behaviors.

Number of Observation Sessions. The ultimate goal of any direct observation assessment is to produce data that accurately represent the behavior(s) of interest (Foster & Cone, 1986). The most important type of validity for direct observational assessment is content validity (Linehan, 1980). Representativeness of observational data depends on both the number of observation sessions and the length of each observation session. As a general rule, the greater amount of data collected on representative behaviors, the more representative the data are of the content domain.

Foster and Cone (1986) pointed out that little attention has been given to the question of the amount of data needed to produce a representative sample of behavior. Practically speaking, a treatment agent can probably get a reasonable idea of a treatment's integrity by conducting three to five observations of 20 to 30 minutes' duration. This extremely rough guideline will vary as a function of the intervention and the settings in which the intervention is implemented.

Reactivity of Observations. An important consideration in assessing treatment integrity is the potential for reactive effects of the observer's presence in the treatment setting, particularly if the treatment agent knows the observer is assessing the integrity of intervention. Foster and Cone (1986) reviewed 17 studies on reactivity in which the conspicuousness and awareness of observer presence was varied. This review showed that 34% of the behaviors investigated were affected by observer presence.

Practical resolutions of potential reactivity of observation in treatment integrity assessments are not easily attained. There are several procedures that may ameliorate reactive effects. First, observers can observe on a random schedule and "spot check" the implementation of treatment plans. Second, observers can try to be as unobtrusive as possible in the treatment setting. Third, observers can simply not communicate the purpose of observation to treatment agents during the treatment integrity assessment phase. After assessing treatment integrity, the observer should provide feedback to the treatment agent regarding the integrity of the treatment.

Some may question the need to minimize observer reactivity if the reactive effects tend to be in the desired direction (i.e., treatment agents tend to implement treatments with greater integrity when observers are present). However, if treatment agents only implement treatment plans while observations are being conducted, the treatment will be less effective or ineffective most of the time (i.e., when observations are not being made). Foster and Cone (1986) provided an extensive discussion of the literature regarding reactivity of direct observations.

Indirect Assessment

Treatment integrity can be assessed using methods other than direct observations. Rating scales, self-monitoring, self-report, and behavioral interviews represent potential candidates for alternative assessment strategies. Self-monitoring has been used to enhance compliance with treatments as well as an assessment device (Bornstein, Hamilton, & Bornstein, 1986). Self-monitoring, however, may be incompatible with the implementation of some treatments and decrease the effectiveness of treatments. Van Houten and Sullivan (1975), for example, found that complex environments such as classrooms interfere with the self-monitoring behaviors of teachers.

Self-monitoring of treatment implementation has received relatively little attention from researchers, probably because it creates an unacceptable concurrent choice situation between treatment implementation and self-monitoring. The current status of self-monitoring research indicates that self-monitoring is most accurate when a concurrently occurring task does not interfere with the subject's self-monitoring or self-recording (Gardner & Cole, 1988).

Several indirect methods for assessing treatment integrity could be constructed. One could construct a self-report measure of treatment integrity to be completed by treatment agents at the end of each treatment session. The items on this measure, each of the operationally defined treatment components, could be rated on a five-point scale ranging from Strongly Disagree to Strongly Agree. Completion of this self-report may produce reactive effects in the desired direction by cuing treatment agents to implement treatments with integrity.

Another assessment strategy would be to use a behavior rating scale completed by an observer after each treatment session. These ratings would be based on observation of the entire treatment rather than the recording of the occurrence/nonoccurrence of implementation of treatment components. These ratings could be on a five-point scale ranging from Low Integrity to High Integrity.

In summary, there are several assessment alternatives to more expensive and potentially reactive direct observations for evaluating treatment integrity. As yet, there is no published research that has investigated the relationships among these alternative methods for assessing integrity. Both research and practical applications of multiple-method integrity assessments should be sure to test the same content in each assessment method to avoid method-content confounds (Cone, 1979).

CONCLUSIONS AND RECOMMENDATIONS

The paucity of studies assessing or reporting treatment integrity limits the confidence in the functional relationships reported. The fact that relatively few studies operationally defined independent variables sets an upper limit on the degree to which the accuracy of the independent variable can be measured. Based on the current status of integrity measurement and the operational definitions of independent variables, the following recommendations are made to improve confidence in our research findings and to promote the integrity of treatments in applied settings:

1. Researchers should provide clear, unambiguous, and comprehensive operational definitions of all independent variables used in experimental studies. The same standards with which dependent variables are operationally defined and measured should be applied to independent variables. Independent variables should be operationally defined along four dimensions: verbal, physical, spatial, and temporal.
2. The integrity with which each component of the independent variable is implemented should be measured using an accuracy criterion. *Accuracy* refers to the extent to which obtained measures approximate or match the "true" state of nature or the objective, topographic features of behavior (Cone, 1981; Johnston & Pennypacker, 1980).

3. Each component of a treatment should be measured by direct observation of component implementation using an occurrence/nonoccurrence observation code. The level of treatment integrity can be obtained by summing the number of components correctly implemented and dividing this number by the total number of components to yield percent integrity. "Correctly implemented" is defined by the operational definition of each component.

4. Two estimates of integrity should be calculated. One, the integrity of each treatment component across days of treatment should be calculated to yield *component integrity*. Two, the integrity of all treatment components within days/sessions should be calculated to yield *daily or session integrity*. Given these two estimates, failure to find significant treatment effects might be explained by poor component integrity over time, poor daily integrity of components, or both. If integrity estimates are high for both component and session integrity and there are no treatment effects, then a reconsideration of the functional analysis is in order.

5. Alternative methods for assessing treatment integrity such as self-monitoring, self-reports, behavior rating scales, and behavioral interviews should be used to supplement direct observations of treatment integrity. Multimethod research studies should be conducted to assess the agreement among these assessment methods to determine whether one or more methods can be substituted for direct observations.

6. Treatment manuals should be developed for all treatments, and treatment agents should be trained to criterion levels on the treatment protocol before implementing a treatment. Recalibration of treatment agents to the treatment protocol should be done periodically for the duration of treatment.

7. Studies reporting treatment outcomes should include treatment integrity data and/or methods used to ensure adherence to treatment protocols. Assessment of treatment integrity in these studies should be given considerable weight in publication decisions.

REFERENCES

Baer, D. (1977). Reviewer's comment: Just because it's reliable doesn't mean that you can use it. *Journal of Applied Behavior Analysis, 10,* 117–120.

Baer, D., Wolf, M., & Risley, R. (1968). Some current dimensions of applied behavior analysis. *Journal of Applied Behavior Analysis, 1,* 91–97.

Becker, W., & Carnine, D. (1980). Direct instruction: An effective approach to educational intervention with disadvantaged and low performers. In B. Lahey & A. Kazdin (Eds.), *Advances in clinical child psychology* (Vol. 3, pp. 429–473). New York: Plenum.

Bornstein, P., Hamilton, S., & Bornstein, M. (1986). Self-monitoring procedures. In A.

Ciminero, K. Calhoun, & H. Adams (Eds.), *Handbook of behavioral assessment* (2nd ed., pp. 176–222). New York: Wiley Interscience.

Brennan, R., & Kane, M. (1977). An index of dependability for mastery tests. *Journal of Educational Measurement, 14,* 277–289.

Campbell, D., & Fiske, D. (1959). Convergent and discriminant validation by the multitrait–multimethod matrix. *Psychological Bulletin, 56,* 81–105.

Clark, L., & Elliott, S. (1988). The influence of treatment strength information on knowledgeable teachers' evaluations of two social skills training methods. *Professional School Psychology, 3,* 241–257.

Cone, J. (1977). The relevance of reliability and validity for behavioral assessment. *Behavior Therapy, 8,* 411–426.

Cone, J. (1979). Confounded comparisons in triple response mode assessment. *Behavioral Assessment, 1,* 85–95.

Cone, J. (1981). Psychometric considerations. In M. Hersen & A. Bellack (Eds.), *Behavioral assessment: A practical handbook* (pp. 38–70). New York: Pergamon.

Cook, T., & Campbell, D. (Eds.). (1979). *Quasi-experimentation: Design and analysis issues for field settings.* Chicago: Rand McNally.

Cronbach, L., Gleser, G., Nanda, H., & Rajaratnam, N. (1972). *The dependability of behavioral measures.* New York: Wiley.

Forehand, R., & McMahon, R. (1981). *Helping the noncompliant child: A clinician's guide to parent training.* New York: Guilford Press.

Foster, S., & Cone, J. (1986). Design and use of direct observation. In A. Ciminero, K. Calhoun, & H. Adams (Eds.), *Handbook of behavioral assessment* (2nd ed., pp. 253–324). New York: Wiley Interscience.

Gardner, W., & Cole, C. (1988). Self-monitoring procedures. In E. Shapiro & T. Kratochwill (Eds.), *Behavioral assessment in schools* (pp. 206–246). New York: Guilford.

Gresham, F. M. (1989). Assessment of treatment integrity in school consultation and prereferral intervention. *School Psychology Review, 18,* 37–50.

Gresham, F. M., Gansle, K., & Noell, G. (1993a). Treatment integrity in applied behavior analysis with children. *Journal of Applied Behavior Analysis, 26,* 257–263.

Gresham, F. M., Gansle, K., Noell, G., Cohen, S., & Rosenblum, S. (1993b). Treatment integrity of school-based behavioral intervention studies: 1980–1990. *School Psychology Review, 22,* 254–272.

Happe, D. (1982). Behavioral intervention: It doesn't do any good in your briefcase. In J. Grimes (Ed.), *Psychological approaches to problems of children and adolescents* (pp. 15–41). Des Moines: Iowa Department of Public Instruction.

Johnston, J., & Pennypacker, H. (1980). *Strategies and tactics of human behavioral research.* Hillsdale, NJ: Lawrence Erlbaum Associates.

Kazdin, A. (1986). Comparative outcome studies of psychotherapy: Methodological issues and strategies. *Journal of Consulting and Clinical Psychology, 54,* 95–105.

Kazdin, A. (1992). *Research design in clinical psychology* (2nd ed.). New York: Macmillan.

Linehan, M. (1980). Content validity: Its relevance to behavioral assessment. *Behavioral Assessment, 2,* 147–159.

Mace, F. C., Page, T., Ivancic, M., & O'Brien, S. (1986). Effectiveness of brief time-out with and without contingent delay: A comparative analysis. *Journal of Applied Behavior Analysis, 19,* 79–86.

Moncher, F., & Prinz, R. (1991). Treatment fidelity in outcome studies. *Clinical Psychology Review, 11,* 247–266.

Peterson, L., Homer, A., & Wonderlich, S. (1982). The integrity of independent variables in behavior analysis. *Journal of Applied Behavior Analysis, 15,* 477–492.

Sidman, M. (1960). *Tactics of scientific research.* New York: Basic Books.

Stark, L., Knapp, L., Bowen, A., Powers, S., Jelalian, E., Evans, S., Passero, M., Mulvihill, M., & Hovell, M. (1993). Increasing calorie consumption in children with cystic fibrosis: Replication with 2-year follow-up. *Journal of Applied Behavior Analysis, 26,* 435–450.

Strosahl, K., & Linehan, M. (1986). Basic issues in behavioral assessment. In A. Ciminero, K. Calhoun, & H. Adams (Eds.), *Handbook of behavioral assessment* (2nd ed., pp. 12–46). New York: Wiley Interscience.

Suen, H. K. (1990). *Principles of test theories.* Hillsdale, NJ: Lawrence Erlbaum Associates.

Van Houten, R., & Sullivan, K. (1975). Effects of an audio cuing system on the rate of teacher praise. *Journal of Applied Behavior Analysis, 8,* 197–201.

Von Brock, M., & Elliott, S. (1987). Influence of treatment effectiveness information on the acceptability of classroom interventions. *Journal of School Psychology, 25,* 131–144.

Williamson, D., McKenzie, S., & Goreczny, A. (1988). Biofeedback. In J. Witt, S. Elliott, & F. Gresham (Eds.), *Handbook of behavior therapy in education* (pp. 547–568). New York: Plenum.

Witt, J. C., & Elliott, S. N. (1985). Acceptability of classroom intervention strategies. In T. Kratochwill (Ed.), *Advances in school psychology* (Vol. 4, pp. 251–288). Hillsdale, NJ: Lawrence Erlbaum Associates.

Wodarski, J., Feldman, R., & Pedi, S. (1974). Objective measurement of the independent variable: A neglected methodological aspect in community-based behavioral research. *Journal of Abnormal Child Psychology, 2,* 239–244.

Wolf, M. M. (1978). Social validity: The case for subjective measurement or how applied behavior analysis is finding its heart. *Journal of Applied Behavior Analysis, 11,* 203–214.

Yeaton, W., & Sechrest, L. (1981). Critical dimensions in the choice and maintenance of successful treatments: Strength, integrity, and effectiveness. *Journal of Consulting and Clinical Psychology, 49,* 156–167.

5

Graphical Display and Visual Analysis[1]

Ronald D. Franklin
Center for Forensic and Neuropsychology, Boca Raton FL and St. Mary's Hospital, West Palm Beach FL

Bernard S. Gorman
Hofstra University

T. Mark Beasley
School of Education and Human Services
St. John's University, New York

David B. Allison
Obesity Research Center
St. Luke's/Roosevelt Hospital
Columbia University, College of Physicians and Surgeons

INTRODUCTION

In this chapter we briefly review literature addressing visual inspection of graphed single-case data. In doing so, we explore graphics perception, considering strategies for enhancing accuracy in visual displays. We review the emergence of applied behavior analysis, present interpretive methods for visually inspected data in applied behavior analysis, review areas of concern in empirically supporting visual analysis and in relating visual analysis to scientific methods of inference, and discuss

---

[1]Parts of this chapter have been taken from Allison, D. B. (1992). When cyclicity is a concern: A caveat regarding phase change criteria in single-case designs. *Comprehensive Mental Health Care*, 2(2), 131–149. Copyright © 1992 by Springer Publishing Company, Inc., New York 10012. Used by permission.

the importance of integrating visual analysis with statistical analysis. Our journey explores interactions of stimulus properties with human information processing. Within this context, we identify strategies for enhancing accuracy in visual display.

Early in human history visual inspection proved important in theory development. As a tool of science, it was the foundation of many significant theories and laws. These scientific models were embraced by early psychologists, eager to separate their science from its origins in religion and philosophy by developing measurable and replicable laws of human behavior. Visual analysts shifted the focus of research away from statistical methods designed to discriminate chance events from causal events and instead developed procedures for demonstrating replicability and generalization.

Many researchers and authors extol the virtues of visual inspection and graphic analysis of data, asserting that an important effect will be manifest in an obvious manner (i.e., Skinner, 1953), and that in applied settings only marked effects have practical significance and utility (Baer, 1977b). However, Kruse and Gottman (1982) challenged the validity of procedures developed by visual inspection proponents. The few existing critical studies comparing graphic and visual inspection with statistical analysis highlight the complexity of this issue.

INTERPRETIVE METHODS

Within single-subject research designs, practitioners frequently infer significant effects from visual inspection of graphed data across one or more treatment conditions. Some measure of time appears on the abscissa and the dependent variable measure appears on the ordinate. The independent variable contains two or more levels of treatment separated by one or more blocks of time (Fig. 5.1). Data are collected and plotted in one of several experimental designs for single-case methods. The most commonly used designs are reversal, withdrawal, alternative treatments, and multiple baseline (Barlow & Hersen, 1984; Kazdin, 1982; Leitenberg, 1973). Kearns (1986) summarized single-case evaluation strategies, which we present in modified form (Table 5.1).

Graphic Display

Graphic analysis of single-case data incorporates three general interpretive principles: *central location* within phases and changes in central location between phases; *variability* in the data, including changes in varia-

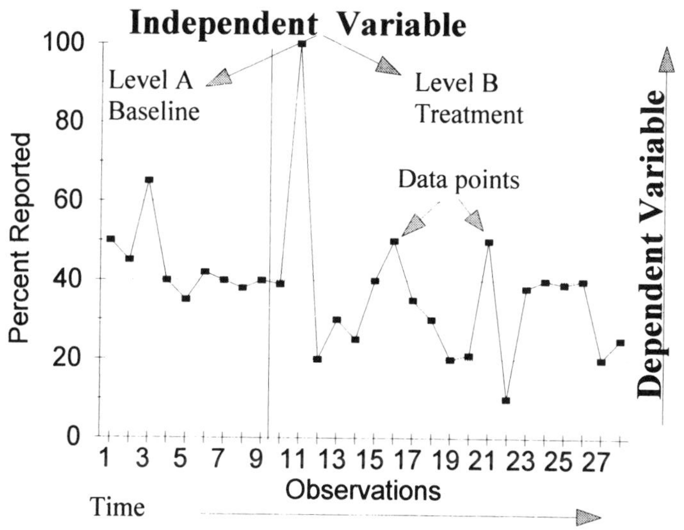

FIG. 5.1. Graphing conventions of independent and dependent variables.

tion over time; and *trend* in central location (linear and nonlinear) within and between different phases of data collection.

Displaying Central Location

Display of Central Location With Single Observations. Many of the visual analysis graphic displays present single observations as data points (Kelly, 1977). For practitioners, differences of data level between and within treatment phases demonstrate treatment effectiveness. For analysts, level represents central location when data are plotted individually (Fig. 5.2). Level can represent the mean, mode, median, or a best fit subjectively estimated (e.g., eyeballed) by the data analyst. Clinicians infer significant change (see section on significance, this chapter) from subjective evaluations of graphic distance separating two or more levels across one or more phase lines.

Vertical phase lines separate conditions of the independent variable (Fig. 5.3). The number and elements of interventions identify the type of research design. For example, the A-B-A-B design consists of two elements, A and B, separated graphically by phase lines. A denotes a baseline, or pretreatment (free operant) phase, and B denotes a treatment phase. By convention, practitioners identify subsequent treatment phases by sequential alphabetic characters. Combined characters, known as *multielement designs*, denote combined treatment conditions.

TABLE 5.1
Single-Case Evaluation Strategies

Evaluation Strategy	*Clinical Research Question*	*Selected Design Options*	*Basic Considerations*
Treatment 1/N no-treatment comparison	Does treatment, with all of its components, result in improved performance relative to no treatment?	Withdrawal and reversal designs	Is the therapeutic effect likely to reverse following the withdrawal of treatment?
		Multiple baseline	Are functionally equivalent behaviors or settings available? Are homogeneous subjects available?
		Multiple probe	Are functionally independent behaviors available? Are long or continuous baselines impractical?
Component assessment	Relative to a treatment package, to what degree do separate components of treatment contribute to improvement?	Interaction	Can the components be examined alone and in combination with the treatment package? Can replication be obtained across subjects?
Treatment–treatment comparison	What is the relative effectiveness of two or more treatments?	Alternating treatments	Can treatments be rapidly alternated for each subject?
Level analysis	Does treatment result in acquisition of successive steps in a chaining sequence?	Multiple probe	Are steps in the treatment sequence independent? Are earlier steps prerequisite to acquiring later steps?
	Does treatment effectively modify a single, gradually acquired behavior?	Changing criterion	Will changes in the dependent variable correspond to changes in the criterion level? Will the dependent variable stabilize at successively more stringent criterion levels?

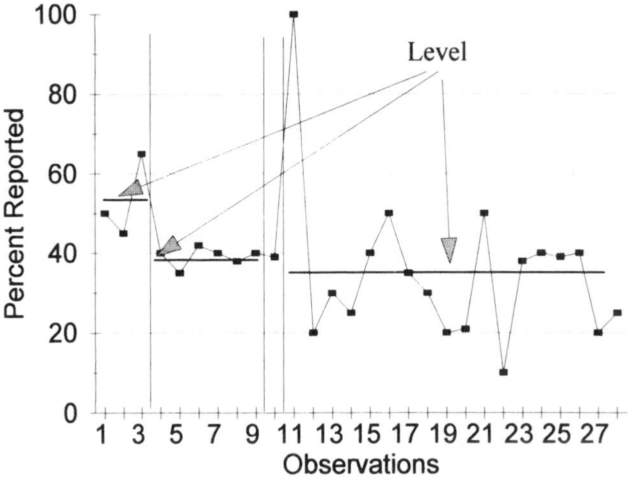

FIG. 5.2. Level indicators.

For example, A-B-A-C-BC-D-DC-DB denotes a single-subject research design consisting of a baseline (A) alternating with six interventions (B, C, BC, D, DC, and DB). Interventions BC, DC, and DB combine treatments B with C, B with D, and C with D (Fig. 5.4).

Phase lines can also connect similar interventions sequentially across

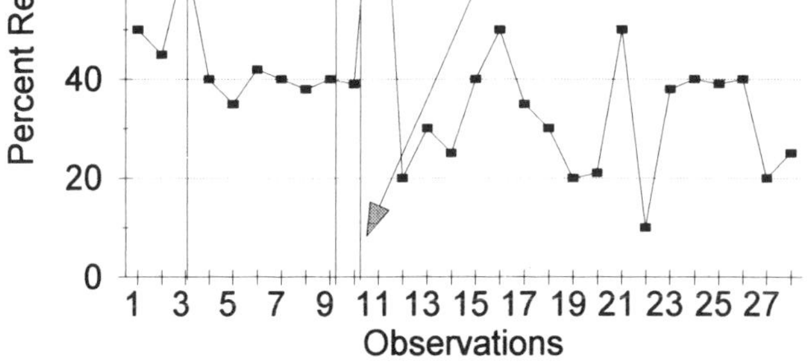

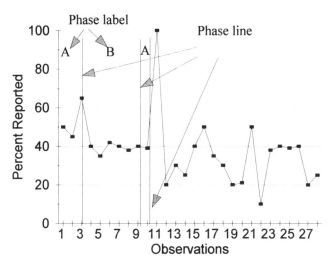

FIG. 5.3. Phase lines.

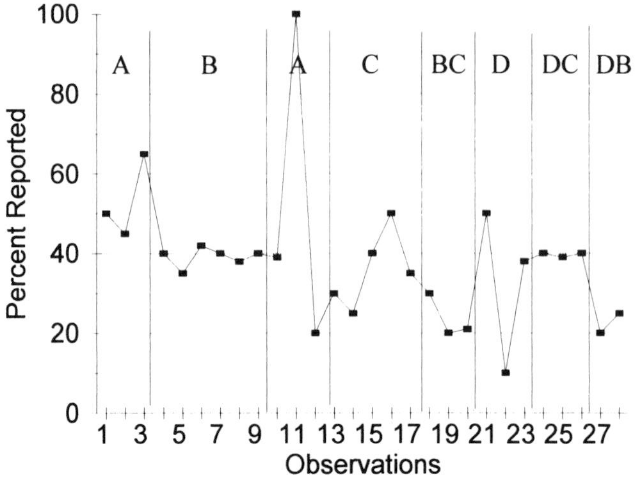

FIG. 5.4. Multi-element design.

multiple designs. These multiple baseline designs can reflect different clients, providers, settings, or exemplars (see Fig. 5.5).

Central Location With Aggregate Data. As the number of observations increases, plotting individual data points becomes less desirable. Visual presentation may be simplified by aggregating data (usually presented as means) within treatment phases. For many data sets encountered in analytic research on behavior, median rather than mean measures of central tendency may be more appropriate. Precise control over data collection is not always possible in clinical situations, and outliers may occur as a consequence. Outliers can unduly bias the estimation of the mean, but the median is resistant to such influence. One problem with the median, however, is that it only takes into account one or two data points. In small samples the median may not reflect the typical score of the sample any more than does the mean. Once solution is to use the broadened median, which averages the three or four middle scores of the distribution (Rosenberger & Gasko, 1983). For simplicity, means and medians are considered appropriate measures of within-phase central location. Overall, the best procedure is to plot the measure of central tendency as a horizontal reference line superimposed on the raw (or smoothed) time-series data. This allows for contextual visual inspection and provides the bases for analyzing variability and trend (see review by Jackson, 1986).

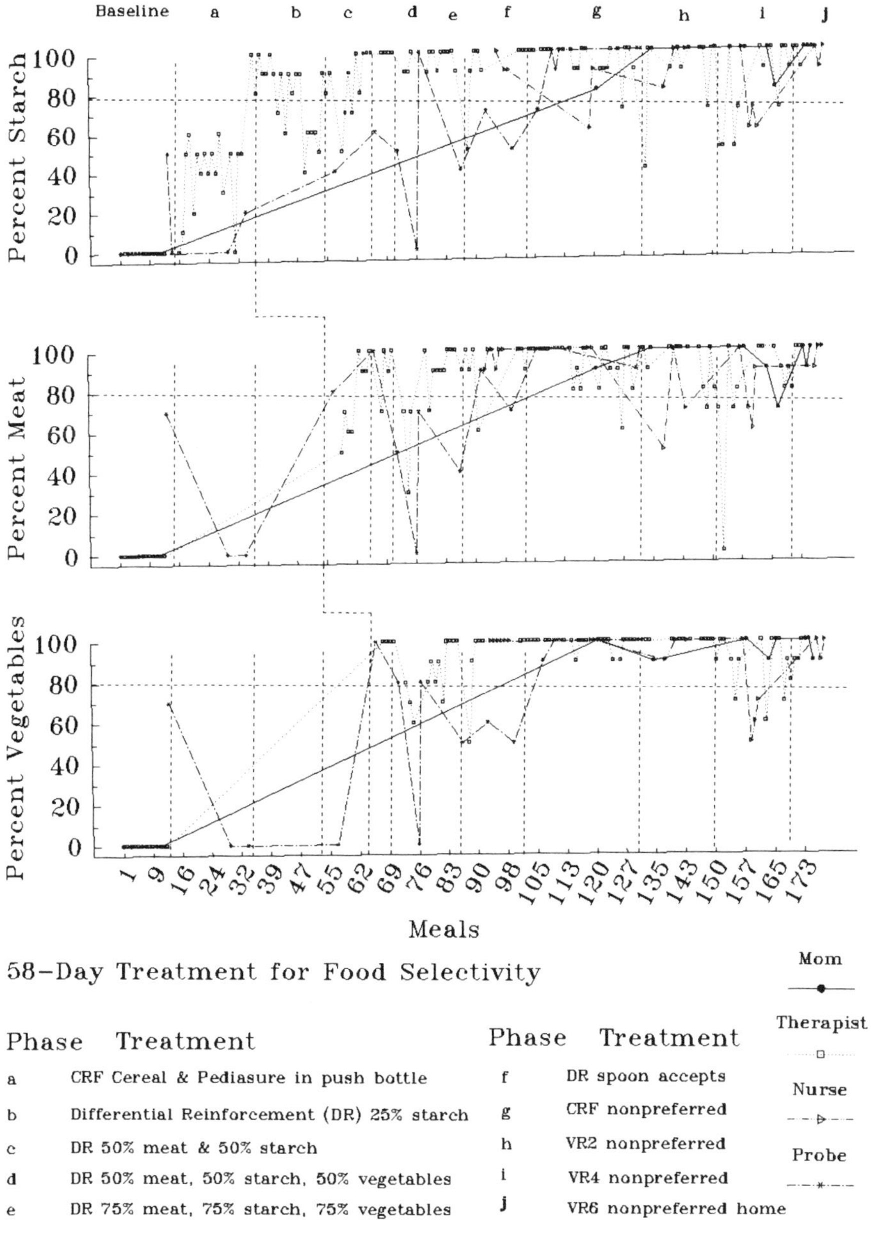

FIG. 5.5. Multiple baseline design.

Displaying Variability

Variability constitutes deviations above and below *level*. Because research on visual inspection of single-case designs suggests that less-sophisticated investigators often ignore (or at least fail to attend to) relative variation within and between phases, it is important to graphically display some estimates of variability. Morley and Adams (1991) suggested that there are only two methods commonly used by behavior analysts to display information about variability: one method uses *range bars* (Parsonson & Baer, 1978), and the other uses *range lines* (Fig. 5.6).

The range bar is typically made by connecting a vertical line through three points (an estimate of central location, the maximum, and the minimum) within each phase; all other data points are usually ignored (not plotted; Fig. 5.6, lower panel). A range line displays the time-series data and a pair of horizontal lines are extended through the minimum and maximum values for each phase (Fig. 5.6, upper panel).

Although informative, these two methods are not entirely satisfactory and have been criticized for the following reasons:

- A single outlier will have undue influence on the range and thus on displays based on the range (Fig. 5.6, first phase, both panels).
- Variability may be confounded with trend (Fig. 5.6, second phase, both panels; variability in the second phase is about the same as in the first); if one considers the increasing trend in these data, however, there is little variability.
- Changes (trends) in variability within phases are not displayed (Fig. 5.6, third phase; within-phase variability ostensibly decreases); this pattern is commonly observed in clinical data and probably reflects an increase in response control as a result of treatment but could also reflect a ceiling (or floor) effect.

The problem with outliers and their influence on displays of variability may be overcome by using a trimmed range (Morley & Adams, 1991). For larger time-series data sets, box-and-whiskers or quartile plots may be used (Leach, 1988; Tukey, 1977; Velleman & Hoaglin, 1981). These approaches, however, do not evade the confounds of trends and changes in variability. If data sets are large enough, repeated range bars, box plots, and so on can be used on subsets of within-case data to avoid these problems. Another approach to overcome the problem of data trends and changes in variability is to plot a *trended range*.

Displaying Trend

Trend consists of lines drawn on a graph that approximate the best linear fit of the data and show how data change over time. Methods for

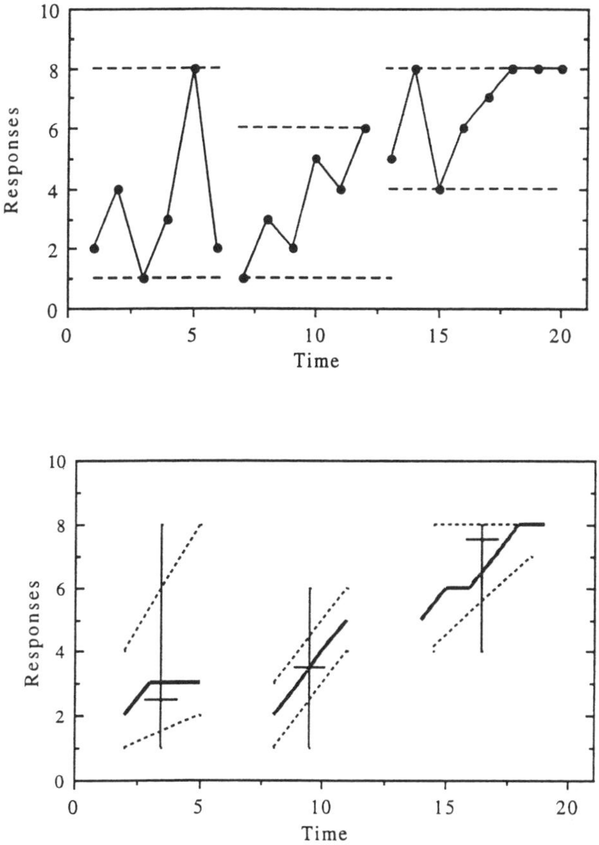

FIG. 5.6. Range bars and range lines. Upper panel: Range lines for hypothetical time-series data. Lower panel: Range bars and median with trend range and running median (RM3) plot superimposed.

superimposing trend lines include linear techniques such as eyeballing, least-squares regression, split-middle method, and resistant line fitting (see also Gorman & Allison, chap. 6, this volume). In the unrecommended practice of eyeballing, an investigator simply draws a line based on the appearance of best fit.

Fitting a Robust Linear Trend: Least-Squares Regression. Least-squares regression minimizes the squared vertical distances between data points by calculation of a regression line from the slope and intercept (Jaccard & Becker, 1990). The regression line is represented algebraically as

$$Y = a + bX \tag{5.1}$$

where slope is represented as

$$b_1 = \frac{\Sigma(x - \bar{x}) * (y - \bar{y})}{\Sigma(x - \bar{x})^2} \tag{5.2}$$

and the intercept is calculated as

$$b_0 = y - (b_1 {}^* X). \tag{5.3}$$

Most spreadsheet programs (e.g., *Lotus 1.2.3*, *Excel*, and *Quattro*) contain built-in functions that calculate least-squares regression. Regression lines are easily produced by spreadsheet graphics (Fig. 5.7).

The confounding factor presented by cyclicity occurs when treatment phases (A–B parings) change in synchrony with a recurring behavior pattern (see chap. 9, this volume). To the extent that the phase may change at the crest or trough of a cycle, cyclicity may be examined through investigating trends within each phase. A trend is a systematic shift in the central location of the data set over time. This should be distinguished from a trend in variance, where the variability of the data sets changes over time. Most commonly, single-case data have linear functions superimposed to indicate increasing or decreasing trends in the target behavior. The simplest way is to "eyeball" a straight line so that it appears to fit the time-series distributions. Unfortunately, even experienced analysts tend to be poor judges when placing a trend line (Mosteller, Siegel, Trapido, & Youtz, 1985). Just as in standard linear

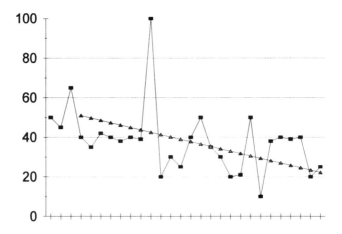

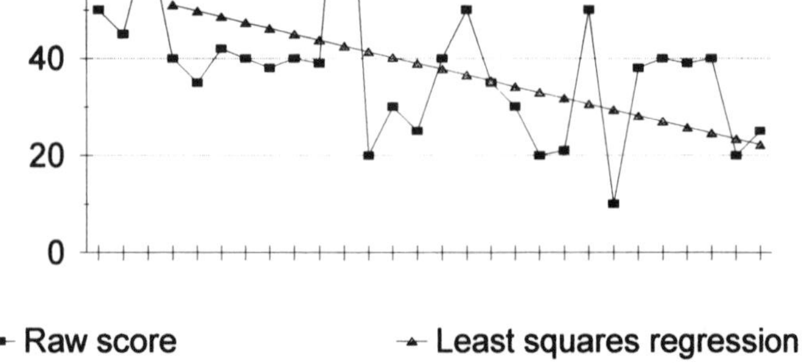

FIG. 5.7. Least-squares regression as trend line (Quattro-PRO/W).

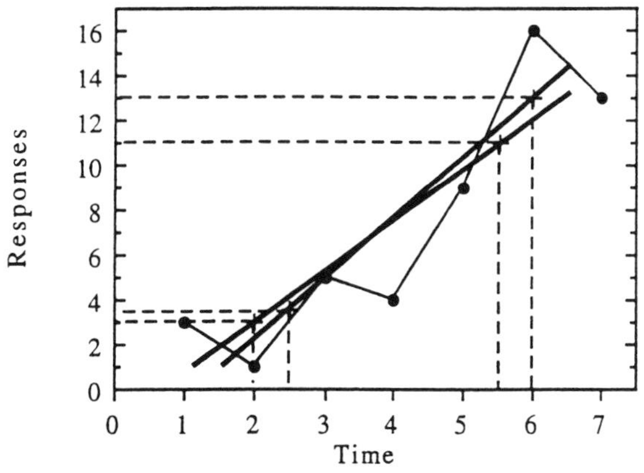

FIG. 5.8. Split-middle trend line for displaying level in trends with an uneven number of data points. The middle data point is assigned to each half and two lines as fit.

regression, outliers tend to exert undue influence on visual perception in the fitting of a trend line.

Fitting a Robust Linear Trend: Split-Middle Method. To construct graphical representations, one usually needs the original data values. Unfortunately, exact values are often unavailable when published graphs are inspected. The split-middle method can be used to sketch a robust trend line for published graphs as well as original data (Kazdin, 1982). The split-middle method progresses as follows:

1. Divide the time-series plot (data) into two halves along the time scale (abscissa).
2. Locate the median time value and median of the dependent variable within each time-series half. If the number of data points in the time series is uneven, the middle points may be randomly assigned to either half or assigned to each half with the line being fitted twice.
3. Make a coordinate out of the intersection of the time and dependent variable medians and extend a line through the coordinates of each half.

Figure 5.8 shows two split middle lines calculated by reallocating the middle time point. Note that the slope changes, although not drastically, with each estimate. Reallocation also has the benefit of providing a rough reliability estimate of the linear fit (slope).

Kazdin (1982) advocated adjusting the fitted line so that the line bisects the data. The rationale for this is that adjusting the slope should minimize the residuals; however, this can rarely be done adequately by eye, especially when there are outliers. It is suggested that the adjusted line provides the basis for a binomial test allowing for a comparison of change over different phases. This test, however, has statistical problems and is not recommended (Crosbie, 1987). Even without a slope adjustment, the split-middle method is usually sufficient in providing an estimate of linear trend for smaller time series (i.e., $4 \leq T \leq 12$). A *trend range* can be displayed by use of this method; however, the coordinates are made from the median time values and the minimum and maximum within each half. One may also choose the trimmed range or quartiles as coordinate values to display *trended variability*. A trended range is displayed for each phase of the data in Fig. 5.6 (lower panel), which demonstrates the previously mentioned problems in interpreting change in variability over time.

Fitting a Robust Linear Trend: Resistant Trend Line Fitting. This method is more often used with larger time series and involves dividing the data into three time-dependent sections: left, middle, and right. When the number of data points are divisible by three, there will be equal numbers of data points in each section. If the remainder is one, the extra point is allocated to the middle section; if the remainder is two, the end sections are allocated the additional points. The same procedure followed in the split-middle method is used to find the median for the dependent variable and time values for each section. A line is fitted by connecting the median coordinates of the two end sections (Fig. 5.9).

From the data in Table 5.2, the slope, b, of this line is calculated by the change in dependent variable medians (M_{dv}) over the change in median time values (M_t):

$$b = \frac{M_{dv(R)} - M_{dv(L)}}{M_{t(R)} - M_{t(L)}} = \frac{2.5 - 13}{20.5 - 4.5} = -0.64 \tag{5.4}$$

The intercept, a, of this line is calculated by using all three sections:

$$a = (1/3)\ [(M_{dv(L)} + M_{dv(M)} + M_{dv(R)}) - b = (M_{t(L)} + M_{t(M)} + M_{dv(R)})]$$
$$b = (1/3)\ [(13 + 5 + 2.5) + 0.64(4.5 + 12.5 + 20.5)] = 15.04 \tag{5.5}$$

This computation fits a linear trend that is easily plotted by substituting any two points into the following linear equation:

$$y_t = a + bT_t = 15.04 - 0.64T_t \tag{5.6}$$

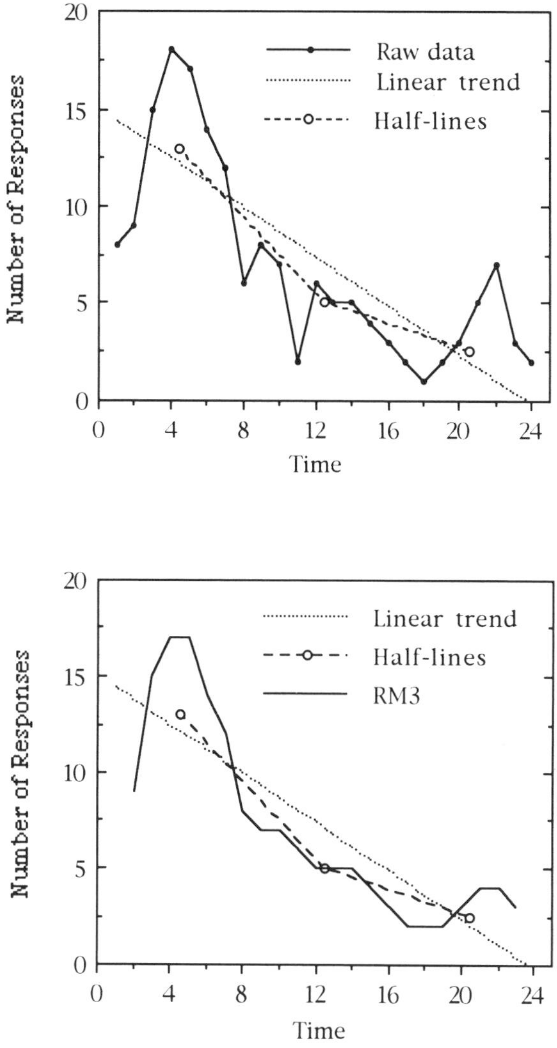

FIG. 5.9. Resistent trend line (linear trend). Half-lines based on the three subsections of the resistant trend line method, and plot of running medians (RM3; lower panel only) for hypothetical time-series data.

The advantage of using this method is that outliers are less influential; lines fitted by eyeballing the data are often biased by the size of even a single aberrant data point (Wampold & Furlong, 1981). This is not to suggest, however, that observations diverging from the general body of the data should be ignored. Indeed, such data may point to interesting and substantive occurrences or to errors in measurement.

TABLE 5.2
Hypothetical Data With Predicted and Residual Values From a Resistant Trend Line

Left Section								
Time	*1*	*2*	*3*	*4*	*5*	*6*	*7*	*8*
Responses	08.00	09.00	15.00	18.00	17.00	14.00	12.00	06.00
Predicted	14.40	13.77	13.13	12.50	11.86	11.22	10.59	09.95
Residual	−6.40	−4.77	01.87	05.50	05.14	02.78	01.41	−3.95
Middle section								
Time	*9*	*10*	*11*	*12*	*13*	*14*	*15*	*16*
Responses	08.00	07.00	02.00	06.00	05.00	05.00	04.00	03.00
Predicted	09.31	08.68	08.04	07.40	06.77	06.13	05.50	04.86
Residual	−1.31	−1.68	06.04	−1.40	−1.77	−1.13	01.50	−1.86
Right section								
Time	*17*	*18*	*19*	*20*	*21*	*22*	*23*	*24*
Responses	02.00	01.00	02.00	03.00	05.00	07.00	03.00	02.00
Predicted	04.22	03.59	02.95	02.32	01.68	01.04	00.41	−0.23
Residual	−2.22	−2.59	−0.95	−0.68	03.32	05.96	02.59	02.23

The fit of this robust line can be checked and improved by examining the residuals and calculating b by using the same method. If the fit of the original trend line based on the raw data is reasonable, then the slope of the residuals is expected to be zero, with no apparent pattern (Velleman & Hoaglin, 1981). The residuals are the distances between the actual data points and the predicted position on the trend line. The residual, r_t at time, T_t, is given by

$$r_t = y_y - (a + bT_t) \tag{5.7}$$

where y_t = observed value at time t, T_t = value on the time axis, and b and a are the slope and intercept defined in Equations 5.5 and 5.6, respectively. When time increments are in units of one, as often occurs with behavioral time-series data, the computation of y_t is simplified by adding the value of b to successive estimates of y_t. Predicted values and residuals for the data in Fig. 5.9 are shown in Table 5.2. Fig. 5.9 displays the first resistant line fitted by the three-group method, along with two half-lines connecting the middle-section median with the medians of the two end sections. This demonstrates one of the major disadvantages of both the split-middle and three-group methods: Connecting two points always creates a straight line but *specification* errors often occur. It is clear that the data in Fig. 5.9 are not described well by a *linear* trend. This is also apparent in Fig. 5.10, which shows that residuals tend to occur in groups and suggests some underlying cyclicity. In such cases, a nonlinear trend should be investigated.

Investigating Nonlinear Trend: Running Medians. A linear trend does not provide a good description of the data in Fig. 5.9, and a specification error is probable. In such situations where there are patterned residuals from a linear trend or in other situations where there is substantial variability among the data, misspecification may be avoided by smoothing the time series by using *running medians* (Morley & Adams, 1991). Because a trend is defined as a systemic change in central tendency over time, plotting estimates of central tendency over time will provide a representation of trend. In smaller time series, it is often preferable to use the median to estimate central location to avoid the influence of outliers (Velleman & Hoaglin, 1981).

Running medians are calculated by segmenting the time-series data into successive batches of a given size and finding the median of each batch. Batch size is often determined by the length of the time series because the length of the plotted trend is reduced by batch size minus one.

For running medians of batch size three (RM3), the medians of successive batches of three data points are determined. The first point is plotted at time $t = 2$ and the last point at $t = T - 1$. The trend is, therefore, reduced by two. RM3 is most useful in small time series (i.e.,

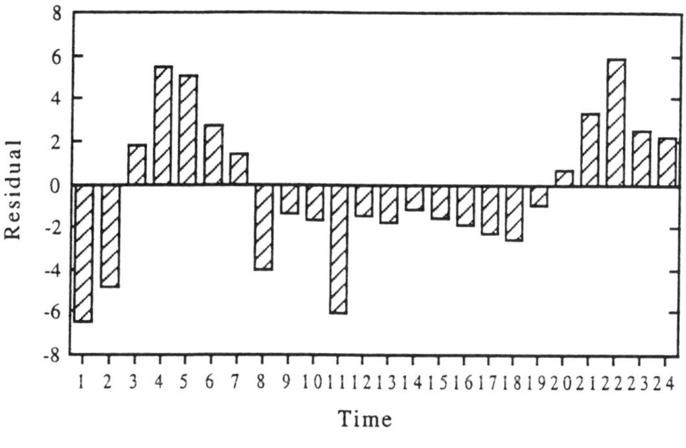

FIG. 5.10. Residuals from the resistant linear trend line for hypothetical data.

$6 \leq T \leq 10$), but for larger time series larger batch sizes are often suggested. RM4 is calculated by finding the medians of successive batches of four data points and plotting them with the median time of each respective batch. Thus, for the first four data points, $RM4_1$ would be plotted with a time of $t = 2.5$ as a coordinate. RM5 is calculated by the same basic procedure of RM3 except that the batches are larger. Using RM5 as an estimate of nonlinear trend has the disadvantage of losing four data points in time-series length. To avoid this loss of data, estimates at $t = 2$ and $t = T - 2$ may be calculated with RM3. Table 5.3 shows RM3, RM4, and RM5 for the data in Fig. 5.9. Figure 5.9 (lower panel) plots a nonlinear trend line using RM3.

Response-Guided Experimentation

Response-guided experimentation involves analyzing data as they are collected and using this analysis to direct subsequent actions (Edgington, 1984). Proponents of this strategy may use rules along with observations to make therapeutic decisions. For example, data showing that an infant accepted 80% of presentations of a nonpreferred food texture for three consecutive meals might result in a presentation of a more-textured food during the next meal. The use of response-guided

TABLE 5.3
Data Showing Running Medians (RM)
With Batch Sizes of 3, 4, and 5

Time	*1*	*2*	*3*	*4*	*5*	*6*	*7*	*8*
Responses	08	09	15	18	17	14	12	06
RM3		09	15	17	17	14	12	08
RM4			12	16	16	15.5	13	10
RM5		09*	15	15	15	14	12	08
Time	*9*	*10*	*11*	*12*	*13*	*14*	*15*	*16*
Responses	08	07	02	06	05	05	04	03
RM3	07	07	06	05	05	05	04	03
RM4	07.5	06.5	06.5	05.5	05	05	04.5	03.5
RM5	07	06	06	05	05	05	04	03
Time	*17*	*18*	*19*	*20*	*21*	*22*	*23*	*24*
Responses	02	01	02	03	05	07	03	02
RM3	02	02	02	03	05	05	03	
RM4	02.5	02	02	02.5	04	04	04	
RM5	02	02	02	03	03	03	03*	

* This symbol indicates that the first and last values of RM5 are calculated with RM3.

experimentation is particularly tempting with changing criterion designs, for example, when change in each phase influences the rate of change in the next (Hartmann & Hall, 1976). The addition of response-guided experimentation has the potential to increase error rate to unacceptable levels.

Visual Inspection

Significance

Interpretation of data by analysts often leads to attributions of causality. Causal attributions rest on the assumption that significant differences exist between treatment conditions. Authors sometimes distinguish between clinical and statistical significance. Clinical significance occurs when an intervention results in important change for the subject irrespective of the intervention's statistical properties. For example, a patient's blood sugar varies insignificantly throughout the week, but on days when it reaches an upper limit the patient becomes comatose. *Clinical significance* is, therefore, a relative term denoting attainment of a critical threshold unique to the problem under study; hence, a criterion reference. *Statistical significance* refers to the probability of nonchance differences occurring across or within interventions. Here, differences in variability occur below or above operationally defined chance levels. For a more complete discussion, see Barlow and Hersen (1984). The concept of clinical significance as distinct from statistical significance was challenged by Silverstein (1993).

Statistical significance is anchored in the null hypothesis. A probability value estimates the possibility that an observed difference between two sample means occurs as a result of chance. If the probability of a difference greater than or equal to the one observed is low, then observed differences are attributed to experimental or treatment effects. Although proponents of visual inspection and analysis view replication and generalizability as the important components of single-case designs (Sidman, 1960), significance attribution in visual inspection also infers causality by applying a set of visual heuristics to data points plotted on graphs (Table 5.4).

Confidence in attributions is greatest when the baseline is stable and there is little variability within phases. Variability between phases is associated with treatment effects, as is the degree of overlap between scores of adjacent phases. The numbers of data points in each phase are also important because a large number can show small but important trends occurring over time.

Internal validity (the ability to isolate an independent variable respon-

TABLE 5.4
Heuristics Described by Parsonson and Baer (1978)

1. Stability of baseline—baseline should not drift toward improvement.
2. Variability within phases—as variability increases, the need for more data increases.
3. Variability between phases—reduced variability in the treatment phase is an indication of control.
4. Overlap between scores of adjacent phases—greater treatment effect is associated with less data overlap.
5. Number of data points in each phase—more are usually better.
6. Changes in trend within phases—collect more data when trends are unclear.
7. Changes in trend between adjacent phases—dramatic changes suggest strong treatment effects.
8. Changes in level between phases—dramatic changes suggest strong treatment effects.
9. Analysis of data across similar phases—consistency in replication indicates treatment effect.
10. Evaluation of the overall pattern of the data—the overall pattern may overcome faults in the data.

sible for therapeutic change) and external validity (the degree to which treatment effects can be generalized) are crucial elements in effective research designs (Campbell & Stanley, 1966). Potential factors in single-case analysis, such as carryover effects and autocorrelated residuals, influence the accuracy of statistical analysis but also affect internal and external validity. Comparisons of dependent variable measures across independent variable conditions provide the objective and replicable data from which the visual analyst infers significant outcomes (Barlow & Hersen, 1984; Kazdin, 1984; Kratochwill & Levin, 1992; Krishef, 1991; Parsonson & Baer, 1978; Tawney & Gast, 1984).

Constraints on the Analysis of Visually Inspected Graphs

Visual analysis is subject to the constraints of other methods of research evaluation. Three constraints on research interpretation viewed as particularly salient to visual inspection and analysis are cyclicity (Allison, 1992), carryover effects (Greenwald, 1976), and outliers. *Cyclicity* refers to behavior change associated with infradian and circadian (viz., biological) timing systems (Moore-Ede, Sulzman, & Fuller, 1982). *Carryover*, or *order effects*, refer to the influence of one treatment phase on the next (Greenwald, 1976). If, for example, an individual learns a new skill as a result of treatment, return to baseline behavior may not be possible. Therefore, carryover from earlier trials can prevent adequate evaluation when inferences originate solely in visual data evaluation.

Cyclicity. Biological rhythms can appear as treatment effects when measured behaviors are affected. Beasley, Allison, and Gorman (chap. 9, this volume) and Allison (1992) presented three possible reasons for the presence of cyclicity: biological rhythms, cyclically chained responses, and schedules of reinforcement (including institutional schedules). Figure 5.11 demonstrates an A-B-A-B design with apparent treatment effects. The graph consists of random error added to a sine wave.

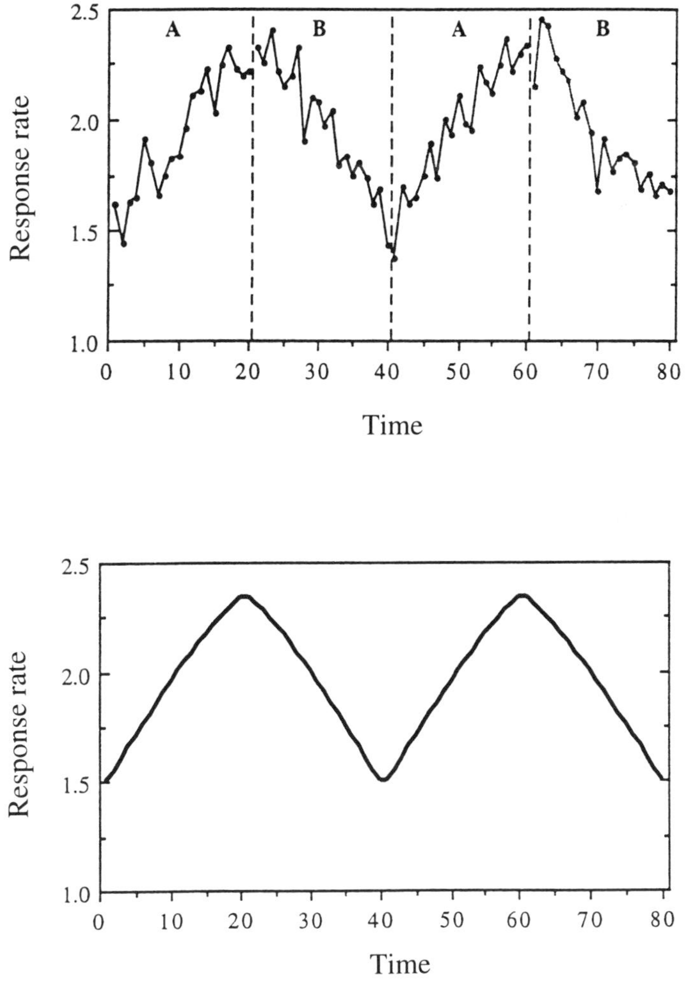

FIG. 5.11. Cyclicity. Upper panel: Results of a hypothetical A-B-A-B experiment designed to decrease the rate of an undesirable behavior. Lower panel: The same data without random error or phase breaks (i.e., sinusoidal wave).

Carryover Effects. When learning or some other treatment that cannot be undone (e.g., drug side effects) changes a response, dependent measures cannot revert to baseline after treatment withdrawal (Greenwald, 1976). These consequences can be temporary or permanent. When carryover effects are temporary, time series can incorporate counterbalance methods in hopes of controlling this confounding factor. When carryover effects cannot be resolved or when their duration is unknown, reversal or withdrawal designs must be replaced with other models, such as multiple baselines.

Outliers. Outliers may represent confounding factors or error (i.e., data collection or data transcription error.) They can be operationally defined as data points lying *x* or more standard deviations from the mean of a series or slope, or in terms of confidence intervals. They may also contain data belonging to a different independent variable but systematically influencing both the independent and dependent variables under study. Regardless of the method for operationally defining them, these data points represent aberrant observations that appear incongruent with other dependent measures taken from the same time series.

Figure 5.12 displays a series of scores with overlaid horizontal lines showing one and two standard deviations. Three data points appear suspect; one of these occurs in the baseline phase. In the absence of this overlay, the return to baseline score could easily be interpreted as evidence of treatment effect. One might question the presence of error variance as the basis for these points, given their degree of discrepancy. Sound treatment integrity (see Gresham, chap. 4, this volume) is the best method for minimizing the presence of outliers. Interpretative constraints include confound factors, or nuisance variables, that systemat-

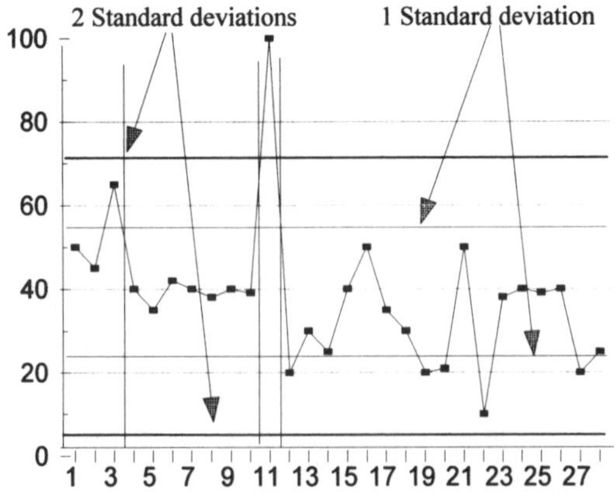

FIG. 5.12. Outliers identified by standard deviation lines.

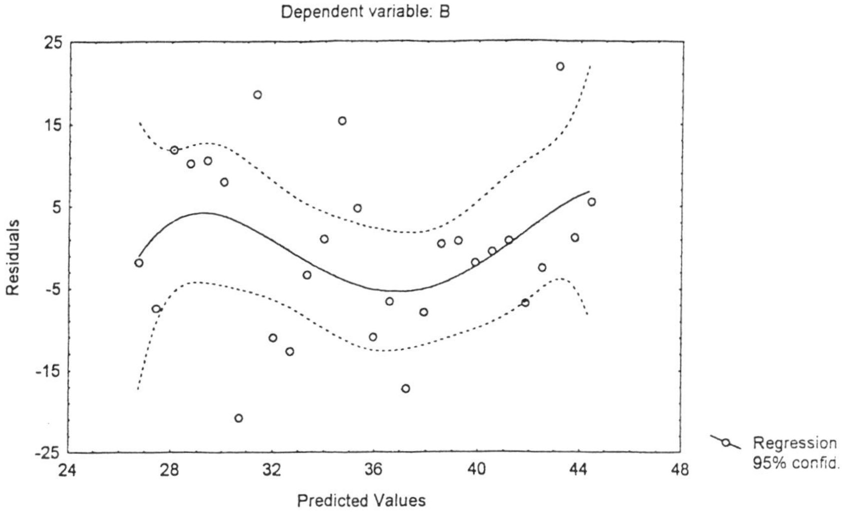

FIG. 5.13. Residuals plotted in nonlinear data.

ically influence the different treatment conditions and are often uncontrolled independent variables (Keppel, 1982).

Residuals. Residuals are useful for identifying constraints on data. A good regression model will have a mean of zero, constant variance, and no autocorrelation. Therefore, plotting residuals can reveal patterns that indicate a poor-fitting model, including the presence of cyclicity, outliers, and nonlinearity. Subtraction of an observed value (value of a data point) from a predicted value (i.e., mean, regression estimate, trend line) produces a residual value. The residual value can be standardized by dividing the result (e.g., the residual) by the square root of the residual mean square (i.e., the standard deviation of the residual). Plottings of residuals against predicted values disclose cyclical patterns in data and allow the evaluator to determine if data are normally distributed (Fig. 5.13) (Statsoft, 1994; Velleman & Hoaglin, 1981).

EVALUATING THE PERFORMANCE OF VISUAL ANALYSIS

Twenty-six books were written about single-case research between 1960 and 1991 (Kratochwill, 1992). During this period, visual inspection gained acceptance among many researchers and practitioners working in schools, developmental centers, hospitals, clinics, and other applied settings. Because of the development of extensive within-, between-, and combined-series designs, practitioners may believe most of the problems associated with visual inspection are resolved (Barrios & Hartmann, 1988; Hayes, 1981). However, we recognize three basic reasons to question sole reliance on visual analysis: equivocal support for the heuristic model, questionable technical performance, and constraints imposed by human physiology.

Equivocal Support for the Heuristic Model

Evaluation of Trend Shift

Trend shift analysis is one way to evaluate the similarity between visual and statistical analysis, thereby establishing a type of criterion-related validity (Parsonson & Baer, 1992). An empirical study was unable to demonstrate that a statistically significant relationship existed between interrater agreement and the visual components of slope and variability appearing in graphed data (Harbst, Ottenbacher, & Harris, 1991). Evaluators in this study were college-trained practitioners (20 physical and 10 occupational therapists) with no special training in visual analysis. All stimulus graphs were simple AB designs that included mean shift, variability, level changes, slope changes, data overlap, and serial dependency. Both least-squares linear regression and split-middle celeration lines were presented as slopes. Subjects rated their view of significant change across treatment phases on a six-point scale. Harbst, Ottenbacher, and Harris concluded that "Interrater reliability of visual analysis augmented with a celeration line is poor" (1991, p. 112). Interrater reliability was better in subjects with both statistical training and single-subject design training than in subjects with only single-subject backgrounds. Interestingly, subjects with no training in statistics or single-subject theory demonstrated interrater reliabilities similar to subjects trained only in single-subject designs. These findings bring into question the effectiveness of trend lines as aids to visual analysis, especially for trained "specialists" without educational foundations in statistics. The problem was noted by Skiba, Deno, Marston, and Casey (1989) who observed, "Judges taught to use trend lines came to rely on them: They then attended much less to all other data-path characteristics . . . " (cited in Parsonson & Baer, 1989, p. 31).

Unfortunately, observers trained in applied behavior analysis have made more rather than fewer errors when interpreting trend lines. Greenspan and Fisch (1992) reported that only 10% of 48 graphs presented to five graduate students in an applied behavior analysis class were correctly identified when both trends and treatment effects were present. When only trends appeared in the graphs, 19% of the graphs were correctly identified. Additionally, different raters in the DeProspero and Cohen (1979) study rated the same trend line as increasing and decreasing. Therefore, if applied behavior analysts rely on trend lines for interpreting graphs and ignore other characteristics of the graph that may attenuate interpretations, and if interpretation of trend lines is unreliable, applied practitioners will need to reduce dependence on trend line interpretation and use supplemental methods of analysis.

Confound of Pre–Post Evaluation

The AB design or variants thereof appear most often in the literature on applied behavior analysis. To this pre–post test model a reversal (or withdrawal) of treatment was added to increase the likelihood of accurate causal inference. When Greenspan and Fisch (1992) examined error rates of AB and ABA designs, their results suggested the reversal increases rather than decreases error. Students consistently recognized error in 62% of AB designs but in only 57% of ABA designs. Group error also increased as the number of sessions per phase increased, and error rates were significantly higher when trends were present (75%) than when trends were absent (47%). Students ($n = 5$) were much better at identifying no treatment effect (70%) than treatment effect (35%). When trends existed with no treatment effects, only 2% of the 48 graphs were correctly identified.

Response-Guided Experimentation

Expanding on the work of others (Armitage, McPherson, & Rowe, 1969; Demets, 1987; Matyas & Greenwood, 1990), Allison, Franklin, and Heshka (1992) demonstrated how response-guided experimentation can easily increase the Type I (or α) error rate to 25%. Matyas and Greenwood (1990) obtained α rates from 16% to 84% in a study of behavior analysis students when data contained lag 1 autocorrelation. (See Gorman & Allison, chap. 6, and Matyas & Greenwood, chap. 7, this volume, for discussions of the meaning and computation of autocorrelation.) Brief *n*-of-1 time series are often autocorrelated (Matyas & Greenwood, 1991).

Questionable Technical Performance

Validity and Reliability

Validity is the extent to which a score measures what it is intended to measure (Barlow & Hersen, 1984; Sattler, 1988). Sattler considered five types of validity (content, criterion-related, concurrent, predictive, and construct), whereas Barlow and Hersen presented three types (content, criterion-related, and construct). Significant validity consists of a relationship between a measure and a criterion when the likelihood of obtaining the relationship by chance is quite small (Kaplan & Saccuzzo, 1982).

Although reliable data are necessary for validity, highly reliable data do not ensure validity. Baer (1977a) observed, "Applied behavior analysis is a discipline deliberately turning away from the detection of weak variables: it systematically filters from its discovery methods the ability to discover variables of less-than-powerful effect . . . it also eventually filters itself of nongeneral variables, through replication across studies rather than replication within studies" (p. 117). Yet, by limiting reliability to interrater measures of dubious veracity, the concept of valid replication of findings across studies is meaningless, because reliability measures across studies remain undefined.

How does one determine or identify "powerful effects"? Which is more powerful, an effect producing immediate and dramatic behavior change requiring significant resources to maintain the change, or an effect requiring few resources that produces graded (although subtle) change that eventually self-maintains?

Validity in single-case designs was studied by using evaluations by 346 raters in four studies (DeProspero & Cohen, 1979; Harbst et al., 1991; Ottenbacher, 1990b; Park, Marascuilo, & Gaylord-Ross, 1990). Reliability measures addressing validity in visual inspection did not exceed .61.

The largest and most concordant study compared 250 reviewers of behavioral journals who evaluated topographic characteristics, data presentation format, and experimental circumstances of 36 graphs (DeProspero & Cohen, 1979). The graphs contained examples of data characteristics considered salient to the determination of visual significance. Changes in mean ratings across phases provided the most concordance when observed changes were consistent with treatment expectations. Their average concordance of .61 (standard deviation = .26) addressed consistency in expert interpretation rather than consistency of data collection.

In a separate study, untrained raters performed almost as well as did journal reviewers (Harbst et al., 1991): Interclass correlations between .37 and .55 were found for a sample of physical and occupational therapists. Their average rating of .47 falls below that of journal reviewers (.55), yet much greater differences might be expected because of the differences in expertise between the two groups. Interestingly, no statistically significant relationship was noted between visual components of graphed data (intraphase variability or changes in slope) and interrater agreement.

Highly expert raters, such as behavior analysts working in applied behavior settings, have attained mean interclass correlations of .60 when evaluating published data (Park et al., 1990). In a comparison of 44 graphs from recently published issues of the *Journal of Applied Behavior Analysis*, the proportion of time all five judges agreed on any one of the three categories rated was only .27. Park et al. (1990) reported 80% concordance between visual inspection and statistical analysis. Most agreements reported by Park et al. were between nonsignificant findings on randomization tests and nonsignificant visual inspection determinations (67%). Therefore, their report of 80% concordance may lead casual readers to erroneous conclusions. Interrater agreement on significant outcome was only 27%. Even more discouraging, of the 80% overall agreement, only 13% ($n = 2$) of expert judges agreed with statistical findings that outcomes were significant; all graphs had been judged to be significant by the peer review process. Less than half of the originally selected graphs ($n = 44$) contained enough data points for statistical analysis, and, contrary to the predictions of Baer (1977b), statistical approaches were more conservative than was visual inspection.

Similar agreement between statistical and visual significance (73%) was reported by Jones, Weinrott, and Vaught (1978) only when data contain low autocorrelation. Jones et al. concluded that "Statistically reliable experimental effects may be more often overlooked by visual appraisals of data than nonmeaningful effects" (p. 280). When moderate-to-high serial dependency exists, accurate judgments from visual inspection were no greater than chance.

Sixteen undergraduate observers coded behaviors of school children from videotape and their agreements compared (Boykin & Nelson, 1981). Observers were paired based on their performance on *Wide Range Achievement Test* scores, hours of training in rating received, and their personal schedules. Pairs of observers were randomly assigned to one of two experimental groups. One group received instruction to obtain a high level of interobserver agreement (.85). The second group was to carefully record observations and reliability calculations. Findings revealed that students inflated their own agreement ratings and erroneously deflated agreements of others. The authors concluded that instructions affected accuracy and interobserver agreement. Accuracy reached .56 and agreement .58 when experimenter, rather than student, calculations were used. Ratings of accuracy and agreement differed significantly between the raters and the experimenter ($p < .05$).

Ottenbacher (1990b) asked 61 teachers and allied health workers to compare six graphs, each representing variations of patterns believed to influence visual interpretation: mean shift, variability, change in slope, change in level, amount of overlap, and degree of serial dependency.

Interrater agreement greater than 80% occurred on only one of the six graphs. Four of the six graphs produced reliabilities below 70%, and half were less than chance. Agreement was greatest when large changes in level or mean shift occurred across phases. Ottenbacher reported .42 as the average rate of disagreement between raters. Presumably, this equals an average rate of interrater agreement of .58. If the interrater agreement of .80 recommended by Kazdin (1982) is used as the "gold standard," then one must conclude that research has failed to demonstrate the presence of acceptable levels of interrater reliability for single-subject models to establish themselves as valid measures. Additionally, all studies reporting interrater reliability appropriate for inferences of validity were conducted using AB designs (Table 5.5). The reliability of alternating treatments, multiple baseline, and others designs remains unknown.

Concepts such as internal and external validity remain difficult to establish when the methods and procedures used to demonstrate their existence are suspect (Campbell & Stanley, 1965).

Specificity

Some researchers believe that visual inspection produces low α error rates (Baer, 1977b; Huitema, 1986a; Parsonson & Baer, 1978; Table 5.6). Analytic techniques with high α error rates are less specific in measuring outcome; the error is often fixed at 5% or 1% in statistical analyses. Alpha error rates are largely unknown when analysts rely on visual inspection. Allison, Franklin, and Heshka (1992) suggested that α rates

TABLE 5.5
Interrater Reliabilities in Single-Subject Research

Author(s)	n	*Subjects*	*Interclass correlation*	*Number of graphs*
Boykin & Nelson (1981)	016	Undergraduates Mean accuracy agreement	.56	10'video[E]
Harbst et al. (1991)	030[1]	10 Occupational therapists 20 Physical therapists	.47	24[E]
Jones et al. (1978)	011	Full-time researchers	.50–.65	24[P]
DeProspero & Cohen (1979)	250	Behavior journal reviewers	.61	36[E]
Ottenbacher (1990a)	061[2]	College graduates	.08–.59	06[E]

[E] = Constructed examples.
[P] = Published in *JABA*.
[1]Untrained in data analysis.
[2]Training unreported.

TABLE 5.6
Predicting the Effects of an Independent Variable on a Dependent Variable*

Actual effect	*Concluded effect*	
	Accept	*Reject*
Accept	1-B Power True positive Sensitivity	B Miss Type II Error
Reject	a False alarm Type I error	1-a True negative Specificity

*Adapted from Demets (1987).

may exceed 25% when evaluators rely on visual inspection alone to infer treatment effect. The α error rate autocorrelation, and the number of looks at the data (i.e., response guided experimentation) interactively affect accuracy specificity. Matyas and Greenwood (1990) demonstrated that high α rates occurred when variability and serial dependence increased, with error rates rising as high as 84% and producing a low specificity of .16.

Sensitivity

The likelihood of finding predicted results is known as power or sensitivity (Table 5.6): The more misses that occur, the less sensitive the measure, and the larger the Type II (or β) error. Studies comparing misses show experienced judges achieve only 48% concordance with statistical measures (Jones et al., 1978).

Evaluations of 27 single-case outcomes by 37 graduate students found β rates were below 10% (Matyas & Greenwood, 1990). With autocorrelation, however, β rates changed less than did α rates.

Constraints Imposed by Human Physiology

Human biology includes susceptibility to illusions, sensory overload, sensory deprivation, and contrast effects, which interact unpredictably with differences caused by genetic endowment and present potential problems for interpreting graphed data. Both visual judgment (Bauer & Johnson-Laird, 1993) and visual memory (Spence & Lewandowsky, 1990) are easily biased by irrelevant information. For example, Furlong and Wampold (1982) compared judgments of 10 randomly selected editors from the *Journal of Applied Behavior Analysis* to determine the criteria they used in identifying an outcome as significant. They found that mathematically equivalent graphs are rated differently, depending on the scaling of the graphs.

The relative superiority of visual memory over other forms of memory in humans presents a potentially alarming problem for visual analysis (Spence & Lewandowsky, 1990). When inaccurate judgments arise from visual analysis, they may persist and significantly bias future evaluations or research more directly than may other types of interpretive errors. As stated by Spence and Lewandowsky (1990), "We do not know how damaging bad graphs are."

Even when graphs convey accurate information by using appropriate elements, they can mislead by truncating scales or presenting different types of scales (Huff, 1954; Lawrence & O'Connor, 1993). Variability within phases of a series result in significantly different interpretations (Lawrence & O'Connor, 1993), as do the presence of horizontal grid lines and the size of values on the dependent-variable axis.

Psychophysical research underscores fallibility in human visual perception. Classical sensory perception research demonstrated that figure-ground, closure, continuity, constancy, and visual suppression can all influence perception of line length, size, and color (McConnell, 1974).

Learning and social influences can also affect interpretation of visual stimuli. People often ignore base rate, ignore important and incorporate irrelevant characteristics of data, overestimate the accuracy of their judgments, and distort judgments because of preexisting expectations (Myers, 1990).

Weber's Law and Stevens' Law are theories of visual perception that must be considered in visual analysis (Cleveland, 1985). Weber's Law provides a mathematical explanation for errors in judgment of position, length, and area:

$$w_p(x) = k_p x \tag{5.8}$$

where **x** represents a line length or some other physical attribute size, $\mathbf{w_p(x)}$ represents a segment of line that has a probability **p** of being longer than the original line length **x** when added to the original line length **x**, and **k** is a constant that does not depend on length **x**; the level of **p** is fixed. This law tells us that our ability to discriminate differences in line length is a function of the percentage differences between the lengths rather than the absolute differences in the lengths. For example, we can easily detect the difference between lines of 2 cm and 2.5 cm, but have difficulty recognizing the difference between lines of 50 cm and 50.5 cm. The absolute differences between the two lines are the same, but the relative differences between the two lines are 25% and 1%.

Similarly, Stevens' Law describes perceived scales for length, area, volume, and other attributes of visual judgment. The equation

$$p(x) = cx^{\beta} \tag{5.9}$$

represents the size of an attribute (e.g., length, area) as **x**. The perceived scale **p(x)** is the actual scale **cx** to a power β. Power values have been empirically derived for a variety of attributes and experiments. The power law exponent for length judgments is about 1.0 and is considerably less for angular (around .7), slope, and volume judgments. Greatest errors occur in comparisons of volume (Baird, 1970).

Figure 5.14 presents an example of angle contamination; the slope ratio in both graphs is equal, yet the graphical perception is very different because angles of the segments are more nearly equal with the horizontal in the right panel than in the left panel (Cleveland, 1985). Analysts comparing percentage data across settings, caregivers, or times of treatment could attribute these graphing differences as treatment effects.

Figures 5.15 and 5.16 appear very similar; yet the two graphs are significantly different: $P(T) = .015$ (one-tail) and .029 (two-tail), even though they are highly correlated ($r = .99$). Graph scaling is equivalent, as is slope. Variance accounts for the difference. Here, level differences between the last four and first four data points best describe observed changes.

Visual analysis of these data can not easily distinguish variability. In

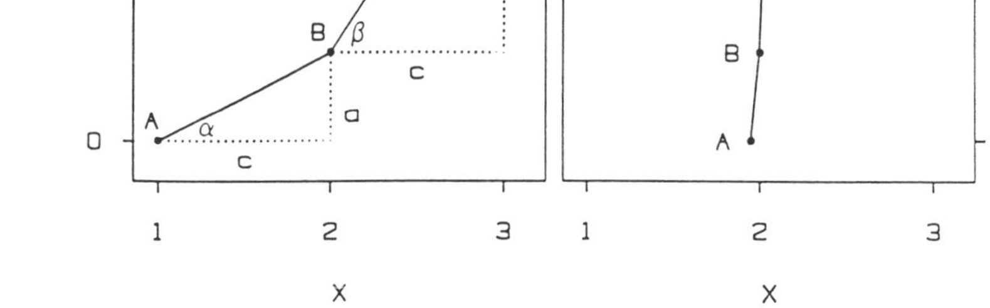

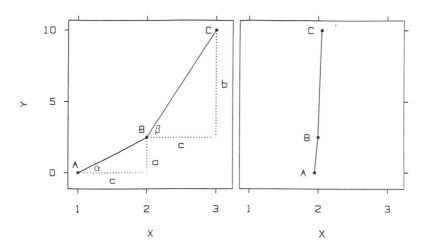

FIG. 5.14. Angle contamination. Ratios in both graphs are equal. From Cleveland (1985). Reprinted with permission of AT&T Bell Laboratories.

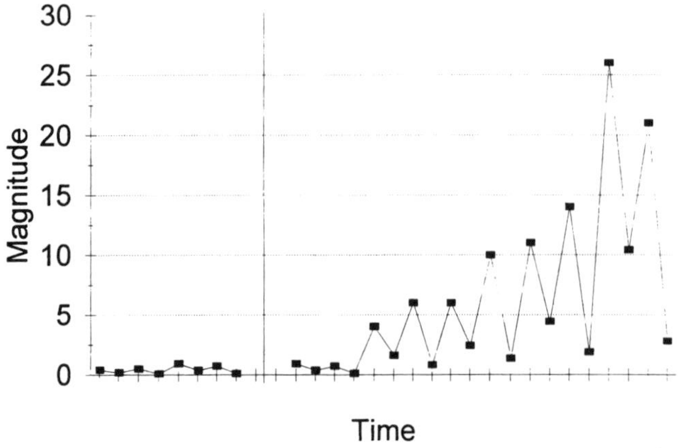

FIG. 5.15. Angle contamination with nonsignificant trend.

retrospect, one might notice the variance. Had fewer data points been available, even anecdotal identification of likely differences would become more limited, and statistical analysis would have been impossible.

Imagine dividing the treatment phase of Fig. 5.16 into three equal observation periods, each independently compared with the baseline phase. Treatment effects occurring in the middle of a graph are more difficult for visual analysts to detect than are effects occurring near the

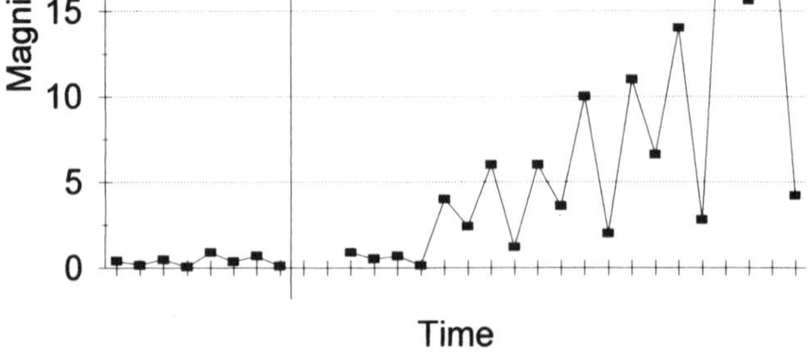

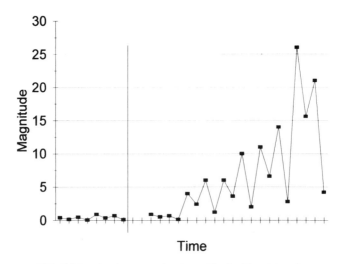

FIG. 5.16. Angle contamination with significant trend.

top or bottom (Lawrence & O'Connor, 1993). Horizontal and vertical lines on graphs may serve as anchors, thereby increasing accurate data interpretation.

Gradual accumulations of imperceptible change eventually reach critical disparity, registering a difference in sensory perception. This phenomenon, known as *just-noticeable differences* (JND), can be influenced in animals by learning. de-Weerd, Vandenbussche, and Orban (1990) compared the efficiency of an adaptive and nonadaptive method in determining JNDs of line orientation in the visual systems of 25 cats, and noted significant JND threshold shifts after training. Perception of JND can be manipulated (Fernandez, 1976), and, in humans, JND varies with the wavelength of luminance (Reitner, Sharpe, & Zrenner, 1992). Under some conditions of field intensity, duration, and diameter, JND appears to have a "U" function, with error increasing as luminance increases or decreases. The addition of color can further increase JND error (Ejima & Takahashi, 1983); a nearly logarithmic transformation occurs with red-green and yellow-blue producing a veiling effect. Errors of interpretation may also increase when graphs contain data points marked in different ways.

One of the simplest and perhaps most common errors in the presentation of data for visual analysis is graphing data without showing the zero point. According to Darrell Huff (1954), any graph without a zero point is dishonest, because such graphs can skew interpretation by a factor of 100. The zero line provides a more accurate proportion for evaluating the graph. Huff also noted that area graphs can skew interpretation, because they display volume rather than length.

The well-known phenomenon of projection also affects visual perception. Frank (1939) proposed that a subject responds to an ambiguous field, such as the ink blots of Rorschach's test (1942) or the drawings of Murray's (1943) Thematic Apperception Test, by "projecting . . . his way of seeing life, his meanings, significance, patterns, and especially his feelings" (p. 403). Researchers, wishing to see meaningful trends and patterns in visual plots, might be more likely to interpret effects as significant than would skeptics. Indeed, treatments considered socially acceptable are more likely than are socially unacceptable treatments to produce effective outcome ratings after visual analysis (Spirrison & Maundy, 1994).

Adjuncts to Visual Inspection

We have demonstrated that the best trained and most experienced visual analysts may have difficulty interpreting graphed data. Change may be consistent but small, autocorrelation may not be evident visually, and learning may affect both responses and interpretation. Specialized training, plotting residuals, and conducting statistical analyses often enhance an analyst's ability to discover patterns of change hidden within data.

Training Effects

Training provided for visual analysts is qualitatively different from training provided for students of statistical analysis (Wampold & Furlong, 1981). Wampold and Furlong compared students trained in visual analysis ($n = 14$) with students trained in multivariate analysis ($n = 10$) to identify their methods of predicting significant differences between phase changes of AB designs. Each subject reviewed 36 randomly presented graphs. The authors found that subjects trained in visual inference attended to large differences between phases, ignoring variation. Subjects trained in multivariate techniques gave more weight to variation across phases in their determinations. Interrater reliability of visual analysts improves with training, even though extensive training fails to produce impressive agreements. Analysts using statistical techniques may disagree about the most appropriate model for evaluating differences in dependent variables but, once identified, statistical models always provide the same result when calculated properly.

Statistics

Applied practitioners and behavioral researchers seem to avoid statistics. Perhaps it is telling that many need reminders of ways to calculate percentage (e.g., 75% of research articles in the 25th anniversary issue of the *Journal of Applied Behavior Analysis* [1993, *26*(4)] provide formulae for calculating percentage).

INTEGRATING VISUAL WITH STATISTICAL ANALYSIS

Synthesis

Kazdin (1982) advocated visual analysis for single-subject or time-series data, calling for statistical analysis under only two circumstances: when a stable baseline cannot be established and when a new treatment is being evaluated. To Kazdin's proscriptions, Huitema (1986b) added "when findings are to be shared with other professionals" (p. 228). Because data are usually subject to review by other professionals, we advocate integrated analysis for all single-subject outcome evaluations.

Practitioners sometimes consider visual analysis and statistical analysis incompatible. According to Neufeld (1977), visual analysis is but one alternative to statistical analysis. The goals of practitioners, whether applied or experimental, should be to explain, predict, and control behavior. Integrative analysis combines statistical and nonstatistical methods whenever possible. Alternatives to statistical analysis other than visual analysis include uncertainty analysis, stochastic process analysis, and correlograms (Neufeld, 1977).

Uncertainty analysis allows prediction of a categorical variable from its position, as described by the following statistic:

$$U(y) = -\sum_{e=1}^{z} P(y_e)Log_2P(y_e) \tag{5.10}$$

"The reduction in uncertainty of one categorical variable, through knowledge of the other, parallels the correlation between the two variables in the usual metric sense" (Neufeld, 1977, p. 52). Stochastic process analysis describes the likelihood that one categorical event will follow another. Correlograms predict relationships between observations as a function of the time separating the observations.

Perhaps future theorists will discover applications for nonlinear models (sometimes referred to as *chaotic models*) in single-subject analysis. Software is now available that allows practitioners easily accessible integrated analysis tools for evaluating single-subject research and time series. Interest in visual analysis will grow as software manufacturers develop inexpensive computer graphics and publishers provide sophisticated data analysis and presentation software. Conscientious practitioners and researchers should insist on integrated analysis of single-subject data.

When statistical analysis is not possible and practitioners must rely on visual analysis alone, then sequential procedures proposed by Furlong and Wampold (1982) should be followed before causal inferences are tendered:

1. Determine the reliability of observed data.
2. Determine the presence or absence of treatment effects.
3. Determine whether the observed change is meaningful.
4. Consider how the treatment effect can be generalized to other settings or other providers.

Huitema (1986b) presented nine "commandments" for avoiding errors in statistical analysis. Visual analysis is subject to most of the errors faced by statistical analysts, and Huitema's commandments are equally important in visual analysis. The following are restatements of his original list:

1. Know the difference between the design and the analysis. Research methodologies vary along three dimensions: frequency of response measurement, analysis method, and design type. The selected analysis must be appropriate for the selected design.
2. Avoid confusing effect size with the statistical significance of the effect. Test statistics represent probability value reflecting the likelihood that two samples come from the same population. Effect size is a descriptive measure of the size of the difference between sample means.
3. Separate speculative conclusions from those based on meaningful data.
4. Avoid confusing statistical significance with replication.
5. Perform an analysis that is consistent with the design.
6. Compare apples with apples and oranges with oranges.
7. Understand the nature of the relation of the data and the analysis method.
8. Respect warnings about small sample size.
9. Communicate findings to others in understandable language.

Visual analysis is important in many of the judgments made by professionals in contemporary society. Air traffic controllers use visual analysis of radar patterns to direct aircraft into and out of busy airports (Costa, 1993). Surgeons rely on visual analysis to locate landmarks, identify damaged tissue, and repair or excise lesions. Cardiologists evaluate electrocardiograms visually, and neurologists rely on visual analysis of the electroencephalograms. Emerging technologies in visual imaging, such as interpretation of magnetic resonance imaging, rely heavily on the analysis of visual information. Still, each of these disciplines has developed statistical adjuncts to assist in decision making (Erdi et al., 1994; Livanov & Rusinov, 1968; Ruben, Elberling, & Salomon, 1976).

As long as clear differences exist between normal and abnormal findings, visual analysis allows but does not guarantee formulation of quick and reliable judgments from highly trained practitioners. When differences in data are less clear, reliance on visual analysis can produce undesirable results.

The long-term effects of decisions made from visual analysis may be very different from the short-term effects most often reported in the scientific literature. Journals reporting visual analysis results rarely consider outcomes beyond several months. Even interventions producing dramatic clinical change, such as the elimination of self-injury, may have unknown consequences a decade later.

Recommendations and Conclusions

Catherine Carswell (1995) described the graphical design conventions used in small sample displays as folk remedies that often work, given sufficient training in interpretation. The most widely used graphic presentation conventions are the seven guidelines used in the *Journal of Applied Behavior Analysis* (Society for the Experimental Analysis of Behavior, 1994):

1. Condition labels (IV levels) are descriptive, centered, and placed above the data.
2. Vertical dashed lines separate conditions; data points are not connected across conditions.
3. Lines between data points do not quite touch the data points; the data points stand out on the graph in relation to the lines.
4. The "0" line is raised slightly so that data points do not rest on the axis.
5. Where more than one set of data appear on a figure, label each and direct an arrow from the label to the data.
6. Subject names are placed in a box small type and go in the bottom right corner.
7. A break in the line is used to indicate that the scale of the axis is not continuous.

These guidelines provide a much-needed model for consistency in graphic presentation for practitioners and researchers. Yet, research indicates that guidelines two and seven need revision, because they often skew visual interpretations. Breaking lines connecting data points across treatment phases may visually enhance inconsequential differences occurring between adjacent phases (Kosselyn, 1994; Spence & Lewandowsky, 1990). Also, breaking the ordinate to indicate that the scale is noncontinuous produces an illusion of greater difference between dependent measures than may exist in reality (Huff, 1954).

We recommend the following:

1. Establish designs that allow adequate hypothesis development in the presence of cyclicity.
2. Balance designs to compensate for unexpected carryover effects.

3. Whenever possible, establish evaluation conditions producing data suitable for statistical as well as visual analysis.
4. Avoid response-guided experimentation methods.
5. Plot residuals to demonstrate how well your data fit a linear model; consider a nonlinear model when the residual mean deviates from zero, shows inconsistent variance, or contains autocorrelation.
6. Provide regression-based estimates of reliability in addition to agreement percentages.
7. When data are aggregated, present median rather than mean values under conditions of unusual variability or in the presence of suspected outliers.
8. Include range bars and trended ranges when possible.

We view visual inspection and statistical analysis as complimentary tools in the development and verification of hypotheses in research and clinical practice. Visual inspection provides techniques for hypothesis generation, increased understanding of the problem, and increased ability to explore alternative explanations. Statistical analysis refines and verifies the hypotheses. Statistical models may be useful in predictions of future events and making probabilistic attributions of causality.

Visual inspection is descriptive in nature. Statistical analysis is inferential and predictive. Panaceas exist in neither, and their combined use may increase validity but never ensure it.

REFERENCES

Allison, D. B. (1992). When cyclicity is a concern: A caveat regarding phase change criteria in single-case designs. *Comprehensive Mental Health Care, 2*(2), 131–149.

Allison, D. B., Franklin, R. D., & Heshka, S. (1992). Reflections on visual inspection, response guided experimentation, and Type I error rate in single-case designs. *Journal of Experimental Education, 61*(1), 45–51.

Armitage, P., McPherson, C. K., & Rowe, B. C. (1969). Repeated significance tests on accumulating data. *Journal of the Royal Statistical Society, Series A, 132*, 235–244.

Baer, D. M. (1977a). Reviewer's comment: Just because it's reliable doesn't mean that you can use it. *Journal of Applied Behavior Analysis, 10*, 117–119.

Baer, D. M. (1977b). Perhaps it would be better not to know everything. *Journal of Applied Behavior Analysis, 10*, 167–172.

Baird, J. C. (1970). *Psychophysical analysis of visual space.* New York: Pergamon.

Barlow, D. H., & Hersen, M. (1984). *Single case experimental designs: Strategies for studying behavior change.* New York: Pergamon.

Barrios, B. A., & Hartmann, D. P. (1988). Recent developments in single-subject methodology: Methods for analyzing generalization, maintenance, and multicomponent treatments. *Progress in Behavior Modification, 22*, 11–47.

Bauer, M. I., & Johnson-Laird, P. N. (1993). How diagrams can improve reasoning. *Psychological Science, 4*(6), 372–378.

Boykin, R. A., & Nelson, R. O. (1981). The effects of instructions and calculation procedures on observers' accuracy, agreement, and calculation correctness. *Journal of Applied Behavior Analysis, 14*, 479–489.

Campbell, D. T., & Stanley, J. C. (1966). *Experimental and quasi-experimental designs for research*. Chicago: Rand McNally.

Carswell, C. M. (1995, March/April). The art and psychological science of graphical communication. *Psychological Science Agenda*, pp. 8–9.

Cleveland, W. S. (1985). *The elements of graphing data*. Monterey, CA: Wadsworth.

Costa, G. (1993). Evaluation of workload in air traffic controllers. *Ergonomics, 36*(9), 1111–1120.

Crosbie, J. (1987). The inability of the binomial test to control Type I error with single-subject data. *Behavioral Assessment, 9*, 141–150.

DeProspero, A., & Cohen, S. (1979). Inconsistent visual analyses of intrasubject data. *Journal of Applied Behavior Analysis, 12*, 573–579.

Demets, D. L. (1987). Practical aspects of data monitoring: A brief review. *Statistics in Medicine, 6*, 753–760.

de-Weerd, P., Vandenbussche, E., & Orban, G. (1990). Staircase procedure and constant stimuli method in cat psychophysics. *Behavioural Brain Research, 40*(3), 201–214.

Edgington, E. S. (1984). Statistics and single-case designs. *Progress in Behavior Modification, 16*, 83–119.

Ejima, Y., & Takahashi, S. (1983). Chromatic valence and hue sensation. *Journal of the Optical Society of America, 73*(8), 1048–1054.

Erdi, Y. E., Wessels, B. W., DeJager, R., Erdi, A. K., Der, L., Chuk, Y., Shiri, R., Yorke, E., Altemus, R., & Varma V. (1994). A new fiducial alignment system to overlay abdominal computed tomography or magnetic resonance anatomical images with radiolabeled antibody single-photon emission computed tomographic scans. *Cancer, 93*(3), 923–931.

Fernandez, D. (1976). Dimensional dominance and stimulus discriminability. *Journal of Experimental Child Psychology, 21*(1), 175–189.

Frank, L. K. (1939). Projective methods for the study of personality. *Journal of Psychology, 8*, 389–413.

Furlong, M. J., & Wampold, B. E. (1982). Intervention effects and relative variation as dimensions in experts' use of visual inference. *Journal of Applied Behavior Analysis, 15*(3), 415–421.

Greenspan, P., & Fisch, G. S. (1992). Visual inspection of data: A statistical analysis of behavior. *Proceedings of the Annual Meeting of the American Statistical Association* (pp. 79–82). Alexandria, VA: American Statistical Association.

Greenwald, A. G. (1976). Within-subjects designs: To use or not to use? *Psychological Bulliten, 8*(2), 314–320.

Harbst, K. B., Ottenbacher, K. J., & Harris, S. R. (1991). Interrater reliability of therapists' judgments of graphed data. *Physical Therapy, 71*(2), 107–115.

Hartmann, D. P., & Hall, R. V. (1976). The changing criterion design. *Journal of Applied Behavior Analysis, 9*(4), 527–532.

Hayes, S. C. (1981). Single-case experimental designs and empirical clinical practice. *Journal of Consulting and Clinical Psychology, 49*, 193–211.

Huff, D. (1954). *How to lie with statistics*. New York: Norton.

Huitema, B. D. (1986b). Statistical analysis and single-subject designs. In A. Poling & R. W.

Fuqua (Eds.), *Research methods in applied behavior analysis: Issues and advances* (pp. 209–232). New York: Plenum.

Jaccard, J., & Becker, M. A. (1990). *Statistics for the Behavioral Sciences*. Belmont, CA: Wadsworth.

Jackson, M. (1986). Robust statistics. In A. D. Lovie (Ed.), *New developments in statistics for social sciences*. London: Methuen/The British Psychological Society.

Jones, R. R., Weinrott, M. R., & Vaught, R. S. (1978). Effects of serial dependency on the agreement between visual and statistical inference. *Journal of Applied Behavior Analysis, 11*(2), 277–283.

Kaplan, R. M., & Saccuzzo, D. P. (1982). *Psychological testing principles, applications, and issues*. Monterey, CA: Brooks/Cole.

Kazdin, A. E. (1982). *Single-case research designs: Methods for clinical and applied settings*. New York: Oxford University Press.

Kazdin, A. E. (1984). Statistical analyses for single-case experimental designs. In D. H. Barlow & M. Hersen (1984). *Single case experimental designs: Strategies for studying behavior change* (pp. 285–321). New York: Pergamon.

Kearns, K. P. (1986). Flexibility of single-subject experimental designs. Part II: Design selection and arrangement of experimental phases. *Journal of Speech and Hearing Disorders, 51*, 204–214.

Kelly, M. B. (1977). A review of the observable data-collection and reliability procedures reported in *The Journal of Applied Behavior Analysis. The Journal of Applied Behavior Analysis, 10*, 97–101.

Keppel, G. (1982). *Design and analysis: A researcher's handbook* (2nd ed.). Englewood Cliffs, NJ: Prentice-Hall.

Kosselyn, S. M. (1994). *Elements of graph design*. New York: Freeman.

Kratochwill, T. R. (1992). *Single case research design and analysis: An overview*. In T. R. Kratochwill & J. R. Levin (Eds.), *Single-case research design and analysis: New directions for psychology and education* (pp. 1–15). Hillsdale, NJ: Lawrence Erlbaum Associates.

Kratochwill, T. R., & Levin, J. R. (Eds.). (1992). *Single-case research design and analysis: New directorns for psychology and education*. Hillsdale, NJ: Lawrence Erlbaum Associates.

Krishef, C. H. (1991). *Fundamental approaches to single subject design and analysis*. Malabar, FL: Krieger.

Kruse, J. A., & Gottman, J. M. (1982). Time series methodology in the study of sexual hormonal and behavioral cycles. *Archives of Sexual Behavior, 11*, 405–415.

Lawrence, M., & O'Connor, M. (1993). Scale, variability, and the calibration of judgmental prediction intervals. *Organizational Behavior & Human Decision Processes, 56*(3), 441–458.

Leach, C. (1988). Guidelines for data presentation. In R. J. Sternberg (Ed.), *The psychologist's companion* (pp. 113). Cambridge, England: Cambridge University Press/The British Psychological Society.

Leitenberg, H. (1973). The use of single-case methodology in psychotherapy research. *Journal of Abnormal Psychology, 82*(1), 87–101.

Livanov, M. N., & Rusinov, V. W. (1968). *Mathematical analysis of the electrical activity of the brain* (J. S. Barlow, Trans.). Cambridge, MA: Harvard University Press.

McConnell, J. V. (1974). *Understanding human behavior*. New York: Holt, Rinehart & Winston.

Matyas, T. A., & Greenwood, K. M. (1990). Visual analysis of single-case time series: Effects of variability, serial dependence, and magnitude of intervention effects. *Journal of Applied Behavior Analysis, 23*, 341–351.

Matyas, T. A., & Greenwood, K. M. (1991). Problems in the estimation of autocorrelation in brief time series and some implications for behavioral data. *Behavioral Assessment, 13*, 137–157.

Moore-Ede, M. C., Sulzman, F. M., & Fuller, C. A. (1982). *The clocks that time us*. Cambridge, MA: Harvard University Press.

Morley, S., & Adams, M. (1991). Graphical analysis of single-case time series data. *British Journal of Clinical Psychology, 30*, 97–115.

Mosteller, F., Siegel, A. F., Trapido, E., & Youtz, C. (1985). Fitting straight lines by eye. In D. C. Hoaglin, F. Mosteller, & J. W. Tukey (Eds.), *Exploring data tables, trends, and shapes* (pp. 225–240). New York: Wiley.

Murray, H. A. (1943). *Thematic Apperception Test manual*. Cambridge, MA: Harvard University Press.

Myers, D. G. (1990). *Social psychology*. New York: McGraw-Hill.

Neufeld, R. W. J. (1977). *Clinical quantitative methods*. New York: Grune & Stratton.

Ottenbacher, K. J. (1990a). Visual analysis of single-subject data: An empirical analysis. *Mental Retardation, 28*, 285–290.

Ottenbacher, K. J. (1990b). When is a picture worth a thousand *p* values? A comparison of visual and quantitative methods to analyze single subject data. *Journal of Special Education, 23*, 436–449.

Paniagua, F. A. (1990). The multiple baseline design across exemplars. *Behavioral Residental Treatment, 5*(3), 177–188.

Park, H., Marascuilo, L., & Gaylord-Ross, R. (1990). Visual inspection and statistical analysis in single-case designs. *Journal of Experimental Education, 58*, 311–320.

Parsonson, B. S., & Baer, D. M. (1978). The analysis and presentation of graphic data. In T. R. Kratochwill (Ed.), *Single-subject research: Strategies for evaluating change* (pp. 101–165). New York: Academic Press.

Parsonson, B. S., & Baer, D. M. (1992). The visual analysis of data, and current research into the stimuli controlling it. In T. R. Kratochwill & J. R. Levin (Eds.), *Single-case research design and analysis* (pp. 15–40). Hillsdale, NJ: Lawrence Erlbaum Associates.

Reitner, A., Sharpe, L., & Zrenner, E. (1992). Wavelength discrimination as a function of field intensity, duration and size. *Vision-Research, 32*(1), 179–185.

Rorschach, H. (1942). *Psychodiagnostics*. Bern: Huber.

Rosenberger, J. T., & Gasko, M. (1983). Comparing location estimators: Trimmed means, medians and trimeans. In D. C. Hoaglin, F. Mosteller, & J. W. Tukey (Eds.), *Understanding robust and exploratory data analysis* (pp. 297–338). New York: Wiley.

Ruben, R. J., Elberling, C., & Salomon, G. (1976). *Electrocochleography*. Baltimore, MD: University Park Press.

Sattler, J. M. (1988). *Assessment of children* (3rd ed.). San Diego, CA: Jerome M. Sattler.

Sidman, M. (1960). *Tactics of scientific research: Evaluating experimental data in psychology*. New York: Basic Books.

Silverstein, A. B. (1993). Type I, Type II, and other types of error in pattern analysis. *Psychological Assessment, 5*(1), 72–74.

Skiba, R., Deno, S., Marston, D., & Casey, A. (1989). Influence of trend estimation and subject familiarity on practitioners' judgments of intervention effectiveness. *Journal of Special Education, 22*, 433–446.

Skinner, B. F. (1953). *Science and human behavior*. New York: The Free Press.

Spence, I., & Lewandowsky, S. (1990). Graphical perception. In J. Fox and J. Long (Eds.), *Modern methods of data analysis* (pp. 13–57). Newbury Park, CA: Sage.

Spirrison, C. L., & Maundy, L. T. (1994). Acceptability bias: The effects of treatment acceptability on visual analysis of graphed data. *Journal of Psychopathology and Behavioral Assessment, 16*(1), 85–94.

Statsoft. (1994). *Statistica/W* (Vol. 1, pp. 1489–2398). Tulsa, OK: Statsoft Inc.

Tawney, J. W., & Gast, D. L. (1984). *Single subject research in special education*. Columbus, OH: Merrill.

Tukey, J. (1977). *Exploratory data analysis*. Cambridge, MA: Addison-Wesley.
Velleman, V. F., & Hoaglin, D. C. (1981). *Applications, basics, and computing of exploratory data analysis*. Boston: Duxbury.
Wampold, B. E., & Furlong, M. J. (1981). The heuristics of visual inference. *Behavioral Assessment, 3*, 79–92.

6

Statistical Alternatives for Single-Case Designs

Bernard S. Gorman
Hofstra University

David B. Allison
Obesity Research Center, St. Luke's/Roosevelt Hospital Center
Columbia University College of Physicians and Surgeons

AN OVERVIEW OF SINGLE-CASE DESIGNS

This chapter discusses statistical approaches for analyzing single-case research designs.[1] These designs and their corresponding statistical analyses span a continuum that ranges from experimental designs to correlational designs. Figures 6.1a and 6.1b display a typology of analyses. By *experimental designs* we mean designs in which researchers manipulate one or more independent variables and in which potentially confounding variables are controlled by randomly assigning treatment conditions to subjects. In quasi-experimental designs, the independent variables are manipulated by natural or historical events. Consequently, there is little direct control of unwanted variation, and treatments are not assigned at random. As one departs from the strict requirements of experimental designs, it becomes more difficult to draw precise conclusions about causal relations between manipulations and outcomes.

We can also draw a distinction within the group of experimental designs between those designs that we call "time-series experimental designs" and those that we call "nontime-series experimental designs." Time-series experimental designs measure behavior over continuous

[1]We wish to thank our colleagues Mark Beasley, Myles Faith, Phillip Good, Jack McCardle, Richard Ittenbach, and David Rindskopf for their astute comments and suggestions as this manuscript was developing.

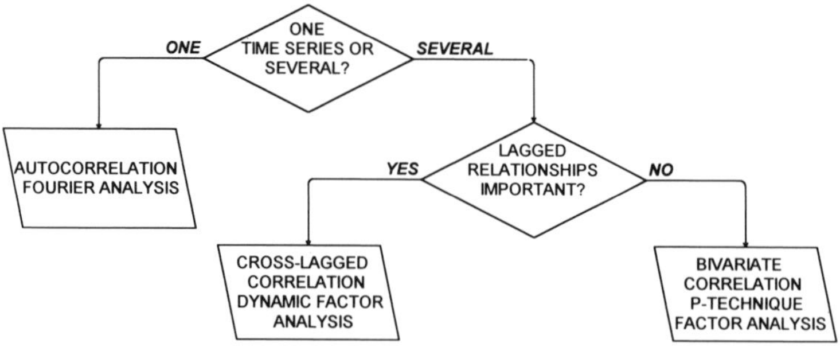

FIG. 6.1A. Correlational strategies.

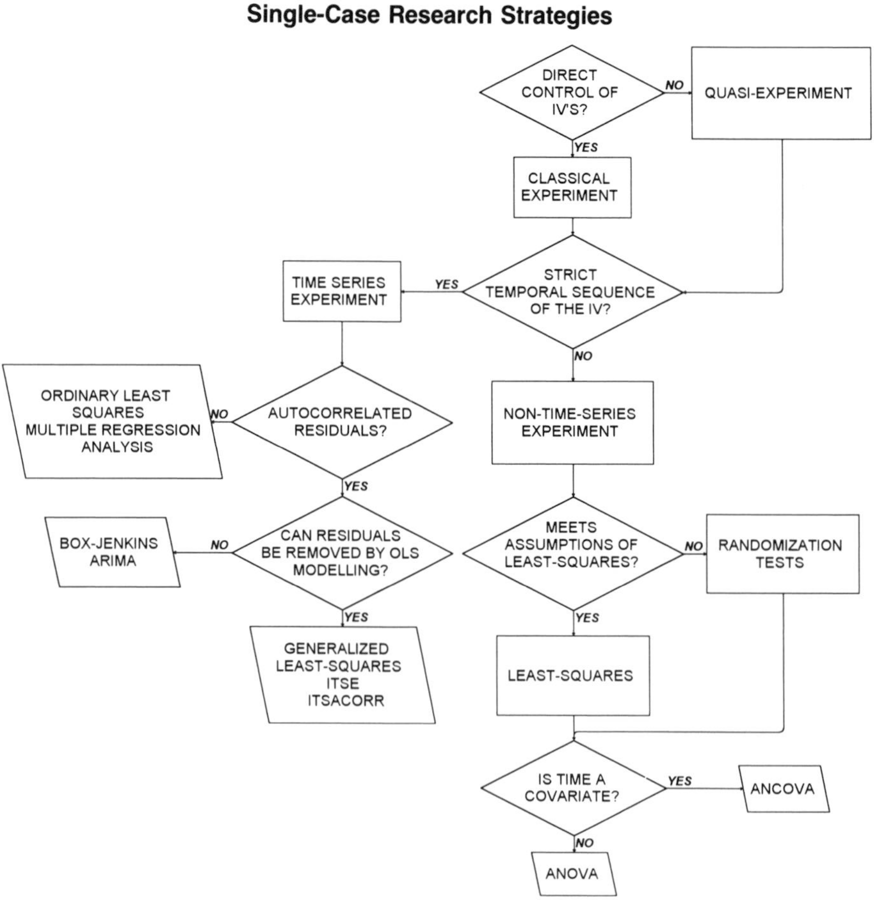

FIG. 6.1B. Experimental strategies.

time spans and introduce one or more treatment interventions at one or more points along a temporal continuum. For example, a researcher evaluating therapy for enuresis might obtain continuous measures of bed-wetting behavior for each of 30 nights during a baseline or control phase (A) and then might intervene during a treatment phase (B) lasting for another 30 days. Depending on ethical and practical considerations, this A-B design might be extended to an A-B-A design or to an A-B-A-B design. A nontime-series experimental design would assign treatments at random throughout the experiment. For example, a researcher might be interested in the effects of medications on a child's activity level. On randomly chosen days, the child might be given Ritalin, placebos, or another medication. Consistent with double-blind procedures, neither the child nor an observer would be aware of the manipulation. Although time might be used as a covariate that serves to statistically control maturation effects, differences in levels of behavior are attributed to the experimental manipulation and not to some temporal effect, per se.

Correlational designs do not classify variables as either independent or dependent variables. Instead, variables are designated as *covariates, predictors*, or *criteria*. Control for unwanted variation is achieved by statistical operations such as partial correlation, blocking, or factor analysis. Assignment of subjects to treatment conditions is nonexistent and/or nonrandom. For example, a researcher might observe correlations among an individual subject's daily self-reports of anxiety, depression, and fatigue, but none of these state variables was directly manipulated by the researcher. In this chapter, we focus mainly on single-case experimental designs.

EXPERIMENTAL DESIGNS

Nontime-Series Experimental Designs

Perhaps the simplest non-time-series experimental design would be an A-B design. In this design, the researcher compares the mean of measurements from a pretreatment or control condition (A) to the mean of posttreatment measures (B) with an independent groups *t*-test or an analysis of variance. These analytic strategies were originally suggested by Gentile, Roden, and Klein (1972). However, these analyses are frequently unacceptable for single-case experiments because some major assumptions of least-squares statistical analysis, including analysis of variance and regression analysis, are likely to be violated. These designs assume normal distributions and equal variances of scores within each level of the independent variable. However, it is possible that interventions will not only change the means of variables within treatments but they will alter other properties of the distributions, such as variance, skewness, and kurtosis.

Perhaps the greatest concern lies in the assumption that residual errors (the components of scores not attributable to treatment effects) should be independent. For example, if we were to conduct a traditional multisubject *t*-test in which 20 subjects were randomly assigned to each of two groups, we would expect a separate data point to come from each subject. We would also expect residual effects to be both normally distributed and independent from subject to subject. In a typical multisubject experiment in which separate subjects are randomly assigned to treatment conditions, these requirements are usually met. However, in single-subject designs, it would be unlikely to find independent and normally distributed residual effects because variables that operate at one point in time will often produce carryover effects that influence later observations. For example, subjects might perseverate on tasks; they may remember concepts from previous sessions; or drug interventions may take some time to metabolize or "wash out." We would say that these behaviors and, possibly, the residuals from the statistical models that we choose are *serially dependent* because successive scores are more similar to each other than would be predicted by chance. We can measure the magnitude of serial dependence of research observations or their residuals by computing autocorrelation coefficients.

The Autocorrelation Problem

Definition of Autocorrelation

Because they play a critical role in all the methods discussed in this chapter, let us digress for a moment to develop the concepts of autocorrelation and serial dependency. An *autocorrelation coefficient* is a modified form of the Pearson product–moment correlation coefficient in which one variable is a series of data values ordered in time and the other variable is the same time series lagged or advanced by k time periods (or "time-lags"). Let us use the data in Table 6.1.

$$\rho_k = \frac{\dfrac{1}{(n-k)} \sum_{1}^{n-k} (x_i - \bar{x})(x_{i+k} - \bar{x})}{\dfrac{1}{n} \sum_{1}^{n} (x_i - \bar{x})^2} \tag{6.1}$$

TABLE 6.1
Illustration of Autocorrelation

Observation	*Original Series*	*K = 1 Lagged Series*	*K = 2 Lagged Series*
1	3	—	—
2	4	3	—
3	4	4	3
4	6	4	4
5	8	6	4
6	8	8	6

In the formula for this autocorrelation coefficient (Kendall & Ord, 1990), n = the number of observations in the original series, k = the number of lags, and X_i is an observation point in the time period i. It should be noted that X is the mean of all observations in the series.

If we carried out Equation 6.1 with the data in Table 6.1, we would see that the zero-order lagged correlation is the correlation of the original time series with itself. That is, the first observation is paired with the first observation; the second observation with the second; and so on. Of course, this correlation coefficient will always be 1.0. To create a first-order lagged series (k = 1), we displace the original series by one time period and pair each observation in the original series with the one that immediately preceded it. We lose one observation and compute the correlation coefficient on the remaining five corresponding pairs of data points. In the present example, the lag-1 autocorrelation is 0.54. This tells us that a data value in the original series can be predicted to a moderate degree from the data value that immediately preceded it. In other words, there is a "serial dependence" in this data set. A second-order lagged series autocorrelation can be created by lagging the original data series by two time periods. In this example, the correlation between the lag-2 series and the original series autocorrelation produces the autocorrelation coefficient of .028. As in the present example, a positive lag-1 autocorrelation often suggests a trend. Negative autocorrelation coefficients often suggest the presence of rapid oscillations. That is, a high data value in one time period may be immediately followed by a low data value at the subsequent time period, and vice versa. Large positive autocorrelations at lags other than the first lag may suggest seasonality or cyclicity. As is common in economic data, a strong autocorrelation at lag 12 in a series of monthly data may show an annual 12-month cycle. Most modern statistical program packages and spreadsheet programs can easily compute autocorrelations for any desired lag.

Problems Produced by Autocorrelation

Residuals from statistical procedures can also be autocorrelated. Unfortunately, it is well known that when residuals are positively autocorrelated, the standard errors for regression analyses, *t*-tests, and ANOVAs will tend to be inflated and the resulting test statistics will be too large (Scheffe, 1959; Suen & Ary, 1987). However, when residuals are negatively correlated, standard errors in *t*-tests and ANOVAS will be too large. Consequently, the resulting test statistics will be too small and *p*-values will be misleading.

Ostrom (1990) showed that as autocorrelation of residuals increases, computed *t*-tests for regression weights values may be severely biased. That is, the computed values may be quite different from their true values. Analyses of variance (ANOVA), *t*-tests, and multiple regression analyses are special cases of the General Linear Model (Cohen & Cohen, 1983). By creating dummy codes or contrast variables to represent levels of experimentally manipulated independent variables, ANOVA problems can be solved as multiple regression problems (Cohen & Cohen, 1983). The *t*-tests for assessing the significance of regression weights can be used as *t*-tests of the effects of levels of the independent variable. Ostrom offered a formula (Equation 6.2) that suggests that in multiple regression, the observed values of the *t*-tests for assessing the significance of regression weights for independent (predictor) variables may be systematically distorted by the presence of autocorrelation of the independent variables themselves, the autocorrelation of residuals of the dependent variable, or both. Although Ostrom's formula would usually be applied for continuous, interval-scale independent variables, there is no reason to assume that it would not be applicable for dummy-coded or effect-coded variables in analyses of variance. In single-case studies it is highly likely that carryover and fatigue effects can introduce autocorrelation.

In Ostrom's formula (Equation 6.2):

$$t' = \sqrt{\frac{1 - pc}{1 + pc}}\, t_{obs} \tag{6.2}$$

t' is the true *t*-test value, t_{obs} = the computed, observed *t*-test statistic, *p*, is the autocorrelation of residuals, and *c* is the autocorrelation of the independent variable. By using this formula, it can be seen that even modest magnitudes of autocorrelation (e.g., > 0.4) in the residual series, the independent variable, or both sets of variables can bias the values of *t*-tests. For example, if both *p* and *c* were .7, then the observed *t*-test value would be more than twice the value of the true *t*-test value. However, also notice that if p or c were zero, then there would be no discrepancy between the true and observed values of t. However, if the levels of the independent variable were randomly assigned to a subject during an experiment, then c would be likely to approach zero and the t-value would not be particularly biased. Ostrom also demonstrated that the variance of the dependent variable may also be biased by autocorrelation. High amounts of positive autocorrelation will tend to show variances that appear to be larger than they actually are. However, the bias of variances becomes smaller as sample sizes increase.

Clearly, the results of ordinary ANOVA and t-test analyses can be biased. Their use should be discouraged unless it can be shown that the assumptions of these tests can be met. Huitema (1985, 1986, 1990) argued that the amount of serial dependency in behavioral data is relatively small. His reanalyses of numerous time series that appeared in behavior modification literature seemed to indicate that most autocorrelations were small and statistically insignificant. However, several articles and empirical studies (e.g., Busk & Marascuilo, 1988; Suen & Ary, 1987) have pointed out that because many studies have small numbers of observations, they lack adequate statistical power to conclude that the autocorrelations are negligible. As an addendum to his earlier findings, Huitema and McKean (1991) showed that autocorrelations are underestimated in small samples. Nonsignificance does not necessarily imply that statistical effects are absent but, rather, that they cannot yet be said to differ from a null value. Further, Huitema's critics argue that even moderate-sized autocorrelations may seriously affect error terms. As Matyas and Greenwood (chap. 7, this volume) showed in detail, Huitema's earlier (1984–1990) conclusions can be questioned.

Randomization Tests

Definitions of Randomization Tests

As we can see, ordinary t-tests and ANOVAs are often inappropriate for single-case studies because they require assumptions about the data that may be difficult to substantiate in practice. Fortunately, a variety of nonparametric approaches, loosely called *randomization tests* or *permutation tests*, can often work effectively with small sample sizes. The tests also dispense with some restrictive assumptions of ordinary t-test and ANOVA analyses, particularly those of normality of distributions. These tests were first developed by Fisher (1935) and Pitman (1937), and were later refined by Edgington (1975, 1979a, 1979b, 1980, 1992), Good (1994), Hubert (1987), Manly (1991), Mielke and Berry (1994), Noreen (1989), and Welch (1990). Mielke and Berry (1994) drew a distinction between three kinds of randomization tests. They classified these tests as permutation tests, per se; approximate randomization tests; and approximation tests that approximate the moments of complete sampling distributions of permutation tests. We provide an example of each type of test with a small data set.

Permutation Tests. We use a small data set in which observations a, b, and c were assigned to Condition 1 and achieved values of a = 2, b = 3, and c = 4. Observations d, e, and f are assigned to Condition 2 and achieve values of d = 6, e = 7, and f = 7 to conduct permutation tests, we first compute a test statistic such as a *t*-test, an *F*-ratio, a chi-square test, or a correlation coefficient on the original data set. In our case, we select a simple statistic, the absolute difference of sums of values in the two groups. In the present example, the difference of sums is 11 (20 − 9). We then systematically rearrange the data into every possible nonredundant arrangement of three objects into two groups and compute the test statistic for each arrangement.[2] Table 6.2 shows the original data set (Arrangement 1) and all possible nonredundant combinations of six observations into two groups (Arrangements 1–9).

For a one-tailed test, we count the number of times that values of the test statistics in the rearranged data sets exceeded or equaled the test statistic obtained from the original data set in a given direction. For a two-tailed test, we would count the number of times that test statistics from the permuted data sets exceed the absolute value of the test statistic of the original data set. If we had a directional hypothesis, we would count the number of times that test statistics from the permuted samples are larger than or equal to the one obtained with the original sample. In any case, we can obtain an exact, empirical probability of the likelihood of finding the result by chance. In the present example, none of the other nine rearrangements had differences of sums that are equal to or greater than 11. Therefore, the probability of finding a test statistic of

[2]There is some confusion about the use of the word *permutation* when discussing this class of tests. To some degree, it would be better to use the word *combination* in some situations. For example, Edgington (1987) provided an example in which 10 subjects were randomly assigned to two treatment conditions, with 5 subjects in each. He then stated that the possible number of "permutations" of 10 subjects into two groups of 5 is 252. However, 252 is the number of combinations of 10 cases taken 5 at a time. The number of permutations of 10 things taken 5 at a time is 30,240. When discussing permutation tests, Mielke and Berry (1994, p. 218) stated that, "Strictly speaking, it is not necessary to generate all possible permutations because the test statistic is not affected by permutations within each sample. Readers will notice that for the 6 case, two-group example above that although there are 20 possible combinations, only 10 are needed for a non-directional test. As a result of this confusion, we choose to use the neutral term *arrangement*."

TABLE 6.2
Arrangements of Six Observations Into Two Groups

	Condition 1		*Condition 2*		
Arrangement	*Members*	*Sum*	*Members*	*Sum*	*Difference of Sums*
1	a, b, c	9	d, e, f	20	11
2	a, b, e	12	c, d, f	17	5
3	a, b, f	12	c, d, e	17	5
4	a, c, d	12	b, e, f	17	5
5	a, c, f	13	b, d, e	16	3
6	a, d, e	15	b, c, f	14	1
7	b, c, d	13	a, e, f	16	3
8	b, c, e	14	a, d, f	15	1
9	b, d, f	16	a, c, e	13	3
10	c, e, f	18	a, b, d	11	7

this size or larger by chance is 1/10, or .10. This probability is an exact probability. It should be noted that the sample size for this example was too small to permit reaching the .05 significance levels or less. However, for two groups and a .05 two-tailed significance level, the test can be used with sample sizes as small as four per group.

Obviously, the previous example was constructed to present a small number of observations and a small number of data arrangements. It would be ideal to forming every possible arrangement of the data values. However, as the number of observations increases, the number of combinations and permutations rises rapidly. In fact, the number of combinations of N objects into two groups of size a and $N - a$ is:

$$C = \frac{N!}{[a!(N - a)!]} \tag{6.3}$$

When there are 100 observations or more, the number of permutations becomes huge. Fortunately, the tedious chore of creating permutations and obtaining their associated test statistics can be managed by computer algorithms. Very fast computers can probably perform all possible arrangements. A more practical strategy, however, would be found in a strategy (to be discussed next) known as the *approximate randomization test strategy,* in which we would create random samples of possible arrangements of observations and then would count the proportions of times that test statistics in the sample of arrangements equaled or exceeded the test statistic in the original data set.

Approximate Randomization Tests. The second kind of randomization test proceeds by first computing the test statistic and then computing statistics for each of a large number of random data rearrangements, in which data are sorted into two groups. In this strategy, at any given sorting, each observation must be assigned once to one and to only one group. A count is obtained of the number of arrangements whose test statistic equaled or exceeded the test statistic of the original data set. We took the data set from Table 6.2 and entered it into a randomization program written by Nakatani (1984). We found that in 5,000 random samples, Condition 2's sum was larger than Condition 1's sum in 95.5% of the samples. The two sums were equal in 4.5% of the samples. Therefore, our empirical significance level is less than .0001.

A related strategy, known as *bootstrapping* (Diaconis & Efron, 1983; Efron & Tibshirani, 1993; Stine, 1990) also depends on random assignments of observations to groups. However, in bootstrapping, a single observation can be assigned several times to the condition to which it belonged in the original sample. That is, if an observation belonged to Condition 1 in the original sample, it will never be assigned to Condition 2. However, in a given sampling, the same observation may be replicated several times or not included at all in Condition 1. In bootstrapping, the differences of the means of Condition 1 and Condition 2 will be evaluated at each sampling and the distribution of thousands of mean differences will be obtained. The empirical significance of a bootstrapped test statistic is defined as the proportion of times that a sample statistic fell in the null value region of a sampling distribution. It should be noted that because randomization and bootstrapping procedures draw random samples, the results of different analyses may produce different findings.

A Clinical Example of a Randomization Test. An example of a test that uses a random sampling of arrangements (without replacement) can be found in Silverstein and Allison (1994), who studied the effects of antecedent exercise (jogging 20 minutes per day), methylphenidate (Ritalin), and a placebo in reducing the hyperactive behavior of Max, a preschool boy. A single-case alternating treatments design was employed for a total of 82 days. The dependent variable was the Conner's Abbreviated Symptom Questionnaire. The independent variable was "treatment" with three conditions: methylphenidate plus attention placebo, antecedent exercise plus medication placebo, and attention plus medication placebo. To control for possible confounding variables, treatments were randomly assigned to days. The only constraint on randomization was the treatments were assigned to days in preselected proportions.The data from this study are displayed in Fig. 6.2.

The *RandPack* program (Edgington, 1990), which implements the an-

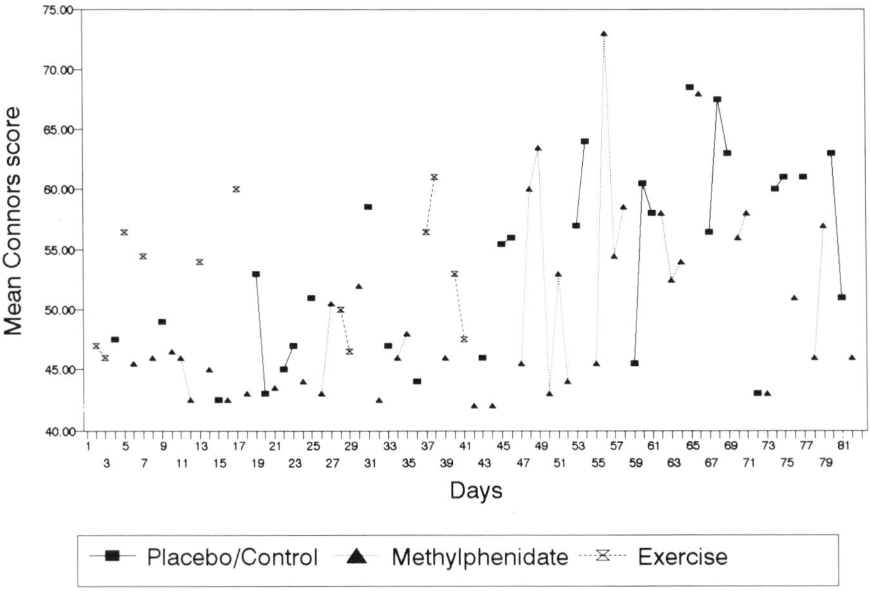

FIG. 6.2. Randomized trial: Ritalin and exercise.

alyses in Edgington's (1987) book, was used. An early stopping rule (see Allison, Silverstein, & Gorman, chap. 10, this volume, for details) was employed to minimize the duration of the study and find the best procedure for Max as quickly as possible. Data were analyzed after each 20 days of experimentation. After the first 20 days, differences among conditions were not significant at the early stopping alpha level. After 40 days, the mean of the exercise condition (M = 52.7; SD = 5.1) was higher than placebo (M = 45.4; SD = 2.7; p = .0001). The means for methylphenidate and placebo were not significantly different. Therefore, the exercise condition was dropped and the remainder of the study compared methylphenidate to placebo/no treatment with an equal allocation of sessions. Finally, after 82 days, hyperactive behavior ratings were lower with methylphenidate (M = 49.7; SD = 7.5) than with no treatment (M = 52.7; SD=5.1; $p < .0238$). It should be noted that although the treatments were randomized, the general upward trend in hyperactivity ratings suggests that carryover effects may have been operating in this experiment.

Moment Approximation Tests. The final class of randomization tests, the moment approximation tests, is based on approximations of the complete permutation sampling distribution of a test statistic. Mielke and Berry (1994) defined a statistic, *delta*, the average within-group difference, weighted by the number of subjects within each treatment level. When groups are well separated, the average within-group difference should be small when compared to differences between groups. If the numbers of observations and groups were small, then it should be possible to obtain a test probability value by finding the proportion of delta values from rearrangements of the original data set that are smaller than or equal to that of the obtained delta value. When the number of observations or groups becomes large, the number of computations of delta becomes prohibitive. Fortunately, Mielke and Berry (1994) found that the sampling distribution of delta values could be approximated by a distribution known as the *Pearson Type III* distribution. Therefore, given the number of observations, the number of treatments, and the number of observations per treatment, the probability of finding a delta value as small as or smaller than the obtained delta can be estimated without having to perform numerous permutations. The data in Table 6.2 were analyzed by a program, MRPP, written by Mielke and Berry (1994), which found the obtained one-tailed probability for the data set in Table 6.2 to be .023.

Assumptions of Randomization Tests:

Randomization tests require fewer assumptions than do parametric tests. However, there may be some confusion about how "assumption free" these tests are. Some authors state that their analyses required no assumptions (e.g., Chen & Dunlap, 1993) and we have been guilty, at times, of these kinds of statements (see Silverstein & Allison, 1994). As we discuss, there are some restrictions to the unbridled use of these tests.

Freedom From Distributional Assumptions. Most authorities on randomization tests state that such tests do not make any assumptions about the shapes of distributions, including variance, skewness, and kurtosis. This is true, but the results from these tests may show the effects of global distributional differences between groups and not necessarily differences in central tendency alone. Boik (1987) showed that when variances are heterogeneous, significance tests that seek differences in central tendency may be confounded by differences in variance. Not only will the probability values for the test be misleading, but the results may not be reflecting the hypotheses that researchers assumed they were testing. In order to pinpoint specific differences, Mielke and Berry (1994) developed tests and computer programs to test for: omnibus combinations of differences in median shifts and variability, variability shifts only, and mean location shifts alone. In other words, although randomization tests for differences in central tendency can be used with distributions of any shape, the two (or more) treatment conditions being compared must have the *same* shape and variance. Similarly, if one wanted to test for variability differences, the distributions should have the same central tendency.

Random Assignment of Treatments. Parametric statistical tests such as *t*-tests and *F*-ratios assume that subjects are selected from the population at random and that subjects are randomly assigned to treatments. In single-case research, it would be unlikely to assume that a clinical client had been randomly selected from the general population or that the observations on that client were randomly selected from the population of observations on that client. However, Edgington (1973) contended that randomization tests for single-case research assume that treatment conditions are assigned to observations at random. Edgington's rationale was that when the order of treatments is randomized over observations, the differences among treatments cannot simply be attributed to history or to maturation effects. Let us imagine two versions of an experimental design that contrast a treatment condition with a control condition within a single subject. In the first version, in which we have nonrandom assignment, all of the control trials were conducted in Sessions 1–5 and all of the experimental treatments were applied in Sessions 6–10. Even if a randomization test showed a statistically significant result in which the mean performance in the treatment condition exceeded the mean performance of the control condition, the validity of our conclusions would be limited. For example, there is the possibility that the subject had a warm-up effect, a habituation or a fatigue effect, or another temporally related effect that was unrelated to the intervention, per se.

To control for unwanted temporal variation we could follow a strict randomization plan for assigning treatments to observation times. For example, we might assign the control treatments at Sessions 2, 3, 7, 9, and 10 and the experimental treatments at Sessions 1, 4, 5, 6, and 8. In this way, we have produced a nonsystematic sequence of control and treatment trials and we would be less likely to conclude that treatment differences were confounded by practice or fatigue artifacts.

One might question Edgington's requirement of random treatment assignment. Of course, it is true that the internal validity of the experiment, that is, the ability to draw causal inferences, may be compromised by nonrandom assignment. It is also true that, under any circumstance, it would be difficult to generalize from the single case to a larger population of individuals. However, the mathematical values of the test will be the same whether the assignment to treatments is random or nonrandom.

Freedom From the Effects of Autocorrelated Residuals. At first glance it seems that, with their relative freedom from restrictions of distributional forms and random selection, randomization tests might also be free from assumptions about autocorrelated errors. However, this might not be the case. In his book, *Permutation Tests*, Good (1994) stated that "All hypothesis-testing methods rely on the independence and/or exchangeability of the observations" (p. 149). Preliminary simulation studies by the present authors (Allison, Faith, & Gorman, 1995) strongly suggested that, as in their parametric counterparts (see Phillips, 1993), true significance probability values are *underestimated* for positive autocorrelated residuals. That is, a researcher might be led to believe that a test was significant at the .05 level when, in fact, it was significant at the .10 (or higher) level.

The opposite effect occurs in the presence of negatively autocorrelated residuals, in which the obtained significance values are *overestimates* of the true values. That is, the result may be too conservative. The authors created random A-B data sets in which the first *N* observations were assigned to treatment A and the last *N* points were assigned to treatment B. Sample sizes were varied from four to six per group and positive lag-1 residual autocorrelations were varied systematically from 0.0 to .90. It was found that the greater magnitude of positive lag-1 correlations, the greater the Type-I error rate. Surprisingly, it was also found that for A-B designs, the larger the sample size, the *greater* the effects of autocorrelations. When autocorrelations were .20 or less, Type I error rates remained at less than .07. By repeating the previous analyses with an alternating treatment design in which *N**2 observations were assigned at random to either treatment A or B, it was also found that autocorrelation increased the Type-I error rate but to a smaller degree than in the A-B design. Unlike the A-B design, the Type-I error rate for the alternating treatment plan *decreased* as sample size increased for a given level of autocorrelation. It appears that in the alternating treatments design with autocorrelations of .30 or less, the Type-I error rate will be less than .07.

The present authors are attempting to tabulate actual and nominal Type-I error rates for a wider variety of combinations of sample sizes and degrees of autocorrelation. Once tables, graphs, or formulas are developed, researchers should be able to correct significance values to be more in line with actual values. Until such time, we can offer some suggestions. One possibility would be to reduce the likelihood of autocorrelation by random assignment of treatments to observation periods—perhaps by using an alternating treatment design. With no apparent pattern, there is a smaller likelihood of serial correlation. Another possibility lies in using larger sample sizes for alternating treatment designs. Yet another tactic might be to choose a conservative significance level, say .01 rather than .05, to offset the inflation of Type-I error rates by positive autocorrelations.

Relaxation of Assumptions and Extensions of Randomization Tests

Although both elegant and desirable, pure random assignments of treatments may not be feasible in many clinical situations. For example, clinicians might only wish to intervene when they can be ensured that baseline behaviors have reached stable levels. They may want to prolong treatment phases for additional observations to maximize a therapeutic effect. Although scientifically desirable, many practitioners believe it may be unethical to return patients to a control condition once improvement seems evident. In an alternating treatment design, in which a Treatment Phase A might alternate with a Treatment Phase B, pure random assignment might produce sequences in which too many Phase A treatments precede or follow B treatments and, thus, produce undesirable carryover effects. Strategies that relax some rigorous demands of strict random assignment were discussed by Edgington (1987, 1993), Ferron (1992), Ferron and Ware (1994), Marascuilo and Busk (1988), and Onghena and Edgington (1994). In these more flexible strategies, investigators can randomly assign the *start* of the treatment phase *after* a stable baseline has been established. For example, suppose that we have 15 observations and we wish to have at least 5 control observations at the beginning of the experiment and 5 treatment observations at the end of the experiment. Therefore, we reserve Observations 1–5 for the control phase, and Observations 11–15 for the treatment phase. We then randomly select the start of the treatment phase at a point in the interval of Observations 6 through 10. If the start was at Observation 8, we would contrast seven successive observations of the control condition A and 8 successive observations of the treatment condition B.

Edgington and others (e.g., Ferron & Ware, 1994; Onghena, 1992; Oghena & Edgington, 1994) extended the use of randomization tests to designs such as ABA designs, ABAB designs, and multiple baseline designs. An especially noteworthy variation can be seen in randomized analysis of covariance in which observation position serves as a covariate and, thus, controls for simple trend effects. Levin, Marascuilo, and Hubert (1978) and Good (1994) also demonstrated that focussed randomization test analyses will be more powerful than general ones. That is, if the researcher can make a priori statements about both the direction of differences and the patterns of differences, then very powerful tests can be constructed. For example, Edgington and Khuller (1992) developed techniques that test for trend effects if the form of the trend has been specified beforehand.

Software for Randomization Tests

In the past, researchers found randomization tests to be appealing. However, the lack of computer resources limited the use of these tests. Today, it is quite possible to carry out these tests on desktop computers with software developed by Cytel, Inc. (1989), Edgington (1987), Hooton (1991), Manly (1991, 1993), and Simon and Bruce (1991). Listings of SAS (1990) programs for computing randomization tests can be found in Ferron and Ware (1994) and Chen and Dunlap (1993). Onghena and Van Damme (1994) developed a special-purpose program SCRT (single-case randomization tests) that analyzes single-case designs and stores individual-case results for further meta-analyses. For those interested in bootstrapping, the SIMSTAT program package (Peladeau, 1994) can produce bootstrap analyses for differences among means, t-test values, and single-factor ANOVAs.

TIME-SERIES EXPERIMENTAL DESIGNS

If the appropriate assumptions can be met, nontime-series analyses, such as those discussed previously, can be used to test mean differences among treatments. However, these analysis methods typically ignore the important fact that changes in behavior are occurring within a dynamic, temporal sequence. For example, mean levels may change abruptly after an intervention and remain at new, permanent levels. Alternatively, a behavior may change immediately after an intervention but then return quickly to preintervention levels. Furthermore, one might consider the possibility that trends within treatment phases may be changing. If we are interested in more than differences in mean performance levels between treatments and we wish to examine dynamic change processes, then a time-series analysis strategy may be preferable.

Characteristics of Time Series

A time series is a mathematical function of the values of observations over time. Time series may vary in four fundamental ways: in trend, in periodicity, in level, and in variability.

Trend

A *trend* is defined as a systematic increase or decrease of observation values over time. Series A displays a positive trend; Series C displays a negative trend, and Series B displays a flat series lacking a trend (see Fig. 6.3).

Periodicity

Periodicity is a pattern of regular, rhythmic, or cyclic fluctuation of values over time. The periodicity of a time series can be defined in two ways: by frequency or by period length. *Frequency* describes periodicity as the number of full cycles per unit time. For example, a series may be described as 10 per day if 10 full cycles were completed within a given day. Periodicity can also be defined by period length, the time that it takes to complete one full cycle. Thus, a series might have a period of 7 days if a complete cycle is completed in one week. Frequency is the reciprocal of period, and vice versa. Figure 6.4 displays two series that differ in their frequencies. Series B has a low frequency and, thus, a long period length, whereas Series A shows a high frequency and small period length. It is possible for a time series to contain several frequency components. In order to assess the relative contributions of each frequency component, a series of techniques collectively known as *Fourier analysis* or *spectral decomposition* (Kendall & Ord, 1990) can be used. For

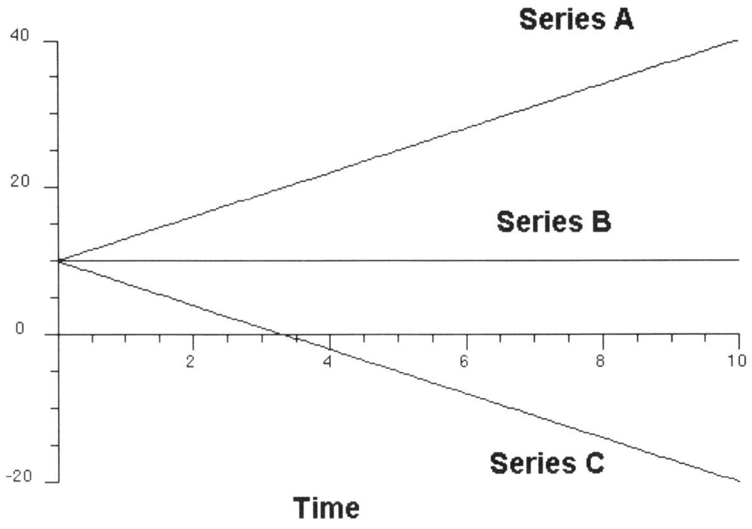

FIG. 6.3. Two series differing in trend.

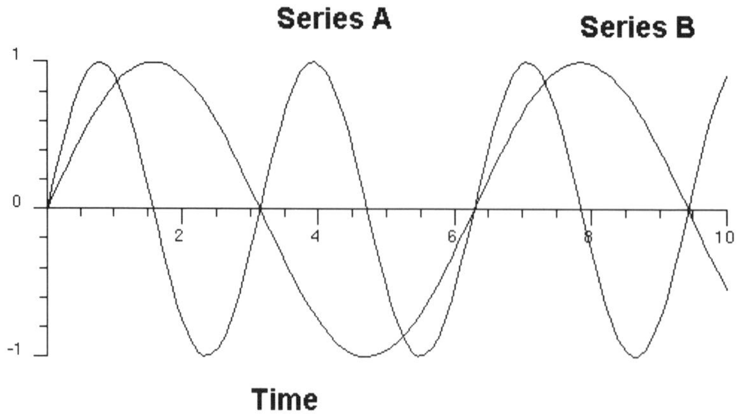

FIG. 6.4. Three series differing in frequency.

example, Fourier analysis of measures of a person's activity level over a long time span might show evidence of a complex combination of rhythms such as several 90-minute cycles, a daily rhythm, a weekly rhythm, and seasonal rhythm.

Level is assessed by the mean value of a series over a given length of time. Figure 6.5 shows two time series that have the same trends but different levels.

Variability

Variability refers to deviations of scores around the mean level of the series. Figure 6.6 displays two series that have the same mean level but differ in variability. In general, most time series will show variations in trend, frequency, level, and variability.

Ordinary Least-Squares Regression Discontinuity Approaches

Time-series intervention designs had their origins in the creative innovations in quasi-experimental designs developed by Campbell (1963) and his colleagues (Cook & Campbell, 1979). Accompanying analyses typically attempt to build an accurate descriptive model of a time series during a baseline period. Then, one or more interventions are attempted and systematic changes from the baseline model are assessed. The rationale for this strategy lies in the premise that if an adequate descriptive model of the baseline time series in Phase A has been built, then it can be assumed that, given no systematic intervention, the series should continue indefinitely. However, given an intervention, the series might

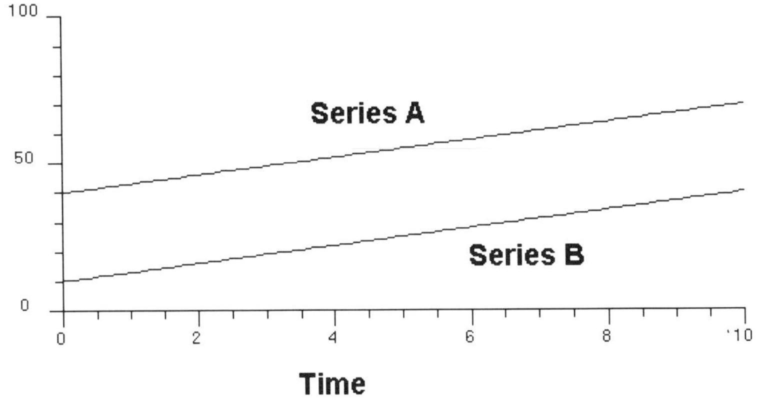

FIG. 6.5. Two series differing in level.

change in trend, level, periodicity, or any combination of these factors. It was hoped that these designs could be assessed by ordinary least-squares methods such as multiple linear regression analysis. However, as we will see, there are problems with such an approach.

Figure 6.7 and Table 6.3 contain data for an interrupted time series. The first 20 observations are in the Baseline Phase (A) and the second 20 observations are in Treatment Phase (B).

Simple Regression Models

Consider some simple models for assessing individual change with ordinary linear least-squares regression models. The first model we look at is:

$$Y_t = b_o + b_1X_t + e_t \tag{6.4}$$

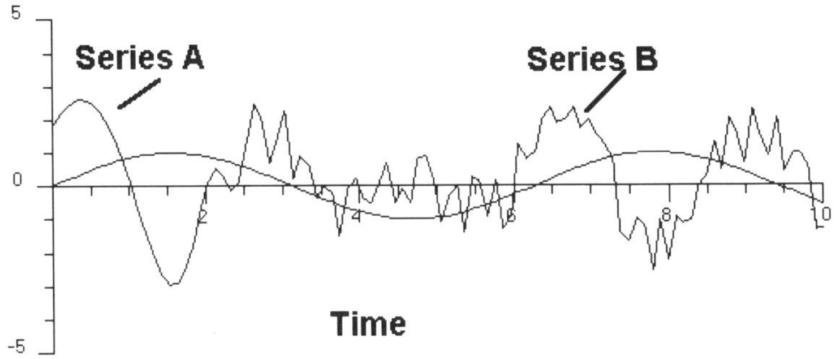

FIG. 6.6. Two series differing in variability.

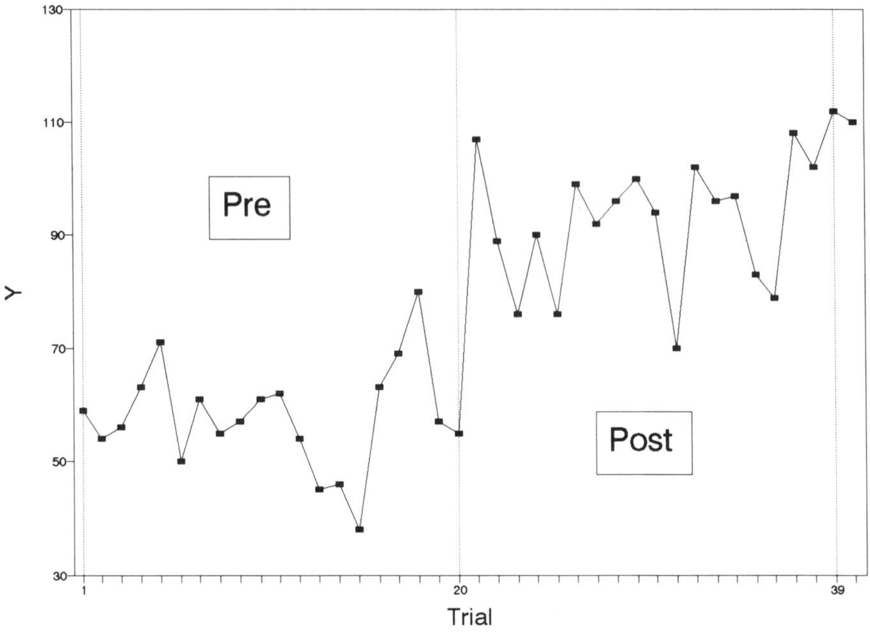

FIG. 6.7. Interrupted time series.

treatment y_t is the value of the dependent variable at time t, and x_t is a dichotomous (dummy) variable that takes on the values zero during the baseline phase and 1.0 during the postintervention phase. The term e_t is a residual error component. An overall significance test for this model would provide the same information as a simple t-test. The intercept, b_0, is the baseline mean, and the value of b_1 will be the deviation of the treatment mean from the baseline mean. The regression formula for the data in Table 6.3 was Y = 57.80 + 36.1X. Thus, the baseline mean is 57.80 and the treatment mean was 36.1 units above the baseline mean. The F-ratio for the regression weight b_1 was 111.11 (df = 1,38, $p < .0001$). Although the model can detect shifts in series level, it is incapable of detecting shifts in a trend from baseline to intervention. If a trend was present in either phase, this model would be confounded by trend effects.

Another simple model might be:

$$Y_t = b_0 + b_1 t + e_t \tag{6.5}$$

In this model, t is a time period. The model describes the time series as a single series with an unvarying linear trend. In this model, b_0 is an intercept term and b_1 is the slope of the trend line. For the data shown in

Table 6.3, the regression formula was $Y = 46.104 + 1.45t$. The F-ratio for the regression weight for trend was statistically significant [$F(1,38) = 68.15$, $p < .0001$], attesting to a general upward trend from the beginning to the end of the series. Although describing an overall trend, this model ignores any shifts in level or trend that may be due to intervention effects.

We can combine the two basic models just described, one that examines changes in level but ignores slope and one that ignores level changes to form more complex models. For example, the model

$$y_t = b_0 + b_1 t + b_2 x_t + e_t \tag{6.6}$$

describes a slope, b_1, that does not vary through the entire series; a shift in levels from baseline to intervention, b_2; and an intercept term, b_0, representing the baseline mean (Gorsuch, 1983). For the present data set, the equation was $Y = 53.73 + .38t + 28.34X$. The F-ratio for X, the term for shift was statistically significant [$F(1,37) = 14.42$; $p < .001$], but the F-ratio for the trend effect, t, was nonsignificant. Although captur-

TABLE 6.3
Sample Data Set for an Interrupted Time-Series Analysis

Phase 1		*Phase 2*	
Observation	*Y*	*Observation*	*Y*
1	59	21	107
2	54	22	89
3	56	23	76
4	63	24	90
5	71	25	76
6	50	26	99
7	61	27	92
8	55	28	96
9	57	29	100
10	61	30	94
11	62	31	70
12	54	32	102
13	45	33	96
14	46	34	97
15	38	35	83
16	63	36	79
17	69	37	108
18	80	38	102
19	57	39	112
20	55	40	110

ing trend and level effects, this model ignores the opportunity to detect trend shifts between phases.

Although they did not plan to use it as an analytic model but, rather, as an effect-size index, Center, Skiba, and Casey (1985–1986) proposed a comprehensive approach in the spirit of analysis of covariance that assesses shifts in level and shifts in slopes between phases. Later, Berry and Lewis-Beck (1986) proposed the model as a data analysis strategy. In this model:

$$Y_t = b_0 + b_1 t + b_2 x_t + b_3 x_t t + e_t \tag{6.7}$$

As before, b_0 is the baseline mean, b_1 is a trend effect for the entire series, and b_2 would indicate the shift in level between phases. The additional term in this model, b_3, would detect a phase by treatment interaction, indicating that slopes differed from one phase to another.

The term $X_t t$ is problematic. At first glance, it would appear that the formula would simply be the product of the dummy code, X, and the value of corresponding time period, t. However, in Berry and Lewis-Beck's (1986) chapter, the term is coded as 0 for all baseline observations and $(t - (n1)X)$, where $n1$ is the number of observations in the baseline phase, for phase 2 observations. In a recent paper by Huitema, McKean, and McKnight (1994), the term is coded 0 for all baseline observations and $(t - (n1 + 1)X)$ for all phase 2 observations. All three codings of the $X_t T$ term provide the same squared multiple correlation coefficient (R^2 = .77) and the same values for the intercept (57.3737), the trend term (.0406), and the trend by time period interaction term (.6947). However, the codings give different values for the level shift term, X. For the simple product coding, the value is 14.10 and it is statistically nonsignificant [$F(1,36) = 1.41$, $p = .243$]. In the coding used by Berry and Lewis-Beck, the level shift term is 27.99 and statistically significant [$F(1,36) = 17.15$, $p = .002$].

Finally, in Huitema et al.'s coding scheme, the value of the level shift term is 28.69 and statistically significant [$F(1,36) = 18.014$, $p < .0001$]. The simple product of an intervention by time period does not seem adequate as a term for detecting shifts in slopes. For one, it seems to underestimate changes in level. For another, in this coding scheme, the product of time by an intervention dummy variable is more highly correlated with the other predictors (level and time) than are Berry and Lewis-Beck's coding or Huitema's coding scheme. The resulting condition, known as *multicollinearity*, will typically provide misleading values of both the regression coefficients and their significance tests.

In an attempt to create effect size measures for further meta-analyses, Allison and Gorman (1993) built on the approach advocated by Berry and Lewis-Beck (1986) and Center et al. (1985–86). Allison and Gorman

(1993) developed a two-stage approach that begins by fitting the baseline series alone using Equation 6.5, the simple trend equation. The resulting baseline equation is then projected into both the baseline and the postintervention phases. Residuals between the original series and the baseline projections for both the baseline and postintervention phases are obtained in order to form a time series consisting of residualized values. These residuals will have values that are independent of effects predicted by the baseline alone. Then, Equation 6.7 is applied to the *residual* series (see Faith, Allison, & Gorman, chap. 8, this volume, for details). The rationale for this procedure is that if the baseline series were to continue indefinitely, then postintervention observations should also be predicted well by the baseline formula. However, with an effective intervention, the postintervention scores might deviate markedly in level and/or slope from projections based on the baseline series alone, as indicated by large residual values.

There is an additional advantage to examining an initial baseline-only regression strategy. It is well known that ordinary least-squares regression analyses can be badly distorted by the presence of even a single outlier value (Chatterjee & Yilmaz, 1992). By performing preliminary analyses of the baseline series and inspecting it for outliers, we can decide whether to use an ordinary least-squares fit or to choose alternative approaches for fitting baselines. For example, we might choose robust regression methods such as the methods developed by Mosteller and Tukey (1977) or the least median of squares (LSMVE) method developed by Rousseau and Leroy (1987). When outliers are present, these robust methods give smaller weights to extreme values and fit more realistic regression lines to the baseline. Although cruder, the split middle line (Kazdin, 1976) or the "celeration line" (Bloom & Fischer, 1982) can also be used to fit outlier-resistant lines through the baseline series.

As we have seen in previous sections of this chapter, no statistical procedure is free from assumptions and restrictions. Least-squares methods are based on several strong assumptions. Researchers who plan to use least-squares should be aware of methods for detecting potential assumption violations. The next section discusses these assumptions and provide methods for detecting assumption violations.

Assumptions of Ordinary Least-Squares Regression. Least-squares methods assume that the residual errors are random, uncorrelated, normally distributed, and have constant variances (Fox, 1991). Perhaps the easiest assumption to check is that of normally distributed residuals. Once residuals from least-squares method are obtained, one could obtain histograms or normal probability plots of the residuals and examine them for departures from normality. For example, in Fig. 6.8,

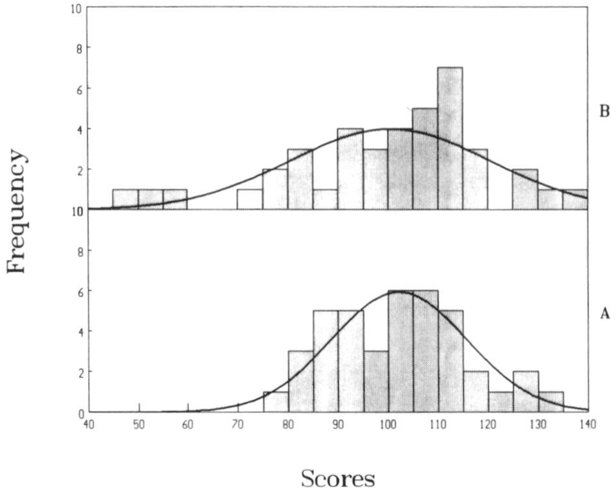

FIG. 6.8. Frequency distributions and departures from normality.

Series A is not perfectly normal, but its distribution is closer to that of a superimposed normal curve based on the same mean and standard deviation than is Series B, which shows highly negative skewness. Many computer programs provide histograms with superimposed normal curves. Alternatively, one might use a normal probability plot to examine departures from normality. Precise statistical tests of departure from normality, like the Wilk-Shapiro test, Lilliefor's test, or Pearson-D'Agostino's omnibus test for normality could be used (D'Agostino, Belanger, & D'Agostino, 1990). All these tests can be performed by Dallal's program ODDJOB (Dallal, 1989). The Pearson-D'Agostino tests, the Kolmogorov-Smirnoff tests, and procedures for transforming distributions to normality can be obtained from the program, UNICORN (Allison, Gorman, & Kucera, 1995).

Ordinary least-squares methods assume that residuals are independent. Because single-case time series come from repeated measures within the same subjects, this assumption is questionable. As we have seen in previous discussions of *t*-test and ANOVA models for assessing changes in level, the error terms for the significance tests of regression weights will be artificially reduced when errors are positively autocorrelated, and will be inflated when the errors are negatively correlated. Although the regression coefficients themselves are unbiased, the significance tests for them may be systematically biased by autocorrelation.

Researchers who plan to use these least-squares methods should examine the patterns of autocorrelations among the residuals to investigate whether assumptions have been violated (Gorsuch, 1983). Fortunately, many modern computer programs can calculate autocorrelations, and most multiple regression programs can compute the Durbin-Watson statistic (Durbin & Watson, 1950), which assesses the presence of first-order autocorrelated residuals. Cromwell, Labys, and Terraza (1994) provided a synopsis of modern quantitative methods for detecting autocorrelated residuals, and Matyas and Greenwood (chap. 7, this volume) offer a full discussion of the implications of autocorrelation. In any case, the presence of autocorrelations should alert users to adopt statistical methods other than ordinary least squares.

Jaccard and Wan (1993) provided some excellent advice on the topic of autocorrelated residuals: "The task of the experimenter is to determine the nature of the dependency in the residuals and to formally remove the dependency from them, creating a new set of residuals that are independent of one another" (p. 44). Gorsuch (1983) noted that the magnitude of autocorrelations in the original time series does not necessarily present a problem. Rather, it is the presence of autocorrelated residuals that causes problems. It is likely that autocorrelated data will produce autocorrelated residuals, but this is not always true. Sometimes, the addition of new variables will substantially reduce the autocorrelations among residuals. For example, one might define a variable that captures the serial dependency and then include that variable in the regression equation. Accurate inferential tests may be possible when the effects of residual autocorrelations are removed. As we explore later, one can apply statistical methods that provide parameter estimates and unbiased standard errors that explicitly consider serial dependency.

Ordinary least squares regression assumes homoscedasticity of residuals. Loosely speaking, this assumption states that the variability of errors of prediction at one point in a time series should be the same as those at other points in the series. More formally, it means that $\sigma_i^2 | X_i$ is constant for all X_i. In some situations, however, subjects may systematically show more or less variability during postintervention than in the baseline period. There are several ways to assess homoscedasticity. One strategy would be to examine plots of residuals in temporal order over the time series. A homosecedastic series should show a uniform spread of residual values around the regression line. If residuals fan out or bulge more at some points in the series than at others, then homoscedasticity is unlikely. Another way to detect heteroscedasticity might be to correlate the absolute values of the residuals, e_i with t_i, the corresponding time periods in which they were obtained. In a homosecedastic series, the magnitude of residuals should not be correlated with their position. Therefore, either a significant positive or a significant negative correlation would indicate a violation of this assumption. More elaborate tests of homoscedasticity, such as Goldfield-Quandt Test (1965), and modified least-squares methods for evaluating heteroscedastic models can be found in Fox (1991), Seber and Wild (1989), Neter, Wasserman, and Kutner (1989), and Judge, Griffiths, Hill, Lütkepohl, and Lee (1985).

The Usefulness of Least-Squares Methods

If their assumptions are met, least-squares methods such as those mentioned previously offer attractive advantages. For one, time-series models can be assessed with multiple regression routines contained in any major statistical computer program or computer spreadsheet. For another, nonlinear effects can be included in the models by transforming variables with power, logarithmic, or trigonometric functions. However, the convenience of ordinary least-squares models may be outweighed by strict assumption requirements.

Modified Least-Squares Methods

Ordinary least-squares methods require researchers to confront some very strict assumptions. Some modifications of these methods, known as *generalized least-square methods,* may enable researchers to meet these assumptions because they can build complex regression models that incorporate autocorrelation and heteroscedasticity effects.

Generalized Least Squares Analyses

The Hildreth-Lu method (Ostrom, 1978) attempts to control autocorrelation effects by incorporating them into the time-series regression equations. In this method, one estimates lag-1 residuals at time period t, $Y_t - \rho Y_{t-1}$, as a function of both an independent variable, X_t, and an autocorrelation component, p. Therefore, the estimation equation is:

$$y_t - \rho_{t-1} = b_0(1 - \rho) + b_1(X_t - \rho X_{t-1}) + e_t \tag{6.8}$$

X can be a dummy variable that might take on the values of 0 for baseline observations and 1 for postintervention observations. As ρ generally is unknown, one estimates an initial value of ρ and then iteratively tries different values of ρ to obtain the smallest residual sum of squares and, thus, the maximum effect size. Once an optimal value of ρ is found, an equation with a new slope, b_1, and a new intercept term, b_0, is formed. The value of b_0 will indicate the number of units by which the mean of the postintervention series differs from that of the baseline. A significance test of b_0 will establish whether X bears any significant relationship to the predicted values of the dependent variable. If needed, Y_t can be found by a simple rearrangement of the formula described previously. If the assumption that only a lag-1 autocorrelation of residuals process is valid, then the residuals from this procedure should not display any significant autocorrelations.

Cochrane and Orcutt (1949; see Ostrom, 1978) and Prais and Winsten (Judge et. al, 1985) developed similar approaches that estimate the values of ρ from the autocorrelation coefficients of residuals of series of iterations of the original regression equation. There are also methods (e.g., Durbin, 1960; Huitema, McKean, & McKnight, 1994) that find the optimum value of ρ by iterative estimation. Major computer programs, such as SPSS' AREG procedure in the TRENDS programs (SPSS, 1990) and SAS's (1994) AUTOREG, can compute generalized least-squares solutions with lag-1 autocorrelated residuals. The results of the Hildreth-Lu, Cochrane-Orcutt, Prais-Winsten, and maximum likelihood methods will usually be similar. Huitema, McKean, and McKnight (1994), however, showed that when sample sizes are small (e.g., $N \leq 30$), these methods may be more biased by autocorrelation than ordinary least-squares methods. As expected, with large sample sizes ($N > 50$) and with intermediate to large amounts of autocorrelation ($r > .30$), these generalized least squares methods are less biased than are ordinary least squares. Huitema, McKean, and McKnight (1994) developed an iterative maximum likelihood method that appears to provide fewer biased results than either ordinary or generalized least squares methods. Thus, if appropriate caution is exercised, these methods may be very useful for exploring simple A-B intervention designs when the researcher has evidence for a simple lag-1 autocorrelation process.

A Generalized Least-Squares Example

As an example of a generalized least-squares analysis, we use a 40-observation series shown in Table 6.3 and Fig. 6.7, in which the first 20 observations are preintervention scores and the remaining 40 observations are postintervention scores.

A maximum-likelihood analysis of this series produced the equation

$$Y_t = 45.49 + 36.79(X_t - .21X_{t-1}) + .21Y_{t-1} + e_t$$

where X is a dummy variable that takes the value of 0 for preintervention and 1 for postintervention. The model fit well ($p < .001$) and the residual series displayed no systematic pattern of autocorrelation or trend. It should be noted that the value of p, the autocorrelation component, was .21 and was not statistically significant but was used for illustration purposes.

Multiphase and Piecewise Regression

Although they are rarely used in the behavioral sciences, there are regression methods known as *piecewise regression models* (Ertel & Fowlkes, 1976), *multiphase regression models* (Hinkley, 1971), or *spline regression models* (Seber & Wild, 1989) that attempt to fit an equation composed of two or more straight lines so that:

$$Y_t = a + b_1(t - c) \text{ when } t > c \tag{6.9}$$

and

$$Y_t = a + b_0(t - c) \text{ when } t \leq c \tag{6.10}$$

In these equations, t is a point along a time continuum and c is a cutoff point on the time continuum. The terms b_0 and b_1 refer to the slopes of the regression lines before and after point c, respectively. Computer programs that carry out this procedure (e.g., Dallal's ODDJOB, 1989; NCSS, Inc.'s CURVEFITTER, 1992) obtain c, b_0 and b_1 and establish the confidence limits for these parameters. The programs also test for differences between the two slopes. It would seem that if the values of slopes were significantly different and if the confidence limits of c included the observation at which intervention occurred, then it could be concluded that a time series had shifted in slope after an intervention point. In the experience of the authors, however, we often found that the values of c obtained from the programs were far from our planned intervention point. For example, using the data set in Table 6.3, the TWO-PHASE procedure in Dallal's (1989) ODDJOB program gave $Y = -.193t + 59.68$ for $t < 13$ and $y = 1.95t + 31.76$ for $t \geq 13$. As the turning point, c, at observation $t = 13$ was further from the actual intervention point at observation 20, we were not satisfied with this outcome. Perhaps the problem lies in the sensitivity of ordinary least-squares methods to outliers. Readers who wish to explore the possibility of using these models should consult Seber and Wild (1989). Alternatively, one might wish to first set the value of c and then compute the previous equations. Finally, the researcher will attempt to establish the goodness of fit of these equations and examine the residuals for autocorrelation.

Box-Jenkins ARIMA Models

Given the challenges of conducting ordinary least-squares analyses, one might wish to have statistical methods besides generalized least-squares approaches that can account for autocorrelated errors. Fortunately, the Box-Jenkins autoregressive integrated moving average (ARIMA) models (Box & Jenkins, 1976; Box & Tiao, 1975) can analyze very complex time series sets if sufficient numbers of data points are available.

The Basic ARIMA Model

The basic Box-Jenkins (1976) ARIMA model is a regressionlike approach that states that a given observation, Y_t, at time t is a function of the values of previous observations and the accumulation and retention of residual errors. This approach combines several techniques discussed in previous sections of this chapter and book, such as building equations with autoregressive terms, differencing values, and modeling residuals. Because several major processes are included in one model, the procedure is known as an autoregressive integrated moving average (ARIMA) approach. By modeling residuals into the equations, many problems that plague ordinary least-squares methods can be reduced. The basic formula for ARIMA models is:

$$Y_t = \phi_1 Y_{t-1} + \phi_2 Y_{t-2} \ldots - \theta_1 e_{t-1} - \theta_2 e_{t-2} \ldots - \theta_q e_{t-q} + c \quad (6.11)$$

Autoregressive Terms. The first components in these equations are the autoregressive terms (AR), phi (ϕ), which state that a given observation can be predicted from past observations, so that:

$$Y_t = \phi_1 Y_{t-1} + \phi_2 Y_{t-2} \ldots \phi_p Y_{t-p} + c \quad (6.12)$$

The values of phi vary between 0 and 1. There may be no phi coefficients in the model at all. However, if the model requires them, there may be as many as p different phi coefficients, where p is the number of lagged terms that the researcher will assess. The phi coefficients are regression weights that account for autoregression up to p units behind the present observation.

Moving Average Terms. The next components are the moving average (MA) components, theta (θ), so that:

$$Y_t = -\theta_1 e_{t-1} - \theta_2 e_{t-2} \ldots - \theta_q e_{t-q} + c \quad (6.13)$$

Moving average parameters are somewhat more difficult to describe than are the autoregressive parameters. They can be considered as coefficients that represent the degree to which the errors or residuals, e, linger in the series and are "remembered" by the series to create a lagged influence. Some time series "drain off" or dissipate their residuals rapidly. Therefore, their theta terms may be small or nonexistent. However, some series have large theta terms because residual errors that linger for awhile will influence subsequent observations. There may be as few as zero theta coefficients or as many as q theta coefficients, where q is the number of moving average lags.

Stationarity

Box-Jenkins ARIMA models assume that time series are "stationary." That is, a time series itself should have the same mean level and the same variability around the mean level throughout the entire time series. This means that a series that displays a systematic trend or that has different variances along the series would be unacceptable for analysis unless it were transformed to stationarity. In order to remove a trend component, ARIMA practitioners often apply a technique known as *differencing*, in which each of the original series values, Y_t, is transformed to a "differenced series," BY_t, by substituting the differences between successive observations for original series values so that: $BY_t = Y_t - Y_{t-1}$. For example, given the ordered series: $Y = 1, 2, 3, 4, 5$ with an obviously rising trend, the differenced series BY becomes $(2 - 1)$, $(3 - 2)$, $(4 - 3)$, and $(5 - 4)$, or 1,1,1,1. Notice that when we use differencing we lose one data point from the previous series. Also, notice that the differenced series has all trends removed and the mean of the series, in the present example, is 1.0. We used one differencing operation in this example. However, if we wished to do so, we could also difference the transformed series. Although one differencing operation is usually sufficient, as many as d differencing operations may be needed. For example, $d = 2$ means that we would difference the first differences. Although differencing is usually adequate for reducing trends, we could also "detrend" a series with a least-squares regression approach in which we find the residuals of an equation that predicted a given observation from observations up to k lags behind. In order to reduce variability around the mean values, practitioners may choose some variance-stabilizing transformation, such as using logarithms or exponents of the original data (Box & Jenkins, 1976).

To summarize, the Box-Jenkins ARIMA model states that any stationary time series can be described by up to p autoregressive terms, d differencing operations, and q moving average terms. If necessary, a nonstationary series may be transformed to a stationary series by up to d differencing operations. The usual notation for describing Box-Jenkins model is ARIMA(p,d,q), where p = the number of autoregressive (AR) terms, d = the number of differencing operations, and q = the number of moving average (MA) terms. A researcher might want to describe a time series as an ARIMA(1,0,1) model or an ARIMA(2,1,2), model, and so on.

Model Identification

Potentially, there are an infinite number of ARIMA models that could be picked for a time series. Only a few of them, however, might adequately fit the data set at hand. At this point, one might wonder how one chooses an accurate ARIMA model. Fortunately, only a few models are usually appropriate. Our task will be to pick a model that has an optimal combination of p, d, and q components so that the residuals from the model will both be small and will show no systematic temporal patterns. That is, we have to say something like "Fit an ARIMA(1,1,1) model." That is, we fit a model with one autoregressive parameter, one differencing term, and one moving average term. Hopefully, the residuals from the model will be small and nonsystematic. Another way of saying this is to say that if we are fortunate, then the model for our series has been "identified" and we have "filtered out" the autoregressive, trend, and moving average components to the point where the remaining series has become random "noise."

Box and Jenkins (1976) provided the major theoretical statements of ARIMA analysis, and Gottman and Glass (1976), Gottman (1981), and McCleary and Hay (1980) made these techniques more accessible to applied researchers. All major statistical program packages have options for ARIMA model fitting, and many specialized computer programs exist for fitting ARIMA and other complex time series models (see Harrop & Velicer, 1990a; Harrop & Velicer, 1990b; and Cromwell, Labys, & Terraza, 1994, for reviews). As a first step in model identification, researchers should plot the time series and examine possible trends and/or uneven variability. Seasonal cycles may also be apparent in the plot. This step will often show that differencing and variance stabilizing transformations will be necessary to create a stationary series. Next, the researcher should obtain the autocorrelation coefficients (ACF) of the series (or differenced series) up to $n/4$ lags behind, where n = the number of data points in the series. In addition, users should obtain partial autocorrelation coefficients up to $n/4$ lags behind. Partial autocorrelation coefficients (PACF) are autocorrelations coefficients between any two time periods, in which the influence of all other time periods has been removed.

One can start to build a preliminary model of the series by examining the patterns of autocorrelation functions and partial autocorrelations. Different patterns of autocorrelation and moving average terms leave their own tell-tale "signatures" in the ACF and PACF plots, much in the way that burning objects leave their particular patterns of spectral bands on the spectroscope. According to McCain and McCleary (1979):

1. If the ACF shows a significant positive peak at lag q and trails off rapidly and/or shows a damped exponential or sine wave and PACF shuts off abruptly, suspect an AR process.
2. If the PACF shows a significant positive peak at lag q and trails off

and shows an exponential or damped sine wave (−) and the ACF is small after lag q, suspect an MA process. (p. 249)

The ACF and PACF functions shown in Fig. 6.9 and 6.10 were obtained from the first 16 lags of the 20 preintervention observations of the series shown in Table 6.3. The ACF plot shows a peak (although nonsignificant) at lag 1 and the beginnings of sine-wave patten at subsequent lags. The PACF shows no significant pattern at any lag. In practice, some time series contain both AR and MA components. Because many series also have seasonal components such as weekly, monthly, or annual cycles, researchers might also examine and consider using seasonal AR, MA, and differencing terms. Attempting the simplest models first is always the best strategy because many time series that appear in behavioral science literature have ps that vary from zero to two, ds that vary from zero to two, and qs between zero and two. Although not necessarily the best model, a reasonable preliminary model for the series shown in Table 6.3 might be ARIMA(1,0,0).

Once a preliminary model is specified, ARIMA programs attempt to fit it. Using the baseline series from Table 6.3, there was a highly significant effect for an autoregressive term [$AR(1) = .92$, $t = 37.54$, $p < .001$]. The standard error for the residuals was 11.2.

The next step in identifying a Box-Jenkins ARIMA analysis will be to assess the fit of the model to the data in order to check if the assump-

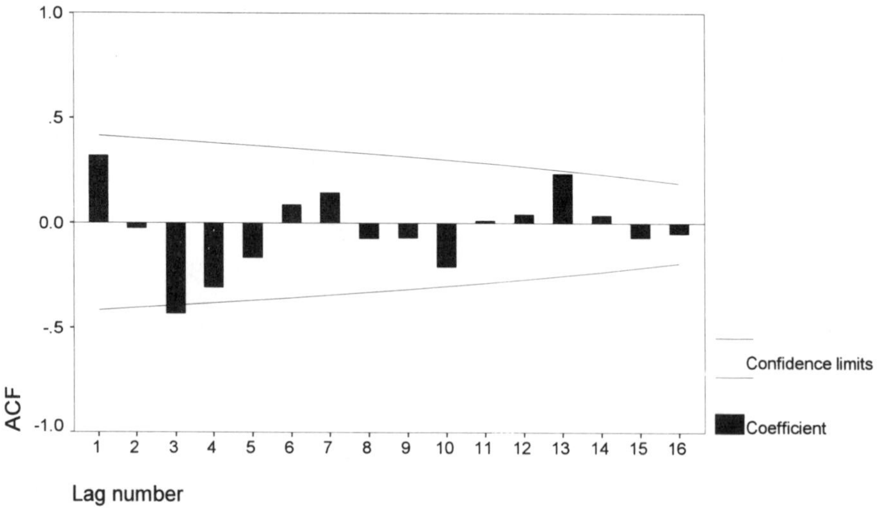

FIG. 6.9. Autocorrelation function for pre-series.

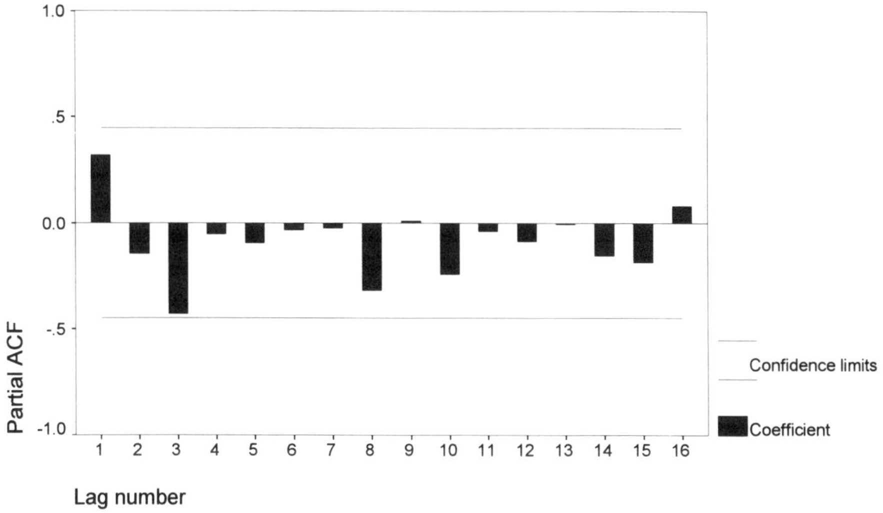

FIG. 6.10. Partial autocorrelation function for pre-series.

tions of ARIMA modeling have been met. Both the AR and MA terms in the model must be within the bounds of 0 to absolute 1.0. In our example, this is true (AR(1)=.92). Hopefully, the model fit the data so well that all that remains in the residual series is random noise. Operationally, this means that the residual series should have mean levels close to zero and small amounts of variance. The residuals should have no significant ACF or PACF patterns. In our example, none of the autocorrelations or partial autocorrelations of residuals from our baseline series was significant at the .10 level or less. Therefore, the initial model of ARIMA(1,0,0) seems plausible.

Intervention Analysis. In order to examine whether a series displays a statistically significant shift after an intervention, we then apply the baseline model to the entire time series and add one or more dummy independent variables to represent the postintervention effects. For example, if we have reason to believe that an intervention effect will be permanent, we could build a "step function" in which a dummy variable would be assigned values of 0 for the baseline phase and 1 for a postintervention phase. If we believe that an intervention had only a short-term effect, we could build a "pulse function" dummy variable in which the value of 1 is assigned for observations shortly after intervention and 0 otherwise. Other weighting schemes could be attempted. Both

BMDP's (1990) 2T program and SPSS's (1990) Box-Jenkins and ARIMA programs can handle models with continuous or dummy independent variables.

An ARIMA Example

Using SPSS's (1990) ARIMA program, the model "ARIMA /VARIABLES Y with X /MODEL (1,0,0) NOCONSTANT," in which X was a step-function dummy variable (0 for Observations 1–20, 1 otherwise) was computed. Both the autoregressive (AR) terms and the effects of X, the intervention variable, were statistically significant, showing that intervention after Observation 20 increased scores and that there was an autoregressive effect. All residual correlations and autocorrelations were small and nonsignificant. The standard error of the residuals, 13.31, was only slightly higher than that of that of the baseline series alone (11.2), again attesting to a good fit. Finally, Fig. 6.11 presents the original series and the model fit by ARIMA. As can be seen, except at the point of intervention, the two series are nearly identical.

Limitations of ARIMA

One typically needs a lengthy series in order to obtain stable ARIMA estimates, but this may be difficult to obtain. For example, some argue that it may be unethical to wait to get baseline data for behaviors that

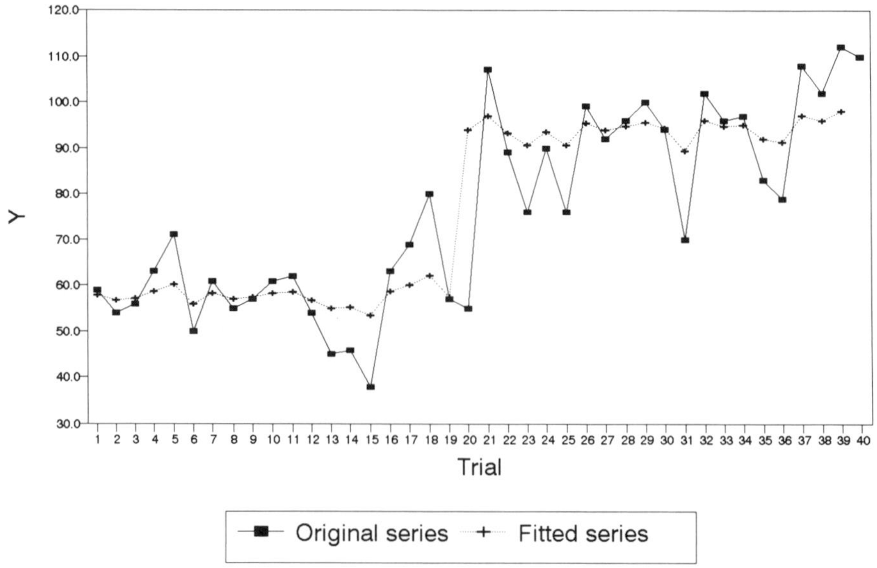

FIG. 6.11. Interrupted time series ARIMA analysis.

may cause harm to self or others. Most applied behavior analytic studies have very few baseline measures and very few postintervention measures (Huitema, 1990; Matyas & Greenwood, 1991; Suen, 1987). The short durations of many projects may limit the use of these powerful methods. Finally, an ARIMA model that adequately fits a time series may not necessarily be the unique, best model, but only one of many plausible models. As sample size increases, it is easier to confirm the adequacy of a model's fit to the data. However, a poor fit may seem acceptable in a short time series because there may be inadequate statistical power to reject the hypothesis of zero residuals.

Although some "expert system" computer programs reduce some of the drudgery of ARIMA analysis by attempting to build plausible models (e.g., see SCITECH, Inc.'s 1995 catalog for advertisements of some current ones: AUTOBOX, Forecast Pro, SmartForecasts). ARIMA analysis is far from an automatic process. Researchers must have some sizable data sets. They must perform extensive checks on the adequacy of both the baseline models and the final fitted baseline-plus-intervention models. Because the requirements for a good ARIMA analysis are so demanding, researchers have sought alternative methods.

ALTERNATIVES TO ARIMA

Overfitting

The tactic of "overfitting" permits researchers to build time-series models without going through the painstaking model identification steps of ARIMA analysis. It is well known that if one includes enough terms, a very irregular time series (or, for that matter, any curve) can be well-fit by complex polynomial equations. For example, we could predict a future value of a time series, Y_{t+1} from past values with an equation such as Equation 6.14:

$$Y_{t+1} = b_1 Y_t + b_2 Y_{t-1} + b_3 Y_{t-2} + \ldots b_m Y_{t-m} + e \qquad (6.14)$$

where t is the present time period and m is the number of lags. In effect, we are saying that we can predict a behavior at a given time if we know nearly everything about past behaviors. It is also a well-established fact that an infinite-length AR series is equivalent to a finite MA series, and vice versa. Glass, Wilson, and Gottman (1978) found that most ARIMA series are simple. They often required one p, one d, or one q parameter or less. Therefore, ARIMA(1,0,0) and ARIMA(1,1,0) models are quite common. If we blindly tried all possible combinations of parameters, even with p, d, and q varying between 0 and 1, there are eight models to be tried and many residual PACF and ACF plots to be examined. However, by taking the nonparsimonious tactic of "overfitting" a time series by including many AR terms (say, up to five) at once, a fairly reasonable "brute force" fit to a data set can be obtained. Methods known as "adaptive filtering" (Trigg & Leach, 1967; Wheelright & Makriadakis, 1973) and the ARAR programs in the interactive time series modeling package, ITSM (Brockwell & Davis, 1991b), can provide forecasts of future time series by using these brute force modeling strategies. Velicer and MacDonald (1984) provided a "general transformation matrix" approach that overfits time interrupted series and circumvents the usual ARIMA model identification stages. The same authors extended their procedure to cross-sectional time-series designs that include multiple subjects (Velicer, 1994; Velicer & McDonald, 1991).

Greenwood and Matyas (1990) and Crosbie (1993) explored the combined effects of autocorrelation, overfitting, and series length and found that in "brief" time series ($n \leq 20$) that overfitting inflated the value of t-tests and F-ratios. However, as large series become longer, especially if the series has 100 observations or more, the effects of overfitting decrease and eventually disappear.

Gottman's ITSE and Crosbie's ITSACORR

ARIMA analyses are mathematically elegant but they require extensive labor and many observations. Least-squares analyses offer computational ease but raise the possibility that statistical tests based on these methods are marred by assumption violations. Clearly, researchers who wish to choose an appropriate time-series method may be faced with a conflict. Fortunately, there are some least-squares methods that combine the best of the ARIMA and regression approaches.

ITSE. Gottman (1981) and Williams and Gottman (1982) developed an approach for the two-phase interrupted time series design that is both rapid and easier to use than ARIMA. Like ARIMA, their interrupted time-series approach (ITSE) uses autocorrelation information, dummy variables, and trend information to analyze an interrupted time series. Unlike ARIMA, the ITSE method uses readily available least-squares methods to assess solutions.

The ITSE Model (Gottman, 1981; Williams & Gottman, 1982) models preintervention data as:

$$Y_t = m_1 t + b_1 + \sum_{1}^{k} a_i y_{t-1} + e_t \qquad (6.15)$$

and models postintervention data as:

$$Y_t = m_2 t + b_2 + \sum_{1}^{k} a_i y_{t-1} + e_t \tag{6.16}$$

In these equations, m_1 and m_2 are the baseline and postintervention slopes, and b_1 and b_2 are baseline and preintervention intercepts. The term a_i represents autocorrelation terms. There may be up to k autocorrelation terms. Gottman and Williams' ITSE program finds the a, b, and m terms and then assesses differences in the preintervention slopes and intercepts. Williams and Gottman (1982) cautioned users that if the sum of autocorrelations exceeds approximately .7, then significance tests and estimates of the regression coefficients might not be accurate. Therefore, researchers who use this approach should probably choose the most parsimonious number of autocorrelation terms, k, and should avoid overfitting. The ITSE program was used to analyze the data in Table 6.3. Using a first-order lag, the program provided the autocorrelation-corrected formula $Y = .069t + 57.052$ for the baseline and $Y = .742t + 86.067$ for the postintervention series. Neither the pre-intervention slope nor the postintervention slope was significantly different from zero. The intercepts were significantly different [$t(34) = 3.62$, $p < .01$] from each other, indicating a shift in level. However, the slopes were not significantly different [$t(34) = 1.1$, $p = .28$].

ITSACORR. Greenwood and Matyas (1990) and Matyas and Greenwood (1991) showed that series length, autocorrelation, and overfitting systematically affect the error terms of t- and F-tests. Crosbie (1993, 1995) developed ITSACORR, a modification of the Gottman and Williams ITSE program, to provide better, less-biased estimates of intervention effects in short series. He noted that the value of the lag-1 autocorrelation is biased by small sample size. Therefore, ITSACORR uses a less-biased estimate of lag-1 autocorrelation and then builds a model similar to an ITSE analysis based on the first-order autocorrelation.

Crosbie (1993, 1995) claimed that statistical power for the ITSACORR model is high for series with as few as 10 observations. Furthermore, resulting t-tests of regression coefficients are less biased for moderate-sized effects. However, he also warned that when a short series ($n < 20$) is combined with a high first-lag autocorrelation ($r > .6$), the test statistics will be inflated. Applying ITSACORR to the data in Table 6.3, the baseline formula was $Y = .057t + 57.06$, and the postintervention formula was $Y = .61t + 88.41$. The intercepts were significantly different [$t(35) = 2.92$, $p < .01$], but the slopes were not significantly different [$t(35) = .60$, $p > .55$].

Dynamic Bayesian Forecasting and State Space Approaches. Interrupted time-series approaches such as the ARIMA approach, ITSE, and ITSACORR assume that the same patterns of autocorrelation and moving average components will be found throughout an entire time series. However, a new technique, dynamic Bayesian forecasting (Pole, West, & Harrison, 1994) permits the slopes and intercepts in a series to change from observation to observation. Consistent with Bayesian statistical analyses, prior forecasts are modified by subsequent information, so that these dynamic procedures "learn" about prior series and adapt their forecasts rapidly. As a result, they can model very complex series. Missing data can easily be accommodated by these procedures because, although missing data will not supply any new information, the procedures can still utilize prior information (albeit, somewhat less accurately). Although the present authors have not yet had extensive opportunities to apply this approach to interrupted time series, it seems promising for producing dynamic forecasts of complex baseline series. Therefore, as in Allison and Gorman's (1993) approach, researchers should be able to project baseline behavior into the postintervention phases and, therefore, analyze a residualized series for shifts in level and slope.

The dynamic Bayesian approach also permits researchers to intervene, so that if they believe that an intervention at a given point should produce a better fit in a series at hand, then this should be reflected in a reduction in residuals in comparison to the residuals for a series that did not account for the intervention.

Haynes, Blaine, and Meyer (1995) introduced psychologists to phase space functions that take into account the value of a variable and its rate of change at any given point in a time series. Although the mathematics underlying phase space analyses differ from dynamic Bayesian analysis, it also seems to provide a valuable means to capture dynamic, complex time series.

Miscellaneous Quasi-Experimental Approaches

Most statistical methods for single-case designs have inherent difficulties, in their restrictions due to autocorrelation, to lack of randomization, or to small sample sizes. Researchers are constantly seeking methods that promise to work with the small samples typically found in clinical practice. Given that some of them have not been fully investigated, we mention a few of them for completeness and suggest that our readers should follow the developing literature that documents their efficacy. Our mention of them should not necessarily be taken as an endorsement.

Tryon's C-Statistic. Tryon's (1982) *C*-statistic (Equation 6.17) is an adaptation of a test known as the *mean-squares successive difference test* (MSD; see vonNeumann, Kent, Bellinson, & Hart, 1941).

$$C = 1 - \frac{\sum_{i=1}^{n-1} (Y_i - Y_{i+1})^2}{2 \sum_{i=1}^{n} (Y_i - \overline{Y})^2} \tag{6.17}$$

In Equation (6.17), Y_i is a score at time i, and n is the total number of time periods. If there is a consistent trend in the data, then the sum of the successive differences in the numerator of the right-side term in the equation will accumulate and the MSD will become large. The standard error of C is:

$$S_e = \sqrt{\frac{n - 2}{(n - 1)(n + 1)}} \tag{6.18}$$

Tryon suggested that users should compute the *C*-value for the baseline series and, hopefully, find that it is insignificant. Then, they should combine the baseline series and the intervention series, obtain the *C*-statistic, and test it for significance. If the combined series has a higher or a lower overall *C*-statistic value than that of the baseline series alone, then a statistically significant *C*-statistic might provide evidence for a shift in level and/or trend.

Blumberg (1984) and Crosbie (1989, 1995) noted several problems with the *C*-statistic. First, the statistic does measure some kind of overall trend in the data series. However, there are many patterns of baseline and postintervention series level and slope changes other than simple trend shifts that can lead to elevated *C*-statistics. Unfortunately, the *C*-statistic is not differentially sensitive to specific kinds of shifts, so that a significant *C*-statistic would only provide an overall measure of nonindependence. Second, the combination of baseline-plus-treatment phases will always have more observations than the baseline series. Therefore, the *C*-statistic will have more power in the longer series and its significance test will be strongly influenced by the number of data points. Crosbie (1989) showed that the *C*-statistic detects lag-1 correlations but not necessarily slope effects. Crosbie (1989) conducted a Monte Carlo study varying slope, autocorrelation, and series length and found that, as in ordinary least-squares and ANOVA results, autocorrelation will inflate the Type-I error rate of the *C*-statistic. Thus, although the *C*-statistic can detect autocorrelation, it seems limited for assessing intervention effects in single-case designs.

Reliable Change Score Indexes

Reliable change indexes (RCIs) bear a close resemblance to *t*-tests and ANOVAs. However, they originated from psychometric rather than from experimental traditions. RCIs attempt to establish whether two or more scores obtained from the same person on two or more occasions can be considered significantly different (Jacobson, Follette, & Revenstorf, 1984). This index and quasi-test is based on the rationale that differences between a subject's scores obtained on two separate occasions should be much greater than score differences due to measurement error. In classical test theory (e.g., Gulliksen, 1950), the standard error of measurement due to unreliability is $s_e = s_x(1 - r_{xx})$, where s_x is the standard deviation of the test and r_{xx} is an estimate of the test's reliability. In Jacobson et. al's (1984) original formulation, r_{xx} was estimated either by coefficient alpha or by measures of rater reliability. The original reliable change index (RCI), shown in Equation 6.19, contrasted preintervention means with postintervention means and used the preintervention standard deviation and an internal consistency reliability estimate. It was assumed that the reliability estimate would be the same for all individuals. The RCI is treated like a standard normal deviate Z-test, so that if the RCI exceeds 1.96, it is significant at the .05 level. If the RCI exceeds 2.58, it is significant at the .01 level, etc. RCIs for individual subjects can be combined in larger meta-analyses.

$$\mathrm{RCI} = \frac{\overline{X}_{pre} - \overline{X}_{post}}{s_{pre}\sqrt{1 - r_{xx}}} \tag{6.19}$$

The original RCI viewed measurement error as caused by a lack of either internal consistency or rater reliability. However, the most important source of measurement error might be attributed to the lack of test–retest reliability. Therefore, an alternative RCI was proposed by Christensen and Mendoza (1986) and later accepted by Jacobson and Truax (1991). In this revised formula (Equation 6.20), r_{xx} is the test–retest reliability, so that their RCI accounts for both pretest and posttest unreliability.

$$\begin{aligned} \mathrm{RCI} &= \frac{\overline{X}_{post} - \overline{X}_{pre}}{s_{diff}} \\ S_{diff} &= \sqrt{2\, s_e^2} \\ s_e &= s_{pre}\sqrt{1 - r_{xx}} \end{aligned} \tag{6.20}$$

Hageman and Arrindell (1993) proposed a more comprehensive reliable change index, $\mathrm{RC}_{\mathrm{id}}$, that attempts to account measurement error due to lack of internal consistency in both the pretest and posttest and to test-retest unreliability. The RC_{id} also compares an individual's change scores to those of a prior norm group. In this index, the preintervention and postintervention means are obtained from an individual subject. The terms M_1 and M_2, however, are the pretest and posttest means of a standardization group. *Se(1)* and *Se(2)* refer to the standard errors of measurement of the pre- and posttests. The terms s_1 and s_2 refer to the standard deviations of pretest and posttest scores and $r_{xx(1)}$ and $r_{xx(2)}$ refer to the internal consistency or rater reliability of pretest and posttest scores. Finally, r_{dd} refers to the reliability of difference scores.

$$RC_{id} = \frac{\overline{X}_{post} - \overline{X}_{pre}\, r_{dd} + (M_2 - M_1)(1 - r_{dd})}{\sqrt{s_{e(1)}^2 + s_{e(2)}^2}}$$

$$r_{dd} = \frac{s_{1_{xx_1}}^2 + S_{2_{xx_2}}^2 - 2s_1 s_2 r_{12}}{s_1^2 + s_2^2 + 2s_1 s_2 r_{12}} \tag{6.21}$$

Yarnold (1988) proposed several change score indices that are similar in spirit to Jacobson and Truax's RCI. For a single variable measured over *T* test periods, Yarnold's formula is:

$$Z = \frac{\overline{Z}_{t1} - \overline{Z}_{t2}}{\sqrt{T(1 - \overline{r_{xx}})}} \tag{6.22}$$

where $\bar{r}_{xx}$ is the average test–retest, split-half, or parallel-forms reliability of the *T* measurements obtained from a prior norm group. Z_{t1} and Z_{t2} are test *Z*-scores either obtained from prior group norms or derived ipsatively from the distribution of an individual's scores around his or her own mean. Yarnold assumed that the tests are parallel. That is, they have equal means and variances and the same true score for each subject. He further assumed that measurement errors between tests are randomly distributed and uncorrelated. As in other RCI measures, the *Z* index is treated as a standard normal deviate.

In an article that reported four single-case studies of therapy outcomes in the treatment of post-traumatic stress disorders, Mueser, Yarnold, and Foy (1991) expanded on Yarnold's earlier index with the formula:

$$Z = \frac{Z_{t1} - Z_{t2}}{\sqrt{J(1 - ACF_1)}} \tag{6.23}$$

for *J* testings over time. The term ACF_1 refers to the first-order autocorrelation among the observations, and *J* refers to the number of desired comparisons. *J* could refer to the number of individual observations, but in their article, Mueser et al. (1991) demonstrated how the *means* of J treatment phases could be compared. Unlike Yarnold's original formula, which used average reliabilities, this formula views the autocorrelation as a substitute for the reliabilities.

To demonstrate the use of Mueser and Yarnold's formulae, we created a simple data set, shown in Table 6.4. In this example, Phase 1 had three observations and Phase 2 had four observations. The data values, Y, were transformed to ipsative Z scores, so that the mean of Phase 1 was 1.02 and the mean of Phase 2 was −0.765. The lag-1 autocorrelation among observations was .64. Applying equation 7 to the data set, the Z-value was 2.10. Thus, the difference between the two phases was significant at the .05, two-tailed level.

Control Chart Techniques

Industrial quality control engineers often use charts to continuously monitor the counts of defects and variations in the mean values of product samples. These sequential charting techniques were developed more than 50 years ago (Shewart, 1931; Wald, 1947). The control charts, such as the Shewart Chart displayed in Fig. 6.12, typically plot values of a time series and then establish control bands (usually ±3 standard deviations around the mean of the series), beyond which a process would be considered "out of control."

Recently, Pfadt, Cohen, Sudhalter, Romanczyk, and Wheeler (1992) discussed the use of the Shewart charts for displaying the stability of baseline series. Extensive discussions of control chart techniques can be found in Grant and Leavenworth (1988), Gitlow, Gitlow, Oppenheim, and Oppenheim (1989), Wheeler (1985), and Wheeler & Chambers (1992).

Most statistical packages have options for producing control charts. Unfortunately, these control chart methods typically assume that the

TABLE 6.4
Illustration of Mueser, Yarnold, and Foy's Change Index

Observation	*Phase*	*Y*	*Z*
1	1	16	1.24
2	1	15	1.02
3	1	14	0.81
4	2	9	−0.24
5	2	6	−0.87
6	2	6	−0.87
7	2	5	−1.08

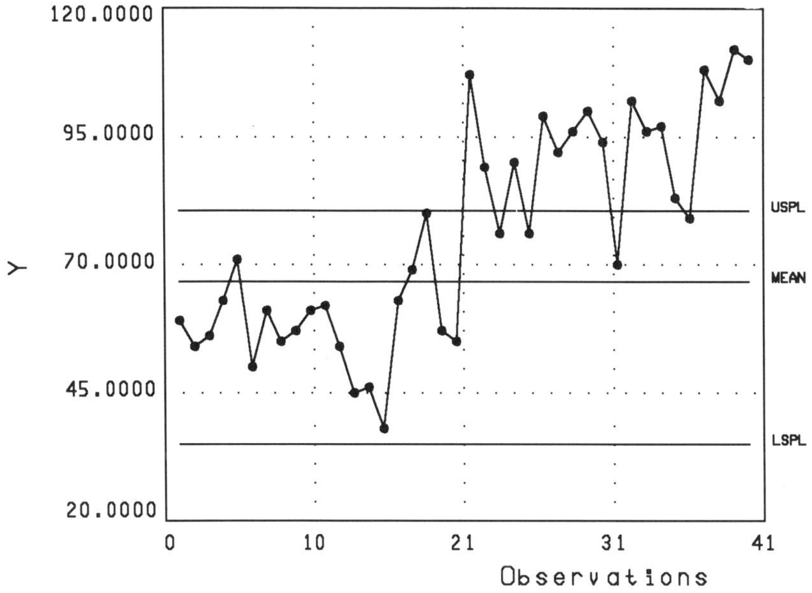

FIG. 6.12. Control chart interrupted time series.

series has no trend, no autocorrelation, and no autocorrelated errors. Wheeler (1990) claimed that control charts are not severely affected by autocorrelation below about .7, and provided methods for adjusting control limits in the presence of large autocorrelations. Given the potential problems that autocorrelation may introduce, readers should probably view control chart techniques as valuable graphic devices but should be cautious about drawing precise statistical inferences from them.

A special charting technique for displaying the results of Wald's (1947) sequential probability ratio test provides a powerful way to examine effects and to terminate a study when the evidence is sufficient either to reject the null hypothesis or to "accept" the null hypothesis. The technique requires researchers to establish clear criteria for scoring the presence of a response. The Type-I error probability (α) and the power (or $1 - \beta$) levels must be set in advance of data collection. As data are collected at each observation, the researcher notes the presence or absence of the criterion effect. With the help of preconstructed table or a predrawn graph, such as the chart in Fig. 6.13, the investigator notes whether the cumulative evidence has crossed a decision boundary; either to reject in favor of the alternative hypothesis or to terminate the study in favor of "accepting" the null hypothesis. Hoffman (1992) presented the details of this method.

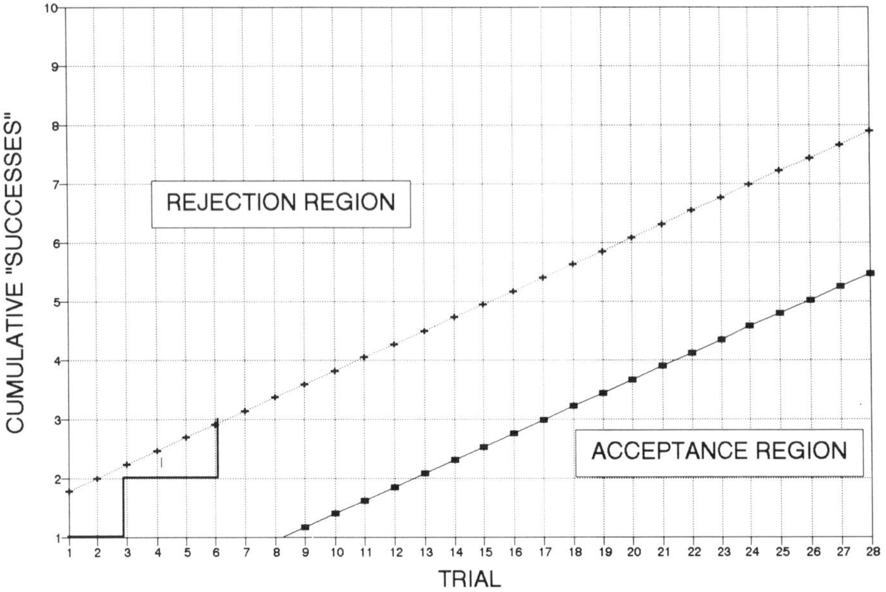

FIG. 6.13. Sequential probability ratio test.

Celeration Line and Split Middle Lines

Other tempting but potentially misleading sets of techniques includes the celeration line (Bloom & Fischer, 1982) and the "split middle" technique popularized by Kazdin (1982). In these techniques, a robust, outlier-resistant line is fitted to the baseline series. The line is then extended past the baseline series into the postintervention series to form an "estimation line." By examining the scatter of points above or below the estimation line, one could get an estimate of the impact of intervention beyond that of continuation of a simple trend effect. For example, if most of the postintervention points lay above or if most of the points lay below the estimation line, then a shift in trend and/or level might be present. Some researchers have attempted to use a binomial test to assess whether the proportions of points above and below the estimation line differ significantly from the expected proportions of 50% above and 50% below the line. However, Crosbie (1987) showed that the binomial test is invalid in the presence of autocorrelated data. Again, these and related techniques (Morley & Adams, 1991) might be useful for visualizing time-series data, but they may be misleading as statistical tests. Further discussion of the use of these techniques for visualizing data can be found in Franklin, Gorman, Beasley, & Allison, chap. 5, this volume.

NONEXPERIMENTAL TIME-SERIES TECHNIQUES

The methods described so far have drawn distinctions between independent and dependent variables. However, it is also possible to consider situations in which patterns of variation occur in a predictable manner but in which no particular variable is given causal priority. In these situations, one examines the correlation between two or more variables over time. For example, a subject could supply daily self-reports rated on three variables—anger, amount of sleep, and depression—each day for 60 days. We would form a data matrix in which the rows are time points and the columns are variables. At the end of this period, correlation coefficients and/or graphs would be computed and patterns of covariation among these variables can be assessed. If desired, patterns of intercorrelation can be reduced to their underlying dimensions by means of multivariate techniques such as factor analysis, principal components analysis, cluster analysis, and multidimensional scaling. For example, we might find that lack of sleep in a given subject might be strongly correlated with depression but uncorrelated with anger.

Let us consider a simple example of what Cattell (1952; 1963) designated *p-technique analysis.* Table 6.5 presents an artificial data set based on the work of Wessman and Ricks (1966) and Gorman and Wessman (1974). Suppose that a subject supplied self-reports of anxiety, depression, sociability toward others, and companionship from others. The intercorrelation matrix of these variables shows strong correlations between anxiety and depression and between sociability toward others and companionship from others. There are negligible correlations between the affect variables and the social behavior variables. A principal components factor analysis suggested that two factors could account for 87% of the total variance in the correlation matrix. The rotated factor loadings show that the first factor was strongly related to the variables that represent social behavior, whereas the second (orthogonal) factor was strongly related to anxiety and depression.

The present example used unlagged variables. If we used some lagged variable, we might have seen some interesting delayed patterns. For example, we might find that a subject's present self-reports of depression are negatively correlated with the previous day's ratings of sociability and companionship.

The number of substantial factors that can be obtained from each subject's correlation matrix might provide some interesting information about individual differences. For example, in previous work on individual patterns of mood fluctuation and stability (Gorman & Wessman, 1974; Wessman & Ricks, 1966), it was found that some subjects provided data that contained several factors, suggesting that their moods varied

TABLE 6.5
Illustration of *p*-Technique Factor Analysis

A. Raw data:

Day	*Anxiety*	*Depression*	*Sociability*	*Companionship*
1	6	7	5	5
2	4	5	1	2
3	4	5	8	9
4	5	5	5	5
5	6	5	6	7
6	8	7	4	8
7	6	5	5	7
8	8	9	3	3
9	8	6	6	6
10	6	4	1	3

	Mean	*Standard deviation*
Anxiety	6.10	1.52
Depression	5.80	1.48
Sociability	4.40	2.22
Companionship	5.50	2.32

B. Correlation Matrix:

	Anxiety	*Depression*	*Sociability*	*Companionship*
Anxiety	1.00			
Depression	.65	1.00		
Sociability	−.05	−.01	1.00	
Companionship	.05	−.10	.84	1.00

C. Roots:

Factor	*Eigenvalue*	*% of trace*
1	1.86	46.4
2	1.64	41.0

D. Varimax Rotated Factor Matrix:

	Loadings	
Variable	*Factor 1*	*Factor 2*
Anxiety	.02	.91
Depression	−.05	.91
Sociability	.96	−.02
Companionship	.96	−.01

along several independent, underlying dimensions. Other subjects, however, provided data that varied along one only underlying dimension, such as elation versus depression. These latter subjects were more global and undifferentiated in their affective experiences.

There can be several interesting advantages of *p*-technique factor analyses. For one, they can use unobtrusive and noninvasive data sources. For another, stable dimensions of covariation might emerge from the data analysis of a series of occasions that would not be obvious on any single occasion. Despite the widespread availability of multivariate software, only a few studies (e.g., Czogalik & Russell, 1995; Gorman & Wessman, 1974; Luborsky, 1995; Nesselroade & Ford, 1985; Stiles & Shapiro, 1995; Wessman & Ricks, 1966; Zevon & Tellegen, 1982) have employed these techniques.

However, *p*-technique analysis is not without its problems. Holtzman (1963) and Cattell (1963) voiced concern about the possibility that patterns of autocorrelation within each variable will distort the patterns of factor loadings in *p*-technique analyses of unlagged variables. Furthermore, they commented that ordinary *p*-technique analysis ignores lagged relationships. As a result, McArdle (1982), Molenaar (1985), and Wood and Brown (1994) developed variants of dynamic factor models that allow for autocorrelation and lagged correlations. The earlier *p*-technique analyses can be viewed as special cases of these newer, more comprehensive approaches. Wood and Brown (1994) provided SAS programs for solving confirmatory dynamic factor analysis problems.

CONCLUSIONS

There are many statistical alternatives available to single-case researchers and practitioners. However, as we hope we have demonstrated, each technique has its inherent assumptions and limitations. It appears the most serious challenges to users of single-case analysis methods revolve around three related issues: sample size, randomization of treatments, and autocorrelation. Table 6.6 summarizes some of the major advantages and limitations of the statistical methods discussed in this chapter.

Although some analysis methods have better small-sample properties than do others, all techniques are severely limited by small sample sizes. As we discuss in the chapter of power analysis (Allison, Silverstein, & Gorman, chap. 10, this volume), all statistical techniques, whether parametric or nonparametric, will produce more precise estimates when sample size increases. However, most single-case studies lack the number of observations needed to achieve the power to validly examine

TABLE 6.6
Applicability of Statistical Techniques for Single-Case Designs

Technique	*Needed Sample Size*	*Circumvents Autocorrelation Assumptions*	*Advantages*	*Disadvantages*
ANOVA & *t*-tests	Small to moderate	No	Familiar to most researchers. Provides simple answer to changes in level	Results may be severely distorted by autocorrelation
Permutation tests	Small	No	Can be used with small sample sizes and nonnormal distributions if some distribution parameters are held equal	May require extensive computation. Not free of assumptions of autocorrelation heterogeneity of variance
Ordinary least-squares regression models	Small to moderate	No, but one can test this assumption. If residuals are not autocorrelated, then models may be adequate	Flexible, many models can be tested, uses readily available software	Unless assumptions about residuals can be met, results may be misleading. Multicollinearity may obscure interpretation of effects
Box-Jenkins ARIMA	Large. Although not a mathematical limitation, 50 or more observations may be needed for an adequate fit of a model	Yes. Estimates of autoregressive components are an integral part of the ARIMA model	Handles complex time series in which autocorrelation is inherently present	The modeling process is very difficult. A feasible model may not necessarily be the best model
Generalized least-squares	Moderate to large (>30). Larger samples provide more power and less-biased estimates of parameters	As in ARIMA, autoregressive components can be included in the statistical model	Can be used for interrupted time series where fairly simple patterns of autocorrelation are present	As in ordinary least squares, model assumptions must be checked

Tryon's C-statistic	Small to moderate	The *C*-statistic is a measure of autocorrelation. Therefore, it is difficult to know whether a *C*-statistic is assessing differences in trend, level, or the presence of autocorrelation	Easily computed	May not adequately answer the researcher's questions about differences in level and trend
Reliable change indexes	Small to moderate	To some degree. Test–retest reliability and autocorrelation may be components of the indexes	Can be used to assess changes above and beyond those caused by unreliability	Assesses changes in level but not necessarily in slope
Control charts	Small to moderate	Estimates of control limits will be affected by autocorrelation. Some correction for autocorrelation may be possible	Provides a simple graphical display of time-varying behavior	Findings may be distorted by violations of assumptions about independence of observations
p-technique factor analysis and dynamic factor analysis	Moderate to large	Basic *p*-technique will be distorted by a autocorrelation. Dynamic factor analysis incorporates autocorrelation	Provides a multivariate means of detecting underlying dimensions of variation over time	Although basic *p*-technique is simple, it may be simplistic. Dynamic factor analysis may require software and analytic skills that are not accessible to most researchers

research hypotheses or establish the boundaries of parameter estimates. Perhaps the strongest suggestion for change that we can make is that researchers should collect a greater number of observations.

No psychologist would debate the notion that behavior changes over time, nor that behaviors are influenced by many interacting variables. Unfortunately, when investigators assess whether a systematic intervention influenced a given behavior that continued over time, there are many uncontrolled variables that can confound research findings. Among these confounds are carryover effects, cyclic behavior (see Beasley, Allison, & Gorman, chap. 9, this volume), and other time-varying events. By randomly assigning treatments to occasions, the effects of these serially dependent events may be reduced or even eliminated. Whenever possible, researchers should consider designs that include random assignments.

As we have seen, every statistical technique is affected by autocorrelated residuals. Because human behaviors typically occur in an ongoing temporal stream, autocorrelation is at least as likely as not. It is well established that statistical test values are overestimated by positive autocorrelation and underestimated in the presence of negative autocorrelation. It seems obligatory for researchers to choose designs, such as those that use randomization, to reduce the influence of autocorrelated effects. Additionally, they should examine results for autocorrelation and, if autocorrelations are present, they should choose statistical techniques that control for them.

When we started to work on this project several years ago, we were far more optimistic about the ease with which we could draw valid conclusions from single-case designs. We thought that if we had sufficient numbers of observations and state-of-the-art statistical techniques, single-case designs should present no more, and possibly even fewer problems, than should multisubject designs. More than 275 years ago, Alexander Pope (1711) penned the phrase, "For fools rush in where angels fear to tread." Somewhat foolishly and, definitely not angelic, we rushed to develop a compendium of techniques. We are more cautious now but we are not pessimistic. Rather, we believe that with better research designs and with the discovery of new statistical techniques, we can profit from the rich sources of information provided by single-case data.

REFERENCES

Allison, D. B., Faith, M. S., & Gorman, B. S. (1995, August). *Type-I error in autocorrelated time series analyzed by randomization tests.* Paper presented at the American Psychological Convention, New York.

Allison, D. B., & Gorman, B. S. (1993). Calculating an estimate of effect sizes for meta-analysis: The case of the single case. *Behavior Research and Therapy, 31*, 621–631.

Allison, D. B., Gorman, B. S., & Kucera, E. M. (1995). UNICORN: A program for transforming data to approximate normality. *Educational and Psychological Measurement, 55*, 625–629.

Berry, W. D., & Lewis-Beck, M. S. (1986). Interrupted time series. In W. D. Berry & M. S. Lewis-Beck (Eds.), *New tools for social scientists: Advances and applications in research methods* (pp. 209–240). Beverly Hills: Sage.

Bloom, M., & Fischer, J. (1982). *Evaluating practice. Guidelines for the accountable professional.* Englewood Cliffs, NJ: Prentice-Hall.

Blumberg, C. J. (1984). Comments on a simplified time series analysis for evaluating treatment interventions. *Journal of Applied Behavior Analysis, 17*, 539–542.

BMDP, Inc. (1990). *BMDP statistical software manual, Vol. I.* Los Angeles: Authors.

Boik, R. J. (1987). The Fisher-Pitman permutation test: A non-robust alternative the the normal theory F test when variances are heterogeneous. *British Journal of Mathematical and Statistical Psychology, 40*, 26–42.

Box, G. E. P., & Jenkins, G. M. (1976). *Time series analysis, forecasting and control.* San Francisco: Holden-Day.

Box, G. E. P., & Tiao, G. C. (1975). Intervention analysis with application to economic and environmental problems. *Journal of the American Statistical Association, 70*, 70–79.

Brockwell, P. J., & Davis, R. A. (1991a). *Time series: Theory and method* (2nd ed.). New York: Springer-Verlag.

Brockwell, P. J., & Davis, R. A. (1991b). *ITSM: An interactive time series modelling program for the PC.* New York: Springer-Verlag.

Busk, P. L., & Marascuilo, L. A. (1988). Autocorrelation in single-subject research: A counterargument to the myth of no autocorrelation. *Behavioral Assessment, 10*, 229–242.

Campbell, D. T. (1963). From description to experimentation: Interpreting trends as quasi-experiments. In C. W. Harris (Ed.), *Problems of measuring change.* Madison: University of Wisconsin Press.

Cattell, R. B. (1952). Three basic factor analytic research designs: Their interrelation and derivatives. *Psychological Bulletin, 49*, 499–520.

Cattell, R. B. (1963). The structuring of change by p- and incremental r-technique. In C. W. Harris (Ed.), *Problems in measuring change* (pp. 163–198). Madison: University of Wisconsin Press.

Center, B. A., Skiba, R. J., & Casey, A. (1985–1986). A methodology for the quantitative synthesis of intra-subject design research. *Journal of Special Education, 19*, 387–400.

Chatterjee, S., & Yilmaz, M. (1992). A review of regression diagnostics for behavioral research. *Applied Psychological Measurement, 16*, 209–227.

Chen, R. S., & Dunlap, W. P. (1993). SAS procedures for approximate randomization tests. *Behavior Research Methods, Instruments, & Computers, 25*, 406–409.

Christensen, L., & Mendoza, J. L. (1986). A method of assessing change in a single subject: An alternative to the RC index. *Behavior Therapy, 17*, 306–308.

Cochrane, D., & Orcutt, G. H. (1949). Application of least-squares regression to relationships containing autocorrelated error terms. *Journal of the American Statistical Association, 44*, 32–61.

Cohen, J., & Cohen, P. (1983). *Applied multiple regression/correlation analysis for the behavioral sciences.* Hillsdale, NJ: Lawrence Earlbaum Associates.

Cook, T. D., & Campbell, D. T. (1979). *Quasi-experimentation: Design & analysis issues for field settings.* Chicago: Rand McNally.

Cromwell, J. B., Labys, W. C., & Terraza, M. (1994). *Univariate time series models.* Los Angeles: Sage.

Crosbie, J. (1987). The inability of the binomial test to control for Type I error with a single case design. *Behavioral Assessment, 9,* 141–150.

Crosbie, J. (1989). The inappropriateness of the C-statistic for assessing stability of treatment effects with single-subject data. *Behavioral Assessment, 11,* 315–325.

Crosbie, J. (1993). Interrupted time-series analysis with brief single-subject data. *Journal of Consulting and Clinical Psychology, 61,* 966–974.

Crosbie, J. (1995). Interrupted time-series analysis with short series: Why it is problematic; How it can be improved. In J. M. Gottman & G. Sackett (Eds.), *The analysis of change* (pp. 361–395). Hillsdale, NJ: Lawrence Erlbaum Associates.

Cytel Software, Inc. (1989). *StatXact: Statistical software for exact nonparametric inference. User Manual.* Cambridge, MA: Authors.

Czogalik, D., & Russell, R. I. (1995). Interactional structures of therapist and client participation in adult psychotherapy: P-Technique and chronography. *Journal of Consulting and Clinical Psychology, 63,* 28–36.

D'Agostino, R. B., Belanger, A., & D'Agostino, R. B., Jr. (1990). A suggestion for using powerful and informative tests of normality. *American Statistician, 44,* 316–321.

Dallal G. E. (1989). ODDJOB: A Collection of Miscellaneous Statistical Techniques. *The American Statistician, 43,* 270.

Diaconis, P., & Efron, B. (1983). Computer-intensive methods in statistics. *Scientific American, 248,* 116–130.

Durbin, J. (1960). Estimation of parameters in time series regression models. *Journal of the Royal Statistical Society, Section B, 22,* 139–145.

Durbin, J., & Watson, M. J. (1950). Testing for serial correlation in least-squares regression. *Journal of the American Statistical Association, 37,* 409–428.

Edgington, E. S. (1973). The random sampling assumption in "Comment on Component-Randomization Tests." *Psychological Bulletin, 80,* 84–85.

Edgington, E. S. (1975). Randomization tests from N = 1 experiments. *Journal of Psychology, 65,* 195–199.

Edgington, E. S. (1979a). Randomization tests for one-subject operant experiments. *Journal of Psychology, 65,* 195–199.

Edgington, E. S. (1979b). The random sampling assumption in "Comment on Component-Randomization Tests." *Psychological Bulletin, 80,* 84–85.

Edgington, E. S. (1980). Random assignment and statistical tests for one-subject experiments. *Behavioral Assessment, 2,* 19–28.

Edgington, E. S. (1987). *Randomization tests* (2nd ed.). New York: Marcel Dekker.

Edgington, E. S. (1990). *RandPack.* Unpublished computer program. Alberta, CA: University of Calgary, Department of Psychology.

Edgington, E. S. (1992). Nonparametric tests for single-case experiments. In T. R. Kratochwill & J. R. Levin (Eds.), *Single-case research design and analysis: New directions for psychology and education* (pp. 33–158). Hillsdale, NJ: Lawrence Erlbaum Associates.

Edgington, E. S., & Khuller, P. (1992). A randomization test computer program for trends in repeated measures data. *Educational and Psychological Measurement, 52,* 93–95.

Efron, B., & Tibshirani, R. J. (1993). *An introduction to the bootstrap.* New York: Chapman and Hall.

Ertel, J. E., & Fowlkes, B. (1976). Some algorithms for linear spline and piecewise multiple linear regression models. *Applied Statistics, 30,* 277–285.

Ferron, J. (1992). *Suggested solutions to problems facing the use of randomization tests with single-case designs.* Poster presented at the American Educational Research Association Convention, Atlanta, GA.

Ferron, J., & Ware, W. (1994). Using randomization tests with responsive single-case designs. *Behavior Research and Therapy, 32,* 787–791.

Fisher, R. A. (1935). *The design of experiments* London: Oliver and Boyd.
Fox, J. (1991). *Regression diagnostics*. Newbury Park, CA: Sage.
Gentile, J. R., Roden, A. H., & Klein, R. D. (1972). An analysis of variance model for intrasubject replication designs. *Journal of Applied Behavior Analysis, 5,* 193–198.
Gitlow, H., Gitlow, S., Oppenheim, A., & Oppenheim, R. (1989). *Tools and methods for the improvement of quality*. Homewood, IL: Irwin.
Glass, G. V., Wilson, V. L., & Gottman, J. M. (1978). *Design and analysis of time series experiments*. Boulder: Colorado Associated University Presses.
Goldfield, S. M., & Quandt, R. E. (1965). Some tests for homoscedasticity. *Journal of the American Statistical Association, 60,* 539–547.
Good, P. (1994). *Permutation tests: A practical guide to resampling methods for testing hypotheses*. New York: Springer-Verlag.
Gorman, B. S., & Wessman, A. E. (1974). The relationships of cognitive styles and moods. *Journal of Clinical Psychology, 30,* 18–25.
Gorsuch, R. L. (1983). Three methods for analyzing limited time-series (N of 1) data. *Behavioral Assessment, 5,* 141–154.
Gottman, J. M. (1981). *Time series analysis: A comprehensive introduction for social scientists*. Cambridge, England: Cambridge University Press.
Gottman, J. M., & Glass, G.V. (1976). Analysis of interrupted time-series experiments. In T. R. Kratchowill (Ed.), *Single-subject research: Strategies for evaluating change* (pp. 199–235). New York: Academic Press.
Grant, E. L., & Leavenworth, R. S. (1988). *Statistical quality control* (6th ed.). New York: McGraw-Hill.
Greenwood, K. M., & Matyas, T. A. (1990). Problems with the interrupted time series for brief single-subject data. *Behavioral Assessment, 12,* 355–370.
Gulliksen, H. (1950). *Theory of mental tests*. New York: Wiley.
Harrop, J. W., & Velicer, W. F. (1985). An comparison of alternative approaches to the analysis of interrupted time series. *Multivariate Behavioral Research, 20,* 27–44.
Harrop, J. W., & Velicer, W. F. (1990a). Computer programs for interrupted time series analysis: I. A qualitative evaluation. *Multivariate Behavioral Research, 25,* 219–232.
Harrop, J. W., & Velicer, W. F. (1990b). Computer programs for interrupted time series analysis: II. A quantitative evaluation. *Multivariate Behavioral Research, 25,* 233–248.
Hageman, W. J. J., & Arrindell, W. A. (1993). A further refinement of the Reliable Change (RC) index by Improving the Difference score: Introducing RCID. *Behavior Research & Therapy, 31,* 693–700.
Haynes, S. N., Blaine, D., & Meyer, K. (1995). Dynamical models for psychological assessment: Phase state functions. *Psychological Assessment, 7,* 17–24.
Hinkley, D. V. (1971). Inference in two-phase regression. *Journal of the American Statistical Association, 66,* 736–743.
Hoffman, H. S. (1992). An application of sequential analysis to observer-based psychophysics. *Infant Behavior and Development, 15,* 271–277.
Holtzman, W. H. (1963). Statistical models for study of change in the single case. In C. W. Harris (Ed.), *Problems in measuring change* (pp. 199–211). Madison: University of Wisconsin Press.
Hooton, J. W. L. (1991). Randomization tests: Statistics for experimenters. *Computer Methods and Programs in Biomedicine, 35,* 43–51.
Hubert, L. J. (1987). *Assignment methods in combinatorial analysis*. New York: Marcel Dekker.
Huitema, B. E. (1985). Autocorrelation in applied behavior analysis: A myth. *Behavioral Assessment, 7,* 109–120.
Huitema, B. E. (1986). Autocorrelation in behavioral research: Wherefore art thou? In A.

Poling & R. W. Fuqua (Eds.), *Research methods in applied behavior analysis* (pp. 187–207). New York: Plenum.

Huitema, B. E. (1990). Autocorrelation: 10 years of confusion. *Behavioral Assessment, 10,* 253–294.

Huitema, B. E., & McKean, J. W. (1991). Autocorrelation estimation and inference with small samples. *Psychological Bulletin, 110,* 291–304.

Huitema, B. E., & McKean, J. W. (1994). Reduced bias autocorrelation estimation: Three jackknife methods. *Educational and Psychological Measurement, 54,* 654–665.

Huitema, B. E., McKean, J. W., & McKnight, S. (1994). *Small-sample time-series intervention analysis: Problems and solutions.* Paper presented at the American Psychological Association Convention, Los Angeles.

Jaccard, J., & Wan, C. K. (1993). Statistical analysis of temporal data with many observations: Issues for behavioral medicine. *Annals of Behavioral Medicine, 15,* 41–50.

Jacobson, N. S., Follette, W. C., & Revenstorf, D. (1984). Psychotherapy outcome research: Methods for reporting variability and evaluating clinical significance. *Behavior Therapy, 15,* 336–352.

Jacobson, N. S., & Truax, P. (1991). Clinical significance: A statistical approach to defining meaningful change in psychotherapy. *Journal of Consulting and Clinical Psychology, 59,* 12–19.

Judge, G. G., Griffiths, W. E., Hill, R. C., Lutkepohl, H., & Lee, T. C. (1985). *The theory and practice of econometrics* (2nd ed.). New York: Wiley.

Kazdin, A. E. (1976). Statistical analysis for single-case experimental designs. In M. Hersen and D. H. Barlow (Eds.), *Single-case experimental designs: Strategies for studying behavior change.* New York: Pergammon Press.

Kazdin, A. E. (1982). *Single-case research designs: Methods for applied settings.* New York: Oxford University Press.

Kendall, M. G., & Ord, J. K. (1990). *Time series* (3rd ed.). New York: Oxford University Press.

Levin, J. R., Marascuilo, L. A., & Hubert, L. J. (1978). N = nonparametric randomization tests. In T. R. Kratochwill (Ed.), *Single-subject research: Strategies for evaluating change* (pp. 167–194). New York: Academic Press.

Luborsky, L. (1995). The first trial of P-technique in psychotherapy research—a still lively Legacy. *Journal of Consulting and Clinical Psychology, 63,* 6–14.

Manly, B. F. J. (1991). *Randomization and Monte Carlo methods in biology.* New York: Chapman and Hall.

Manly, B. F. J. (1993). *RT: A program for randomization testing.* Cheyenne, WY: West.

Marascuilo, L. A., & Busk, M. (1988). Combining statistics for multiple baseline A and replicated ABAB designs across subjects. *Behavioral Assessment, 10,* 1–28.

Matyas, T. A., & Greenwood, K. M. (1991). Problems in the estimation of autocorrelation in brief time series and some implications for behavioral data. *Behavioral Assessment, 13,* 137–157.

McArdle, J. J. (1982). *Structural equation modelling of an individual system: Preliminary results from "A case study of alcoholism."* Unpublished manuscript. University of Denver, Psychology Department.

McCain, L. J., & McCleary, R. (1979). The statistical analysis of simple interrupted time-series quasi-experiments. In T. D. Cook & D. T. Campbell (Eds.), *Quasi-experimentation: Design and analysis for field experiments* (pp. 233–293). Chicago: Rand McNally.

McCleary, R., & Hay, R. A., Jr. (1980). *Applied time series for the social sciences.* Beverly Hills, CA: Sage.

McDowall, D., McCleary, R., Meidinger, E. E., & Hay, R. A., Jr. (1980). *Interrupted time series analysis.* Beverly Hills, CA: Sage.

Mielke, P. W., & Berry, K. J. (1994). Permutation tests for common locations among samples with unequal variances. *Journal of Educational and Behavioral Statistics, 19,* 217–236.
Molenaar, P. C. M. (1985). A dynamic factor model for the analysis of multivariate time series. *Psychometrika, 50,* 181–202.
Morley, S., & Adams, M. (1991). Graphical analysis of single-case time series data. *British Journal of Clinical Psychology, 30,* 97–115.
Mosteller, F. & Tukey, J. W. (1977). *Data analysis and regression: A second course in statistics.* Reading, MA: Addison-Wesley.
Mueser, K. T., Yarnold, P. R., & Foy, D. W. (1991). Statistical analysis for single-case designs: Evaluation of outcome of chronic PTSD. *Behavior Modification, 15,* 134–158.
Nakatani, K. (1984). Monte Carlo statistics on personal computers: A random permuation test for difference of means. *Hiroshima Forum for Psychology, 10,* 25–30.
Nesselroade, J. R., & Ford, D. (1985). P-technique comes of age: Multivariate, replicated, single-subject designs for research on older adults. *Research in Aging, 7,* 46–80.
Neter, J., Wasserman, W., & Kutner, M. H. (1989). *Applied linear regression models* (2nd ed.). Homewood, IL: Irwin.
Noreen, E. W. (1989). *Computer-intensive methods for testing hypotheses: An introduction.* New York: Wiley.
Onghena, P. (1992). Randomization tests for extensions and variations of ABAB single-case experimental designs: A rejoinder. *Behavioral Assessment, 14,* 152–171.
Onghena, P., & Edgington, E. S. (1994). Randomization tests for restricted alternating treatment designs. *Behaviour Research and Therapy, 32,* 783–786.
Onghena, P., & Van Damme, G. (1994). SCRT 1.1: Single-case randomization tests. *Behavior Research Methods, Instruments, and Computers, 26,* 369.
Ostrom, C. W., Jr. (1990). *Time series analysis: Regression techniques* (2nd ed.). Beverly Hills, CA: Sage.
Ostrom, C. W., Jr. (1978). *Time series analysis: Regression techniques.* Beverly Hills: Sage.
Peladeau, N. (1994). *SIMSTAT user's guide.* Montreal: Provalis Research.
Pfadt, A., Cohen, I. L., Sudhalter, V., Romanczyk, R. G., & Wheeler, D. J. (1992). Applying statistical process control to clinical data: An illustration. *Journal of Applied Behavior Analysis, 25,* 551–560.
Phillips, J. P. N. (1993). Serially correlated errors in some single-subject designs. *British Journal of Mathematical and Statistical Psychology, 36,* 269–280.
Pitman, E. J. G. (1937). Significant tests which may be applied to samples from any populations. *Journal of the Royal Statistical Society: Section B, 4,* 119–130.
Pole, A., West, M., & Harrison, J. (1994). *Applied Bayesian forcasting and time series analysis.* New York: Chapman and Hall.
Pope, A. (1711). *An essay on criticism, pt. III, l.66.* Cited in Microsoft Corp. (1992). *Microsoft Bookshelf © 1987–1992*: Redmond, WA: Microsoft Corp.
Rousseau, P. O., & Leroy, A. M. (1987). *Robust regression and outlier detection.* New York: Wiley.
SAS, Inc. (1990). *SAS language reference, Version 6.* Carey, NC: Authors.
SAS, Inc. (1994). *SAS/ETS user's guide, Version 6* (2nd ed.). Carey, NC: Authors.
Scheffe, H. (1959). *The analysis of variance.* New York: Wiley.
SCITECH, Inc. (1995). *Software for science.* Chicago: Authors.
Seber, G. A. F., & Wild, C. J. (1989). *Nonlinear regression.* New York: Wiley.
Shewart, W. A. (1931). *Economic control of quality of manufactured products.* New York: Van-Nostrand.
Silverstein, J. M., & Allison, D. B. (1994). The comparative efficacy of antecedent exercise and methylphenidate: A single-case randomized trial. *Child: Care, Health, and Development, 20,* 47.

Simon, J. L., & Bruce, P. C. (1991). *Resampling stats: Probability and statistics in a radically different way*. Arlington, VA: Resampling Stats., Inc.

SPSS, Inc. (1990). *SPSS/PC+: Trends*. Chicago: Authors.

Stiles, W. B., & Shapiro, D. A. (1995). Verbal exchange structure of brief psychotherapy—interpersonal and cognitive-behavioral psychotherapy. *Journal of Consulting and Clinical Psychology, 63*, 15–27.

Stine, R. S. (1990). An introduction to bootstrap methods: Examples and ideas. In J. Fox & J. S. Long (Eds.), *Modern methods of data analysis* (pp. 325–373). Newbury Park, CA: Sage.

Suen, H. K. (1987). On the epistemology of autocorrelation in applied behavior analysis. *Behavioral Assessment, 9*, 113–124.

Suen, H. K., & Ary, R. (1987). Autocorrelation in applied behavior analysis: Myth or reality? *Behavioral Assessment, 9*, 125–130.

Trigg, D. W., & Leach, A. G. (1967). Exponential smoothing with adaptive response rate. *Operational Research Quarterly, 18*, 53–59.

Tryon, W. W. (1982). A simplified time-series analysis for evaluating treatment interventions. *Journal of Applied Behavior Analysis, 15*, 423–429.

Velicer, W. F. (1994). Time series models of individual substance abusers. In L. M. Collins & L. A. Seitz (Eds.), *Advances in data analysis for prevention intervention research (NIDA Research Monographs), 142*; pp. 264–299). Rockville, MD: National Institute on Drug Abuse.

Velicer, W. F., & MacDonald, R. P. (1984). Time series analysis without model identification. *Multivariate Behavioral Research, 19*, 33–47.

Velicer, W. F., & MacDonald, R. P. (1991). Cross-sectional time series designs: A general transformation approach. *Multivariate Behavioral Research, 26*, 247–254.

von Neumann, J., Kent, R. H., Bellinson, H. R., & Hart, B. J. (1941). The mean successive difference. *Annals of Mathematical Statistics, 12*, 153–162.

Wald, A. (1947). *Sequential analysis*. New York: Wiley.

Welch, W. J. (1990). Construction of permutation tests. *Journal of the American Statistical Association, 85*, 693–698.

Wessman, A. E., & Ricks, D. F. (1966). *Mood and personality*. New York: Holt, Rinehart, & Winston.

Wheeler, D. J. (1985). *Keeping control charts*. Knoxville, TN: SPC Press.

Wheeler, D. J. (1990). *Correlated data and control charts*. Knoxville, TN: SPC Press.

Wheeler, D. J., & Chambers, D. S. (1992). *Understanding statistical process control*. Knoxville, TN: SPC Press.

Wheelright, S. C., & Makriadakis, S. (1973). *Forecasting methods for management*. New York: Wiley.

Williams, E. A., & Gottman, J. M. (1982). *A user's guide to the Gottman-Williams time series analysis computer programs for social scientists*. New York: Cambridge University Press.

Wood, P. W., & Brown, D. (1994). The study of intraindividual differences by means of dynamic factor models: Rationale, implementation, and interpretation. *Psychological Bulletin, 116*, 166–186.

Yarnold, P. R. (1988). Classical test theory methods for repeated measures designs. *Educational and Psychological Measurement, 48*, 913–919.

Zevon, M. A., & Tellegen, A. (1982). The structure of mood change: An idiographic/nomothetic analysis. *Journal of Personality and Social Psychology, 43*, 111–122.

7

Serial Dependency in Single-Case Time Series

Thomas A. Matyas and Kenneth M. Greenwood
La Trobe University

INTRODUCTION

The idea that behavior is not random is fundamental to the concept of psychological and behavioral sciences. Behavior emanates from an individual organism and inevitably forms a chronological sequence. Thus, psychological science needs to establish, *inter alia*, models of the patterns of behavior as ordered in time. The same may be said of the underlying psychological and physico-chemical substrates that have been presumed to be involved in the causation of this behavior. In the ideal of science these models are thought to be valuable both as representations of knowledge about the causal phenomena and as tools for building an applied science, a technology of prediction and evaluation. Indeed, this technological goal is exemplified in this book, wherein time-series designs are discussed as a tool for investigation and management of individual cases.

The purpose of this chapter, therefore, is to review the issue of predictability across time in behavioral time series. To achieve this aim, the chapter considers the definition of serial dependence and examines how it can arise out of a variety of patterns over time. This is a necessary prelude to an informed and detailed discussion of both why serial dependence matters and whether it is present in behavioral time series. The chapter shows how the presence and nature of serial dependence is not only an issue in our conceptualization of behavior, but also a practical problem in the analysis of single-case data. Serial dependence patterns reflect the mathematical structure and graphic shape of the time series. Not surprisingly, therefore, it has been shown to affect the statistical analysis of single-case data. In addition, serially dependent data form nonrandom trend patterns when graphed, and because the human observer may be suspected of reacting to pattern, the ability of serial dependence to influence visual analysis of single-case graphs has also been debated. Although a number of strong a priori arguments can be envisaged, the evidence on visual analysis is more limited and inconsistent than that determining impact on statistical analysis.

Although the impact of serial dependence on visual analysis is less clear at present, there is sufficient argument and evidence to be concerned about serial dependence in visual analysis. Furthermore, the existence and nature of serial dependence in individual behavior has been an issue of controversy in the psychological literature on single-case design (Busk & Marascuilo, 1988; Huitema, 1985, 1986; Sharpley & Alavosius, 1988; Suen, 1987; Suen & Ary, 1987). The chapter therefore, reviews the literature on the presence of serial dependence and provides new analysis incorporating the use of a recent procedure claimed to reduce the bias of estimation (Huitema & McKean, 1991). The review and analysis show that serial dependence in single-case time series is not distributed according to the theoretical distribution obtained by assuming null autocorrelation, as proposed by Huitema (1985, 1988). The implications of the observed distribution of serial dependence are considered in the final section. Issues in both statistical and graphical judgment analysis are considered in that context.

CAUSATION AND QUANTIFICATION OF SERIAL DEPENDENCY

A variable whose future is predictable to some degree from its own values or from the passage of time possesses statistical serial dependence (see also chaps. 6 and 9, this volume). The presence and nature of the serial dependence can be quantified and investigated via the pattern of autocorrelation and partial autocorrelation (e.g., Box & Jenkins, 1976; Glass, Wilson, & Gottman 1975). Autocorrelation is the extent to which values of the observed behavior at time t (Y_t) are correlated with values at time $t - i$ (Y_{t-i}). For example, when $i = 1$ the autocorrelation is termed the lag one autocorrelation. Time series may exhibit autocorrelation at various time lags, depending on the underlying nature of the series. Partial autocorrelation is analogous to the partial correlation, familiar to readers of the psychological and educational research methods literature. Partial correlation is the extent to which two variables X and Y are correlated when the effects of a third variable Z have been removed. Similarly, partial autocorrelation is the extent to which values at time t and $t - i$ are correlated when the shared variance with values of t at all other lags except i have been removed (Box & Jenkins, 1976; Glass, Willson, & Gottman, 1975).

It is important in the context of this chapter to recall that autocorrelation can arise as a result of a wide range of nonrandom processes. For example, mathematical structures such as straight lines, sinusoids, and other cyclic series, and a multitude of curvilinear growth models such power functions and logarithmic functions, all show a pattern of autocorrelation. All the previous examples can be represented as equations of functions relating Y, the response, to X, the time. Thus, the power function $Y = aX^n$, or the straight line $Y = aX + b$, or the sinusoid $Y = a\sin X$ all claim that the value of the response Y can be predicted by knowing the value of time X. Figure 7.1 presents a range of familiar time-series models and their corresponding autocorrelograms. It should be clear from the figure that particular mathematical structures have identifiable autocorrelograms and partial autocorrelograms.

When variable error, in the form of a normally distributed random residual (ϵ), is added to make the model realistic, the autocorrelation pattern remains, but in diluted form. This is illustrated in Fig. 7.2, which shows the familiar linear model incorporating error residuals: $Y = a + bX + \epsilon$. When some degree of determinism is present in the time series, the autocorrelogram detects this serial dependence provided the sample is large enough.

The discussion so far has encompassed only so-called deterministic models of behavior, where the response is predictable from values of time. However, the theoretical possibilities for representing behavior are very broad. Another class of mathematical models, which will also generate their own patterns of serial dependence in data, are the so-called stochastic models (e.g., Gottman, 1981). These models are distinct from the deterministic models in that they represent behavior as a function of itself at previous points in time. This is most simply exemplified by the first order autoregressive model $Y_t = a + b_1Y_{t-1} + \epsilon$ (Fig. 7.3). Here the first order autoregressive coefficient b_1 introduces serial dependence compared to the random series (Fig. 7.3). Comparison with the random series $Y_t = a + \epsilon$ (bottom of Fig. 7.3), shows that the first order autoregressive function tends to drift up and down at unpredictable points, and there is a tendency to linger at the higher or lower values longer than does the random example. The autocorrelograms and partial autocorrelograms (Fig. 7.3) indicate the nonrandom nature of the autoregressive series very clearly, although examination of the time-series chart may not suggest anything special to the uninitiated. A wide range of stochastic models exist (e.g., Glass et al., 1975; Gottman, 1981; chap. 6, this volume), including higher order autoregressive models and moving average models (in the latter, Y_t is a function of earlier values of ϵ). These

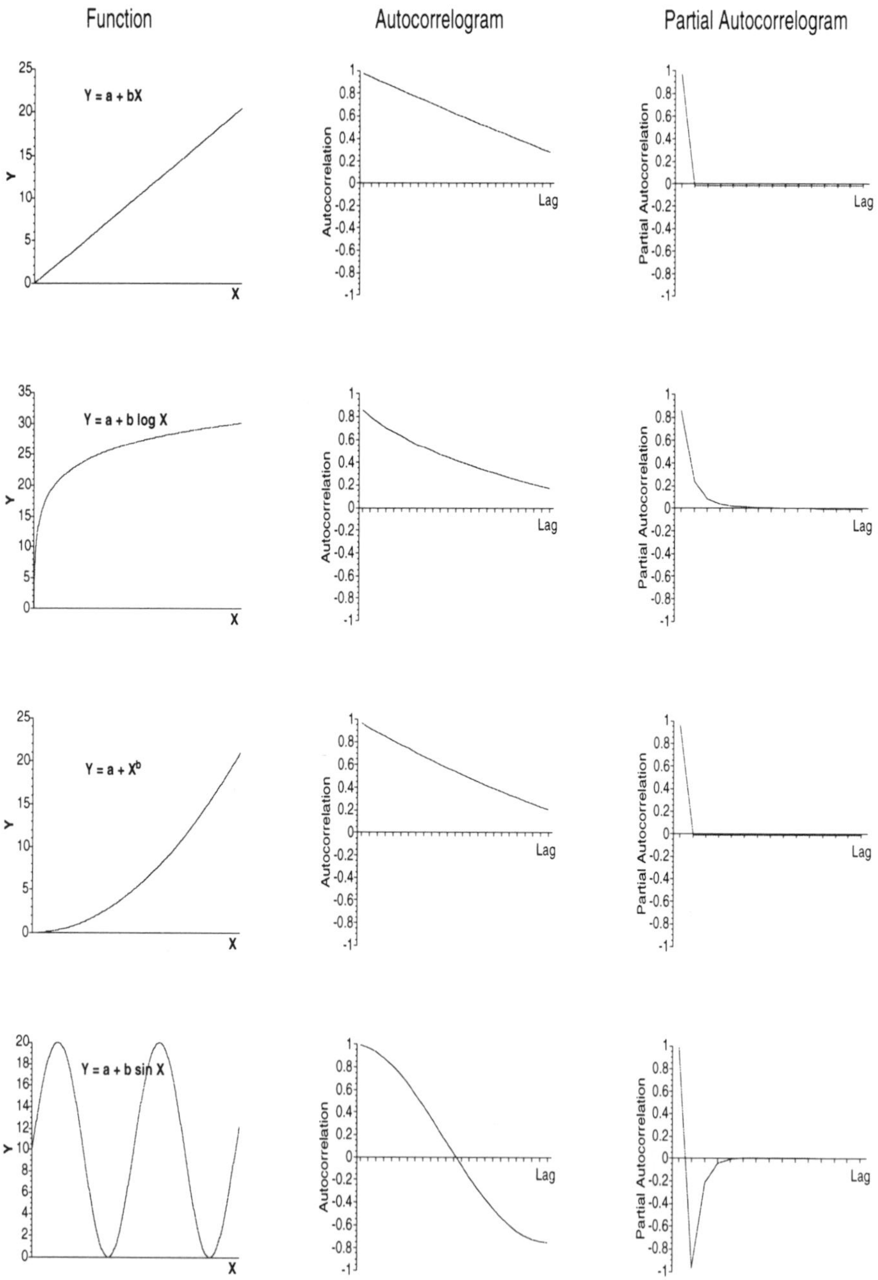

FIG. 7.1. Autocorrelograms and partial autocorrelograms for four common mathematical functions encountered in time-series analysis. Each row of three panels presents the function, its autocorrelogram, and its partial autocorrelogram.

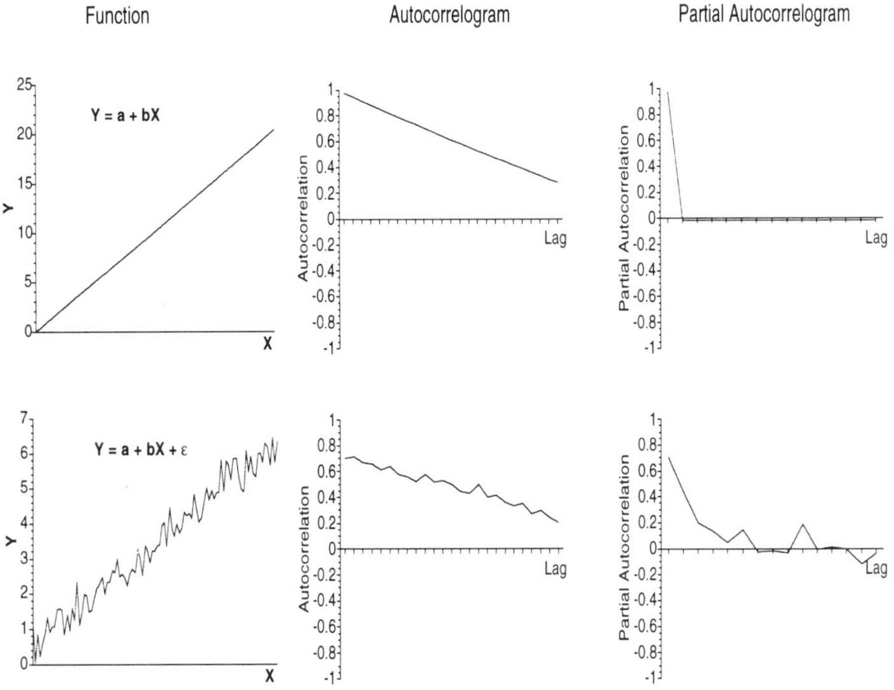

FIG. 7.2. The effect of adding noise to a linear model and the resulting change in the autocorrelogram and partial autocorrelogram of the linear model.

models also are associated with particular patterns of autocorrelation and partial autocorrelation (e.g., Glass et al., 1975; Gottman, 1981).

All of the previous examples relate behavior either to time or to the history of the behavior itself. It may appear that although these two types of models cover a very broad range, the idea of serial dependence doesn't encompass a familiar way of thinking causally about behavior, which is the reductionist model. This is not so. In the reductionist model behavioral variables need to be related to underlying psychological or physiological variables. A simple illustration of this idea is the equation $Y_t = a + bZ_t$, where Z_t is the underlying causal variable. However, the temporal structure of Z_t must be considered also. For example, Z_t may well follow one of the deterministic or stochastic models depicted in Fig. 7.1 and 7.2, all of which are ordered in time to some degree. If Z_t follows the first order autoregressive model form, so that $Z_t = \alpha + \beta_1 Z_{t-1} + \epsilon$, then by simple algebraic substitution we have $Y_t = a + b(\alpha + \beta_1 Z_{t-1} + \epsilon)$. This will convert to the familiar regression form $Y_t = k + mZ_t + b\epsilon$, comprising an intercept constant $k = a + b\alpha$ and a regression parameter

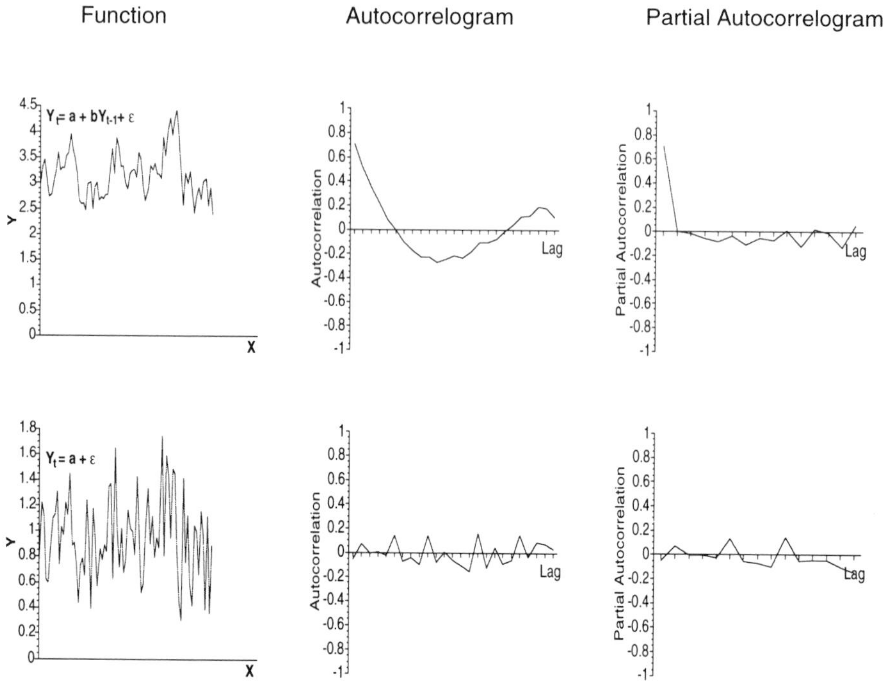

FIG. 7.3. A series composed of random fluctuations around a mean value and the series' autocorrelogram and partial autocorrelogram (bottom row) contrasted with a first order autoregressive time series and its autocorrelogram and partial autocorrelogram.

$m = b\beta_1$; $b\epsilon$, of course, is a random variable as it simply consists of the random variable ϵ multiplied by the constant b. As β_1 is a first order autoregression it will engender a degree of autocorrelation via m into the behavior of Y_t. Thus, the autocorrelogram for Y_t will not be null.

WHY DOES THE PRESENCE OF SERIAL DEPENDENCY MATTER?

Serial dependence can be quantified and is a property of a wide range of mathematical time series models. Does this necessarily imply that knowledge about its presence is important in single-case methodology? At least three powerful arguments conclude that knowledge about the presence and structure of serial dependence in single-case time series is important. From the perspective of this volume, and that of pragmatism, the two most important arguments are that both graphical judgment and statistical modes of analyzing single-case design data have been shown to be affected by the presence of serial dependence. These arguments are detailed later.

There is also a third argument, more theoretical in nature, that can be only briefly canvassed in this context: Serial dependence announces nonrandom structure in time series, the pattern of serial dependence is more than a tool for empirical model identification and model diagnosis when fitting time series. Thus, the presence and pattern of serial dependence should be of interest to those seeking to build models about the nature of human behavior, either for purely predictive reasons or in the quest for causal models. The idea that a behavior follows a time series that is essentially random around a fixed level seems most unlikely a priori (Busk & Marascuilo, 1988). Nevertheless, this idea has been argued (Huitema, 1985, 1986) and defended (Huitema, 1988).

We return now to the other two important issues, the influence of autocorrelation on statistical and graphical analyses of data from single-case designs. That the presence of serial dependence in data affects the statistical analysis of single-case interrupted time-series designs is beyond doubt. The tests based on means, such as the t and F tests once proposed (Gentile, Roden, & Klein, 1972), are invalidated by serial dependence, because these distributions are known to be incorrect for data that do not have serially independent residuals (Scheffé, 1959), and this theoretical position has been confirmed by simulation (Greenwood & Matyas, 1990). Moreover, serial dependence in the data can occur because the time series is nonergodic; that is, that its statistical parameters, such as the mean, are changing over time. The most obvious illustration of this point is that of a baseline depicted by a linear model with slope, a model exhibiting an autocorrelogram composed of positive autocorrelations that gradually diminish with increasing lag (Fig. 7.2). Clearly, a straight baseline with positive slope that continues unchanged into the intervention phase will have a different mean, but it would be fallacious to argue that this represents an intervention effect if the slope doesn't change. Thus, for several reasons, the presence of serial dependence invalidates the use of traditional t and F tests.

Interrupted time-series analysis (ITSA) can cope with time series that are serially dependent (Glass, Wilson, & Gottman, 1975; Gottman, 1981), but this implies a need to know if there is serial dependence. Moreover, ITSA requires that an appropriate model be identified for the baseline data to see if intervention has produced a change from the preexisting trend. The pattern of autocorrelation is not only a signal against oversimplistic analysis. Knowledge of the autocorrelation and partial autocorrelation patterns is also useful for model identification and, once a model has been fitted, the autocorrelation function can be used to investigate if residuals are now serially independent (Glass, Wilson, & Gottman, 1975; Gottman, 1981). Thus, knowledge about serial dependence in data is essential for choosing statistical method. Moreover, further analyses of serial dependence are an inherent part of the proper conduct of ITSA.

This argument is not confined to the use of ITSA. Other proposals for statistical analysis are in fact affected by the presence of serial dependence. For example, the split-middle technique, in conjuction with use of the binomial test (White, 1974), has been presented as a quick and simple method for analysis of intervention effects (e.g., Kazdin, 1982). The split-middle technique uses a graphical nonparametric procedure, based on locating the medians for the data in the first and second halves of the baseline phase, to fit a straight line. This "celeration line" is then extended into the intervention phase and the number of points falling above or below the extrapolated line are counted. The binomial test is then applied to this count. Crosbie (1987) already demonstrated that the binomial distribution is affected by the presence of serial dependence. More important from the present perspective, the literature on the split middle approach has not taken sufficient cognizance of the fact that a particular model, the linear model, is assumed and extrapolated. The possibility of nonlinear deterministic or stochastic trends is simply not considered. The presence of autocorrelation in data may be due to linear trend, but this is clearly not the only possibility. The ubiquitous adoption of a linear model with which to account for any serial dependence, as advocated by the split-middle method, seems premature to say the least. Moreover, the split-middle method contains no procedure for examining the residuals to test the assumption that a linear model properly represents the data and no procedure to ensure that there is no additional source of serial dependence.

As another example, consider the randomization test (Edgington, 1987). Although this test is forgiving of distributional assumptions because it employs a simulation approach (Edgington, 1987), serial dependence nevertheless could be an issue. The randomization test obtains the difference between baseline and experimental trials administered in random order. This difference is then compared with the distribution of differences calculated from random permutations of trials allocated to imaginary baseline and experimental conditions. It is argued that the difference between the actual experimental and baseline trials should be greater than the difference observed in the vast (> 95%) majority of permutations that create imaginary sets of baseline and experimental trials. However, it is well known (Edgington, 1987; Kazdin, 1980) that this conclusion rests on the assumption that there is no carryover effect.

In the event of carryover effects, the scores of baseline trials that follow experimental trials would be artificially changed to be closer in value to the preceding experimental trial, diluting the comparison. A carryover effect is an example of serial dependence. To our knowledge, there is no provision in current procedures for assessing the serial dependence in a randomization design, to test for possible carryover effects, prior to application of randomization tests. Devising such a test does not appear, however, to present any unusual problems.

Similar to statistical analysis, the results of visual analysis may also be suspect when serial dependence is present in data. As reviewed previously, serial dependence in time series can arise from a range of underlying processes that manifest graphically as either deterministic trends or stochastic trends. The simplest deterministic trend is linear trend. Other deterministic trends of relevance to single-case analysts are likely to be the curvilinear trends of adaptation and learning processes and seasonal or cyclic trends. When a random residual is added to these phenomena, and relatively brief samples of the total time series are encountered, the difference between the linear and nonlinear possibilities is obscured. This unfortunate conjunction can be reasonably speculated to increase the probability of judgment error.

Perhaps even greater risk could be suspected from data possessing stochastic trend, such as that generated by autoregressive or moving average models. Stochastic trend may be particularly problematic for the human judge because it comprises drifts of variable magnitude, and direction. For example, in a first order autoregressive model $Y_t = a + bY_{t-1} + \epsilon$, the occurrence of a particularly large value of e will continue to affect the series for several points, depending on the value of b. Thus, random shocks in such a series could be perceived as nonrandom effects by visual analysts (see the following discussion and Fig. 7.4).

Textbooks describing single-case visual analysis have often promoted concepts of level and trend changes exemplified with linear models (e.g., Hersen & Barlow, 1976; Kazdin, 1982). Proposals to calculate trend lines and draw them as visual aids (e.g., Hojem & Ottenbacher, 1988; Kazdin, 1982; White & Haring, 1980) are further testimony to the dominance of linear modeling in this literature. Such simple models seem likely to promote a cognitive set toward perception of changes in a linear trend or level when other (nonlinear) deterministic trends are in place, or when stochastic trends transform random variation into apparent systematic variation. This seems particularly likely when the sample size is too brief to expose a temporary variation, and single-case data is characteristically composed of brief time series (Huitema, 1985).

As an example, consider the hypothetical data presented in Fig. 7.4. Panel A shows a first order autoregressive time series where the lag 1

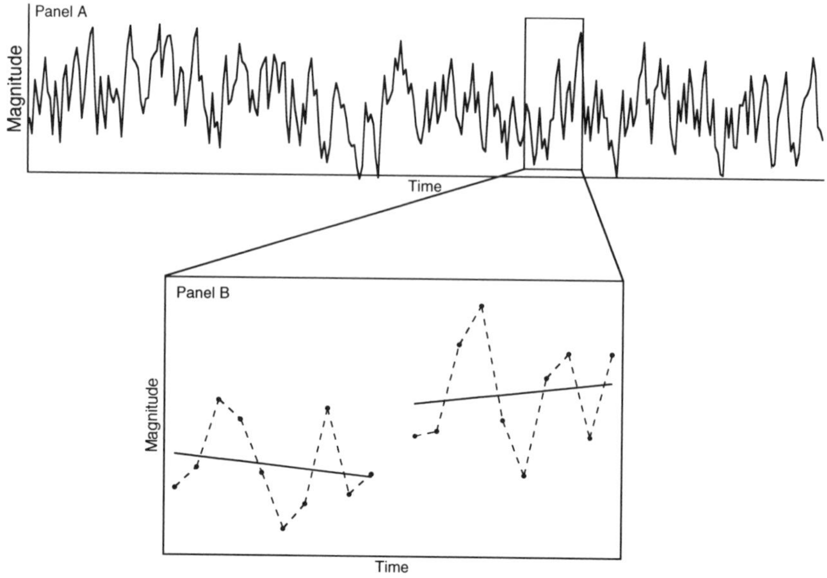

FIG. 7.4. A large sample from a first order autoregressive time series with an autoregression coefficient of 0.6. The exploded panel illustrates what could happen if two phases of an AB design (N = 10 per phase) were conducted and no intervention effect occurred, but the analyst plotted the data with an expectation of a linear model and used linear trend lines as aid to visual judgment.

autoregression coefficient is 0.6. Panel B shows what would appear if the highlighted sample of 20 points were observed in a single-case AB design and then fitted with a linear model. The temptation to infer an interphase change seems very strong. Incidentally, note that if the next 10 points in Panel A were also sampled, as part of a withdrawal phase (ABA design), we would probably continue to be fooled. Nevertheless, the true nature of the series is quite clear on examination of panel A. No visual analyst, we hope, would be fooled into imagining a linear model displaced at the point of intervention given the pattern established in the previous hundred plus points. However, in the visual analysis of single-case data we are rarely in possession of large samples, baselines of five to six trials being a median (Huitema, 1985). Of course, this example was deliberately selected to highlight the possibility of misinterpretation. It would be legitimate to consider the probability of apparent effects given an experimental start at any of the points in the series of Panel A. Although this probability is not easy to estimate, the example should suffice to highlight the potential danger when small samples are encountered by visual analysts whose cognitive maps are dominated by linear models. Given the state of the literature indicated previously, it is not unreasonable to fear that the problem of nonlinear data may be too common.

Indeed, some of these hypothetical fears about error in visual analysis have been empirically supported. Matyas and Greenwood (1990a) used computer-generated AB charts with known intervention effects and degrees of autocorrelation, generated with a first order autoregressive model. They found that charts with higher positive autocorrelation produced higher false alarm rates than did those with low autocorrelation. This effect interacted with the degree of random variability (ϵ) in the data, as hypothesized previously. The combination of medium to high values of autocorrelation and amplitude of random shock to the time series produced the worst visual judgment, with false alarm rates in excess of 40%. Serial dependence combined with low values of ϵ produced low error rates, as might be expected under the analysis of the previous paragraph. Data obtained by Ottenbacher (1986) also show that serial dependence in charts increases judge unreliability (Matyas & Greenwood, 1990b).

Despite these findings, there are also results suggesting that some patterns associated with certain types of serial dependence do not affect visual analysis adversely (e.g., DeProspero & Cohen, 1979; Jones, Weinrott & Vaught, 1978) but this issue was discussed in greater length in chap. 5 of this volume. Moreover, the study of the effect of serial dependence on visual analysis is still in its infancy. The data reviewed previously cover only a small portion of the time series that produce serial dependence. For example, there are no data on the effect of cyclicity and stochastic models with negative autocorrelation, nor on the effect of curvilinear deterministic trends, such as might occur during adaptation unrelated to intervention (e.g., natural recovery).

Although the issues have not always been simple, and some remain to be resolved more clearly in the empirical arena, the presence of serial dependence in single-case baselines is of significance from the perspective of both statistical analysis and graphical judgment. The issue also needs to be addressed in order to establish a proper understanding of the time series that are characteristic of the fields of interest. The methodological interest in single-case time series analysis subsumes a more fundamental question about the variables being investigated. Of course, these problems are of theoretical interest only if autocorrelation does not in fact exist in behavioral data. Although it may appear strange to imagine that psychological and behavioral time series pervasively comprise random fluctuations around a mean value, this argument has been canvassed and the resulting autocorrelation debate has been of sufficient interest to generate a spirited literature (Busk & Marascuilo, 1988; Huitema, 1985, 1986, 1988; Sharpley & Alavosius, 1988; Suen, 1987; Suen & Ary, 1987). The next section reviews this literature and presents new results pertaining to this discussion.

IS THERE SERIAL DEPENDENCE IN BEHAVIORAL BASELINE SERIES?

Early Evidence Concerning the Presence of Serial Dependency

The biasing effects of serial dependency on classical methods of statistical analysis have been known for some time. For example, Scheffé (1959) showed that the *F* test is too liberal in the presence of positive autocorrelation and too conservative in the presence of negative autocorrelation. Despite this, it is only relatively recently that attention has been given to the question of whether behavioral time series are serially dependent.

Jones, Vaught, and Weinrott (1977), in a paper that aimed to encourage the use of time-series analysis for single-case time series, pointed to the importance of serial dependency in behavioral time series. Gentile, Roden, and Klein (1972) had earlier proposed the use of analysis of variance models to analyse time-series data. Jones et al. (1977) and others (Glass, Wilson, & Gottman, 1975; Hartmann, 1974; Thoresen & Elashoff, 1974) argued that the presence of serial dependence invalidated the use of such an analytic method. Jones et al. (1977) went further to claim that visual analysis would also be influenced by the presence of serial dependence.

More important for the present discussion, Jones et al. (1977) claimed that "Serial dependency is a common property of behavioral scores, such as repeated observations of the same subject" (p. 153) and went further to state that "It could be argued that serial dependency should always be found in repeated measurements for individual subjects" (p. 154). Such claims were not uncommon in writings of that time, although these claims were not supported by empirical data. However, unlike the majority of authors, Jones et al. (1977) did provide some empirical support for their assertions.

They applied time-series analyses to data from 24 graphs of experimental results sampled from the *Journal of Applied Behavior Analysis* (JABA) and reported that 20 (83%) of the graphs displayed significant lag 1 autocorrelation with coefficients ranging from .40 to .93. Of these, 9 graphs (45%) had first order autocorrelation coefficients in excess of .70. On the basis of these findings Jones et al. concluded that "Serial dependency is a common property of behavioral scores obtained in operant research" (p. 154).

Hartmann et al. (1980) reiterated the view that serial dependency is a common property of behavioral time series, and reported on an unpublished study by Kennedy in 1976 in which 29% of time series in a sample of series selected from JABA were found to have significant serial correlations. Hartmann et al. (1980) noted the discrepancy in the figures (83% vs. 29%) provided by Jones et al. (1977) and Kennedy and, although unable to account for it, concluded that it was clear that a substantial number of published single-case charts were serially dependent.

We became intrigued by this discrepancy and, when we examined closely the sampling procedure of Jones et al. (1977), we discovered (Jones, Weinrott, & Vaught, 1978) that their sample of charts had been deliberately biased to include time series where serial dependency was apparent from a visual inspection of the charts. Although we had some sympathy with their reasons for choosing such charts to compare the results of visual and statistical analysis of time series, as was the aim of their 1978 paper, we did not believe that such a sampling procedure was a sensible method to use to determine the prevalence of serial dependency in behavioral time series.

Therefore, we decided to conduct a proper survey of the serial dependency found in the baseline phases of behavioral time series published in JABA. We surveyed 182 baseline phases of single-case studies published in JABA between 1977 and 1983 (Matyas & Greenwood, 1985). We found that 31% of baseline series displayed significant positive lag 1 autocorrelation, but that only 6% of series had $\Sigma a_i \geq 0.6$, a value that Gottman (1981) suggested invalidated the use of his ITSE procedure for analysis. At that time, we concluded that although serial dependence seemed not to be as much a problem as had previously been thought, a significant number of series displayed levels of serial dependence likely to be problematic for analysis.

The Huitema Survey

Around the same time, Huitema (1985, 1986) conducted a similar survey that also involved data from graphs published in JABA during a nonoverlapping period (1968–1977). Huitema exposed a more serious flaw in the work of Jones et al. (1977) than that described previously. He pointed out that Jones et al. had erroneously calculated the lag 1 autocorrelations they reported from a combined series of raw pre- and postintervention data. Where an intervention effect is present (i.e., the mean scores of the phases differ), such an approach will result in greatly inflated autocorrelation estimates. Huitema correctly pointed out the error in this method of calculating autocorrelation.

Huitema proceeded to reanalyze the 24 data sets used by Jones et al. (1977). He calculated the lag 1 autocorrelation coefficient within each phase found in the 24 charts (a total of 61 phases). Of the 61 autocorrelation coefficients calculated, only one was found to differ significantly from zero using Bartlett's test (1946), and the largest lag 1 autocorrelation coefficient was .47, not the .93 reported by Jones et al. (1977).

Having demonstrated the errors with the method of calculating autocorrelation coefficients used by Jones et al. (1977) and the spurious results produced, Huitema proceeded to conduct a proper survey of serial dependence in behavioral time series. He studied all time series published in JABA between 1968 and 1977 that contained more than five points in the baseline and in which there were nonzero values (some other exclusion criteria were also applied; see Huitema, 1985). A total of 441 data sets were included, which yielded a total of 1748 phases. Huitema concentrated on the 441 baseline phases, because these were the phases that tended to contain the most points and, of course, each chart selected must have had a baseline phase. The distribution of raw autocorrelation coefficients and Fisher *Z* transformed coefficients were presented.

So far, the method used by Huitema in his survey was the same as that used by us (Matyas & Greenwood, 1985), and the resulting distributions were very similar (compare Huitema, 1985, Fig. 3 and Matyas & Greenwood, 1991, Fig. 4). However, the conclusions drawn by Huitema were very different from ours. To explain the discrepancy, it is necessary to describe Huitema's approach to answering the question of whether serial dependence exists in behavioral time series.

Huitema (1985) reasoned that if there were no serial dependency in all behavioral time series, then the distribution of lag 1 autocorrelation coefficients should be normally distributed with a mean of zero. He was also able to predict the standard deviation of the distribution of autocorrelation coefficients assuming that all series contained 10 data points (which was the median number of baseline points in the series he sampled). His distribution of raw lag 1 autocorrelation coefficients appeared to deviate little from these predictions. The mean lag 1 autocorrelation coefficient was −0.01, and there was no significant deviation from the obtained and expected frequencies of coefficients found using a chi-square test.

Huitema admitted that this was a crude test and that a better test would be provided by analysing standardized autocorrelation coefficients, which would deal with the problem of different number of points in the series. The distribution of standardized autocorrelation coefficients was then examined and the obtained and expected (standard normal distribution) frequencies compared using a chi-square test. This test identified a significant discrepancy between the observed and theoretical distributions. However, using an unspecified "intensive analysis" Huitema (1985, p. 114) attributed the discrepancy to 10 studies with standardized autocorrelation values greater than 2.7. When these series were fitted with linear and nonlinear regression models to remove trend, their residuals were found to have low lag 1 autocorrelation values. Huitema concluded that there was "little or no autocorrelation problem in applied behavioral data" and that "a wide range of conventional statistical methods can be employed" (Huitema, 1985, p. 116).

Criticisms of the Huitema Survey

Huitema's 1985 paper, entitled "Autocorrelation in Applied Behavior Analysis: A Myth," attracted a variety of comment and criticism, which became known as the autocorrelation debate. Given the beliefs previously expressed in the literature (see previous discussion) concerning the existence of serial dependence, the heat developed in this debate is not surprising. A number of counterarguments were put forward, most of which related to the lack of power present in tests of whether autocorrelation is significant in brief time series.

Lack of Power. All of the critics (Busk & Marascuilo, 1988; Sharpley & Alavosius, 1988; Suen, 1987; Suen & Ary, 1987) pointed to the problems of lack of power inherent in dealing with behavioral time series where there are typically very few points. They argued that tests for autocorrelation are likely to have very little power and that Huitema's observation that few lag 1 autocorrelation coefficients were significant was simply a result of low power rather than a reflection of the true state of behavioral time series.

Busk and Marascuilo (1988) conducted a survey of autocorrelation coefficients from JABA series and demonstrated, using a power analysis method proposed by Suen and Ary (1987), that the power for detecting significant autocorrelation was very low in behavioral time series with small ($n = 6 - 15$) and medium ($n = 16 - 30$) sample sizes.

The Fallacy of Accepting the Null. Suen (1987) challenged the logic of Huitema's analytic approach. To conclude that serial dependence was a feature of behavioral time series, Huitema required the empirically obtained distribution of autocorrelations to deviate by a statistically significant amount from the distribution expected under null autocorrelation assumptions. Suen argued that failure to reject the null hypothesis could not be interpreted to indicate the truth of the null hypothesis. He concluded that the burden of proof should be on the nonexistence of autocorrelation rather than on its existence.

A related point was made by Sharpley and Alavosius (1988), who argued that the issue is not whether the autocorrelation coefficient is statistically significant or not, but whether the degree of autocorrelation present will distort the results of classical statistical procedures.

Incorrect Standardization Procedure. Busk and Marascuilo (1988) pointed out that the Bartlett test (1946) is a large sample procedure and should not have been used to standardize the autocorrelation coefficients or as a significance test. (This criticism is dealt with in more detail later in this chapter.)

Inconsistent Use of the Meta-Analytic Stance. Both Busk and Marascuilo (1988) and Matyas and Greenwood (1991) criticized Huitema for his inconsistent use of the meta-analytic stance he chose. As detailed earlier, Huitema relied on a failure to find a difference between the observed and theoretical distributions of standardized autocorrelation coefficients. When a significant deviation was found, he switched from the populationwide approach to an "intensive analysis," which resulted in the elimination of 10 problematic series. Of course, any distribution that deviates from normality can be made normal by the removal of values that do not fit (Matyas & Greenwood, 1991).

The Busk & Marascuilo Survey

Busk and Marascuilo (1988), dissatisfied with Huitema's methodology, conducted a "counter" survey. They examined 44 studies published in JABA between 1975 to 1985 that had a baseline phase and more than 5 points per phase. From these studies, 101 baseline phases and 125 intervention phases were available. To avoid a problem they considered to be inherent in Huitema's approach, they examined the autocorrelation coefficients in three groups with similar numbers of points per phase: "small" samples, 6–15 points; "medium" samples, 15–30 points; and "large" samples, more than 30 points. Binomial tests comparing the number of positive and the number of negative autocorrelation coefficients were used. They reasoned that, if Huitema was correct and autocorrelation coefficients are randomly distributed around zero, an approximately equal number of positive and negative values should be observed. The null hypothesis was rejected for the total sample of baseline phase autocorrelation coefficients and for the large sample subset because of an excess of positive autocorrelation coefficients. The tests for small and medium sample subsets did not reach significance. For intervention series, analysis of the total sample and all three subsets resulted in significance indicating an excess of positive autocorrelation coefficients.

Busk and Marascuilo (1988) concluded that "Many single-subject research studies are based on data where the autocorrelation tends to be larger than zero" (p. 238). They further demonstrated that 40% of baselines phases and 59% of intervention phases had autocorrelation coefficients greater than 0.25, a value that has been argued to result in substantial increases in the Type-I error rate of classical statistical methods.

Huitema's Response

Huitema (1988) provided an extremely detailed reply to his critics. His main point was that, in focusing on the power issue, the critics had failed to understand his meta-analytic approach. Huitema did not rely on the significance testing of his autocorrelation coefficients, but instead on their distribution. Although power problems might influence the number of significant values found, they should not influence the distribution of standardized autocorrelation coefficients. We believe that Huitema's response here was justified.

Huitema also pointed to some problems in the criticisms concerning the logic of accepting the null hypothesis, although he did skirt the issue of whether there were alternative models of the structure of autocorrelation in behavioral time series that could result in a distribution such as he observed.

Huitema's response concerning the incorrect standardization procedure is of interest. Busk and Marascuilo (1988) simply stated that the procedure was designed for large samples and therefore inappropriate. Huitema (1988) agreed that the procedure had been used for large samples but argued that many large sample tests perform adequately in the small sample situation, alternative tests for the small sample case were not developed for use with the autocorrelation coefficient, and that the Bartlett test's large sample properties are well known. However, as Matyas and Greenwood (1991) demonstrated and as confirmed by Huitema and McKean (1991), the Bartlett statistic was not an appropriate choice for use in standardization.

Huitema's sole response to the criticism of inconsistent use of the meta-analytic stance was that the nonstationarity of the offending series justified his procedure. This argument would have been more convincing if Huitema had applied the same procedures to all series before examining the distribution of autocorrelation in the residuals. It is quite possible that the measured autocorrelation of a number of series that did not show large autocorrelation coefficients would change after "intensive" analysis and that, therefore, the distribution of standardized coefficients would alter. For example, if linear trend were removed from all series (whether there was "genuine" linear trend or not) before the autocorrelation were assessed, then the measured autocorrelation coefficients would have tended to have decreased magnitude. This would have had the effect of reducing the mean of the autocorrelation distribution and also of reducing its standard deviation. These changes would have resulted in a poorer fit between the actual distribution and the theoretical distribution proposed by Huitema.

Huitema's response to the criticism of the lack of serial dependency being due to data acquisition artifacts seems reasoned and, in any case, it seems very unlikely that such an explanation could be responsible for the results he found.

Although Huitema made many valid criticisms of the Busk and Marascuilo countersurvey, the fact remains that they found a median raw autocorrelation coefficient of around 0.20 compared to Huitema's median values of .03 to .07. Huitema claimed, without providing any empirical data, that Busk and Marascuilo's more recent sample had longer baseline phases with steeper slopes. The median values reported by Busk and Marascuilo do present a problem for Huitema's position, unless one is willing to argue that baseline slopes were steeper in this sample. That the data reported in JABA has changed so much in that period of time seems unlikely. However, it should be noted that the median values reported in our survey of autocorrelation coefficients, which we sampled from the same period as did Busk and Marascuilo, were more similar to the values reported by Huitema. This finding casts some doubt on the meaning of the Busk and Marascuilo (1988) survey.

Matyas and Greenwood's Criticisms

Although Huitema responded well to the criticisms reviewed previously, addressing all of the points raised and exposing some weaknesses in the arguments, we remained intrigued by Huitema's basic argument. Our 1985 survey had resulted in a distribution of autocorrelation coefficients similar to that of Huitema (1985), but we had not employed his meta-analytic approach. Although we found it difficult to accept the idea that all behavioral time series shared a similar null autocorrelation parameter, we appreciated the logic of Huitema's approach. Our view was also that the criticisms made during the autocorrelation debate did not clearly demonstrate any major flaw in his argument. This state of affairs motivated us to examine more closely the methodology used by

Huitema. In doing so, we noted several flaws indicating that his conclusions were not correct (Matyas & Greenwood, 1991).

Standard Deviation Estimation Problems. The first problem we found related to the method used to standardize the raw autocorrelations. A major aspect of Huitema's argument is that the distribution of r_1 was centered on zero. This, he implied, is evidence that behavior is not autocorrelated. However, it is also possible to envisage behaviors and individuals as being very heterogeneous, with some time series positively autocorrelated and others negatively. It can be imagined that the populations of time series characteristic of particular individuals, particular target behaviors, and particular sampling intervals are melded into a superpopulation, which is then arbitrarily sampled. There seems to be no reason to argue that it would be impossible, or even unlikely, for the sampling distribution of r_1 from this superpopulation to be quasi-normal with a mean autocorrelation around zero. Thus, Huitema's distribution may not have been uniquely determined by a single underlying process with $r_1 = 0$.

Consideration of this alternative hypothesis suggests that a larger variance in the distribution of r_1 might be a more appropriate nonnull prediction than hypotheses about central tendency shifts. Not only will there be the variance in r_1 due to sampling error, but also that due to the systematic variation between the processes characteristic of particular individuals, behaviors, and sampling intervals. This reasoning suggests in turn that determination of the distribution variance should be carefully examined.

Huitema (1985) reported that he standardized the autocorrelations before examining the obtained distribution for departure from normality. The formula employed for the standardization process will influence the shape of the distribution. A number of formulae appear in the literature. Huitema (1985) used the Fisher-*z* method to standardize. Another commonly used formula for the standard deviation of r_1, which Huitema used to test for significance of individual autocorrelations but not to standardize them, is that provided by Bartlett (Bartlett, 1946). Davies, Triggs, and Newbold (1977), using arguments derived from Moran (1947, 1948), pointed out that a more precise formula exists. This is the formula employed for time-series analysis by the SPSS subprogram Box-Jenkins. Following Davies et al., we also examined the early literature. We found that Moran (1948) had presented two expectations for the standard deviation of r_1, one based on a cyclic definition suggested by Hotelling (Anderson, 1942; Dixon, 1944).

In order to compare the performance of these formulae, we computed their values over the range $n = 5$ to $n = 80$ and found that the formulae deviate nontrivially at sample sizes of $n \leq 20$. We further found that the Fisher-z method, followed by Bartlett's formula, gave the largest values and would, therefore, provide less sensitive significance tests. When employed to generate standardized distributions, such distributions would have a lower variance than if the alternative standardization techniques were used. This is because each r_1 would be divided by a larger estimate of the standard deviation, thus resulting in a lower variance of the distribution of standardized values. Huitema standardized using the least sensitive method and used the next least sensitive method to test for significance of individual r_1s.

Central Tendency Estimation Problems. Huitema also argued that behavioral data are not autocorrelated because his r_1 distribution was centered close to zero. Although not explicitly stated, Huitema (1985) seems to have expected the central tendency to be zero and used this expectation in his standardization and in significance testing. Is an expectation of zero central tendency the appropriate null hypothesis for r_1?

Reexamination of the literature yielded a number of early papers (Anderson, 1942; Dixon, 1944; Moran, 1948) that all obtained the expectation $-(n - 1)^{-1}$ for the null distribution of r_1. At small sample sizes, the central tendency expectation will be nontrivially below zero. Huitema, at least by 1988, was aware of this negative expectation. In his 1988 paper, he made the point several times (pp. 261, 262, 266, 272) that the autocorrelation coefficient is a biased estimator at small sample sizes. However, he did not take this negative expectation into account in his survey. This negative bias not only challenges Huitema's assumption of null expectancy for the sample autocorrelation, but also indicates a further difficulty in his approach of having to obtain a composite null expectancy based on different sample sizes. Huitema's (1985) meta-analysis did not take the negative bias into account, nor the fact that the negative bias would vary according to sample size. This raises the possibility that his distribution of r_1s was in fact centered significantly above what would be expected under the null hypothesis.

Having identified these problems in the way in which Huitema conducted his meta-analysis (but not in the basic approach), we decided to replicate his approach using the values from our survey but to correct for the problems associated with central tendency expectation and standard deviation estimate. To achieve this, we first conducted a number of large simulation studies to determine empirically the appropriate standard deviation formula to use in the procedure and also to examine the degree of bias in the estimation of the population autocorrelation coefficient when the true value was not equal to zero (which was the only theoretically known case). We found that Moran's (1948) cyclic formula provided the best fit to the empirically derived standard deviation. We furthermore found that the shape of the distribution of measured autocorrelation coefficients was not normal (as Huitema expected) at small sample sizes.

In summary, our work demonstrated that, if Huitema's theory of zero autocorrelation in behavioral time series were correct, he should have obtained a distribution of autocorrelation coefficients that had a mean of less than zero (because of the negative bias of the autocorrelation coefficient) and that had much less spread than he reported (because he used an inappropriate standard deviation estimate). The obtained distribution supported better the idea proposed earlier that a variety of true autocorrelation coefficients exist in behavioral data according to the individual studied, the behavior assessed, and the sampling characteristics employed.

The Matyas and Greenwood Survey

Using our empirically derived central tendency and standard deviation estimates, we reexamined the series in our 1985 survey and found that 23.1% of them showed significant autocorrelation. This is a tenfold increase over the 10 series out of 441 (2.3%) reported by Huitema. This incidence of significant autocorrelations was clearly inconsistent with Huitema's argument that behavioral time series have a true autocorrelation coefficient of zero and that deviations from zero in measured autocorrelation are solely due to error fluctuation.

Huitema and McKean's Unbiased Estimator

Huitema and McKean (1991) reported on further work into autocorrelation estimation and inference with small samples. In this paper they examined in detail the bias in the autocorrelation estimator and provided empirical evidence that a correction factor of 1/N be added to r_1 to provide a estimator of lag 1 autocorrelation that is unbiased when $\rho = 0$ (but, *importantly*, not when $\rho \neq 0$). They also demonstrated, as had Matyas and Greenwood (1991), that the Bartlett test used by Huitema (1985) is inappropriate with small samples. They proposed using a standard deviation estimate of $[(N - 2)^2/(N^2(N - 1)]^{1/2}$ when $\rho = 0$.

It should be noted that nowhere in this paper (Huitema & McKean, 1991) were the implications of these findings for the earlier conclusions discussed. It is clear, however, that the degree of bias demonstrated in the autocorrelation coefficient at small n and the inappropriateness of standard deviation estimate used in Huitema's meta-analysis invalidated his earlier conclusions.

A New Analysis Based on Huitema's "Unbiased" Estimator

To demonstrate the problems for Huitema's earlier conclusions posed by his work on a less biased estimator of r_1 and a better standard deviation estimate, we applied these formulae to the series in our 1985 survey. First order autocorrelation coefficients, calculated using the less biased method ($r_1 + 1/N$) proposed by Huitema and McKean (1991), were obtained for the 182 single-case time series published in the *Journal of Applied Behavior Analysis* between 1977 and 1983 (Matyas & Greenwood, 1991). Each coefficient was converted to a standard (Z) score by dividing it by the standard deviation proposed by Huitema and McKean (1991). The distribution of Z scores in shown in Fig. 7.5.

If Huitema's (1985) theory is correct, this distribution of Z scores should be normal with a mean of 0 and a standard deviation of 1. It is clear from an inspection of Fig. 7.4 that the obtained distribution of Z

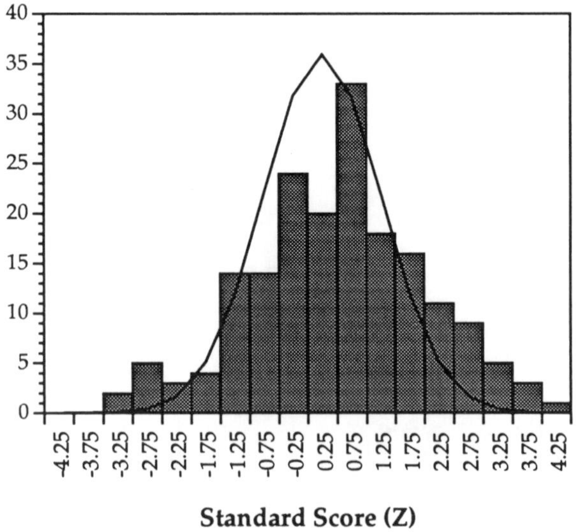

FIG. 7.5. Distribution of standardized first order autocorrelation coefficients calculated using Huitema & McKean's (1991) improved estimators of r_1 and its standard deviation.

scores deviates from the standard normal curve overlaid on the figure. The mean obtained Z score was 0.521, not zero as predicted by Huitema's theory. The standard deviation of the Z scores was 1.476, not 1.0. The obtained distribution of Z scores was found to deviate significantly from a standard normal curve using a Kolmogorov-Smirnov test, $Z = 3.078$, $p < .001$. Moreover, 22.5% (rather than the expected 5%) of the Z scores exceeded the critical Z of 1.96 appropriate for a type 1 error rate of .05; 17.0% of these were positive autocorrelations and 5.5% were negative.

Conclusion

In summary, the previous analysis shows, using Huitema's meta-analytic approach, that his conclusion that behavioral time series are not autocorrelated is untenable. Although autocorrelation at lag 1 does not seem to be as frequent nor as large as once believed, it is clear that the general hypothesis of null autocorrelation cannot be sustained.

IMPLICATIONS OF THE PRESENCE OF AUTOCORRELATION IN BASELINES

The distribution of the lag 1 autocorrelation in behavioral baselines is not centred where the null predicts, and is more heteregeneous. These findings suggest that we may be dealing with more than one population of time series that have been melded in the exercise of overall analysis, a position we have previously canvassed (Matyas & Greenwood, 1991). This, in turn, indicates that neither statistical nor visual analyses can assume a priori a simple "flat straight line plus random residual" model.

The nonnull tendency toward positive lag 1 autocorrelation was much more pronounced than that toward negative autocorrelation, although both exceeded the expected 2.5%. When the autocorrelation of residuals is positive, tests based on the t or F distributions will be too liberal (Matyas & Greenwood, 1991). Similarly, visual analysis tends to become too liberal (Matyas & Greenwood, 1990a) when first order autoregressive models generate positive r_1 values. This may not be the case with positive autocorrelation in the context of other models, but a potential problem does appear to exist, which deserves further investigation.

Negative autocorrelation tends to engender conservatism of both statistical analysis (Greenwood & Matyas, 1990) and visual judgment (Gregg, Matyas, & Greenwood, 1990) when data are generated by a first order autoregressive process. However, the key issue is correct model identification for the purpose of forecasting and comparing, rather than the fact that the lag 1 autocorrelation is positive or negative. It is for this purpose of indicating the type of time series that the detailed nature of deviations in the autocorrelogram from null are principally significant and, in this respect (that of understanding the underlying temporal pattern of relevant behavioral or psychological variables), the literature suggests a surprising degree of ignorance. Unlike many other disciplines, we seem to lack an extensive description of the temporal pattern for many key variables.

The rejection of an ubiquitous model for behavioral baselines is unlikely to surprise, but does raise the issue that statistical analysis for single-case designs will need to conduct specific model identification as a prelude to ITSA. It is premature to recommend the simple panacea of conducting interrupted time-series analyses as if autocorrelation was null, or using only linear regression models, as Huitema (1985) did. The consequences of this conclusion are nontrivial. Statistical analysis of single-case data where the model is unknown has presented serious difficulties because behavioral baselines are usually very brief. As Huitema (1986) very cogently pointed out, it is not simply a power limitation issue. The model identification problem demands a longer baseline than typically collected by single-case analysts (Glass, Wilson, & Gottman, 1975; Gottman, 1981; Huitema, 1986). The distinction between a linear deterministic process with random residual versus other possibilities, such as the various stochastic processes, or the various nonlinear deterministic models, is not possible to detect when very little data are available.

In this respect it is worth noting that the tools of model identification described in classic texts on the analysis of time series (Box & Jenkins, 1976; Glass, Wilson, & Gottman, 1975) work poorly when brief samples are all that is available, although this has not been broadly acknowledged in the behavioral literature. For example, the autocorrelogram shown in Fig. 7.3 is based upon a large sample ($n > 100$) of the autoregressive time series. In the majority of the behavioral literature, time series are much shorter (Huitema (1985). Autocorrelograms calculated from brief samples are severely distorted. This is illustrated in Fig. 7.6, which presents the autocorrelograms and partial autocorrelograms for the autoregressive model in Fig. 7.4. In Panel A of Fig. 7.6, the autocorrelogram is based on the full large sample ($n = 300$) and clearly indicates the characteristic pattern for first order autoregressive series seen also in Fig. 7.3. Note, however, that the lower panels of Fig. 7.6, which depict the autocorrelograms for shorter samples ($N = 10$) of the same data or residuals from linear modeling depart radically in appearance from the expected large sample pattern. Fig. 7.6 illustrates an aspect of the diffi-

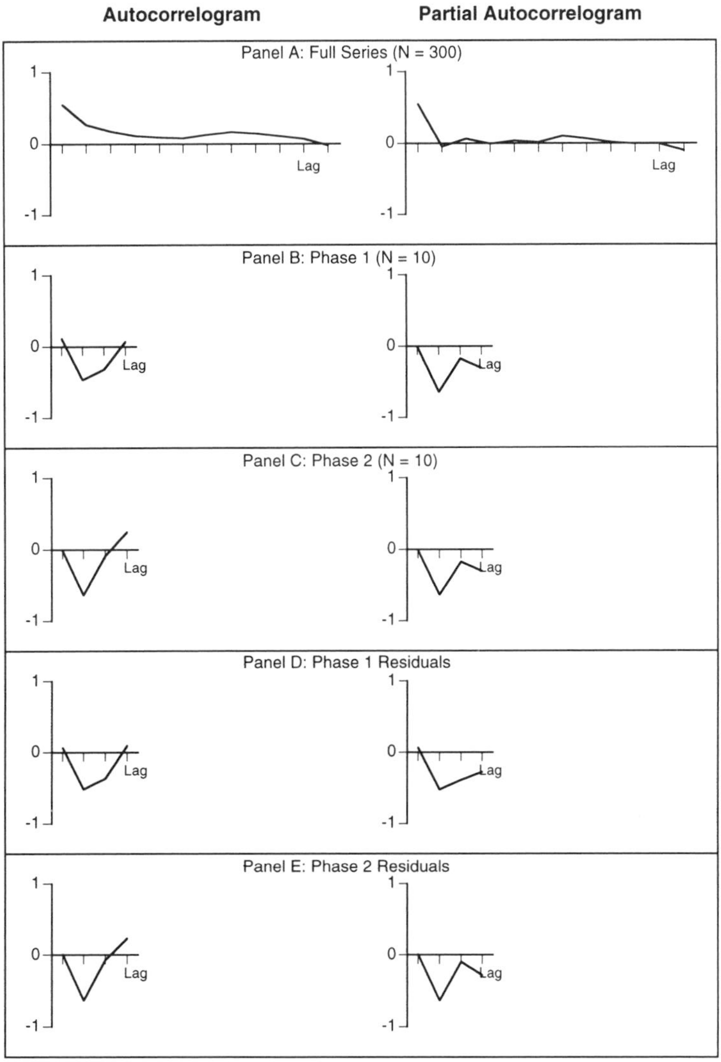

FIG. 7.6. Autocorrelograms and partial autocorrelograms calculated from the the first order autoregressive series depicted in Fig. 7.4 (Panel A), the two phases of the subsample identified in the inset of Fig. 7.4 (Panels B and C), and the residuals from linear regression models fitted to the subsample phases (Panels D and E).

culties encountered in correct model identification with brief samples, such as may be found in the behavioral literature.

Although a number of attempts to avoid the model identification process have been suggested (Gottman, 1981; Simonton, 1977; Velicer & MacDonald, 1984), these do not seem appropriate. One already has been empirically demonstrated to fail (Greenwood & Matyas, 1990), but these methods are a priori problematical. The proposals of Velicer and MacDonald (1984) and Simonton (1977) are based around the idea of applying high order equations which adapt well to complex forms. For example, Simonton proposed that a seventh order autoregressive model be used; that is, a model with a constant and seven autoregressive parameters (representing lags 1–7). "Approximative" models require both the assumption that fitting higher order models (overfitting) will not adversely affect the type 1 error estimation and that a large number of parameters can be estimated. The effect of overfitting has not been extensively studied. However, fitting a higher order autoregressive model to data generated by a lower order model has been shown not to be robust (Greenwood & Matyas, 1990). More directly, the problem of estimating a large number of model parameters when relatively few within phase values are available prevents the idea of high order models from being effective solutions. A model with seven autoregression coefficients would often have more parameters than data, if Huitema's (1985) survey of the length of previously published baselines is an indication of the future! On the contrary, the analysis of brief time series such as are collected during single-case experimental designs should examine very carefully the use of the *simplest* possible models.

Because model identification with a single brief time series cannot be done well, the obvious alternative is to investigate sets of long series and determine if a homogeneous model can be applied for a particular type of outcome measure. Such investigations seem long overdue. They would address the methodological issue of model identification and provide valuable insight into the nature of the target behavior. If model selection were based on prior investigative modeling and on theory about the target behavior, then statistical analysis of single-case data would be freed of its major conundrum.

The presence of serial dependence in behavioral baselines also raises issues for visual analysis. The performance of human judges using case charts has been shown to be influenced by serial dependence interacting with random variability in the context of a first order autoregressive model (Matyas & Greenwood, 1990a, 1991). However, the issue is not yet clear. Because serial dependence merely reflects the presence of nonrandom trend in data, the more complex questions are what aspects of nonrandom variation influence error of judgment. Autocorrelation is only a crude measure, and serial dependence arises from a very wide range of time-series models, some of which may be problematical for the visual analyst and some of which may be much less so. For example, when a linear model, which is highly familiar to human judgment, is in fact generating the autocorrelation, human judges may cope well. This appeared to be the case in DeProspero and Cohen's (1979) study, where tilting a linear model by 30° had little impact on interjudge agreement rates. The study of how different time series influence human judges is only just beginning. It would be useful to know much more about the ability of human judgment confronted by data generated under a range of realistic models other than the linear or first order autoregressive types, which have characterized the literature to date (see section 3 in this chap., and chap. 5 of this volume).

In concluding this chapter, it should be noted that despite the substantial debate raised to date by the issue of serial dependence in single-case baselines, the analysis of such dependence nevertheless remains in its infancy. All analyses so far, including our own, have been restricted to examination of the lag 1 coefficient. The deeper analysis of the time-series structure, based on techniques such as portmanteau tests, autocorrelograms, partial autocorrelograms, model fitting, and examination of residuals (Box & Jenkins, 1976; Glass, Wilson, & Gottman, 1975; Gottman, 1981) remains to be conducted. We presume debate has centered around the lag 1 autoregression because the primary question has been the rather crude one of whether a null hypothesis could be sustained and the lag 1 autocorrelation is a simple first test of that proposition. However, it is not by any means a complete assessment of that issue, nor does it address the question of more fundamental value: What is the nature of the underlying series? If the answer to that question is not "Mean plus a random normally distributed residual," then several possibilities with distinct characteristics arise. These distinct characteristics are important methodologically because both statistical and graphical approaches to the analysis of single-case data can be influenced by the nature of the underlying series, as reviewed in earlier sections of this chapter and elsewhere in this volume (chaps. 5, 6, 9). The distinctions are also likely to be of conceptual value, because different equations can signify important differences in the causal processes of behaviors of interest. This latter issue has not received the attention it deserves in the literature on single-case design. Single-case time series are not only a methodological device, they are also an evaluation tool. The pattern of individual behavior over a sustained period is a fundamental phenomenon that a science of human behavior ought be able to predict and ultimately explain. Improvements in technology are likely once improvements in fundamental science are achieved.

REFERENCES

Anderson, R. L. (1942). Distribution of the serial correlation coefficient. *Annals of Mathematical Statistics, 13,* 1–13.

Bartlett, M. S. (1946). On the theoretical specification of the sampling properties of autocorrelated time series. *Journal of the Royal Statistical Society, B8,* 27–41.

Box G. E. P., & Jenkins G. M. (1976). *Time series analysis: Forecasting and control.* San Francisco: Holden-Day.

Busk, P. L., & Marascuilo, L. A. (1988). Autocorrelation in single-subject research: A counterargument to the myth of no autocorrelation. *Behavioral Assessment, 10,* 229–242.

Crosbie, J. (1987). The inability of the binominal test to control type 1 error with single-subject data. *Behavioral Assessment, 9,* 141–150.

Davies, N., Triggs, C. M., & Newbold, P. (1977). Significance levels of the Box-Pierce portmanteau statistic in finite samples. *Biometrika, 64,* 517–522.

DeProspero, A., & Cohen, S. (1979). Inconsistent visual analyses of intrasubject data. *Journal of Applied Behavior Analysis, 12,* 573–579.

Dixon, W. J. (1944). Further contributions to the problem of serial correlation. *Annals of Mathematical Statistics, 15,* 119–144.

Edgington, E. S. (1987). *Randomization tests* (2nd ed.). New York: Marcel Dekker.

Gentile, J. R., Roden, A. H., & Klein, R. D. (1972). An analysis-of-variance model for the intrasubject replication design. *Journal of Applied Behavior Analysis, 5,* 193–198.

Glass, G. V., Wilson, V. L., & Gottman, J. M. (1975). *Design and analysis of time-series experiments.* Boulder: Colorado Associated University Press.

Gottman, J. M. (1981). *Time-series analysis: A comprehensive introduction for social scientists.* Cambridge, England: Cambridge University Press.

Greenwood, K. M., & Matyas, T. A. (1990). Problems with the application of interrupted time-series analysis for brief single-subject data. *Behavioral Assessment, 12,* 1–16.

Gregg, M. E., Matyas, T. A., & Greenwood, K. M. (1990, July). *Reduction of false alarm rates in visual analysis of single-case charts by training with a programmed text.* Paper presented at the 13th National Conference of the Australian Behavior Modification Association, Melbourne.

Hartmann, D. P. (1974). Forcing square pegs into round holes: Some comments on an analysis of variance model for the intrasubject design. *Journal of Applied Behavior Analysis, 7,* 635–638.

Hartmann, D. P., Gottman, J. M., Jones, R. R., Gardner, W., Kazdin, A. E., & Vaught, R. S. (1980). Interrupted time-series analysis and its application to behavioral data. *Journal of Applied Behavior Analysis, 13,* 543–559.

Hersen, M., & Barlow, D. H. (1976). *Single case experimental designs: Strategies for studying behavior change.* Oxford, UK: Pergamon.

Hojem, M. A., & Ottenbacher, K. J. (1988). Empirical investigation of visual-inspection versus trend-line analysis of single-subject data. *Physical Therapy, 68,* 983–988.

Huitema, B. E. (1985). Autocorrelation in applied behavior analysis: A myth. *Behavioral Assessment, 7,* 107–118.

Huitema, B. E. (1986). Autocorrelation in behavioral research: Wherefore art thou? In A. Poling & R. W. Fuqua (Eds.), *Research methods in applied behavior analysis: Issues and advances* (pp. 187–208). New York: Plenum.

Huitema, B. E. (1988). Autocorrelation: 10 years of confusion. *Behavioral Assessment, 10,* 253–294.

Huitema, B. E., & McKean, J. W. (1991). Autocorrelation estimation and inference with small samples. *Psychological Bulletin, 110,* 291–304.

Jones, R. R., Vaught, R. S., & Weinrott, M. (1977). Time-series analysis in operant research. *Journal of Applied Behavior Analysis, 10,* 151–166.

Jones, R. R., Weinrott, M. R., & Vaught, R. S. (1978). Effects of serial dependency on the agreement between visual and statistical inference. *Journal of Applied Behavior Analysis, 11,* 277–283.

Kazdin, A. E. (1980). Obstacles in using randomization tests in single-case experimentation. *Journal of Educational Statistics, 5,* 253–260.

Kazdin, A. E. (1982). *Single-case research designs: Methods for clinical and applied settings.* New York: Oxford University Press.

Matyas, T. A., & Greenwood, K. M. (1985). *A survey of serial dependence in behavioral baselines.* Paper presented at the 8th annual conference of the Australian Behaviour Modification Association, Melbourne.

Matyas, T. A., & Greenwood, K. M. (1990a). Visual analysis of single-case time-series: Effects of variability, serial dependence and magnitude of intervention effect. *Journal of Applied Behavior Analysis, 23,* 1–11.

Matyas, T. A., & Greenwood, K. M. (1990b). The effect of serial dependence on visual judgment of single-case charts: An addendum. *American Journal of Occupational Therapy, 10,* 308–320.

Matyas , T. A., & Greenwood, K. M. (1991). Problems in the estimation of autocorrelation and some implications for behavioral data. *Behavioral Assessment, 13,* 137–157.

Moran, P. A. P. (1947). Some theorems on time series. I. *Biometrika, 34,* 281–291.

Moran, P. A. P. (1948). Some theorems on time series. II. The significance of the serial correlation coefficient. *Biometrika, 35,* 255–260.

Ottenbacher, K. J. (1986). An analysis of serial dependency in occupational therapy research. *Occupational Therapy Journal of Research, 6,* 211–216.

Scheffé, H. (1959). *The analysis of variance.* New York: Wiley.

Sharpley, C. F., & Alavosius, M. P. (1988). Autocorrelation in behavioral data: An alternative perspective. *Behavioral Assessment, 10,* 243–251.

Simonton, D. K. (1977). Cross-sectional time-series experiments: Some suggested statistical analyses. *Psychological Bulletin, 84,* 489–502.

Suen, H. K. (1987). On the epistemology of autocorrelation in applied behavior analysis. *Behavioral Assessment, 9,* 113–124.

Suen, H. K., & Ary, D. (1987). Autocorrelation in applied behavior analysis: Myth or reality? *Behavioral Assessment, 9,* 125–130.

Thoresen, C. E., & Elashoff, J. D. (1974). An analysis of variance model for intrasubject replication design: Some additional comments. *Journal of Applied Behavior Analysis, 7,* 639–641.

Velicer, W. F., & MacDonald, R. P. (1984). Time series analysis without model identification. *Multivariate Behavioral Research, 19,* 33–47.

White, O. R., & Haring, N. G. (1980). *Exceptional teaching* (2nd. ed.). Columbus, OH: Merrill.

8

Meta-Analysis of Single-Case Research

Myles S. Faith
David B. Allison
Obesity Research Center
St. Luke's/Roosevelt Hospital Center
Columbia University College of Physicians and Surgeons

Bernard S. Gorman
Hofstra University

INTRODUCTION

Meta-analysis is a collection of methods designed to quantitatively summarize the results of separate studies. Unlike previous "box-score" techniques that simply tabulated the number of research studies passing some criterion (such as statistical significance or another a priori criterion of improvement), meta-analysis employs quantitative measures of the magnitude of effect of each study.

Meta-analyses generally have three basic goals. First, meta-analytic studies strive to provide a point estimate of the average effect size; that is, an overall, quantitative summary. The need for a point estimate not withstanding, it has been said that "A statistician is someone who can drown in a stream whose average depth is six inches," implying that an average can obscure a great deal of variability. Obviously, it is also desirable to establish boundaries around a point estimate. Therefore, as a second goal, meta-analyses strive to provide confidence intervals in which the "true" population effect size is likely to be found. Given confidence intervals, one could easily establish whether the average effect size is significantly different from a null value. Finally, if there is substantial variability around an average effect size, then meta-analytic techniques also permit the researcher to search for variables that moderate effect sizes. Thus, a third goal of meta-analysis is to identify the variables that lead to larger or smaller effects.

Meta-analysis has several strengths and advantages over traditional narrative reviews. First, conducting a meta-analysis often forces the reviewer to become far more familiar with the data being reviewed than does a narrative review (Rosenthal, 1991a). Second, traditional narrative reviews have been shown as overly conservative (Cooper & Rosenthal, 1980; Rosenthal, 1979). That is, reviewers frequently underestimate the extent to which the data support clear conclusions. It seems that reviewers too often mistake sampling error for real between-study variation. Thus, traditional reviews often end with vague statements that more research is needed. In contrast, meta-analyses more often end with more interesting and informative statements such as "X clearly affects Y by such-and-such an amount on average, but more research is needed on how or under what circumstances." These more definitive statements are frequently made possible by the greater power that meta-analyses can achieve by pooling data from multiple sources. Third, meta-analyses foster greater objectivity by requiring meta-analysts to explicitly state their criteria for study inclusion and analyze all studies meeting those criteria (Cooper, 1982).

Single-case research has traditionally been neglected in meta-analytic reviews (Giles, 1990). This is, no doubt, due in part to a lack of agreed-upon and widely disseminated methods for meta-analyzing single-case research. Fortunately, methods have begun to emerge in recent years (Allison & Gorman, 1993; Busk & Serlin, 1992; Center, Skiba, & Casey, 1985–1986; Gingerich, 1984; Scruggs, Mastropieri, & Casto, 1987a; White, Rusch, Kazdin, & Hartmann, 1989), and several single-case meta-analyses have been published (Allison, Faith, & Franklin, 1995; Andrews, Guitar, & Howie, 1980; Scruggs, Mastropieri, & McEwen, 1988; Skiba, Casey, & Center, 1986; White et al., 1989). Meta-analyzing single-case research seems essential for two reasons. First, many treatments, particularly behavioral treatments, have been tested primarily in single-case designs. Therefore, evaluation of these treatments necessitates meta-analysis of the single-case literature. Second, single-case research frequently leaves readers wondering whether observed treatment effects would generalize to individuals other than the one being studied. By meta-analyzing data from many individuals, one obtains a better picture of the expected average effect.

Scope of This Chapter

This chapter contains four major sections. We begin with an overview of the steps involved in conducting a meta-analysis. Most of these issues are not unique to single-case meta-analyses; therefore, they are covered only briefly and other sources are referenced for more detail. Next, we discuss methods for the calculation of effect sizes, discussing two broad categories—nonregression approaches and regression approaches. The section ends with a discussion of the strengths and weaknesses of the various methods. Following this, we present four issues unique to the meta-analysis of single-case research. These issues include the appropriateness of combining single-case and group effect sizes, the handling of multiple effect sizes, alternative strategies for weighting effect sizes, and the selection of design phases to compare. In the final section, we review available software useful for meta-analytic work.

STEPS AND FEATURES OF A GOOD META-ANALYSIS

In this section, we discuss some of the features that produce a well-done meta-analysis. Most of the issues we discuss are not limited to the meta-analysis of single-case research and are discussed in greater detail in other sources (Cooper, 1982, 1989; Ellis, 1991; Green & Hall, 1984; Jackson, 1980; Wampold, Davis, & Good, 1990). Figure 8.1, adapted from Chalmers and Lau (1993), provides an overview of the steps involved in conducting a meta-analysis. This figure serves as a focus for the present discussion.

Defining the Question

Defining the research question must be the first step. In our experience, meta-analyses that address more focused and specific questions generally are more tractable and yield more informative results than do general questions. For example, broad research questions often become difficult to manage and analyze (e.g., What is the effect of behavioral treatment on undesirable behavior?). On the other hand, focused research questions often permit a more fine-tuned dissection of the data (e.g., What is the effect of overcorrection on self-stimulatory behavior?). Once the question has been defined, researchers specify inclusion criteria for potential studies. Here, sound operational definitions of the independent variable(s) (treatment; see Gresham, chap. 4, this volume) and the dependent variable(s) (outcome; see Primavera, Allison, & Alfonso, this volume) of interest must be defined. Additionally, the meta-analyst may wish to establish other necessary criteria. These might include some minimal score on a quality scale (see later discussion) or a minimum number of data points.

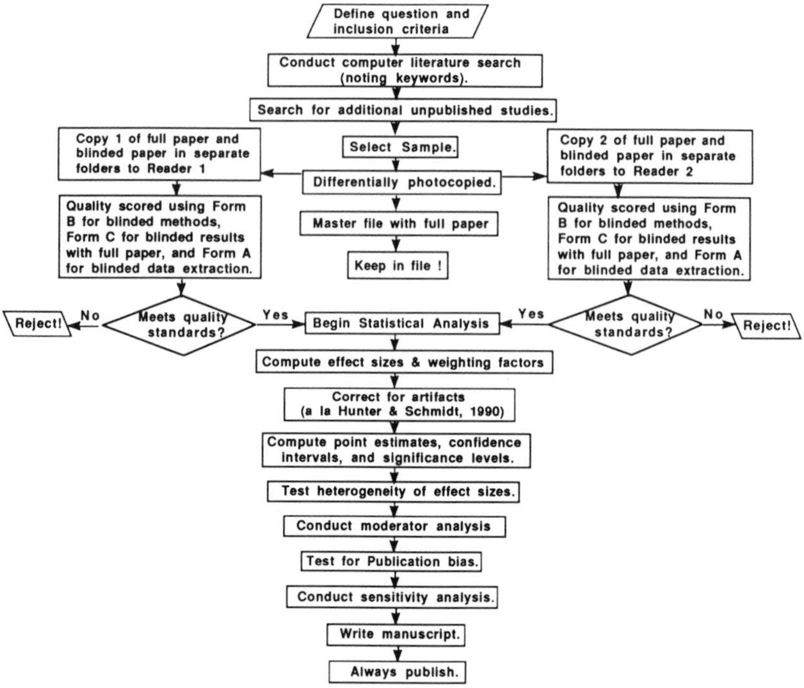

FIG. 8.1. An overview of the steps involved in conducting a meta-analysis. From Chalmers, T. C., & Lau, J. (1993). Meta-analytic stimulus for changes in clinical trials. *Statistical Methods in Medical Research, 2,* 162. Copyright © 1992 by the Cambridge University Press. Adapted with permission.

Searching the Literature

Once researchers define inclusion criteria, they search the literature for acceptable studies. The best way to start a search is by accessing a computer literature database, such as *MEDLINE, PsychLit, ERIC,* etc. It is also important to search for unpublished studies. One of the best sources for this is *Dissertation Abstracts,* also available in machine-readable form. The Internet is another excellent option that should not be overlooked. When conducting computer searches, it is helpful to record keywords used in the search strategy, because many meta-analysts publish this information in the methods section of their reports. Following computer database searches, it is generally necessary to conduct an "ancestry analysis" for older literature by checking reference lists of retrieved publications. Additionally, it is often useful to use the "invisible college"; that is, to contact investigators working in the area to check for further unretrieved (especially unpublished) articles. More discussions on conducting thorough literature searches can be found elsewhere (Dickersin, 1994; Reed & Baxter, 1994; Rosenthal, 1994; White, 1994).

Coding and Extracting Data

Once located, studies must be coded for relevant features, and the data necessary to calculate an effect size must be extracted. (Details on the latter aspect are contained in the following section on how to calculate effect sizes.) Regarding coding in general, it is essential to have a clear coding sheet with precise instructions for recording information about aspects of the studies. Figure 8.2 is an example of a coding sheet used by Allison et al. (1995) to study the effects of antecedent exercise on disruptive behaviors. Obviously, the nature of the coding sheet will vary from one meta-analysis to the next. Additional coding schemes for study quality can be found in Glass, McGaw, and Smith (1981) and Wortman (1994).

As Fig. 8.2 indicates, the data extraction and coding ideally are conducted independently by two people so that the reliability of the coding and extraction procedures can be assessed. This intercoder reliability can be quantified using the methods described by Primavera et al. (chap. 3, this volume).

Analyzing the Data

Computing Effect Sizes and Weighting Factors. The first step in analyzing the data is to compute effect sizes and weighting factors. (The computation of effect sizes is discussed later in considerable detail.) Weighting factors can be tricky, particularly when meta-analyzing single-case research. Meta-analysts typically weight each observation by the inverse of the variance of the observation's effect size (Hedges & Olkin, 1985). In single-case meta-analytic research, exact expressions for effect size variances have not been derived and development of such expressions is made difficult by the autocorrelation problem (Gorman & Allison, chap. 6, this volume; Matyas & Greenwood, chap. 7, this volume). Thus, in lieu of the inverse of the variance, one might weight each effect size by N, where N is the number of data points on which the effect size was calculated. (Alternative weights based on "pseudo-standard errors" are discussed later in the section addressing special issues in single-case meta-analysis.)

Additionally, investigators may wish to calculate other weighting factors. In particular, numerous investigators have suggested weighting by studies' quality scores (Chalmers et al., 1981; Felson, 1992; Fleiss, 1993;

Coding Form

Study ID#: ______________________

Authors: ____

____

Publication year: ____________________________

Was study published _______ or unpublished _______?

Were the majority of subjects (≥50%) diagnosed as:

[ ] Developmentally disabled only

[ ] Developmentally disabled plus other psychological diagnoses

[ ] not Developmentally disabled

Were the majority (>50%) of the subjects adults (≥21 years) _______ or children (<21 years) _______?

How many minutes did the exercise period last? _______

What type of exercise was employed? (check all that apply)

[ ] Jogging	[ ] Weight lifting
[ ] Walking	[ ] Other ____________________ (specify)
[ ] Aerobic dancing	
[ ] Cycle ergometer	

On how many subjects was the effect size derived? _______

Was the comparison on which the effect size was based (that which specifically evaluated the efficacy of AE) one that occurred between groups _______, within groups _______, or within single cases over time _______?

Which of the following DVs were measured?

Direct Observation	*Rating Scale*
[ ] Aggression (physical)	[ ] Hyperactivity
[ ] Self-stim/stereotypy	[ ] General "maladaptive" behavior
[ ] Self-injury	[ ] Other
[ ] Tantrumming	
[ ] Out-of-seat	
[ ] Talk outs/inappropriate verbalizations	
[ ] Other	

Describe how the effect size was calculated: ________________________________

____

____

____

What was the effect size? _______

What was the mean number of exercise sessions per subject? _______

Was some attention/activity control condition used? _______

Control for expectancy effects (if not stated assume not).

1) Were data collectors blind to experimental hypotheses? _______
2) Were data collectors blind to experimental conditions? _______
3) Were people interacting with subjects blind to experimental hypotheses? _______
4) Were people interacting with subjects blind to experimental conditions? _______

Was interrater reliability on the DV assessed? _______

Was some measure of treatment integrity taken? _______

Was some measure of social or clinical validity assessed? _______

FIG. 8.2. Example of a coding sheet from Allison et al.'s (1995) meta-analysis.

Rosenthal, 1991; Sacks, Berrier, Reitman, Ancona-Berk, & Chalmers, 1987). Methods for scoring the quality of a study can be found in Glass et al. (1981) and Wortman (1994). However, as Fleiss pointed out, because there is an "absence of rigorous and validated statistical methods for analyzing the resulting data, weighting by quality must be considered a descriptive rather than an inferential procedure until statistical models for quality scores are developed" (Fleiss, 1993, p. 143).

Correcting Effect Sizes for Artifacts

Hunter and Schmidt (1990, 1994) and Hunter, Schmidt, and Jackson (1982) provided extensive discussions about correcting effect sizes for various sources of error and bias. In the context of single-case intervention research, a bias of concern is attenuation due to unreliable measurement of the dependent variable. If r_{obs} is the observed effect size expressed as a correlation coefficient and r_{yy} is the estimated reliability of the dependent measure also expressed in a correlation metric, the disattenuated or "corrected" effect size, r_{corr}, is given by Equation 8.1:

$$r_{corr} = \frac{r_{obs}}{\sqrt{r_{yy}}} \qquad (8.1)$$

Compute Point Estimates, Confidence Intervals, and Significance Levels. One of the main goals of any meta-analysis is to provide a point estimate of the treatment's effect size. This is traditionally provided by the mean effect size from all studies. It is often helpful to provide this estimate as a straight arithmetic mean and as a weighted mean. Additionally, it is helpful to display confidence intervals (CI)(e.g., 95%) around the obtained mean. According to Hedges and Olkin (1985, p. 86), the 95%CI can be computed as follows:

$$95\%CI = \underline{d} \pm (1.96)(\sqrt{\sigma^2}) \qquad (8.2)$$

In this formula, $\underline{d}$ is the weighted mean effect size of n studies and σ^2 is the variance of effect sizes across n studies. As previously mentioned, exact expressions for single-subject effect size variances have not yet been derived. For now, meta-analysts might utilize formulae traditionally used for group designs (see formulae 8.10 and 8.12 in this chapter). Finally, the significance of the mean effect size can be obtained by conducting a single-sample $\underline{t}$-test examining whether the mean effect size is different from zero.

Testing for Heterogeneity. Meta-analysts are occasionally accused of "combining apples and oranges." One way of dealing with this is to test whether the sample of observed effect sizes is statistically homogeneous. If effect sizes are homogeneous, it means that all studies appear to be estimating a common parameter, that the variation among observed effect sizes is simply due to sampling error, and that it is legitimate to combine the studies under consideration. In contrast, if the results are heterogeneous, these assumptions are not valid. Unfortunately, conventional procedures for testing the homogeneity of effect sizes are dependent on knowing the standard errors of the individual effect sizes (Hedges & Olkin, 1985). However, these values have not been derived for single-case meta-analysis. Therefore, strict tests of homogeneity are not possible. However, one of the main of goals homogeneity testing, assessing whether the effect size varies systematically with other specified factors, can often be met by conducting moderator analyses.

Moderator Analyses. In moderator analyses, one assesses whether the magnitude of the effect size varies systematically as a function of other study characteristics. These characteristics might be methodological (e.g., study design, degree of treatment integrity, overall study quality, etc.) or substantive (e.g., study population, treatment intensity) in nature. The goal is to develop a quantitative coding system for any proposed moderators and then regress effect size on the codes. Details can be found in Glass et al. (1981) and more recently in Hedges (1994). This sort of analysis is perhaps the strongest response meta-analysts might have to the "apples-and-oranges" criticism. As Green and Hall (1984) stated, the comparison of apples and oranges "is what quantitative reviewers do and *should* do, but they code apples as apples and oranges as oranges; they do not just throw all the fruit in the basket" (p. 51).

Assessing Publication Bias. One particularly important kind of moderator analysis is a test of whether effect size varies systematically with publication status (published versus unpublished). Publication bias occurs whenever the probability of a study being published is conditional upon the results of the study (Hedges & Olkin, 1985; Iyengar & Greenhouse, 1988). The most common form of publication bias is the greater propensity to publish statistically significant findings than nonsignificant findings. Such bias has been shown to occur in other areas of research (Dickersin, 1990; Easterbrook, Berlin, Gopalan, & Matthews, 1991), although the extent to which it is present in the single-case literature remains unexplored. To the extent that such bias occurs, it will cause reviewers who examine only (or primarily) the published literature to overestimate the actual efficacy of treatments (assuming that the actual population effect size is positive). Thus, it is important to assess the evidence of publication bias. The simplest way to test for publication bias is to conduct a t-test evaluating whether the mean effect size is greater among published than unpublished studies.

Sensitivity Analyses. The final statistical procedure in a meta-analysis is really a loose collection of procedures referred to as "sensitivity analysis" (Greenhouse & Iyengar, 1994). The goal here is to determine how "sensitive" the results are to varying the procedures or methods employed in the analysis. Examples include reconducting the analyses with different weighting schemes, while excluding outliers, with different methods of managing missing data, and so on. More details can be found in Greenhouse and Iyengar (1994).

Publication

As indicated by the final steps in Fig. 8.1, the meta-analysis is not complete until the manuscript is written and the results are published. As Chalmers and Lau (1993) emphasized, it is essential to publish the meta-analysis regardless of its results so as to avoid any further publication bias.

HOW TO CALCULATE EFFECT SIZES

There have been several methods proposed for the calculation of effect sizes within single-case studies. In this section, we briefly describe some of the more popular techniques, comment on their strengths and weaknesses, and cite published reviews which have used the respective methods. Examples using simple A-B designs are presented for pedagogical purposes.

To underscore the commonalities and differences among methods, we have broadly divided them into (1) nonregression approaches and (2) regression approaches to meta-analysis. The nonregression approaches include standardized difference methods and the percent of nonoverlapping data points (PND). Regression approaches include methods proposed by Gorsuch (1983), White et al. (1989), Center et al. (1985–1986), and Allison and Gorman (1993). After discussing the strengths and limitations of each method, it is tentatively concluded that regression approaches are the best ones currently under development, although there is clearly no "gold standard" to date.

Before delving into specific techniques, we describe how data can be extracted from graphs. With few exceptions, these techniques must be used irrespective of the specific meta-analytic method.

Extracting Data From Graphs

In order to compute effect sizes, one must first derive numeric values for each individual data point. Unfortunately, the original data are rarely published in research reports. However, such data can be extracted from the graphs that accompany these reports. This potentially tedious task can be accomplished through one of several means. Ultimately, the value for each data point is determined by its direct distance from the abscissa of the graph. Thus, the meta-analyst generates a ratio scale of values in which data points that are further from the x-axis take on larger values.

To extract values for individual data points, "architect's dividers" are typically used. Using this compasslike tool, the meta-analyst places one prong in the center of the individual data point and extends the other prong directly to the abscissa. This distance between prongs represents the value for that data point and can be represented in millimeters or any other metric of length. This method had been used by Allison et al. (1995), Huitema (1985), and Skiba et al. (1886) with excellent reliability.

Automated tools sometimes referred to as "digitizing tablets" or "computer aided drafting" (CAD) might also be used to extract values and reduce the amount of time spent on this task. Although we have not tried them ourselves, these tools might be especially useful for studies that present many data points. Programs are available from major companies such as Calcomp, Kurta, Hitachi, Summa Graphics, and Software for Scitech. Prices generally range from $200 to $1,800. For either method of data extraction, it is preferable to have multiple recorders and to report interrater reliability coefficients.

Nonregression Approaches

Standardized Difference Approaches

Several authors (Gingerich, 1984; Jayaratne, Tripodi, & Talsma, 1988) have argued that effect sizes be calculated as the following standardized difference:

$$\underline{d} = \frac{(M_t - M_b)}{s} \tag{8.3}$$

where M_t is the mean during treatment phases, M_b is the mean during baseline phases, and s is the standard deviation of baseline phase data points. This method is borrowed from the traditional methods used for the analysis of group designs (Glass, 1978) and thus provides an index which is apparently comparable to that used in group meta-analyses.

Andrews et al. (1980) used this method to evaluate the efficacy of treatments for stuttering.

Two advantages of this method are its apparent compatibility with traditional methods for group meta-analysis and its ease of implementation. However, results gleaned from this method must be interpreted with caution because of several issues. First, this method does not appear to bypass the autocorrelation problem (Busk & Marascuilo, 1988; Huitema, 1985, 1988; Suen, 1987). As Gorman and Allison (chap. 6, this volume) indicated, positive or negative autocorrelation can result in biased significance testing. In regard to meta-analysis, this translates into a $\underline{d}$ that is either too large or too small depending on the nature of the serial dependency. In particular, this method fails to take any time trends into account.

Another concern with the standardized difference approach is that it only compares *levels* of behavior across phases, while apparently dismissing other important parameters such as the *slope* of behavior. This limitation has several implications. First, this method may be insensitive to any preexisting trends in the data (see Allison, 1992). In other words, the simple comparison of mean differences is questionable if behavior shows a steady process (e.g. a sine wave or declining slope) during the baseline phase before any intervention has been implemented. Baseline cyclicity might be due to a number of factors that were reviewed by Allison (1992) and Beasley, Allison, and Gorman (chap. 9, this volume).

Another implication is that this technique might be insensitive to the effects of intervention on the slope of behavior. This parameter often provides important information and should not be excluded from consideration. For example, consider the researcher who is testing a new drug designed to stop the cognitive deterioration associated with Alzheimer's disease. Hypothetical data for such an example are presented in Table 8.1 and graphed in Fig. 8.3. In this example, a generic dependent variable, cognitive functioning, is presented over time and as a function of treatment phase. This intervention seems to be effective, because intervention appears to stop a pronounced downward trend in cognitive functioning. Using Formula 8.3, one obtains a $\underline{d}$ value of −1.25, which suggests an ineffective intervention. However, one might suspect that this $\underline{d}$ value is an inaccurate estimate of the "true" effect size because it does not parameterize the effect of intervention on slope of behavior. In other words, our eyes clearly tell us that the treatment is beneficial and has stopped cognitive deterioration. However, Equation 8.3 tells us that the treatment is detrimental because the *mean* value of cognitive functioning is lower during treatment than control days. At the least, one might argue that this effect size does not capture the full picture of this intervention. To better understand the multifaceted ef-

TABLE 8.1
Hypothetical Data Illustrating the Effects of an Intervention for Alzheimer's Disease on Cognitive Functioning in a Single-Case Design

Time	*Phase*	*Data Point*
1	Baseline	17
2	Baseline	16
3	Baseline	15
4	Baseline	15
5	Baseline	13
6	Baseline	11
7	Baseline	9
8	Baseline	6
9	Treatment	8
10	Treatment	9
11	Treatment	7
12	Treatment	8
13	Treatment	8
14	Treatment	9
15	Treatment	7

fects of this treatment (i.e., effects on both level and slope of behavior), the meta-analyst might choose one of the regression approaches discussed later.

Alternative methods have attempted to overcome some of these shortcomings while still working within the confines of a standardized difference metric (Busk & Serlin, 1992; Corcoran, 1985; Strube, Gardner, & Hartmann, 1985). For example, Busk and Serlin (1992) presented three approaches for computing effect size that differ in terms of the stringency with which underlying assumptions are met. These assumptions include the homogeneity of variance and intercorrelations across treatment phases. These alternative methods deserve consideration when conducting meta-analysis, although it remains questionable as to whether they adequately model trends in the data.

Percent of Nonoverlapping Data (PND)

Scruggs, Mastropieri, and Casto (1987a) developed a nonparametric method for the analysis of single-case data. Their method requires computing the PND between phases. Assuming the goal of treatment is to increase behavior, the PND is calculated as follows in the simple A-B design: First, the number of data points in the treatment phase that exceeds the highest data point in the previous baseline phase is divided by the total number of data points in the treatment phase. Second, the resulting number is multiplied by 100, yielding a percentage score. Higher percentage scores reflect more efficacious interventions. This method has been used in several published meta-analyses by its authors (Scruggs & Mastropieri, 1994; Scruggs, Mastropieri, Forness, & Kavale, 1988; Scruggs, Mastropieri, & McEwen, 1988).

To illustrate the PND method, consider a study by Ohlsen (1987) that tested the effects of an exercise program on quiet time among blind adolescents. The data for one subject are presented in Table 8.2 and are graphed in Fig. 8.4. Using the PND technique, one obtains a PND of 87.5%, thus suggesting an efficacious intervention.

The strongest feature of the PND method is its ease of computation and interpretability. Results can be generated with a simple hand calculator and can be computed more quickly than most other methods. Furthermore, a percentage score is readily understood by most readers. Despite these strengths, the PND method has several drawbacks. First, PND can yield quite misleading results when outlying data points are present. For example, imagine an intervention designed to reduce a child's cursing behavior. Furthermore, imagine that among a set of nonzero baseline phase data points, one data point is zero. Although this intervention might be very effective and reduce *all* treatment phase data points to zero, the PND here would still be zero and suggest an ineffective treatment.

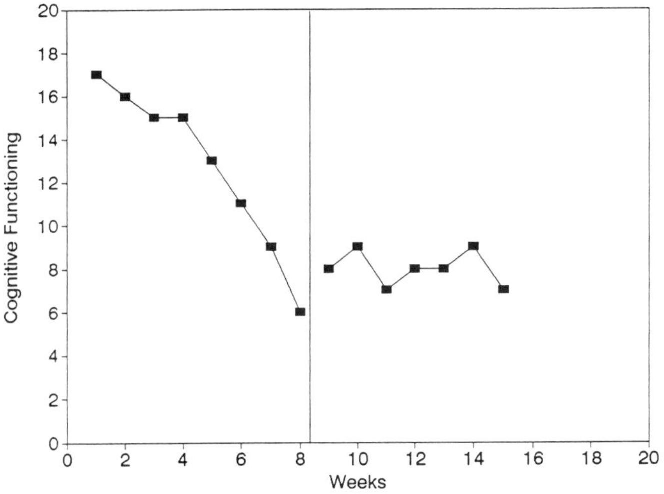

FIG. 8.3. Hypothetical data of the cognitive functioning of an individual with Alzheimer's disease graphed over time and as a function of treatment intervention.

TABLE 8.2
Data Illustrating the Effects of an Exercise Program on Quiet Time among One Adolescent

Time	*Phase*	*Data Point*
1	Baseline	9
2	Baseline	11
3	Baseline	13
4	Baseline	14
5	Baseline	9
6	Baseline	14
7	Baseline	16
8	Baseline	13
9	Treatment	19
10	Treatment	19
11	Treatment	20
12	Treatment	21
13	Treatment	24
14	Treatment	18
15	Treatment	24
16	Treatment	13

Note. Data taken from Ohlsen (1987).

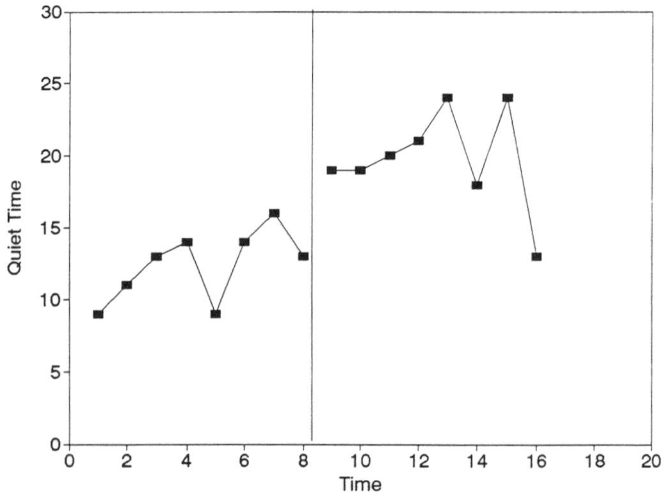

FIG. 8.4. Percentage of quiet time displayed by a blind adolescent graphed over time and as a function of an exercise treatment intervention.

Another problem is that the PND statistic is strongly affected by sample size. Specifically, as the number of baseline data points increases, the PND statistic systematically decreases regardless of the actual effect (Allison & Gorman, 1994). These concerns and others are discussed elsewhere in greater detail (Allison & Gorman, 1993, 1994; Scruggs & Mastropieri, 1994; Scruggs, Mastropieri, & Casto, 1987a, 1987b; White, 1987). Recognizing these limitations, some other researchers have turned to linear regression for solutions.

Regression Approaches

Regression approaches offer sophisticated and flexible methods for research synthesis by fitting statistical models to observed data. Regression models offer better descriptions of trends in the data as well as the multifaceted effects of intervention on behavior. These methods vary in the complexity of the regression models and the number of parameters that are fit. More complex regression coding approaches could also be adopted for more complex designs (Simonton, 1977), although they are not reviewed here due to space limitations. Ultimately, for any regression model, the resulting $\underline{F}$ or R^2 change can be converted to $\underline{d}$ through the use of standard formulae (Friedman, 1982; Rosenthal, 1991a; Wolf, 1986; Formulae 8.4, 8.8, and 8.9, this chapter) and integrated across studies.

Four methods are now presented. These are the methods introduced by: Gorsuch (1983), White et al. (1989), Center et al. (1985–1986), and Allison and Gorman (1993). The methods are presented roughly in historical order. As the reader can see, the methods build upon one another in a logical progression.

Gorsuch (1983) and White et al. (1989)

Gorsuch (1983) evaluated the effects of three data analytic strategies for brief interrupted time-series designs: trend analysis, autoregressive analysis, and differencing analysis. Gorsuch concluded that trend analysis was the most appropriate analysis in terms of minimizing both Type-I and Type-II errors. Trend analysis is conducted by evaluating the effects of one's experimental intervention in a regression *after* entering time as a covariate. This procedure is conceptually analogous to ANCOVA (Maxwell & Delaney, 1990). The R^2 change associated with the treatment intervention once time has been partialed out can be used as the effect size or converted to $\underline{d}$. Specifically, Formula 8.4 can be used for such a conversion:

$$\underline{d} = \sqrt{\frac{4R^2}{(1 - R^2)}} \tag{8.4}$$

To illustrate this method, data from Table 8.1 were reanalyzed accordingly. Ordinary least-squares regression reveals that, after controlling for the effects of time, the resulting R^2 change is .02, which corresponds to a $\underline{d}$ of .31. Thus, the intervention appears to have a small effect after partialing out variance due to the passage of time.

A conceptually similar model was proposed by White et al. (1989). Their formula for $\underline{d}$ is as follows:

$$\underline{d} = \frac{(\bar{X}_e - \bar{X}_c)}{SD'} \quad (8.5)$$

where $\bar{X}_e$ is the predicted level of the target measure on the last day of the treatment phase *estimated from the within treatment phase regression* of the dependent measure on day or session of observation, and $\bar{X}_c$ is the predicted level of the target measure on the last day of the treatment phase *estimated from the within baseline phase regression* of the target measure on the day or session of observation (White et al., 1989, p. 289). SD' equals $[SD(1 - r^2)]^{.5}$, where SD is the pooled within phase standard deviation and r is the correlation of the dependent measure with the day (or session) of observation. In essence, this method uses regression to "project ahead" *specifically* to the last day of treatment. The $\underline{d}$ value results from the comparison of two scores—one projected from baseline phase data and the other projected from treatment phase data.

Ohlsen's (1987) data were reanalyzed using this method. Analysis of the data from Table 8.2 yielded $\bar{X}_e = 18.92$, $\bar{X}_c = 19.36$, $SD' = 1.20$, and $\underline{d} = -0.37$.

The major advantage of the methods advocated by Gorsuch (1983) and White et al. (1989) is that they statistically adjust for the effects of time. In doing so, the meta-analyst can answer the question of whether there is a nonzero difference that exists *above and beyond the mere passage of time*. Unfortunately, Gorsuch's method tests *only* for differences in levels of observed behavior (i.e., mean differences). It does *not* test for differences in slope. As mentioned previously, it is possible to have an intervention that affects not only the level of behavior, but the slope as well. However, Gorsuch's (1983) method does not model this parameter and therefore would not detect such effects. Therefore, meta-analysts might prefer alternative methods when interventions are hypothesized to affect the slope of behavior. In such situations, one of the following regression models might be preferable.

Center et al. (1985–1986)

Center et al. (1985–1986) developed a more sophisticated regression model for computing effect size, in which the independent or joint effects of level, trend, and changes in slope can be calculated. The resulting equation is:

$$Y = b_0 + b_1X + b_2t + b_3X(t - n_a) + e \tag{8.6}$$

where Y is the observed value of the dependent variable; b_0 is the regression constant; X is a dummy coded variable for treatment; t is the day or session of observation; n_a is the number of data points in the baseline phase; and e represents error.

To calculate an effect size one first computes the full model and then obtains the associated R^2. The model is then recomputed without the parameters whose effects one wishes to estimate and the R^2 associated with this reduced model is obtained. These R^2s can then be converted to an incremental $\underline{F}$-ratio via the formula:

$$\underline{F} = [(R_f^2 - R_r^2/\underline{M})]/[(1 - R_f^2)/(\underline{N} - \underline{k} - \underline{1})] \tag{8.7}$$

where R_f^2 is the R^2 from the full model, R_r^2 is the R^2 from the reduced model, $\underline{M}$ is the number of parameters whose effects one is estimating, $\underline{N}$ is the total number of data points, and $\underline{k}$ is the number of parameters in the full model (not including b_0). The resulting $\underline{F}$ value can then be converted to a $\underline{d}$ statistic using the following formulae:

$$\underline{d} = 2\sqrt{\frac{F}{df_d}} \tag{8.8}$$

$$\underline{d} = 2\sqrt{\frac{df_nF}{df_d}} \tag{8.9}$$

Formula 8.8 should be used when the degrees of freedom in the numerator of the $\underline{F}$ ratio equals one (i.e., when one parameter is being estimated); Formula 8.9 should be used whenever the degrees of freedom in the numerator of the $\underline{F}$ ratio is greater than one. Skiba et al. (1986) used this method to evaluate the effectiveness of nonaversive interventions in classrooms.

To illustrate this method, the data from Table 8.1 were reanalyzed to estimate the unique effects of treatment on slope of behavior. In this case, $R_f^2 = .94$, $R_r^2 = .76$, $\underline{M} = 1$, $\underline{N} = 15$, and $\underline{k} = 3$. These values yield an $\underline{F}$ value of 32.73, which corresponds to a $\underline{d}$ of 3.45.

The major advantage of this method is its flexibility for modeling additional parameters, such as treatment on slope of behavior. However, the following issues should be considered when using this method. First, under certain circumstances, the b_2 parameter may overestimate the effects of trend and the model thereby underestimate the magnitude of $\underline{d}$. That is, because the b_2 parameter is calculated from *all* data points across *all* treatment phases, data variation that is really due to intervention could erroneously be attributed to the effects of time. Although one could estimate the b_2 parameter just from baseline phase data, Center argued that the small number of baseline data points typically provided would not yield a relatively stable estimate of trend. Consequently, Center et al.'s method may yield a trend parameter that is stable but systematically biased.

A second point is that $\underline{d}$ will be systematically inflated when changes in the level and slope of behavior occur in opposite directions. This bias exists because Center et al.'s method is sensitive to *any* improvement in the predictability of the dependent measure, including changes in parameter signs. Thus, for example, if an intervention designed to decrease slapping successfully *decreases* the average amount of slapping across phases, but *increases* the rate of slapping (in spite of the average decrease in slapping), one's resulting $\underline{d}$ might be artificially large.

One minor point to note is that $\underline{d}$ or $\underline{r}$ cannot be negative when using Formula 8.5. That is, $\underline{d}$ is an index of how much better a model with more parameters fits the data compared to a model with fewer parameters. Because a higher order model can never provide a poorer fit than a reduced model, $\underline{d}$ can never be smaller than zero *even if treatment has a detrimental effect*. However, this issue is easily resolved by assigning + or − signs depending on the signs of the regression weights.

Center et al.'s method represents a significant improvement over previous techniques and warrants serious consideration when conducting a meta-analysis. Recently, Allison and Gorman (1993) modified this method to address concerns with the original formula. This method is now presented in detail. However, we emphasize that it is best conceptualized as a working model that is still being refined and improved. It is by no means the "definitive solution" to single-case meta-analysis.

Allison and Gorman (1993)

Table 8.3 presents an algorithm for the calculation of effect sizes using this method. Steps 1 through 4 respond to the concern of overestimating the effects of trend. Trend is only computed based on baseline data but compensated for in both the baseline and treatment phases. Steps 6 through 8 allow for detrimental treatment effects to be represented by a negative $\underline{d}$ value. Note that Step 7 recommends using the adjusted-R^2, instead of the unadjusted R^2. This modification to the original procedure (Allison & Gorman, 1993) serves to correct for small sample bias (Darlington, 1990). The problem posed by changes in level and slope that occur in opposite directions is addressed in Step 10. It should be recognized that the resulting adjusted R^2 from Step 7 or the resulting adjusted

TABLE 8.3
Algorithm for Regression Based Effect Size Estimation in Single-Case Designs.

Step 1.	Compute regression equation of $\underline{Y}$ on $\underline{T}$ in baseline phase only where $\underline{T}$ is time or observation number and $\underline{Y}$ is the dependent variable.
Step 2.	Compute residuals for baseline data.
Step 3.	Use regression equation generated in step 1 to generate predicted Y values for treatment phase.
Step 4.	Compute "residuals" for the treatment phase by subtracting the predicted values in Step 3 from the actual Y values in the treatment phase. The residual or "detrended" data from Steps 2 and 4 are then used in all subsequent analyses.
Step 5.	Compute the zero-order *r*s of X and $(T)X$ with the detrended Y values where X is a dummy code for the independent variable. If the signs of both zero-order *r*s are the same proceed with Step 6. If they are different, go to Step 10.
Step 6.	Simultaneously regress the detrended Y values on both X and $(T)X$, via the model: $$Y = b_0 + b_1X + b_3X(t) + e;$$
Step 7.	Obtain the adjusted-R^2 for the regression equation in Step 6. This statistic is available in the output of most major statistical packages (if not see any major multivariate statistics text).
Step 8.	Convert the adjusted R^2 to a $\underline{d}$ or $\underline{r}$ via standard formulae (see, for example, Friedman, 1982; Wolf, 1986).
Step 9.	Assign the same sign to $\underline{d}$ that the zero order correlations had in Step 5. The resulting $\underline{d}$ is the effect size.
Step 10.	In the event that the level and slope zero order $\underline{r}$s have different signs, simply estimate the effect of level since the change in slope will automatically attenuate its effects. As in Step 8, convert the adjusted-R^2 to $\underline{d}$ or $\underline{r}$ by standard formulae.

R^2 from Step 10 estimate the proportion of *residual* variance in the dependent variable that is due to treatment effects. Some of the total variance has been removed in Steps 1 through 4.

To illustrate this method, Ohlsen's data were reanalyzed using the algorithm in Table 8.3. First, the meta-analyst regresses quiet time onto time *for baseline phase only* to get the following equation, Quiet time = 9.64 + .607*time. Predicted quiet time is then subtracted from actual quiet time to create a new variable, "residualized quiet time." Residualized quiet time is then regressed onto treatment phase (0 or 1) and the treatment phase by trend interaction, thus yielding a R^2 of .15, an adjusted R^2 of .09, and a corresponding $\underline{d}$ of .63. Because of the signs on the beta weights, we assign a positive sign to our effect size. In this example, the beta weights for level and slope were in the same direction, and so slope was included in the final regression model (see Step 5).

This method has been used in at least one published meta-analysis to date (Allison et al., 1995). However, several caveats should be mentioned. The first issue involves baseline regression equations that make "out of bounds" projections into subsequent treatment phases. For example, percentage scores have a finite range of possible values (i.e., 0 to 100). However, it is possible for baseline regressions to project values that exceed these limits. What predicted scores should be used when they fall out of these natural limits?

This point is illustrated by the hypothetical example of a school psychologist who implements a fixed ratio reinforcement schedule in order to improve a student's performance on homework assignments. Baseline and treatment phase data are plotted in Fig. 8.5, where time is represented in days and the dependent variable is percentage of homework correct. As one sees, there is a pronounced increase in homework performance even before the treatment was implemented. These baseline phase data are fit by the regression line percentage homework correct = 41.10 + 10.9*time. With simple arithmetic, one sees that this student's performance is predicted to exceed 100% on approximately the fifth day of intervention. Of course, this is impossible because one cannot get greater than 100% of the problems correct.

One way to resolve this problem is a sort of "windsorization" of the data. That is, predicted values that exceed natural limits are fixed at those limits. Thus, predicted percentages that fall below 0 or exceed 100 are set to 0 or 100, respectively. Therefore, for the data presented in Fig. 8.5, all projected observation coming after the fifth day of intervention would be fixed to 100.

A greater concern with Allison and Gorman's (1993) method is the small number of baseline data points typically presented in single-case research. That is, primary sources *ideally* should provide a large number of baseline data points to allow for a stable regression model. Unfortunately, this ideal is rarely met, with most studies providing only three to four baseline data points (Huitema, 1985). There is no simple solution to this problem, which is not unique to the Allison and Gorman approach but is common to virtually any quantitative method. Indeed, this common obstacle underscores the need for good research design at the level of the individual study.

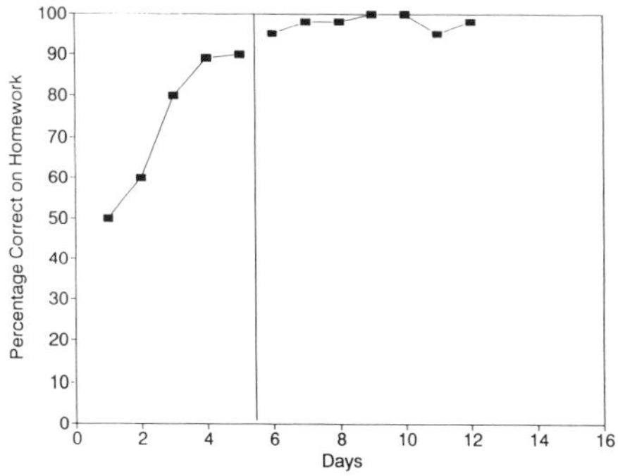

FIG. 8.5. Hypothetical data of the percentage of homework problems correctly solved over time by as a function of a behavioral intervention.

To address this problem, one might choose more stringent study inclusion criteria for the particular meta-analysis (e.g., only studies reporting at least $\underline{n}$ baseline data points). Also, when averaging effect sizes the meta-analyst might weight each effect size by the number of data points used in that study—an issue discussed in the final section of this chapter.

Despite the limitations of the various regression approaches, they appear to be promising methods and deserve consideration. As meta-analysis becomes more common among single-case studies, we believe that these methods will be further developed and improved upon.

SPECIAL ISSUES IN SINGLE-CASE META-ANALYSIS

Can Group and Single-Case Studies Be Combined?

In many areas, the research question is addressed via both group and single-case research studies. For example, in reviewing the effects of antecedent exercise on disruptive behavior, Allison et al. (1995) meta-analyzed 16 group studies and 26 single-case studies. The approach undertaken in that project, and the one currently espoused, is that both types of studies should be meta-analyzed but that this should be done separately. The reason is that the effect size parameters being estimated in group and single-case studies are two fundamentally different estimands. Even though both may be expressed in similar metrics (e.g., $\underline{d}$ or $\underline{r}$), studies using between-group designs estimate the degree to which *among-person* variation in the dependent measure is due to the independent variable. Even in the case of the repeated measures (i.e., pretest–

posttest) design, data are averaged across subjects in computing effect sizes for change over time (Gibbons, Hedeker, & Davis, 1993; Looney, Feltz, & VanVleet, 1994). In contrast, single-case experiments solely estimate the extent to which *within-person* variation in the dependent measure is due to the independent variable.

Thus, one can conduct parallel analyses within each type of study (group vs. single-case) and compare the results in terms of overall direction of effect and moderator relationships. However, a direct combining or comparison of effect sizes does not seem reasonable at this time. One promising approach that may eventually allow more formal integration of within-subject effects and between-subjects effects may lie in the use of hierarchical linear models (Panel on Statistical Issues And Opportunities For Research in the Combination of Information, 1992; Raudenbush, 1994). We look forward to future developments in this regard.

Multiple Effect Sizes per Study

An issue that confronts virtually every meta-analyst is how to manage studies that (potentially) yield more than one effect size. This can occur when there are more than two conditions being compared, when there is more than one dependent variable,[1] or, in the context of single-case research, when there is more than one subject per study. In the context of group meta-analysis, the issue of statistically dependent effect sizes is treated in some detail by Gleser and Olkin (1994) and the references therein. The main problem is that if one uses each separate effect size in subsequent analyses, one tends to overestimate the amount of independent information that one has. This leads to an overestimation of the precision of one's results. Moreover, unless each study yields the same number of separate effect sizes, some studies may unjustly receive more weight than may others.[2]

There are several ways to handle multiple effect sizes. These include (a) using generalized least squares (GLS) approaches in moderator analyses (see Gleser & Olkin, 1994; Gorman & Allison, chap. 6, this volume), (b) computing an average effect size for each study, and (c) arbitrarily or randomly selecting one effect size to represent each study. The first approach (GLS) may be the best in terms of conducting moderator analyses (Gleser & Olkin, 1994), although it is certainly the most com-

[1]Multiple baseline designs across behaviors or settings can be seen as special cases of the multiple dependent variables situation.

[2]Although, in the case of multiple subjects rather than multiple variables, this unequal weighting is probably appropriate.

plex. In contrast, the second method is probably the simplest and best approach for deriving point estimates of the overall effect size (Rosenthal & Rubin, 1986). We see little justification for the third approach.

Weighting Effect Sizes

As mentioned previously, average effect sizes in meta-analyses are typically weighted averages. Similarly, other statistics calculated from several effect sizes such as beta weights in meta-regression are also based on weighting each effect size differentially. The rationale for weighting is that estimates from larger studies and estimates with more precision should be valued more, and this should be reflected in the analysis.

The generally accepted practice in such analyses entails weighting ES_i by $1/V_i$, where ES_i is the effect size for study i and V_i is the variance of ES_i.[3] The variance of a statistic is usually some function of N and σ^2, where σ^2 is the variance of the variable on which the statistic is calculated. In serially dependent data, variances of statistics will also be affected by the degree of serial dependency (autocorrelation).

Because $\underline{d}$ and $\underline{r}$ are the two most common effect size metrics, weights are presented only for these statistics. (For the moment, the autocorrelation issue is tabled, but we return to it shortly.) For $\underline{d}$, Hedges and Olkin (1985) showed that the approximate variance is given by:

$$Var(\underline{d}) = \frac{N_e + N_c}{N_e N_c} + \frac{d^2}{2(N_e + N_c - 3.94)} \tag{8.10}$$

where N_e is the N in the experimental condition and N_c is the N in the control condition.[4] Therefore, the weight applied to a given $\underline{d}$ would simply be the inverse of the right hand side of Equation 8.10.

Weighting effect sizes expressed as $\underline{r}$ is slightly trickier. The reason is that the distribution of $\underline{r}$ is bounded by -1 and 1. This means that $\underline{r}$ cannot be normally distributed, because every normal distribution extends from positive to negative infinity. Moreover, this results in strict arithmetic averages of $\underline{r}$s being biased estimates of the average $\underline{r}$ (Rosenthal, 1991a). Because of these factors, averaging and statistical analyses

---

[3]Every sample statistic has a variance. The variance is the square of the statistic's standard error. The statistic's standard error is simply the standard deviation of the statistic's sampling distribution.

[4]Note that Hedges and Olkin (1985) referred to $\underline{d}$, that is the standardized mean difference, as $\underline{g}$ and use $\underline{d}$ to refer to an unbiased estimator of the standardized mean difference. We have presented $\underline{d}$ here for simplicity but fully support the use of Hedges and Olkin's (1985) unbiased estimator and encourage the reader to pursue their writing on the topic.

with $\underline{r}$s is not done. Rather, the accepted practice is to convert $\underline{r}$ to a $\underline{Z}$ using the Fisher $\underline{r}$-to-$\underline{Z}$ transformation. The Fisher $\underline{r}$-to-$\underline{Z}$ transformation is:

$$Z = \frac{1}{2} ln \left[\frac{1 + r}{1 - r} \right] \tag{8.11}$$

where *ln* stands for the natural log (log to the base *e*). All analyses and averaging are then done on the $\underline{Z}$s. Average $\underline{Z}$s can then be back transformed to average $\underline{r}$s.

Thus, for analyses involving $\underline{r}$s (actually $\underline{Z}$s) the meta-analyst needs the variance of $\underline{Z}$, which is:

$$Var(Z) = \frac{1}{N_e + N_c - 3} \tag{8.12}$$

Therefore, the weight applied to a given $\underline{Z}$ should simply be $N_e + N_c - 3$.

Until now we have ignored any possible autocorrelation. However, positive autocorrelations (the kind more commonly encountered) will cause formulae 8.10 and 8.12 to underestimate the variance of effect sizes and negative autocorrelation will cause overestimation. Thus, a more appropriate expression for the variance of $\underline{d}$ and Fisher's $\underline{Z}$ might be:

$$Var(\underline{d}) = \left[\frac{N_e + N_c}{N_e N_c} + \frac{d^2}{2(N_e + N_c - 3.94)} \right] C \tag{8.13}$$

$$Var(Z) = \left[\frac{1}{N_e + N_c - 3} \right] C \tag{8.14}$$

where C is some function of the degree of autocorrelation. Because these weights are ultimately used in a multiplicative fashion, ignoring C is essentially equivalent to setting C to be equal across all studies. If one had no information the degree of autocorrelation or the function relating C to autocorrelation, ignoring C in the weighting might be a very reasonable alternative.

However, in single-case meta-analyses information is almost always available on the degree of autocorrelation because the raw data are usually necessary to calculate the effect size. Thus, if we knew the function relating C to autocorrelation, it would be wise to incorporate C into our weighting scheme. Wheeler (1990) suggested the possibility of adjusting standard errors by a factor of $[1/(1 - \underline{r}_1^2)]^{.5}$, where $\underline{r}_1$ is the lag-1 autocorrelation of residuals. It is assumed that autocorrelated residuals are positive. This implies that variances be corrected by the square of this term, that is:

$$C = \frac{1}{1 - r_1^2} \quad (8.15)$$

It should be noted that no proof is offered for this correction and, therefore, it should only be used as a heuristic and not as a method for obtaining an exact expression for the variance of the effect size. Unfortunately, ignoring C is also not quite correct. Thus, meta-analysts might conduct their analysis using the variances uncorrected by C but then also try repeating analyses incorporating C as a form of sensitivity analysis. Hopefully, future research efforts will produce more formal expressions for the variance of effect sizes under autocorrelation.

From Which Phases Should Effect Sizes Be Computed?

A final issue that confronts the single-case meta-analyst is to determine on which phases to base the effect size computation. Consider the case of an A-B-A-B design. One could use both A and both B phases, or alternatively use only the first A and the last B. The advantage of the former is that it uses all of the data and, therefore, should provide more precise estimates overall. Alternatively, one could argue for the latter approach because, if there are carryover effects of treatment, the second A phase may no longer truly represent "baseline." Moreover, in the first B phase, the behavior may not be fully decreased (or increased) because the experimenter may be concerned that if it is, it may not revert to baseline levels in the second A phase. In the case of a changing criterion design (Barlow & Hersen, 1988; Hartmann & Hall, 1976), comparing the first and last phases may be the only reasonable alternative. In determining which phases to select for computation, no definitive statements can be offered. Whichever strategy is selected, however, it is essential that the meta-analyst clearly state and consistently maintain that rule for all studies in the analysis. Perhaps the best strategy is for the energetic meta-analyst to conduct the analysis several ways as a form of sensitivity analysis.

SOFTWARE FOR COMPUTING META-ANALYSES

Effect Size Computation

Meta-analysis requires investigators to combine estimates of effect sizes from a wide variety of experimental and statistical designs. In order to do so, statistical results must be reduced to a common metric, usually *d* or *r*. Fortunately, computer programs can relieve some of the burden of computing effect sizes from results that have been reported with different statistical tests. At present, none of the program packages will compute all of the effect size estimates mentioned in this chapter; therefore, readers may wish to gather several programs for their personal libraries.

As part of their meta-analysis package, Gorman, Primavera, and Karras (1983) included a BASIC program, EFFECT, that converts correlation coefficients, *Z*-, *t*-, and *F*-test values, and chi-square values to Friedman's (1982) *rm*, a correlation-based effect size index. A spreadsheet version of the program that performs all transformations is also available from the authors. Because nearly all statistics, including nonparametric and multivariate statistics, can be expressed or approximated by one of these distributions, it lends itself to a multiplicity of designs. Gorman, Primavera, and Allison (1995) performed a major overhaul on Gorman et al.'s (1983) EFFECT program. The new program, POWPAL, has all of the capabilities of the earlier program, but it now can accept *d*-values, Cohen's (1988) f and f^2 effect sizes, probability values, and can output *d* values and Fisher's *Z* values. Because effect size indexes are integral components of statistical power analyses and sample size estimation, the program also provides power and sample size estimates. Both EFFECT and POWPAL rely solely on summary statistics and, therefore, assume that the researcher has chosen an appropriate statistical model for the study at hand. However, because the program does not accept means, standard deviations, or pretest versus posttest correlations, it cannot compute effect sizes from raw data or intermediate results.

Curlette (1987) developed a BASIC program, "The Meta-Analysis Effect-Size Calculator," that provides raw and unbiased *d* measures for a wide variety of between-subjects and within-subjects two-group designs. Researchers can enter means, standard deviations, sample sizes, *F*-values, *t*-values, gain scores, residual scores, probability values, and pretest versus posttest correlation coefficients into the program. Unlike Gorman et al.'s (1983, 1995) programs, it does not rely solely on summary data. However, except for input of probabilities, the program is limited to two-group comparisons with interval and ratio-scale data.

McDaniel (1986) supplied SAS routines, based on Hunter et al. (1982), for calculating *d* and *r* indices from *t*-tests, *F*-values, chi-square values, and means and standard deviations. At the user's option, the programs can provide corrections for unreliability and restrictions of range.

Mullen and Rosenthal (1985) and Mullen (1989, 1993) provided a series of BASIC programs for summarizing and contrasting effect sizes based on the work of Rosenthal (1991a). Although none of their programs were specifically designed for calculating effect sizes, many have subprocedures for computing effect sizes from means, standard deviations, sample sizes, and statistical test values.

Schwarzer (1988) presented an extensive program package for combining and contrasting effect sizes. One of the subprograms within the package obtains *r* and *d* indices from *F*-, *t*-, and chi-square values. As in the Gorman et al. (1983) package, this feature may permit a wider variety of designs to be considered.

Johnson (1989) produced DSTAT, an extensive program package that estimates effect sizes from many statistics, stores them in a database, summarizes them, and performs model testing using the models described in Hedges and Olkin (1985). Many useful techniques can be found in the sections of the package that compute *d* and *r* effect sizes. For example, users can enter standard deviations for each group and have the option of using the control group or pooled standard deviation. The *t*-test and *F*-test sections provide options for both between-subjects and within-subjects designs.

The previously mentioned programs will aid in computing effect sizes. However, researchers will also come across infrequently used designs that have not yet been incorporated in existing packages. In these cases, simple programs can typically be written for microcomputers in BASIC or as routines for programmable calculators or computer spreadsheets. Ordinary least-squares regression might also be appropriate for analyzing data from nontraditional single-case designs (see Simonton, 1977).

Programs for Integrating Information

Once effect size measures have been obtained and transformed to a common metric, researchers will typically wish to achieve three goals. The first goal is to combine effect sizes from similar studies to obtain an "average" effect size. In order to form such aggregates, the effect sizes from individual studies are typically weighted by such characteristics as sample sizes, reliability of measures, and variances of the dependent variables. The second goal is to search for sources of heterogeneity among the effect sizes. If all of the effect sizes remain close to the average effect size, then there is little reason to suspect that other variables are related to variations in effect size. If, however, effect sizes vary considerably around the average effect size, then researchers might find it useful to seek variables that are theoretically related to variations in effect size. If there are variations among the effect sizes, then the third goal will emerge. This goal will be to perform inferential tests of the impact of other variables on differences among effect sizes.

Several computer packages are available for managing files of effect sizes. Nearly all of them can easily achieve the first goal of providing a weighted average effect size. However, the program packages differ considerably when it comes to achieving the second and third goals, those of detecting heterogeneity and performing inferential tests.

Gorman et al. (1983) included a BASIC program, CUMANAL in their meta-analysis package that employed formulas from Stoffelmayr, Dillavou, and Hunter (1983) for providing a weighted average effect size, a significance test of this average, and a breakdown of the variance among the studies into the variance attributable to sampling error and to the variance attributable to true differences among studies. A second program in their package, ROSENTHAL, implements Rosenthal's formulas for assessing overall heterogeneity among studies and for providing specific pairwise and groupwise contrasts among studies. On a more ambitious level, the program REGSYN, uses the weighted least-squares regression synthesis approach outlined in Hedges and Olkin's (1983) article to assess linear models for the main effects and interactions of several variables upon effect sizes.

Mullen (1989, 1993) and Mullen and Rosenthal (1985) provided source listings and executable BASIC programs for performing a wide variety of procedures for averaging effects sizes, for performing overall tests of study heterogeneity, and for performing contrasts among specific studies. Schwarzer's (1988) meta-analysis program provides a comprehensive system for obtaining average effect sizes from individual $\underline{r}$ and $\underline{d}$ statistics and probability values. The program assesses heterogeneity among studies and performs cluster analyses to detect subgroups of studies with similar effect sizes. However, the program does not perform focussed tests among studies.

Finally, Johnson's (1989) D-STAT program provides a database system for recording and computing effect sizes from different studies. It offers routines for achieving all three goals of meta-analysis: providing average affect sizes, assessing heterogeneity, and providing inferential tests of factors capable of influencing effect sizes.

It should be mentioned that all of these software packages were developed for the meta-analysis of group designs. As the field develops a better understanding of the issues involved in meta-analyzing single-case designs, we anticipate the development of more sophisticated software programs to facilitate the hands-on labor of data extraction and analysis.

SUMMARY

Single-case designs historically have played a prominent role in the evaluation of clinical trials and will continue to do so (Wachter & Straf, 1990). Unfortunately, single-case data have been excluded from most quantitative literature reviews due to insufficient meta-analytic techniques. However, as this chapter illustrates, methods are under development and being implemented. Although there is no gold standard to date and several data analytic issues remain unresolved, meta-analysts can be encouraged by these developments and need no longer think it *necessary* to disregard single-case studies from quantitative literature reviews.

REFERENCES

Allison, D. B. (1992). When cyclicity is a concern: A caveat regarding phase change criteria in single-case designs. *Comprehensive Mental Health Care, 2,* 131–149.

Allison, D. B., Faith, M. S., & Franklin, R. (1995). Antecedent exercise in the treatment of disruptive behavior: A review and meta-analysis. *Clinical Psychology: Science and Practice, 2,* 279–303.

Allison, D. B., & Gorman, B. S. (1993). Calculating effect sizes for meta-analysis: The case of the single case. *Behavior, Research, and Therapy, 31,* 621–631.

Allison, D. B., & Gorman, B. S. (1994). "Make things as simple as possible, but no simpler." A rejoinder to Scruggs and Mastropieri. *Behavior, Research, and Therapy, 32,* 885–890.

Andrews, G., Guitar, B., & Howie, P. (1980). Meta-analysis of the effects of stuttering treatment. *Journal of Speech and Hearing Disorder, 45,* 287–307.

Barlow, D. H., & Hersen, M. (1988). *Single case experimental designs.* New York: Pergamon.

Busk, P. L., & Marascuilo, L. A. (1988). Autocorrelation in single-subject research: A counterargument to the myth of no autocorrelation. *Behavioral Assessment, 10,* 22–242.

Busk, P. L., & Serlin, R. C. (1992). Meta-analysis for single-case research. In T. R. Kratochwill & J. R. Levin (Eds.), *Single-case research design and analysis: New directions for psychology and education* (pp. 187–212). Hillsdale, NJ: Lawrence Erlbaum Associates.

Center, B. A., Skiba, R. J., & Casey, A. (1985–1986). A methodology for the quantitative synthesis of intra-subject design research. *Journal of Special Education, 19,* 387–400.

Chalmers, T. C., & Lau, J. (1993). Meta-analytic stimulus for changes in clinical trials. *Statistical Methods in Medical Research, 2,* 161–172.

Chalmers, T. C., Smith, Jr., H., Blackburn, B., Silverman, B., Schroeder, B., Reitman, D., & Ambroz, A. (1981). A method for assessing the quality of a randomized trial. *Controlled Clinical Trials, 2,* 31–49.

Cohen, J. (1988). Statistical power analysis for the behavioral sciences. Hillsdale, NJ: Lawrence Erlbaum Associates. Design research. *Journal of Special Education, 19,* 387–400.

Cooper, H. M. (1982). Scientific guidelines for conducting integrative research reviews. *Review of Educational Research, 52,* 291–302.

Cooper, H. M. (1989). *Integrating research: A guide for literature reviews* (2nd ed.). Newbury Park, CA: Sage.

Cooper, H. M., & Rosenthal, R. (1980). Statistical versus traditional procedures for summarizing research findings. *Psychological Bulletin, 87,* 442–449.

Corcoran, K. J. (1985). Aggregating the idiographic data of single-subject research. *Social Work Research and Abstracts, 21,* 9–12.

Curlette, W. J. (1987). The meta-analysis effect size calculator: A basic program for reconstructing unbiased effect sizes. *Educational and Psychological Measurement, 47,* 107–109.

Darlington, R. B. (1990). *Regression linear models.* New York: McGraw-Hill.

Dickersin, K. (1990). The existence of publication bias and risk factors for its occurrence. *Journal of the American Medical Association,* 263, 1401–1405.

Dickersin, K. (1994). Research registers. In H. Cooper & L. V. Hedges (Eds.), *The handbook of research synthesis* (pp. 71–83). New York: Russell Sage Foundation.

Easterbrook, P. J., Berlin, J. A., Gopalan, R., & Matthews, D. R. (1991). Publication bias in clinical research. *Lancet, 337,* 867–872.

Ellis, M. V. (1991). Conducting and reporting integrative research reviews: Accumulating scientific knowledge. *Counselor Education and Supervision, 30,* 225–237.

Felson, D. T. (1992). Bias in meta-analytic research. *Journal of Clinical Epidemiology, 45,* 885–892.

Fleiss, J. L. (1993). The statistical basis of meta-analysis. *Statistical Methods in Medical Research, 2,* 121–145.

Friedman, H. (1982). Simplified determinations of statistical power, magnitude of effect and research sample sizes. *Educational and Psychological Measurement, 42,* 521–526.

Gibbons, R. D., Hedecker, D. R., & Davis, J. M. (1993). Estimation of effect size from a series of experiments involving paired comparisons. *Journal of Educational Statistics, 18,* 271–279.

Giles, T. R. (1990). Bias against behavior therapy in outcome reviews: Who speaks for the patient? *The Behavior Therapist, 13,* 5–86–90.

Gingerich, W. J. (1984). Meta-analysis of applied time-series data. *Journal of Applied Behavioral Science, 20,* 71–79.

Glass, G. V. (1978). Integrating findings: The meta-analysis of research. *Review of Research in Education, 5,* 351–379.

Glass, G. V., McGaw, B., & Smith, M. L. (1981). *Meta-analysis in social research.* Beverly Hills, CA: Sage.

Gleser, L. J., & Olkin, I. (1994). Stochastically dependent effect sizes. In H. Cooper & L. V. Hedges (Eds.), *The handbook of research synthesis* (pp. 339–355). New York: Russell Sage Foundation.

Gorman, B. S., Primavera, L. H., & Allison, D. B. (1995). POWPAL: A program for estimating effect sizes, statistical power, and sample sizes. *Educational and Psychological Measurement, 55,* 773–776.

Gorman, B. S., Primavera, L. H., & Karras, A. (1983). A microcomputer program package for metaanalysis. *Behavior Research Methods and Instrumentation, 15,* 617.

Gorsuch, R.L. (1983). Three methods for analyzing limited time-series (N of 1) data. *Behavioral Assessment, 5,* 141–154.

Green, B. F., & Hall, J. A. (1984). Quantitative methods for literature reviews. *Annual Review of Psychology, 35,* 37–53.

Greenhouse, J. B., & Iyengar, S. (1994). Sensitivity analysis and diagnosis. In H. Cooper & L. V. Hedges (Eds.), *The handbook of research synthesis* (pp. 383–398). New York: Russell Sage Foundation.

Hartmann, D. P., & Hall, R. V. (1976). The changing criterion design. *Journal of Applied Behavior Analysis, 9*, 527–532.

Hedges, L. V. (1994). Fixed effects models. In H. Cooper & L. V. Hedges (Eds.), The handbook of research synthesis (pp. 285–299). New York: Russell Sage.

Hedges, L. V., & Olkin, I. (1983). Regression models in research synthesis. *American Statistician, 37*, 137–140.

Hedges, L. V., & Olkin, I. (1985). *Statistical methods for meta-analysis*. Orlando, FL: Academic Press.

Huitema, B. E. (1985). Autocorrelation in applied behavior analysis: A myth. *Behavioral Assessment, 7*, 107–118.

Huitema, B. E. (1988). Autocorrelation: 10 years of confusion. *Behavioral Assessment, 10*, 253–294.

Hunter, J. E., & Schmidt, F. L. (1990). *Methods of meta-analysis*. Newbury Park, CA: Sage.

Hunter, J. E., & Schmidt, F. L. (1994). Correcting for sources of artificial variation across studies. In H. Cooper & L. V. Hedges (Eds.), *The handbook of research synthesis* (pp. 323–336). New York: Russell Sage Foundation.

Hunter, J. E., Schmidt, F. L., & Jackson, G. B. (1982).*Meta-analysis: Cumulating research findings across studies*. Beverly Hills, CA: Sage.

Iyengar, S., & Greenhouse, J. B. (1988). Selection models and the file drawer problem (with discussion). *Statistical Science, 3*, 109–135.

Jackson, G. B. (1980). Methods for integrative research. *Review of Educational Research, 50*, 438–460.

Jayaratne, S., Tripodi, T., & Talsma, E. (1988). The comparative analysis and aggregation of single-case data. *Journal of Applied Behavioral Science, 24*, 119–128.

Johnson, B. T. (1989). *DSTAT: Software for the meta-analytic review of research literatures*. Hillsdale, NJ: Lawrence Erlbaum Associates.

Looney, M. A., Feltz, C. J., & VanVleet, C. N. (1994). The reporting and analyzing of research findings for within-subjects designs: Methodological issues for meta-analysis. *Research Quarterly for Exercise and Sport, 65*, 363–366.

Maxwell, S. E., & Delaney, H. D. (1990). *Designing experiments and analyzing data*. Belmont, CA: Wadsworth.

McDaniel, M. A. (1986). Computer programs for calculating meta-analysis statistics. *Educational and Psychological Measurement, 46*, 175–177.

Mullen, B. (1989). *Advanced basic meta-analysis*. Hillsdale, NJ: Lawrence Erlbaum Associates.

Mullen, B. (1993). *Advanced basic meta-analysis: Version 1.10*. Hillsdale, NJ: Lawrence Erlbaum Associates.

Mullen, B., & Rosenthal, R. (1985). *BASIC meta-analysis: Procedures and programs*. Hillsdale, NJ : Lawrence Erlbaum Associates.

Ohlsen, R. L., Jr. (1987). Control of body rocking in the blind through the use of vigorous exercise. *Journal of Instructional Psychology, 5*, 19–22.

Panel on Statistical Issues and Opportunities for Research in the Combination of Information. (1992). *Contemporary Statistics: Statistical issues and opportunities for research* (Vol. 1). Washington, DC: National Academy Press.

Raudenbush, S. W. (1994). Random effects models. In H. Cooper & L. V. Hedges (Eds.), *The handbook of research synthesis* (pp. 301–321). New York: Russell Sage Foundation.

Reed, J. G., & Baxter, P. M. (1994). Using reference databases. In H. Cooper & L. V. Hedges (Eds.), *The handbook of research synthesis* (pp. 57–70). New York: Russell Sage Foundation.

Rosenthal, M. C. (1994). The fugitive literature. In H. Cooper & L. V. Hedges (Eds.), *The handbook of research synthesis* (pp. 85–94). New York: Russell Sage Foundation.

Rosenthal, R. (1979). The "file-drawer" and tolerance for null results. *Psychological Bulletin, 86*, 638–641.

Rosenthal, R. (1991a). *Meta-analysis procedures for social science research*. Beverly Hills, CA: Sage.

Rosenthal, R. (1991b). Quality-weighting of studies in meta-analytic research. *Psychotherapy Research, 1*, 25–28.

Rosenthal, R., & Rubin, D. B. (1986). Meta-analytic procedures for combining studies with multiple effect sizes. *Psychological Bulletin, 99*, 400–406.

Sacks, H. S., Berrier, J., Reitman, D., Ancona-Berk, V. A., & Chalmers, T. C. (1987). Meta-analyses of randomized controlled trials. *New England Journal of Medicine, 316*, 450–455.

Schwarzer, R. (1988). Meta-analysis programs. *Behavior Research Methods, Instruments, and Computers, 20*, 338.

Scruggs, T. E., & Mastropieri, M. A. (1994). The utility of the PND statistic: A reply of Allison and Gorman. *Behavior, Research, and Therapy, 32*, 879–883.

Scruggs, T. E., Mastropieri, M. A., & Casto, G. (1987a). The quantitative synthesis of single-subject research: Methodology and validation. *Remedial and Special Education, 8*, 24–33.

Scruggs, T. E., Mastropieri, M. A., & Casto, G. (1987b). Reply to Owen White. *Remedial and Special Education, 8*, 40–42.

Scruggs, T. E., Mastropieri, M. S., Forness, S. R., & Kavale, K. A. (1988). Early language intervention: A quantitative synthesis of single-subject research. *Journal of Special Education, 22*, 259–283.

Scruggs, T. E., Mastropieri, M. S., & McEwen, I. (1988). Early intervention for developmental functioning: A quantitative synthesis of single-subjects research. *Journal for the Division of Early Childhood, 12*, 359–367.

Skiba, R., J., Casey, A., & Center, B. A. (1986). Nonaversive procedures in the classroom behavior problems. *Journal of Special Education, 19*, 459–481.

Simonton, D. K. (1977). Cross-sectional time-series experiments: Some suggested statistical analyses. *Psychological Bulletin, 84*, 489–502.

Stoffelmayr, B. E., Dillavou, D., & Hunter, J. E. (1983). Premorbid functioning and outcome in schizophrenia: A cumulative analysis. *Journal of Consulting and Clinical Psychology, 51*, 338–353.

Strube, M. J., Gardner, W., & Hartmann, D. P. (1985). Limitations, liabilities, and obstacles in reviews of the literature: The current status of meta-analysis. *Clinical Psychology Review, 5*, 63–78.

Suen, H. K. (1987). On the epistemology of autocorrelation in applied behavior analysis. *Behavioral Assessment, 9*, 113–124.

Wachter, K. W., & Straf, M. L. (Eds.). (1990). *The future of meta-analysis*. New York: Russell Sage Foundation.

Wampold, B. E., Davis, B., & Good III, R. H. (1990). Hypothesis validity of clinical research. *Journal of Consulting and Clinical Psychology, 58*, 360–367.

Wheeler, D. J. (1990) *Correlated data and control charts*. Knoxville, TN: SPC Press.

White, D. M., Rusch, F. R., Kazdin, A. E., & Hartmann, D. P.(1989). Applications of meta-analysis in individual subject research. *Behavioral Assessment, 11*, 281–296.

White, H. D. (1994). Scientific communication and literature retrieval. In H. Cooper & L. V. Hedges (Eds.), *The handbook of research synthesis* (pp. 41–55). New York: Russell Sage Foundation.

White, O. R. (1987). Some comments concerning "The quantitative synthesis of single-subject research." *Remedial and Special Education, 8*, 34–39.

Wolf, F. M. (1986). *Meta-analysis: Quantitative methods for research synthesis*. Beverly Hills, CA: Sage.

Wortman, P. M. (1994). Judging research quality. In H. Cooper & L. V. Hedges (Eds.), *The handbook of research synthesis* (pp. 97–109). New York: Russell Sage Foundation.

9

The Potentially Confounding Effects of Cyclicity: Identification, Prevention, and Control

T. Mark Beasley
School of Education and Human Services
St. John's University, New York

David B. Allison
Obesity Research Center
St. Luke's/Roosevelt Hospital
Columbia University, College of Physicians & Surgeons

Bernard S. Gorman
Department of Psychology
Hofstra University, Nassau Community College

Among behavior analysts, single-case designs have become a popular alternative to more traditional group experiments. Although single-case designs have numerous strengths both philosophically and practically, they also have potential weaknesses in the areas of analysis and inference. In attempts to address a major analytic issue (i.e., the limited numbers of observations), the use of frequent and repeated measures is often suggested (Barlow & Hersen, 1984). The collection of data at several points in time, however, creates the potential for "testing" and "instrumentation" (Campbell & Stanley, 1966) as threats to internal validity (Horn & Heerboth, 1982). The primary focus of this chapter is that undetected cyclical trends in behavior (or factors correlated with the target behavior) may confound estimates of treatment effects. Moreover, cyclicity, even when detected, complicates the interpretation of data and remains one of the most neglected issues in single-case research (Barlow & Hersen, 1984).

Cyclicity can be defined as any recurrent patterns or fluctuations in the dependent variable (i.e., the subject's behavior) that are not direct results of the independent variable (i.e., intervention). Allison (1992) proposed that certain conventional criteria for changing baseline (A) and intervention (B) phases in single-case designs maximize the likelihood of confounding treatment effects with cyclicity, whereas less typical methods minimize this possibility. Under circumstances where a cyclical trend in behavior is a strong possibility, researchers should employ strategies that control or account for cyclicity in order to avoid confounded effects.

To make this reasoning clear, a description of some of the circumstances under which cyclical trends might be suspected is followed by a discussion of procedures for detecting cyclicity. Finally, methods for determining when to change phases and the extent to which each of these criteria reduce or increase the threat of confounding treatment effects with cyclicity are discussed, and recommendations for research are made.

HOW CYCLICITY CAN CONFOUND INTERPRETATIONS

In the interpretation of results from a single-case design, history and maturation are the most obvious potentially damaging threats to internal validity when cyclicity is suspected. Campbell and Stanley (1966, pp. 7–8) defined maturation as "all those biological or psychological processes which systematically vary with the passage of time, independent of specific external events." Although maturational processes are generally considered to have monotonic trends, any dynamic process causing cyclical variations over time meets this definition. Campbell and Stanley also argued that the effects of season or "institutional schedule" might be classified under either maturation or history effects.

To counter the twin threats of history and maturation, practitioners of single-case research arrange multiple A-B pairings. Most obviously, the A-B-A-B design consists of two consecutive A-B pairings employed with one subject. Alternating-treatment designs consist of many A-B pairings, where the phase lengths are quite short (on average the time interval required to collect one datum). Multiple baseline designs can be viewed as separate A-B designs where the independent variables are introduced at varying times across several behaviors, subjects, or settings (Barlow & Hersen, 1984). This arrangement rules out threats to interval validity in much the same way that the pretest–posttest control group experiment does. To elaborate, the multiple baseline design allows not only for A-B comparisons within subjects (behaviors or settings), but also allows for between-subject A-B comparisons and thus controls for history and maturation as threats to internal validity. For example, the B phase data of the subjects receiving treatment first is compared to the behavior of the subject(s) who have had treatment withheld on order to extend the baseline.

Although cyclicity can confound the interpretation of experimental effects in A-B-A-B alternating-treatment and certain multiple baseline designs (described briefly later), for simplicity primary focus is placed on the A-B-A-B withdrawal design. Texts on single-case research suggest that this design controls for the effects of history and maturation. Barlow and Hersen (1984) stated:

> Whereas the A-B design permits only tentative conclusions as to a treatment's influence, the A-B-A design allows for an analysis of the controlling effects of its introduction and subsequent removal. If after baseline measurement (A) the application of treatment (B) leads to improvement and conversely results in deterioration after it is withdrawn (A), one can conclude with a high degree of certainty that the treatment variable is the agent responsible for changes in the target behavior. Unless the natural history of the behavior under study were to follow identical fluctuations in trends, it is *most improbable* that observed changes would be due to any influence other than the treatment variable that is systematically changed. (pp. 152–153)

It is this possibility of "identical fluctuations in trends" that makes cyclicity a problem in estimating treatment effects.

If the period of a cyclic pattern (the full length of one cycle in time; the distance from crest to crest) exceeds the length of experimental phases, then different experimental phases would sample different portions of a single cycle (Johnston & Pennypaker, 1980). Because a second variable (cycle position) would systematically covary with the independent variable (experimental condition), the experiment would be confounded. The most extreme confounding would occur if phase changes coincided with crests and troughs of a wave pattern.

A graphic depiction of this phenomenon can be found in the data in Figs. 9.1A and 9.1B. Figure 9.1A shows the results of a hypothetical A-B-A-B experiment designed to decrease an undesirable behavior. At first glance, the treatment may appear to be quite effective. The behavior reliably falls and rises with the introduction and withdrawal of treatment, respectively. Inspection of Fig. 9.1B, however, reveals that the pattern of the behavior over time is a sinusoidal wave and no true effect of treatment exists. The phase changes merely capitalize on a preexisting pattern. In fact, the 16 observations in the Fig. 9.1B time series is based on the function:

$$Y_t = 10 \sin(i) + 20,$$

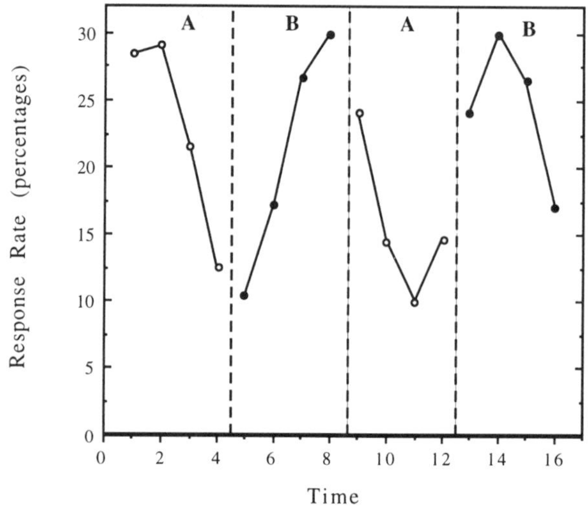

FIG. 9.1A. Results of a hypothetical A-B-A-B experiment designed to decrease the rate of an undesirable behavior. Reprinted with permission.

where i is t expressed in radians. The series has a wavelength or period of $2\pi = 6.28$ and a frequency of $1/2\pi = 0.159$.

The effects of cyclicity are of equal concern in alternating-treatment designs in that it is possible that the period of the cycle could be brief enough to coincide with the unit of alternation. For example, this would occur if the daily behavior of an individual exhibited a negative lag-one autocorrelation (i.e., days with better-than-average behavior tended to follow days with worse-than-average behavior, and vice versa) and conditions alternated on a daily basis. Nonconcurrent multiple baseline designs across subjects are also vulnerable if subjects' cycles are not synchronous and baseline periods for subjects are not sufficiently long for researchers to observe cyclical fluctuations (Watson & Workman, 1981). In contrast, concurrent multiple baseline designs across behaviors or settings should be robust to such confounding except in the unlikely event that each response or responses in each setting were cyclical but fluctuated with a different period and/or on a different schedule. Although this is possible, it seems rather remote. Truly simultaneous treatment designs should be impervious to cyclicity. Although often taken to be synonymous with the alternating-treatment design, the simultaneous treatment design is distinctly different (Barlow & Hersen, 1984). The simultaneous treatment design is conceptually equivalent to the analysis of concurrent schedules of reinforcement described by Ferster and Skinner (1957). Similarly, it does not seem that cyclicity could easily con-

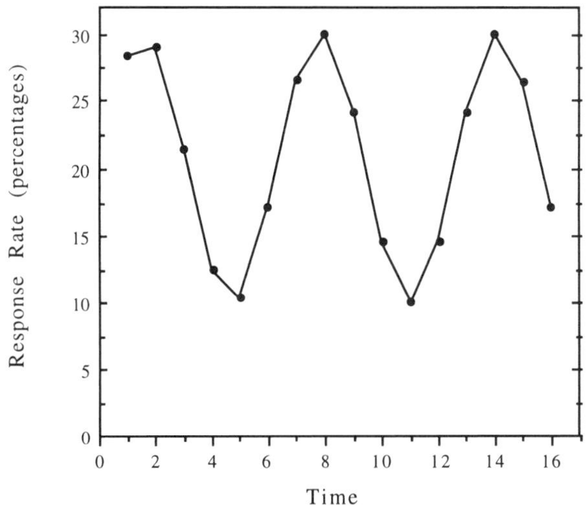

FIG. 9.1B. The same data as in Fig. 9.1A without random error and phase breaks (i.e., sinusoidal wave). Reprinted with permission.

found the interpretation of changing criterion designs (e.g., Hall & Fox, 1977; Hartmann & Hall, 1976).

WHY CYCLICITY MIGHT BE PRESENT

Cyclical patterns may be present in time-series data for many reasons. Although this discussion is by no means exhaustive, three broad categories related to cyclicity are presented: biological rhythms, cyclically "chained" responses, and schedules of reinforcement/institutional schedules. Where possible, we cite examples from the literature where these cycles have been recognized and dealt with appropriately.

Biological Rhythms

When one investigates individual human behavior (as in psychotherapy research), cyclical patterns may be a function of underlying biological processes. In particular, the 90-minute (Klietman, 1982), 25-hour, 28-day, and 365-day cycles are common to humans (Aschoff, 1984). These cycles can have profound effects on symptoms of psychopathology (Gerada & Reveley, 1988), arousal (Freeman & Hovland, 1934), attention (Colquhoun, 1971), reaction time (Kleitman, Titelbaum, & Feiveson, 1938), judgment of time duration (Hoagland, 1933), nicotine tolerance and addiction (Leaventhal & Cleary, 1980), and other behaviors dependent on physiological negative feedback loops or opponent processes (i.e., Solomon & Corbit, 1973).

Other cycles have also been observed. For example, some persons with affective disorders have been reported to "rapidly" cycle (Alarcon, 1985), such that four or more cycles occur per year. Among normative samples, a seven-day cycle in positive and negative affect has been observed (Almagor & Ehrlich, 1990). Also, the attention of children has been noted to cycle through peaks and troughs throughout the schoolday to the extent that it affects academic achievement (Biggers, 1980). Moreover, nonhuman animals, frequently studied in basic operant research, also exhibit periodicity in their estrous cycles as well as cycles corresponding to circadian rhythms and lunar and annual cycles (Aschoff, 1984).

Biological cycles may be caused by seasonal, climatic, or internal hormonal changes. Alternatively, operant mechanisms may be viewed as causal when emission of the behavior reduces subsequent rates of that same behavior through "satiation" and the passage of time increases "drive" and the likelihood that the behavior will be emitted (Skinner, 1953).

The importance of considering these biological rhythms becomes even more apparent when one considers the possibility that the effects of the operant mechanisms may depend on the portion of the cycle being investigated. Roberts, Bennett, and Vickers (1989) demonstrated that such treatment by cycle-phase interactions can occur. For instance, among female Wistar rats, the effects of a progressively escalating ratio schedule of reinforcement depended greatly on the phase of the subject's estrous cycle.

Researchers have also observed that some behavior exhibited by persons with developmental disabilities is cyclic in nature. Akyurek (1985) suggested that "clocklike processes" and "biological rhythms" may govern some of the behavior of autistic children. Fisher and colleagues (e.g., Cataldo & Fisher, 1991; Fisher, Piazza, Harrell, & Chinn, 1990) reported several cases of individuals with severe aggressive or self-injurious behavior disorders that clearly had cyclical components. In one case, the behavioral cycle coincided with the menstrual cycle. Recognition of these cycles not only suggested the need for experimental designs that could control for cyclicity, but also led to the development of successful treatments (Cataldo & Fisher, 1991).

Human body weight has also been shown to vary cyclically on a seasonal basis. Although these effects are relatively small, they are statistically significant when aggregated over many individuals (Hardin et al., 1991; Rico et al., 1994; Taylor & Stunkard, 1993). Similarly, in many "community" weight loss studies an entire community serves as a single case. Such studies generally produce small weight losses, often no larger than seasonal fluctuations. Thus, researchers conducting such experiments would need to ensure that pre- and posttreatment weights were not taken during different seasons of the year.

Some persons with mental retardation have also been suggested to have "rapidly cycling" affective disorders (Glue, 1989). Morley and Adams (1991) reanalyzed data from Lavender (1981) on the rate of seizures among persons with epilepsy and found an underlying periodicity that was not obviously apparent on visual inspection of the raw data. Meier-Koll, Fels, Kofler, Schulz-Weber, and Thiesses (1977) demonstrated that the stereotypic behavior of one girl with mental retardation appeared to vacillate on a 90-minute cycle. Sorosky, Ornitz, Brown, and Ritvo (1968) also observed that stereotypic behavior among persons with mental retardation tended to fluctuate cyclically with a period of 90 minutes. It seems especially important to be cognizant of these possibilities, given the frequent use of single-case research among persons with developmental disabilities.

For example, the functional analysis method developed by Iwata, Dorsey, Slifer, Bauman, and Richman (1982) entails observing a subject under four different conditions for 15 minutes per condition. Because an entire session takes place in fewer than 90 minutes, different conditions would take place during different portions of a 90-minute cycle, and the potential confounding could be great. Iwata et al. (1982), however, wisely conducted several sessions per subjects and randomized the order of presentation within each session. Not only did this control for order effects, but the likelihood that the condition would covary systematically with cycle position was thereby greatly reduced. Randomization (discussed later) represents one method of minimizing the confounding of treatment effects with cyclicity.

Cyclically Chained Responses

Occasionally, several responses may be causally linked either within the individual or among more than one individual. Suen and Ary (1989) referred to these phenomena as "cyclical chains." For example, if response X causes response Y, which causes response Z, which in turn causes response X, then responses X, Y, and Z are said to be cyclically chained. Such chains are frequently observed among family members by "systems" therapists.

An excellent example is provided by Snyder (1987), who treated an adolescent boy for inconsistent diabetic self-care though behavioral family therapy. Snyder conducted an "extended baseline" (45 days) during which data were collected on the subject's self-care, "antisocial" behavior, and school attendance, and the rate of mother–son aversive interactions (nagging, arguing, etc.). Data were analyzed both visually and statistically through lagged correlations, which:

> suggested a cyclic positive feedback process. At the beginning of a cycle, the son would engage in relatively good self-care but frequent antisocial behavior. In response to his frequent antisocial behavior, the mother would increase her nagging and threats. This would result in an immediate reduction in appropriate self-care by the son, a countercontrol strategy. However, her nagging also led to a reduction in antisocial behavior because poor self-care interfered with such behavior. Thus her nagging was negatively reinforced. . . . This continued until a diabetic crisis occurred which terminated the mother's nagging and threats (negatively reinforcing the son's countercontrol), and the cycle will begin again. (p. 25)

Despite the serious nature of the diabetes, Snyder's (1987) decision to run such an extended baseline appears to have been quite beneficial. The analysis made possible by this long baseline not only facilitated the design of an efficacious treatment but also allowed a determination of the period of the cycle. Thus, phases that were consistently longer than the period of the cycle could be employed and thereby reduce the possibility of confounding treatment effects with cyclicity.

A situation which may frequently occur in educational research was elaborated by Wacker, Steege, and Berg (1988). In their example, a subset of children in one classroom were learning math on a microcomputer. These children spent a larger proportion of time on-task but frequently sought the attention of the teacher to ask for instructions. But the latter behavior (attention seeking) was counterproductive to the goal of computer assisted instruction: to have the children work on-task independently so that the teacher could devote time to other students. Giving attention to the computer students allowed them to progress, which increased time on-task, but also reinforced their disruptive attention-seeking behavior. In turn, this reduced the amount of time the teacher could spend with the other students, which consequently reduced their amount of time on-task. The experimental solution postulated was to improve the instructional design of the computer program so that instruction were available at every step.

During individual communications, people speak, listen, and then respond to what they hear. Warner and Mooney (1988) used this cyclicity to explain individual differences in percent of time spent talking in dyadic conversations. Although physiological rhythms and cognitive capacities could not be seen as potential causes, the chain of reinforcements associated with social approval and attention were proposed to affect the cycles of individual's commmunication (Warner, 1979) and positive affect (Warner, Malloy, Schneinder, Knoth, & Wilder, 1987) within group settings. Furthermore, the complimentary or compatability of communication rhythms has been suggested to influence interpersonal attraction (Chapple, 1970).

Institutional Schedules/Schedules of Reinforcement

Ferster and Skinner's (1957) *Schedules of Reinforcement* is replete with examples and explanations of how certain schedules produce repetitive and predictable waxing and waning of response rate. Although these patterns are rarely sinusoidal in shape, their recurrent nature over time clearly qualifies them as cycles.

Allison (1992) presented a hypothetical example involving the mean progress note-writing rate of a group of therapists at a community mental health clinic. In addition to a base salary, these therapists are paid piece-rate on a combined fixed-interval, fixed-ratio schedule (offering mental health workers monetary performance incentives and focusing on note writing are both practices that have been reported in the organizational behavior management literature; see Allison, Silverstein, & Galante, 1992; Calpin, Edelstein, & Redmon, 1988). Specifically, they receive 50 cents per progress note (fixed-ratio), which is provided to them in their paycheck at the end of each month (fixed-intervals). Because response rate is, in part, a function of immediacy of reinforcement, response rates increase toward the end of each month as reinforcers become more immediate. Additionally, the expected post reinforcement pause or decrement in response rate (Ferster & Skinner, 1957) would constitute a trough of the cycle.

Let us suppose further that an organizational behavior management (OBM) consultant is hired by the clinic management to increase progress note writing, which is somewhat sporadic. An intervention is devised and evaluated with an A-B-A-B design. The consultant begins collecting baseline data on the first of the month and predetermines that each phase will be of equal length, lasting two weeks. The implications of this should be obvious. Baseline phases will always sample the first two weeks of the month when response rate is low, and intervention phases will always sample the last two weeks of the month when response rate is high. Given that the intervention attempts to increase note writing, a blatant Type-I error could occur.

Certainly no competent OBM practitioner would be caught by so simple a trap. In the applied world, however, things are rarely so simple. To take the hypothetical example further, because note writing requires attendance (patient records may not be removed from the clinic), attendance would probably cycle synchronously with response rate. If the same consultant were hired to decrease absenteeism, it is not hard to imagine overlooking the possible effects of pay schedule.

Pay schedules are perhaps the most obvious but by no means the only possible cycles in institutional settings. For example, researchers in organizational behavior have observed that employee satisfaction may vary cyclically of a periodicity of about five years (Shirom & Mazeh, 1988). Certainly, OBM researchers are aware that economic trends can vary cyclically, which may have profound effects on their dependent variables (e.g., sales). In school organizations, factors such as subject matter, testing, and even lunch have definite schedules that are reinforced in educational institutions. Therefore, effective time management and scheduling must take into account the schoolday cycles experienced by students and teachers alike (Biggers, 1980). Furthermore, Weidlich (1988) used cyclicity to explain macrosystems such as long-term economic recovery and the prosperity and decline among restaurants.

Finally, Gouse (1984) reported a case in which the dose of neuroleptic agents administered to an entire psychiatric ward varied cyclically with a period of four weeks under "ordinary" circumstances and with a period of two weeks during times of organizational stress. Moreover, during one time of stress the amplitude of the wave (the distance from crest to trough) was equivalent of approximately 800 milligrams of chlorpromazine! Clearly, this cycle could greatly influence many variables. However, it is questionable whether a behavior analyst planning a wardwide intervention at this institution would anticipate, recognize, or control for such a cycle.

DETECTING CYCLICITY AND OTHER TRENDS IN DATA

As stated previously, our discussion of cyclical patterns was not intended to be exhaustive. In part, this discussion is limited because cyclical patterns in behavioral research have been minimally explored. Further investigations in which cyclical patterns were treated as the focus rather than as a nuisance would certainly be a welcome addition to the field. Moreover, individual researchers may wish to evaluate their own data for possible cyclical patterns. Such exploration would generate a body of knowledge regarding common cycles on which applied researchers could draw.

Graphic and Visual Inspection for Detecting Cyclicity

One approach to examining potential cyclicity is through visual inspection of extended series of graphed data. Although practically simple, the validity of this procedure is questionable (Kruse & Gottman, 1982). Many researchers and authors extol the virtues of visual inspection and graphic analysis of data, asserting that an "important" effect will be manifest in an obvious manner (i.e., Skinner, 1963) and that in applied settings only marked effects have practical significance and utility (Baer, 1977). Comparative studies of graphic/visual inspection versus statistical analysis highlight the complexity of this issue (DeProspero & Cohen, 1979; Furlong & Wampold, 1982; Jones, Weinrott, & Vaught, 1977; Park, Marascuilo, & Gaylord-Ross, 1990). For example, Wampold and Furlong (1981) found that the orientation and background of the analyst determined which features of a graph were most salient. As might be expected, researchers with a statistical background focused on the size of change between phases in consideration with the variability of the data, whereas applied behavior analysts often attended simply to the magnitude of change in location or central tendency. Despite those who eschew visual inspection as an analytic procedure, such graphic methods do provide an essential, interpretive adjunct to statistical analyses (Morley & Adams, 1991).

In analyzing single-case data, there are three general aspects to consider when constructing graphs:

1. *Central location* within phases and changes in central location between phases.
2. *Variability* in the data, including changes in variation over time.
3. *Trend* in central location (linear and nonlinear) within and between different phases of data collection.

Graphical methods for visually inspecting all three of these aspects are presented by Franklin, Gorman, Beasley, & Allison (chap. 5, this volume). It should be noted, however, that the graphical display of *trend* most directly addresses the detection of *cyclicity.* For example, running medians for the data from Fig. 9.1B would show a strong cyclical trend.

Statistical Analyses for Detecting Cyclicity

Because of the apparent problems with the reliability of "eyeballing" for analyzing time-series data, it has been widely suggested that some form of statistical analysis be employed in addition to visual/graphical inspection. As mentioned earlier, the confound that cyclicity presents occurs when treatment phases (A-B pairings) are changed in a manner synchronous with the recurrent behavioral pattern. To the extent that the phase may be changed at the crest or trough of the cycle, cyclicity may be examined through statistical analyses that model each phase. Yet, no consensus on what constitutes an appropriate analysis has been reached. Variants of the repeated-measures ANOVA have been suggested in which the within-phase observations are treated as cases (Gentile, Roden, & Klein, 1972; Shine & Bower, 1971). An important assumption of linear models, however, is independence of error terms for all observations. Because it seems reasonable to assume that successive observations of the same organism are somehow dependent, a number of authors have suggested that it is likely that the residuals of these observations are also related (see Matyas & Greenwood, chap. 7, this volume); thus, the ANOVA and most other parametric methods may be inappropriate in many experiments which incorporate time-series data. (Gottman & Glass, 1978; Hartmann, 1974; Jones et al., 1977).

To circumvent the violation of the independence of errors assumption (i.e., serial dependency), *interrupted time-series analysis* based on the Box and Jenkins (1976) autoregressive integrated moving averages (ARIMA) model has been recommended for the analysis of single-case data (Glass, Wilson, & Gottman, 1975; Jones et al., 1977). An ARIMA model develops a model of the data, after removing serial dependency and other sources of irrelevant variation, that can then be tested through a least-squares approach. Although this approach has the advantage of accounting for serial dependency, it raises new difficulties (see Gorman & Allison, chap. 6, this volume for more details). Namely, the modeling process may become quite complex, to the point that it is difficult to make inferential decisions or even identify the null hypothesis being tested (Gorsuch, 1983). However, many single-case researchers contend that data from behavioral experiments can be analyzed with the simplest of the ARIMA models (McDowall, McCleary, Meidinger, & Hay, 1980). Thus, developing a full ARIMA model for single-case data may not always be appropriate; however, ARIMA statistics can provide very useful diagnostics for assessing the potential of cyclicity.

Huitema (1985, 1986) contended that little evidence exists to indicate that serial dependency is a major threat to single-case behavioral researchers; however, this contention has met with substantial resistance and rebuttal (Matyas & Greenwood, chap. 7, this volume). Moreover, although time-series analyses typically require a minimum of 50 to 60 data points per phase (Glass et al., 1975), most behavioral single-case experiments provide far fewer observations for the entire study.

Gorsuch (1983) suggested three parametric, least-squares alternatives to time-series analysis: *autoregressive analysis, differencing,* and *trend analysis.* Several nonparametric approaches to time-series data have also been suggested (see Edgington, 1992; Levin, Marascuilo, & Hubert, 1978); however, most of these tests were developed to assess treatment effects rather than trends. Because the detection and control of cyclicity and its correlates involve an investigation of overall and within-phase trends, our discussion focuses on ARIMA models, nonparametric tests that assess trend, spectral analysis, cross-correlation functions, coherence analysis, and trend analyses (e.g., Gorsuch, 1983; Kelly, McNeil, & Newman, 1973).

Time-Series Analysis: ARIMA Models. Time-series analysis is actually a collection of statistical techniques, but arguably its most useful component in the analysis of single-case behavioral data is the estimation of serial dependency through an autoregressive analysis. This is because autocorrelation can be caused by several observations being affected by the same influence, even though that influence is unrelated to the dependent variable. If this influence is unmeasured then the errors are considered correlated, which is termed a *moving average.* This is distinct from an *autoregressive component,* in which previous observations influence later observations. Thus, autoregressive observations create autocorrelation but not all autocorrelated time-series are autoregressive.

Cyclicity is often considered an autoregressive process. For example, hormonal levels today may be considered a function of yesterday's level or behavioral responses may be determined by the previous reinforcement of those behaviors. This is not to rule out the possibility of cyclical moving averages, however. In fact, a researcher who uncovers the "cause" of the moving average has found a useful covariate. In either case, the serial correlation, autocorrelative function (ACF), and partial autocorrelative functions (PACF) are used in evaluating autocorrelation regardless of its origin.

The serial correlation is a correlation coefficient derived from the T values of a data series with the same series up to k lags behind. To elaborate, when $k = 1$, the lag-one serial correlation is computed by pairing the first observation with the second, the second with the third, until the last observation has been paired with the penultimate. For $k = 2$, a lag-two serial correlation pairs the first observation with the third, the second with the fourth, and so on. The ACF shows a collection of k zero-order serial correlation between successive observations at different lags from 1 to k. Although several lags are available in the ACF, a lag-one autocorrelation is the most common in behavioral research. Huitema and McKean (1991) observed that the coefficient is underestimation in short series. Based on their suggestion, the formula for the serial correlation or ACF at lag-k is:

$$\mathrm{ACF}_{(k)} = \frac{\sum_{t=1}^{T} (Y_t - \overline{Y})(Y_{t+k} - \overline{Y})}{\sum_{t=1}^{T} (Y_t - \overline{Y})^2} \tag{9.1}$$

The standard error for the serial correlation or ACF at lag-k is:

$$S_e[\mathrm{ACF}_{(k)}] = \sqrt{1/N\left(1 + 2 \sum_{i=1}^{k} \mathrm{ACF}^2_{(k)}\right)} \tag{9.2}$$

Thus, a Z-test can be computed and compared to the unit normal distribution; however, one must be careful in performing multiple tests and inflating the Type-I error rate. Therefore, one may consider adjusting the alpha with the Bonferroni correction of dividing alpha by k, the number of lags analyzed. However, this correction will be conservative because of the correlation between tests. Another popular test for the ACF at each lag is the Box-Ljung test (e.g., Ljung & Box, 1978), which appears in the SPSS ARIMA module. It tests the null hypothesis that the ACF at each lag does not differ from a white noise (random) process.

The PACF gives the correlation of successive observations with all other observations controlled or partialed out. The computational formula is similar to other formulae for partial correlations and becomes complex rapidly with increasing lags. Therefore, it is best to rely on computer packages to compute the PACF. However, the standard error for the PACF is simple:

$$S_e[\mathrm{PACF}_{(k)}] = \sqrt{1/N} \tag{9.3}$$

The exact interpretations of ACFs and PACFs are outside the scope of this chapter, but the reader may refer to Gorman and Allison (chap. 6, this volume).

Figure 9.2 shows the output from a SAS PROC ARIMA (SAS Institute, 1993a) analysis performed on the data from Fig. 9.1A. It should be noted that a variety of other packages would yield similar output; however, the results may vary slightly, based on which algorithms are used for the ACF and PACF. Also, the SAS package has been criticized for its limited output and that significance tests such as a Box-Ljung test do not appear (Harrop & Velicer, 1990). However, SAS is used because of its populartiy in a wide variety of analytic contexts. Figure 9.2 indicates that the total time-series from Fig. 9.1A is *nonstationary*—it has some systematic trend.

```
                             ARIMA Procedure


                    Name of variable = X.

                    Mean of working series = 21.47712
                    Standard deviation     =  7.37899
                    Number of observations =       16

                            Autocorrelations

Lag Covariance Correlation -1 9 8 7 6 5 4 3 2 1 0 1 2 3 4 5 6 7 8 9 1
  0  54.449489     1.00000 |                    |********************|
  1  26.909416     0.49421 |          .         |**********          |
  2 -12.572869    -0.23091 |        .      *****|           .        |
  3 -35.941842    -0.66010 |       *************|            .       |
  4 -26.817132    -0.49251 |    .     **********|               .    |
  5   6.990038     0.12838 |   .                |***             .   |
  6  26.364001     0.48419 |   .                |**********      .   |
  7  16.573204     0.30438 | .                  |******            . |
  8  -4.093164    -0.07517 | .                **|                  . |
  9 -21.278605    -0.39080 | .          ********|                  . |
                           "." marks two standard errors


                        Partial Autocorrelations

           Lag Correlation -1 9 8 7 6 5 4 3 2 1 0 1 2 3 4 5 6 7 8 9 1
             1     0.49421 |          .         |**********          |
             2    -0.62871 |       *************|         .          |
             3    -0.35779 |          .  *******|         .          |
             4    -0.02892 |          .        *|         .          |
             5     0.28395 |          .         |******   .          |
             6    -0.16038 |          .      ***|         .          |
             7    -0.23959 |          .    *****|         .          |
             8     0.16756 |          .         |***      .          |
             9    -0.10034 |          .       **|         .          |
```

FIG. 9.2. ACF and PACF for the time-series data in Fig. 9.1A.

This is important because ARIMA models are appropriate only for stationary (nontrending) time series. A nonstationary process is suspected when the ACF gradually decays rather than having a few larger autocorrelations in the earlier lags and near zero autocorrelations in the later lags and the lower-order PACF lags are large. For an autoregressive component, the autocorrelations will decay slowly to 0 for increasing lags, and the PACF will drop abruptly to 0 when the appropriate lag (k) is reached. In Fig. 9.2, the ACF decays gradually and the PACF drops to 0 at a lag of $k = 4$, which gives an indication of seasonality. Also, the strong lag-six correlation indicates a six-observation cycle. This should come as no surprise, because the data points were based on a sinusoidal wave with a period of 2π and four observations in each phase. In fact, if a true sinusoidal wave were analyzed, the ACF itself would show a sinusoidal pattern, which is observable in Fig. 9.2. When autocorrealtion is detected, the time series must be *differenced*. Differencing, which will be discussed in more detail later, involves subtracting successive observations until the nonstationary trend has been removed from the ACF and PACF.

In the scenario presented, the data were to represent an A-B-A-B design in which phases should be analyzed separately. However, there are only four observations per phase. Therefore, only lag-one autocorrelation coefficients (1) and standard errors (2) were calculated for each phase, which are shown in Table 9.1. Although statistical significance was not reached (most likely due to low sample size), the autocorrelation for these within-phase data suggest a nonstationary process that should be differenced. Although we do not present a comprehensive and exhaustive coverage, ARIMA models and diagonostics, as well as simply computing the ACF and PACF, can be effective means for identifying cyclicity in behavioral research. A major concern, however, is that most behavior analytic experiments lack a sufficient number of observations to obtain stable autoregressive estimates and accurate ACFs.

Differencing. Although the differencing of scores is included in the rubric of ARIMA models, it has been a long-established procedure in econometric literature (e.g., Ezekiel & Fox, 1959). In differencing, the transformed dependent variable is:

$$Y^{\Delta}{}_t = Y_t - Y_{t-1}, \tag{9.4}$$

which called the "first difference" of Y. The number of first differenced observations is one less than the total number of observations. For example, if the series is $\boldsymbol{Y}$ = [2, 3, 5, 9, 13, 18, 24], then

$$\boldsymbol{Y}^{\Delta} = [(3\text{-}2), (5\text{-}3), (9\text{-}5), (13\text{-}9), (18\text{-}13), (24\text{-}18)] = [1, 2, 4, 4, 5, 6]$$

TABLE 9.1
Lag-One Autocorrelation Coefficients with Standard Errors for Each Phase in Fig. 9.1A.

Phase	*ACF(1)*	*Se(1)*
1. A	0.152	0.489
2. B	0.210	0.479
3. A	−0.237	0.474
4. B	−0.120	0.493

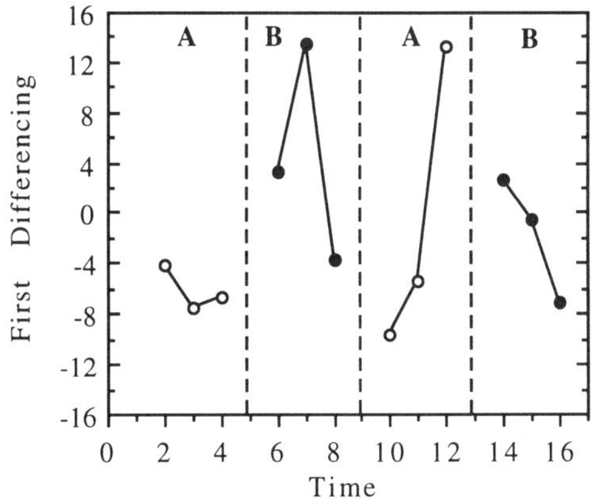

FIG. 9.3. Time-series data from Fig. 9.1A after within-phase first differencing.

If the first differences do not eliminate the autocorrelative, nonstationary process, the second differences may be taken:

$$Y^{\Delta\Delta}{}_t = Y^{\Delta}{}_t - Y^{\Delta}{}_{t-1}$$

$$Y_t^{\Delta\Delta} = [(2\text{-}1), (4\text{-}2), (4\text{-}4), (5\text{-}4), (6\text{-}5)] = [1, 2, 0, 1,1] \qquad (9.5)$$

The first difference procedure is related to both the notions of trend and autoregression in time-series data. The first differencing approach is used to correct for a linear trend; however, it also corrects for a special case of autoregression, when the autoregressive parameter is 1.0. Thus, to the extent that cyclicity confounds interpretation because of its modulation with phase changes, within-phase differencing may help control cyclicity and improve the estimation of treatment effects.

Figure 9.3 shows the response rates from Fig. 9.1A after they have been first-differenced within each phase. Although it is not presented, an ARIMA analysis of each of these differenced within-phase data still show some autocorrelation. Thus, a second differencing may be necessary. Because of the limited number of observations, we refrain from such a transformation. As it stands, it is obviously much more difficult to infer a treatment effect after this transformation. However, the researcher must be cautious not to difference every time series for interpretation. Differencing is a procedure used for detrending data; that is, removing systematic, autocorrelative effects. Thus, differencing can always be performed, but differenced data should only be interpreted when nonstationary processes such as cyclicity are suspected on logical or theoretical grounds. Otherwise, the differencing process may remove the treatment effect, especially in situations where intervention effects have a gradual onset or cause changes in the slope rather than the level of a behavior (Allison & Gorman, 1993). For example, if the data in Fig. 9.1A were to represent a "true" treatment effect rather than a cyclical fluctuation, then the within-phase differencing shown in Fig. 9.3 would obscure any effects and interpretation. However, it appears that differencing as a general heuristic rather than a statistical algorithm is effective when within-phase trends or cyclicity are strongly suspected.

Nonparametric Tests of Serial Dependency. Although the serial correlation formula in Equation 1 is the most popular, it is often limited to longer time series and the assumptions of parametric test statistics. Therefore, a few lesser-known tests that do not rely as heavily on parametric assumptions are presented. Each test is designed to detect serial dependency or cyclicity. If detected transformation options such as differencing may be necessary. For the sake of simplicity, the 16 data points from Fig. 9.1A are displayed in Table 9.2 and are used for computational examples. Also, unit normal approximations are calculated for demonstration purposes regardless of whether the sample size permits a reasonable approximation.

It should also be noted that Edgington (1992) elaborated many non-

TABLE 9.2
Nonparametric Computational Examples Based on the Data from Fig. 9.1A.

Raw Data	*Median Sign*	*Turning Points*	*Successive Differences*
32.59	+		
28.48	+		−4.12
21.02	+		−7.46
14.44	−		−6.57
13.80	−	trough	−0.65
17.03	−		3.23
30.49	+	peak	13.47
26.81	+		−3.69
20.90	−		−5.91
11.21	−		−9.68
5.79	−	trough	−5.42
19.00	−		13.21
25.67	+		6.67
28.25	+	peak	2.57
27.65	+		−0.60
20.51	−		−7.14
$M = 20.96$	$R = 6$	$P = 4$	$S = 5$

Note. M = Median, R = number of runs, P = number of turning points, S = number of successive differences.

parametric and randomization tests for statistical analyses of single-case experiments. However, the majority of these procedures test for changes in behavioral level rather than trends in behavior (Onghena, 1992). To this extent, these tests are not helpful when detecting cyclicity is a concern. Therefore, these methods are not presented. The interested reader is referred to Gorman and Allison (chap. 6, this volume).

The Mean-Square Adjacency Test of Successive Differences was originally developed by vonNeumann (e.g., vonNeumann, 1941; vonNeumann, Kent, Bellinson, & Hart, 1941) and adapted by Tryon (1982). Tryon's C-statistic tests the null hypothesis that adjacent (or lag-one) fluctuations in a time series have a random pattern and is calculated as:

$$C = 1 - \frac{\sum_{t=1}^{T-1} (Y_{t+1} - Y_t)^2}{2 \sum_{t=1}^{T} (Y_t - \bar{Y})^2} \tag{9.6}$$

where Y_t is the observed value at time t and T is the total number of observations. As can be inferred from Equation 9.6, if there is a consistent trend in the time series, then the sum of squared successive differences will accumulate and become large relative to the total variability in the denominator. For $T > 25$, a unit normal approximation test can be developed from the standard error of C. Because the expected value of C is zero, then the test statistic is simply C divided by its standard error:

$$S_e(C) = \sqrt{(T - 2)/(T - 1)(T + 1)} \tag{9.7}$$

which approximates the normal distribution under the null hypothesis. For $T < 25$, critical values are tabled for C (Tryon, 1982) and for $L = 2(1 - C)$ (Kanji, 1993). In the present example, $C = 0.4343$, which exceeds its critical value at the $\alpha = .05$ level of significance. Therefore, the null hypothesis of no trend is rejected. When C is divided by its standard error, a value of $z_C = 1.85$ results, which indicates marginal significance (two-tailed $p = .0644$). It should be noted that the results of the ARIMA analysis indicated a strong lag-one serial correlation which is consistent with these results for Tryon's C. However, because the C statistic only uses lag-one information, it has been criticized for being insensitive to more complex dependencies. Although lag-one serial correlation is often the most important type of serial dependency, researchers must be aware that the C statistic may not detect time series trends for higher order lags (Crosbie, 1989).

The runs test for randomness in a sample is based on the idea that a random time series should not have too many or too few successive values (runs) above or below the median. Too few runs indicates a low frequency cycle or a linear/monotonic trend in the time series, which can be determined upon visual inspection. If there are too many runs, a rapidly oscillating cycle is indicated. To calculate the number of runs, one first finds the median value in the data and then assigns positive signs (+) to observations greater than the median. Negative signs (−) are assigned to observations below the median. A sequence of similar signs is considered a "run." Thus, if there are three consecutive +s in time series sequence, it is a run. The first observation starts the first run and every time the sign changes, a new run is counted. Tables of critical values for runs are available in many sources (e.g. Kanji, 1993; Siegel & Castellan, 1988). For longer times series (i.e., $T > 30$), the test statistic can be compared to a normal distribution with a mean of $(T/2 + 1)$ with a variance of $T^3(T - 2)/4T^2(T - 1)$. Therefore, a single sample z-test can be calculated:

$$z_R = \frac{R - (T/2) + 1)}{\sqrt{T^3(T - 2)/4T^2(T - 1)}} \tag{9.8}$$

In either case, if the observed value exceeds the critical value at a given significance level, the null hypothesis of no cyclicity is rejected. For the sinusoidal time series in Table 9.2, the number of runs about the median, $R = 6$, is not statistically significant at the .05 level. The unit normal approximation, which equals -1.55 also fails to indicate that the time series has significantly fewer than expected runs (two-tailed $p = .1212$).

The runs test for successive differences is based on a similar concept. That is, successive differences in random data should have no particular order. To calculate the number of runs for a sequence of data, find successive differences between adjacent observations by subtracting observation $Y_{(t-1)}$ from observation Y_t, then find the algebraic signs of the differences. As before, a sequence of similar signs is called a *run*. For example, in a time series with an increasing monotonic trend, each value, Y_t, is larger than the previous observation, $Y_{(t-1)}$, and all successive differences would be positive and therefore, there is only one run. To elaborate, if there is a low-frequency cycle or a long-term monotonic trend there will be fewer runs than expected. Conversely, if there are rapid oscillations, there will be more runs than expected. For $5 < T < 40$, critical values for the number of runs for successive differences S can be found in Kanji (1993). For longer time series (e.g., $T > 40$) the expected number of runs is $(2T - 1)/3$ with a variance of $(16T - 29)/90$. Therefore, a single-sample z-test is formed:

$$z_S = \frac{S - ((2T - 1)/3)}{\sqrt{(16T - 29)/90}} \tag{9.9}$$

In either case, if the observed value exceeds the critical value, then the null hypothesis of no cyclicity is rejected. In the present example the number of successive runs for successive difference, $S = 5$ (see Table 9.2), is significantly lower than expected, $p < .05$. The presence of cyclicity is also confirmed by the unit normal approximation, $z_s = -3.36$, $p = .0008$, which exceeds the two-tailed critical value for significance at $\alpha = .05$.

The Turning point test is based on the notion that the higher and lower values in random time series data should not occur in any sequence. If the value of an observation in a sequence is below the value of the observation that immediately preceded it and also below the value of the observation that immediately followed it, it is called a *trough* turning point. If a the value of an observation in a sequence is above the value of the observation that immediately preceded it and also above the value of the observation that immediately followed it, it is called a *peak* turning point. Starting with the second observation and preceding to the next to last observation, count the number of turning points. Time-series data that have negative autocorrelations or rapidly oscillating trends have higher numbers of turning points than expected, whereas positive autocorrelations or low frequency cycles have fewer than expected turning points. For shorter series, a table of critical values for the number of turning points, P, can be found in Kanji (1993). For longer series, the expected mean is $2(T - 2)/3$ with a variance of $(16T - 29)/90$. Therefore, a single-sample z-test that under the null hypothesis approximates the unit normal distribution can be formed:

$$z_P = \frac{P - (2(T - 2)/3)}{\sqrt{(16T - 29)/90}} \tag{9.10}$$

In the present example, the number of turning points, $P = 4$ (see Table 9.2), is significantly lower than expected, $p < .05$; thus, the null hypothesis of no cyclicity is rejected. The unit normal approximation, $z_P = -3.36$, $p = .0008$, also indicates a significant low frequency cycle.

Spectral Analysis. A collection of procedure under the rubric of "spectral analysis" are often suggested for the analysis of time-series data (Horne, Yang, & Ware, 1982). The idea is that trends in time-series data, regardless of the complexity of their functions, can be described by a series of sine and cosine functions. That is, behavior over time can be viewed as a superposition of sinusoidal waves (Bohrer & Porges, 1982). Therefore, spectral analysis attempts to decompose trends in data and find component waves that represent cyclicity, even for extremely "noisy" patterns of data. It is based on Fourier's spectral decomposition theorem. Although the mathematics of the Fourier analysis are beyond the scope of this chapter, one can easily appreciate the output of computer packages that produce these analyses. Typically, a spectral plot is examined. The frequency or the period, which is the reciprocal of the frequency, is plotted on the abscissa. In the literature, this is often referred to as the *frequency* or *time domain*. The spectral density, which describes the amount of "power" in the spectrum plotted on the ordinate (y-axis). Note that the frequency is, at most, half the length of the number of observations. The spectral density plot (or periodogram) is examined for the frequencies or periods at which peaks occur. In general, time-series data with a linear trend will result in a spectral density plot with a linear trend (i.e., peaks at the ends), whereas random data will show no discernible peaks. Time-series data with a cyclical pattern, however, will show peaks at points related to their period. Thus, the spectral density plot can be viewed as a partition of variance of the original time series into the amount of variance that is accounted for by each periodic component. In some cases, peaks may be difficult to locate or multiple peaks may exist due to harmonic or overtone frequencies. In such cases one of several smoothing procedures may be implemented (Bloomfield, 1976); however, these issues are beyond the scope of this chapter.

For the data in Table 9.2 (Fig. 9.1A), the results of a spectral analysis from SAS PROC SPECTRA (SAS Institute, 1993a) are displayed in the form of a spectral density plot (Fig. 9.4) with period on the x-axis. As can be seen, a peak occurs between periods of five and six, which indicates a strong five/six-observation cycle in these data. This is to be expected, because treatment phases are changed approximately every four observations and/or the data were based on a sinusoidal wave with a period of 2π. As with the time-series analyses, some statistical software that perform spectral decompositions is available.

Statistical Analyses for Detecting Correlates of Cyclicity

Behavioral research is not always concerned with the description of independent response systems. Rather, the statistical demonstration of two systems that are temporally related and covary over time is of interest, especially if cyclical response patterns are likely. For the researcher, however, it may be difficult to determine the cause of cyclicity. Detecting

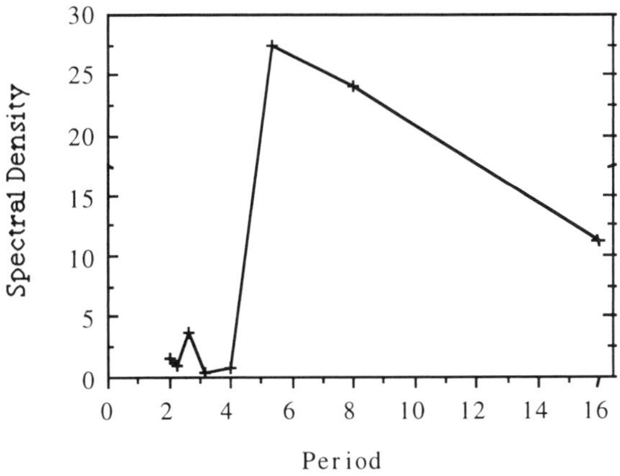

FIG. 9.4. Spectral density plot of time-series data in Fig. 9.1A.

correlates of the cyclical process, however, is important, because it may be incorporated into the analysis of data or used to qualify the interpretation of results. In the A-B-A-B design, one correlate of cyclical trends may be the application and removal of treatment. Yet, in some cases, the presence of another underlying process that influences the dependent variable is possible. In this section we present three methods for analyzing, statistically controlling, and detecting correlates of cyclicity. An overview is presented for each method and followed by a reanalysis a data set supplied by David Barlow.

Does Cyclicity Ever Go Undetected? Providing definite examples of research in which cyclicity has gone undetected and instead has "masqueraded" as treatment effects is not easy. If researchers present data in such a way that their cyclical nature is clear, then cyclicity is no longer undetected. Instead, we can only examine examples in which cyclicity may have gone undetected and possibly masqueraded as treatment effects.

Barlow, Leitenberg, and Agras (1969) provided an illustration of potential confounding by cyclicity in which a male pedophile was treated through covert sensitization. Two dependent variables were employed: frequency of sexual urges for young girls, and scores on a card-sort task measuring sexual arousal to vignettes involving young girls. The design was an A-B-A-B reversal design, and the results are reproduced in Fig. 9.5. The criterion for determining phase length was not specified.

The reader may note the striking similarity in the appearance of Fig. 9.5 compared with Fig. 9.1A. That is, Barlow et al.'s (1969) results are not

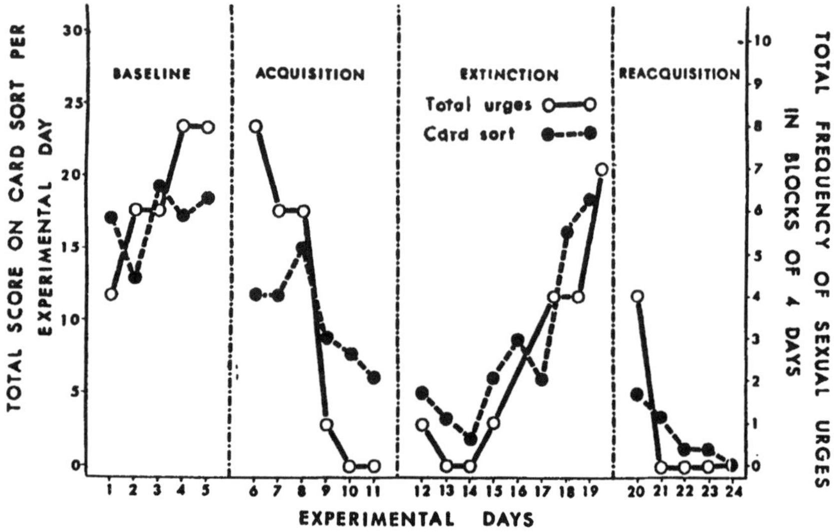

FIG. 9.5. Total score on card sort per experimental day and total frequency of pedophilic sexual urges in blocks of 4 days surrounding each experimental day (lower scores indicate less sexual arousal). From Barlow et al. (1969). Reprinted with permission.

unlike a sinusoidal wave with some random variability added. This potential confound of cyclicity becomes more plausible when we consider the nature of the dependent variables. Both dependent variables are measures of sexual arousal or desire, which are known to fluctuate with hormonal levels. Furthermore, both men and women exhibit cyclicity in hormonal levels and sexual interest (Kruse & Gottman, 1982). This being the case, we cannot be completely confident that the apparent results in Fig. 9.5 are a function of the treatment and not merely a function of hormonal cycles that are correlated with sexual urges, desire, and interest.

In deference to Barlow and his associates, however, three comments are in order. First, the aforementioned suggestion does not prove that the treatment was not effective, only that an alternative explanation has not been ruled out. Second, the conclusions about the effectiveness of covert sensitization were strengthened by a constructive replication with an ego-dystonic homosexual man in their study, as well as by conceptually similar but methodologically different research by other investigators (Earls & Castonguay, 1989). Finally, selection of this example is not meant to imply that the method was particularly poor. On the contrary, the study is methodologically sound overall. It was selected only because of the pattern of data obtained.

Most of the nonparametric tests discussed in the previous section indicated significant cyclical trends for both overall data patterns in Fig. 9.5. It should be noted that these tests were also performed for each phase separately and that the cyclical nature of the trends was substantiated. Thus, differencing (Equation 9.4) the within-phase data was performed to control cyclicity. Fig. 9.6 shows the Barlow et al. data after being differenced once. After differencing, treatment effects, especially for the card sort data, are difficult to infer. As stated earlier, however, if

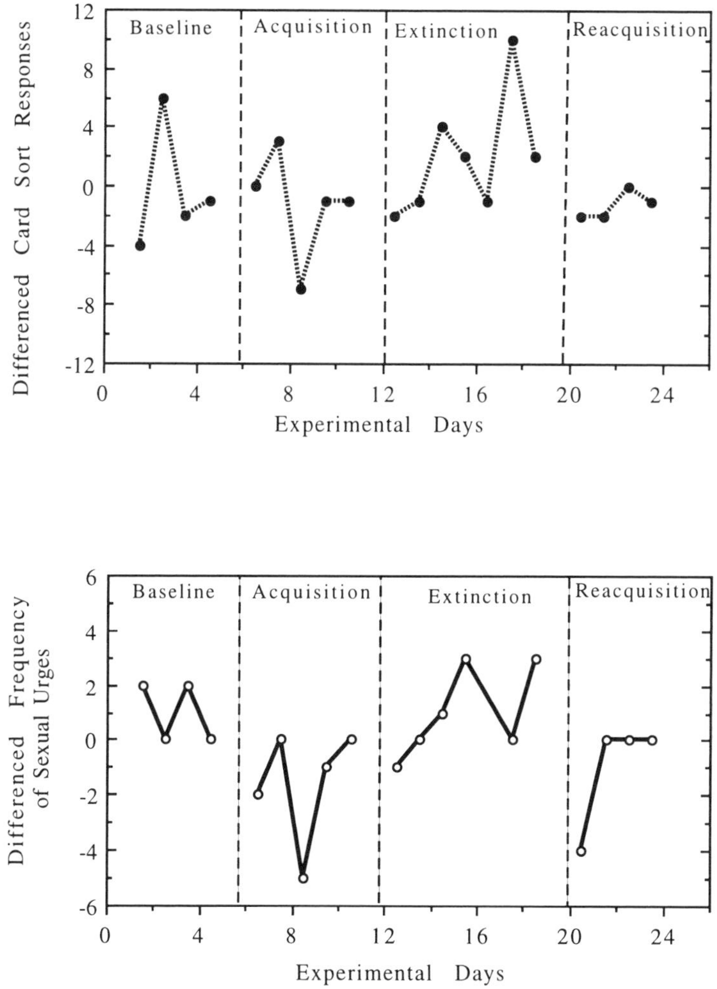

FIG. 9.6. Data from Barlow et al. (1969) after within-phase differencing.

covert sensitization, as a means of reducing pedophilic tendencies, has a gradual onset, the data will naturally exhibit some trend. Therefore, differencing may remove and thus obscure the treatment effect.

Cross-Correlation Functions. The cross-correlation function is an attempt to establish temporal precedence in time-series data when more than one variable is measured. The basic idea involves inspecting autocorrelation patterns for two variables, X and Y, over several lags. At a zero-lag, the correlation of X and Y is symmetric. At lag-one, however, the correlations between X_t and Y_{t+1} as opposed to the correlation between Y_t and X_{t+1} are not necessarily identical. The asymmetry between the cross-correlations of "X leading Y" and "Y leading X" indicates temporal precedence. That is, the variable that causes the other should have higher cross-correlations over several lags when it is the leading variable. As intuitively appealing as this sounds, it should be noted that strong autocorrelations within the time-series variables can obscure the underlying causal relationship to the point of suggesting the wrong direction of causality. In such cases, procedures typically called "prewhitening" should be performed. Basically, before computing the cross-correlation function, the methods suggested for identifying and detrending autocorrelative data (i.e., ARIMA modeling and differencing) should performed.

Figure 9.7A shows the SAS PROC ARIMA output for the cross-correlation function of the card sort and sexual urges data. Because there were strong autocorrelative trends in both data sets, the within-phase differenced scores shown in Fig. 9.6 were used. In Fig. 9.7A, negative lags indicate that the differenced sexual urges values were the leading variable. Likewise, positive lags indicate the differenced card sort scores as the leading variable. From these results, one might conclude that sexual urges have temporal precedence over the card sort scores, which seems reasonable given the nature of these variables. That is, it seems more likely for an appetitive behavior (i.e., sexual urges) to have temporal precedence over its manifestation in a psychological test that measures sexual preferences. Interestingly, the cross-correlation function of the undifferenced data indicated that the card sort scores had temporal precedence, which demonstrates how within-variable autocorrelation can affect the cross-correlation function (see Fig. 9.7B).

In single-case research, one may use a dummy-coded variable to represent the application of treatment which is the basis for interrupted time-series analysis (see Gorman & Allison, chap. 6, this volume). In using the dummy variable, the cross-correlation indicates the strength of the treatment across the range of k lags. Because the research question of interest involved both card sort scores and sexual urges as dependent

```
                    Correlation of DIFCSORT and DIFURGE
                    Variance of input = 3.609977
                    Number of observations =   24

                            Cross-correlations

Lag Covariance Correlation -1 9 8 7 6 5 4 3 2 1 0 1 2 3 4 5 6 7 8 9 1
 -6   -3.000907   -0.45011  |           *********|       .            |
 -5    1.957823    0.29366  |            .       |****** .            |
 -4   -0.612245   -0.09183  |            .     **|       .            |
 -3   -1.816780   -0.27250  |            .  *****|       .            |
 -2   -0.677296   -0.10159  |            .     **|       .            |
 -1    1.448579    0.21727  |            .       |****   .            |
  0    1.918367    0.28774  |            .       |****** .            |
  1    3.207683    0.48113  |            .       |**********          |
  2    1.200680    0.18009  |            .       |****   .            |
  3    0.091156    0.01367  |            .       |       .            |
  4    1.659864    0.24897  |            .       |*****  .            |
  5   -1.496145   -0.22441  |            .   ****|       .            |
  6   -1.515193   -0.22727  |            .  *****|       .            |
                            "." marks two standard errors
```

FIG. 9.7A. Cross-correlation function of card sort and sexual urges data after within phase first differencing.

```
                            ARIMA Procedure
                    Correlation of CSORT and URGE
                    Variance of input =  35.3184
                    Number of observations =  25

                          Cross-correlations

Lag Covariance Correlation -1 9 8 7 6 5 4 3 2 1 0 1 2 3 4 5 6 7 8 9 1
 -6   -3.724800   -0.20754  |            .   ****|       .            |
 -5   -0.972800   -0.05420  |            .      *|       .            |
 -4    2.539200    0.14148  |            .       |***    .            |
 -3    5.971200    0.33271  |            .       |*******.            |
 -2    8.966400    0.49960  |            .       |**********          |
 -1   13.921600    0.77570  |            .       |***************     |
  0   15.240000    0.84916  |            .       |****************    |
  1   11.795200    0.65721  |            .       |*************       |
  2    7.470400    0.41624  |            .       |********            |
  3    3.225600    0.17973  |            .       |****   .            |
  4    0.500800    0.02790  |            .       |*      .            |
  5   -2.097600   -0.11688  |            .     **|       .            |
  6   -2.611200   -0.14549  |            .    ***|       .            |

                                "." marks two standard errors
```

FIG. 9.7B. Cross-correlation function of card sort and sexual urges data from Barlow et al. (1969). Negative lag values indicate sexual urges as the leading variable.

variables, rather than one being a control variable, their cross-correlation function with a dummy-coded treatment variable may also be of interest. In the present example, a single dummy code variable representing the presence of treatment was created. Thus, for observations that occurred during baseline or extinction (see Fig. 9.5), the treatment variable was assigned a value $X = 0$. For observation within treatment phases, a value $X = 1$ was assigned. Figures 9.8A and 9.8B show the cross-correlation functions for the card sort scores and sexual urges with the treatment variable, X. Again, within-phase differenced scores were used because of the strong autocorrelation in both series. Also, because treatments within an experiment are considered the potential cause, they must also be considered a leading variable. Therefore, only lags with the "treatment leading" (positive lag values) are interpreted. The results indicate that treatment had significant impact on reducing inappropriate sexual urges and their manifestations in the card sort task. For sexual urges, the effect rapidly decayed at the second and fourth lags, indicating a more immediate but relatively temporary effect of treatment. For the card sort data, the effect of treatment was not initially as strong; however, the effect extended to the third lag, which indicates a moderate but relatively permanent treatment effect.

```
                        Correlation of DIFCSORT and X
                        Variance of input =    0.2464
                        Number of observations =  24

                                 Cross-correlations

Lag Covariance Correlation -1 9 8 7 6 5 4 3 2 1 0 1 2 3 4 5 6 7 8 9 1
 -6   0.750744     0.42939  |              .    |*********           |
 -5   0.538866     0.30821  |              .    |****** .            |
 -4   0.421218     0.24092  |              .    |*****  .            |
 -3   0.841270     0.48117  |              .    |**********          |
 -2   0.087719     0.05017  |              .    |*      .            |
 -1  -0.363393    -0.20784  |              . ****|      .            |
  0  -0.585034    -0.33461  |              .*******|    .            |
  1  -0.709226    -0.40565  |              ********|    .            |
  2  -0.597744    -0.34188  |              .*******|    .            |
  3  -0.844246    -0.48287  |            **********|    .            |
  4  -0.215336    -0.12316  |              .    **|     .            |
  5   0.087185     0.04987  |              .    |*      .            |
  6   0.026042     0.01489  |              .    |       .            |
                             "." marks two standard errors
```

FIG. 9.8A. Cross-correlation function of card sort data and treatment variable (X) after within-phase first differencing.

```
                    Correlation of DIFURGE and X
                    Variance of input =    0.2464
                    Number of observations =  24

                            Cross-correlations

Lag Covariance Correlation -1 9 8 7 6 5 4 3 2 1 0 1 2 3 4 5 6 7 8 9 1
 -6   0.538566    0.56889  |            .       |***********         |
 -5   0.541083    0.57155  |            .       |***********         |
 -4   0.482260    0.50942  |            .       |**********          |
 -3   0.166005    0.17535  |            .       |****   .            |
 -2  -0.266082   -0.28106  |            . ******|       .            |
 -1  -0.404960   -0.42776  |           *********|       .            |
  0  -0.530612   -0.56049  |         ***********|       .            |
  1  -0.509127   -0.53780  |         ***********|       .            |
  2  -0.275480   -0.29099  |            . ******|       .            |
  3  -0.242725   -0.25639  |            .  *****|       .            |
  4   0.092904    0.09814  |            .       |**     .            |
  5   0.087302    0.09222  |            .       |**     .            |
  6   0.100694    0.10636  |            .       |**     .            |
                           "." marks two standard errors
```

FIG. 9.8B. Cross-correlation function of sexual urges data and treatment variable (X) after within-phase first differencing.

Spectral Coherence. The assessment of covariation of response systems has been a paramount question in much of the behavioral sciences. However, the use of typical methodologies to detect cyclicity may obscure the relationship between rhythmic behaviors. If it is reasonable to describe the systems in terms of periodicities, then cross-spectral analysis may contribute a functional methodology to evaluate shared variance between two systems. For example, constructs such as arousal are dependent on a statistical assessment of the relationship among physiological response systems. However, analyzing these variables without considering the cyclical nature of each may bias the statistical estimates and thus threaten construct validity. Because many behavioral and physiological systems are manifested at more than one frequency, the calculation of a summary statistic describing the *coherence* between the two systems across frequencies is necessary.

Coherence is a frequency-dependent measure that quantifies the magnitude of shared power between two signals. Coherence values are normalized between 0 and 1. Thus, the square of this function most accurately describes the proportion of variance shared between the two processes when both have cyclical patterns. If they have little in common at a given frequency, the coherence magnitude is 0. That is, even if both time series look alike in time and/or frequency domain, the series may be independent. If two signals have exactly the same amount of a given frequency in their composition, the coherence at that frequency will be 1, which suggests that the two series may be two effects of the same cause. Thus, coherence analysis provides a methodology for developing constructs that depend on the relationship of more than one response system, even if these systems cycle at different frequencies.

When there is high coherence between two systems at a specific frequency, there is also a constant phase between their cyclicity. The phase provides information about the lead lag time between the two series. The measure of relative phase between two signals yields information about the synchrony of the signals at a specific frequency. The two signals may be in perfect synchrony (a relative phase of 0 degrees or 0 radians) or be exactly out of phase or perfect syncopation (180 degrees or π radians). This analysis provides a means of quantifying the relative degree of synchrony between any two signals at each of the frequencies of interest (Bohrer & Porges, 1982). A plot with the period or frequency on the x-axis and the cross spectral phase on the y-axis will typically show the points at which the two trends are most and least synchronous. Thus, as was the case with the cross-correlation function, it may be possible to generate causal hypotheses.

The cross-spectrum of the card sort and sexual urges data from Barlow et al. (1969) had an extremely high squared coherence value (0.9774), which suggests that the series are at least related to the same cause. In examining the cross-spectrum plot it can be seen that many values are near zero for larger periods indicating a great deal of synchrony, which further supports the results of the cross-correlation analysis. Also, there is synchrony at periods between 4 and 7, which is not surprising given that Barlow and his associates changed phases after four to six observations and the treatment seemed to affect both measured variables. There was also some syncopation at lower periods, indicating that the behaviors are not always synchronous at that one may lead or cause the other (see Fig. 9.9).

Similar to the use of dummy-coded variable to represent treatment condition in the cross-correlation function to perform interrupted time-series analysis, attempts to incorporate binary variable in coherence analysis have been proposed (Brillinger, 1975). It should be noted that if dummy-coded data are used in behavior change research, then the researcher should expect some syncopation in the cross-spectrum. That is, the dummy-coded values stay the same during the phase; however, the behavior is expected to increase or decrease. Thus, the synchrony of the cross-spectrum in behavioral change research is dependent on the length of each phase and whether the treatment has an immediate or gradual impact on behavior. In using the dummy-coded variable, X, to

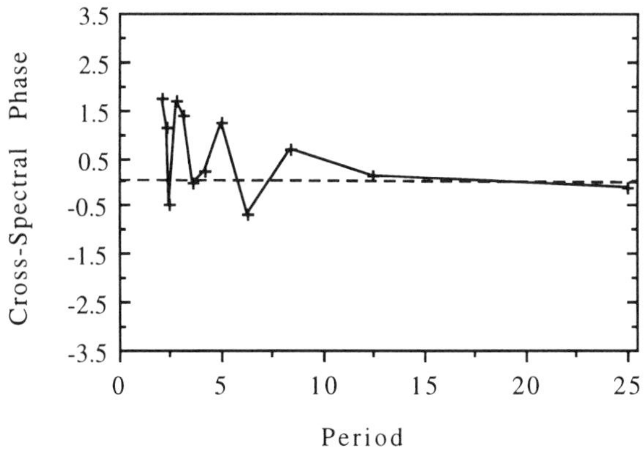

FIG. 9.9. Cross-spectral phase plot for card sort and sexual urges data.

represent treatment conditions (i.e., $X = 1$ for treatment, $X = 0$ for baseline), the squared coherence values for both the card sort (0.9880) and sexual urges (0.9619) data with a dummy-coded treatment variable were also high. In examining the cross-spectral functions, both show synchrony at the largest period, which indicates that the overall changes in behavior coincided with changes in treatment (i.e., the treatment changed the behavior). For the sexual urges data (see Fig. 9.10), syncopation is noted throughout the domain especially at frequencies of about 3 and 6. However, at a period of 5, there seems to be synchrony. Again, considering that phases were changed after four to six observations, a finding consistent with the cross-correlation analysis is indicated. That

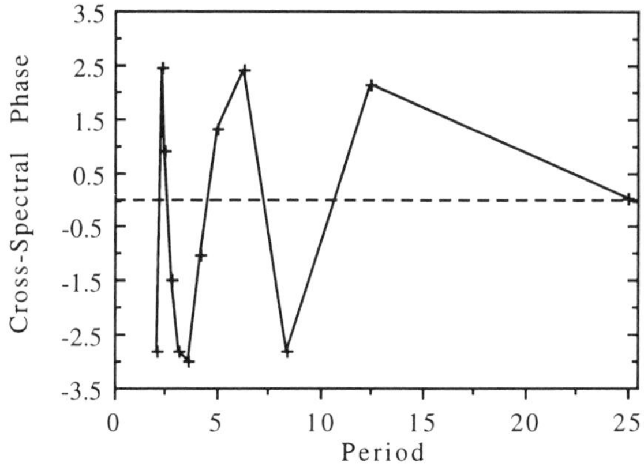

FIG. 9.10. Cross-spectral phase plot for card sort data with treatment variable (X).

is, the treatment had an immediate but rather temporary effect on inappropriate sexual urges. To explain, consider a behavior that changed immediately when phases were changed. In such a case, the trend in behavior would be synchronous with the frequency of phase change. If this effect were permanent, the synchrony would be evident throughout the domain. If this immediate effect were not permanent, then less synchrony would occur at larger period values. In contrast, a gradual effect would not show synchrony with phase changes but rather at periods removed from the phase change. This is can be seen in the card sort data in which synchrony is observable at the largest period, but syncopation is notable throughout the rest of the domain (see Fig. 9.11).

Another approach to this issue is to use the Fourier transformed variables from the periodogram as dependent variable in other statistical analyses, such as MANOVA or discriminant function analysis (e.g., Warner & Mooney, 1988). Although this methodology has intuitive appeal, its statistical properties have yet to be established. Thus, this topic remain outside the scope of this chapter.

It should be noted that the peaks occurring at periods of 6 and 12 in Fig. 9.10 suggest the existence of harmonic overtones, which may obscure the interpretation of treatment effects. Harmonic overtones are often corrected through a variety of smoothing procedures; however, these methods are beyond the scope of this chapter.

Trend Analysis. One cause of serial dependency or autocorrelation in single-case observations is the failure to specify elements in the model that represent all the influences at work. It may be that the dependent

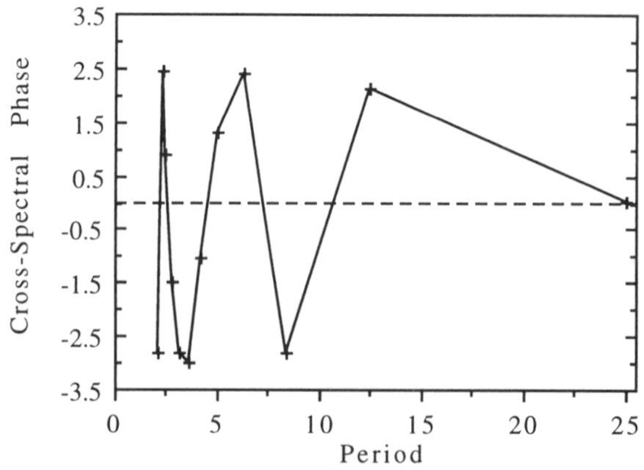

FIG. 9.11. Cross-spectral phase plot for sexual urges data with treatment variable (X).

variable is influenced not only by intervention but also by effects or cycles that vary systematically across time. If the statistical model is a regression analysis, the trends can be included as a covariate. Gorsuch (1983) suggested a linear regression model that takes overall slope into account:

$$Y_{it} = b_0 + b_1 X_i + b_2 t + e_{it} \tag{9.11}$$

where t is variable representing time (coded 1 to T for the T successive observations in the entire experiment), Xi is dummy variable (coded $Xi = 0$ for baseline and $Xi = 1$ for intervention), and e_{it} is the residual from the model. For this model, b_0 is a zero intercept, b_2 estimates the average slope, and b_1 estimates the average treatment effect. The effect of an intervention, however, may result in a change in slope as well as a change in level or in some cases just a change in slope (Kazdin, 1984; Parsonson & Baer, 1978). Again, the data in Fig. 9.1A, if considered to have a valid treatment effect, shows little change in average level across phases, but there are drastic changes in slope. Yet, no provisions are made for a change in slope in Equation 9.11.

Although not planned as an analytic model, but rather as an index of effect size, Center, Skiba, & Casey (1985–86) proposed a comprehensive approach that assesses shifts in level and slope. As compared to Equation 9.11, this approach adds an interaction term involving the multiplication of t and Xi which estimates the change in slope. However, t and Xi are necessarily correlated in the A-B design, which often makes the separation of baseline and posttreatment effects difficult. Therefore, the use of a piecewise regression, akin to regression discontinuity models (Trochim, 1984), has been recommended (Center et al., 1985–86; Green, 1978):

$$Y_{it} = b_0 + b_1 X_i + b_2 t + b_3 X_i(t - n_a) + e_{it} \tag{9.12}$$

where n_a represents the number of points in the baseline phase. In this model, b_1 estimates the change in level, whereas b_3 estimates the change in slope due to intervention. Although t and Xi are still correlated, their correlation with the interaction (change in slope term) is reduced. An alternative suggestion to this approach is to rescale t such that $t = 1$ at the start of each phase. However, this suggestion, although reducing the correlation of t and Xi, ensures that the interactive slope term is correlated to the time variable. Also, centering as a means of reducing multicollinearity and increasing the precision of parameter estimates has been suggested (Yi, 1989; Smith, & Sasaki, 1979). However, this method for standardizing main and interactive effects is typically used as a means to overcome the problem of artibrary scales. In the case of single-case data, however, centering the time variable, may obscure the metric.

That is, time as a variable may not be arbitrary, it may have definite meaning to the researcher. Therefore, inappropriate centering may obscure interpretation of the parameter estimates (Tate, 1984). For the purposes of this demonstration, the time value, t, will be rescaled within each phase for the multiplicative interaction term, whereas for the main effect of time t values will vary from 1 to T (Green, 1978).

Another approach to such statistical analyses is built on Center et al.'s approach (Allison & Gorman, 1993). In this two-stage approach, the baseline data are fitted separately using ordinary regression procedures. The resulting baseline equation is then projected into subsequent phases. Residuals between the baseline projections and the original time series data form a time series of residualized values on which regression models (i.e., Center et al., 1985–86) are performed. The rationale for this procedure is that if the baseline series were to continue indefinitely, then in the absence of treatment effects, postintervention observations should be predicted well by the baseline formula. However, with an effective treatment, the postintervention scores should deviate markedly in level and/or slope from the baseline projections.

Neter and Wasserman (1974) as well as Kelly, McNeil, and Newman (1973), showed that the analysis in Equation 12 can be extended to A-B-A-B designs. To estimate an averaged, overall effect, the consecutive A-B phases can be dummy coded and Equation 9.12 can be used. However, a researcher interested in more specific hypotheses may use some variant of the following model:

$$Y_{it} = b_0 + b_1X_{1i} + b_2X_{2i} + b_3X_{3i} + b_4t + b_5X_{1i}\,(t - n_{a1}) + b_6X_{2i}\,(t - n_{b1}) + b_7X_{3i}\,(t - n_{a2}) + e_{it} \tag{9.13}$$

where X_{1i}, X_{2i}, and X_{3i} are dummy codes for each phase following the initial baseline and n_{a1}, n_{b1}, and n_{a2} are the number of data points up to the treatment change for the first three respective phases. To elaborate, observations in the first treatment (B) phase are assigned an X_1 value of 1, all other observations are given zeros. Observations in the second baseline (A) phase and final B phase are assigned values of 1 for X_2 and X_3, respectively, otherwise zeros are given. Therefore, the initial baseline level of behavior is estimated by b_0. Also, in this model b_1, b_2, and b_3 estimate the respective changes in level and b_5, b_6, and b_7 estimate changes in slope. For those more familiar with other types of analyses, it is noted that Equation 9.13 gives parameter estimates equivalent to an ANCOVA with time (t) as a covariate. However, it should be noted that in ANCOVA models, a significant time by phase interaction indicates that slopes change (are not parallel) across treatment. This is analogous to a significant heterogeneity of regression effect that may obscure the interpretation of phase main. This has particular bearing on the statistical analysis of single-subject data. That is, the interpretation of main effects (i.e., changes in level across phases) must be qualified in the presence of significant interactions (i.e., changes in slope across phases).

In ANCOVA models, when a significant interaction of the independent variable and the covariate is present, the use of some follow-up analysis such as the Johnson–Neyman (1936) technique or Rogosa's (1980) pick-a-point method is suggested. The basic idea for either of these procedures is to determine regions of the covariate where the groups differ. In single-case research this means that one searches for observation points within a phase where the values of the dependent variable are significantly changed, while statistically controlling the effects of the covariate (time). Rogosa (1980) argued that one should pick points of theoretical interest. In single-case research, an experimenter may wish to test all observation points in the phase for significance. However, this requires many statistical tests. Thus, for any of these analyses, it is suggested that if multiple tests using Equations 9.12 or 9.13 are performed, some form of Type-I error rate correction (i.e., Bonferroni adjustment) should be used. Jennings (1988) provided a very usable guide to ANCOVA follow-up procedures. Examples of Equation 9.13 and follow-up analyses are provided in the next section.

It should also be noted that if nonlinear processes are suspected with phases they can also be modeled statistically (i.e., Kelly, McNeil, & Newman, 1973; Neter & Wasserman, 1974; Trochim, 1984). In the presence of cyclicity, as with other analytic models, it would be important to obtain a sufficient number of baseline observations so that the cycle could be modeled. In situations where the baseline series were not of adequate length, one might consider using these models on differenced data in which case the change in slope parameter may not be necessary and nonparametric tests of single-case intervention effects may be employed (e.g., Edgington, 1980, 1982; Levin et al., 1978). Detailed discussions of these issues are beyond the scope of this chapter. The interested reader is referred to Gorman and Allison (chap. 6, this volume), Green (1978), and Center et al. (1985–86).

To control and assess cyclicity in the Barlow et al. (1969) data, a statistical trend models such as Equation 9.13 was employed. In this case, dummy coding was used so that all parameter estimates were compared to the first baseline phase and an α level of .05 was used for significance testing. For the card sort data this yielded the following solution:

$$Y_{it} = 15.000 - 2.800X_{1i} - 21.498X_{2i} - 20.700X_{3i} + 0.600t - 2.086X_{1i}(t - n_{a1}) + 0.961X_{2i}(t - n_{b1}) - 1.700X_{3i}(t - n_{a2}) \quad (9.14)$$

Descriptively, one might choose to plot each phase separately. Because in the dummy coding process baseline measures were given a value of zero across X_1, X_2, and X_3, their respective regression coefficients are not weighted. Thus, for the baseline data:

$$Y_{tA1} = 15.000 + 0.600t$$

For the data in the first acquisition phase, only X_1 was assigned values of 1, X_2 and X_3 were assigned zeros; thus, the regression equation for the acquisition phase is:

$$Y_{tB1} = 15.000 - 02.800 + 0.600t - 2.086(t - n_{a1})$$

$$Y_{tB1} = 12.200 + 0.600t - 2.086t + 2.086n_{a1}$$

Because $n_{a1} = 5$, then:

$$Y_{tB1} = 22.263 - 1.486t$$

To determine the within-phase regression, consider that when the acquisition phase begins $t = (n_{a1} + 1) = 6$; thus, the *zero* intercept for the acquisition phase is when $t = n_{a1} = 5$. Thus, the intercept for the acquisition phase is:

$$12.200 + 0.600t - 2.086(t - n_{a1})$$

$$12.200 + (0.600 \times 5) - 2.086\ (5 - 5) = 15.200$$

Therefore, the within-phase regression solution is:

$Y\ t^*_{B1} = 15.200 - 1.486t^*$, where t^* is the within-phase time.

Using this same process the regression solutions for the extinction phase are:

$$Y_{tA2} = -17.074 + 1.561t;$$

$$Y\ t^*_{A2} = 0.102 + 1.561t^*;$$

and for the reacquisition phase:

$$Y_{Bb2} = 24.900 - 1.100t;$$

$$Y\ t^*_{B2} = 5.700 - 1.100t^*;$$

Table 9.3 (Panel A) shows test statistics indicating that the total score on the card sort task was significantly reduced by the time of the extinction (X_2), but not in the initial acquisition (X_1) or reacquisition (X_3) phases. However, in the presence of significant interactions (i.e., changes in slope), one should be cautious in the interpretation of these main effects. The rate of reduction was only significantly greater during the acquisition phases, $X_{1i}(t - n_{a1})$, which indicates an immediate effect of covert

TABLE 9.3
Statistical Analysis of the Barlow et al. (1969) Card Sort Data.

Panel A: Model 9.13 Analysis

Variable	*DF*	*Parameter Estimate*	*Standard Error*	*T for H_0: Parameter = 0*	*Prob > |T|*
INTERCEPT	1	15.000	2.488	6.029	0.0001
X1	1	−2.800	2.872	−0.975	0.3452
X2	1	−21.498	6.380	−3.369	0.0042
X3	1	−20.700	12.303	−1.683	0.1131
T	1	0.600	0.750	0.800	0.4363
X1*(T-NA1)	1	−2.086	0.940	−2.218	0.0424
X2*(T-NB1)	1	0.961	0.851	1.130	0.2763
X3*(T-NA2)	1	−1.700	1.061	−1.603	0.1299

Panel B: Analysis of Card Sort Time-Series Using Rogosa's (1980) Method

Test	*Numerator*	*df*	*F-value*	*p-value*
Acquistion				
Observation 1	14.7001	1	2.6127	0.1268
Observation 2	23.1958	1	4.1226	0.0604
Observation 3	28.4739	1	5.0607	0.0399
Observation 4	31.1893	1	5.5433	0.0326
Observation 5	32.4351	1	5.7647	0.0298
Observation 6	32.9216	1	5.8512	0.0287
Extinction				
Observation 1	48.3290	1	8.5896	0.0103
Observation 2	36.5804	1	6.5015	0.0222
Observation 3	27.7595	1	4.9338	0.0422
Observation 4	21.1335	1	3.7561	0.0717
Observation 5	16.1355	1	2.8678	0.1110
Observation 6	12.3438	1	2.1939	0.1593
Observation 7	9.4497	1	1.6795	0.2146
Observation 8	7.2279	1	1.2846	0.2748
Observation 9	5.5139	1	0.9800	0.3379
Reacquisition				
Observation 1	16.8943	1	3.0026	0.1036
Observation 2	17.6538	1	3.1376	0.0968
Observation 3	18.2367	1	3.2412	0.0919
Observation 4	18.6728	1	3.3188	0.0885
Observation 5	18.9898	1	3.3751	0.0861
Error		15	5.6265	

sensitization on reducing the rate of sexual arousal to "pedophilic vignettes."

Furthermore, because the rate reduction was significantly different across phases, Rogosa's (1980) pick-a-point method was used to investigate the time during the phase that pedophilic sexual arousal significantly changed. These results indicate that significant reductions in sexual arousal did not occur until the third observation in the acquisition phase. These significantly lower levels remained until the fourth observation of the extinction phase. Statistically significant reduction in sexual arousal to pedophilic vignettes did not occur through the rest of the time series including the five reacquisition observations (Table 9.3, Panel B).

For the frequency of sexual urges, the following equation was solved:

$$\hat{Y}_{it} = 3.400 + 1.400X_{1i} - 15.237X_{2i} - 19.200X_{3i} + 1.000t - 2.800X_{1i}(t - n_{a1}) - 0.399X_{2i}(t - n_{b1}) - 1.800X_{3i}(t - n_{a2}) \quad (9.15)$$

For the full model and within-phase baseline, acquisition, extinction, and reacquisition phases, the regression solutions are respectively as follows:

Full Model	*Within-Phase*
$Y_{tA1} = 3.400 + 1.000t$	$Y_{tA1} = 3.400 + 1.000t^*$
$Y_{tB1} = 18.800 - 1.800t$	$Y_{tB1} = 9.800 - 1.800t^*$
$Y_{tA2} = -7.448 + 0.601t$	$Y_{tA2} = -0.837 - 0.601t^*$
$Y_{tB2} = 16.600 - 0.800t$	$Y_{tB2} = 3.200 - 0.800t^*$

Table 9.4 (Panel A) shows significant changes in frequency of sexual urges from baseline to extinction (X_2) and from baseline to reacquisition (X_3), but not from baseline to acquisition (X_1). Significant changes in the reduction rate of pedophilic urges was detected between the baseline and acquisition, $X_{1i}(t - n_{a1})$, and between baseline and reacquisition, $X_{3i}(t - n_{a2})$, but no slope differences were found between baseline and extinction, $X_{2i}(t - n_{b1})$. These results suggest a gradual impact of covert sensitization on the frequency of pedophilic urges and that treatment significant reversed the rate of sexual urges.

As with the card-sort data, the rate of reduction was significantly different across phases and the pick-a-point method was used to investigate at what time during the phase did pedophilic sexual urges significantly change. These results indicated that pedophilic urges were significantly reduced by the second observation of the acquisition phase and remained at a significantly lower level through the rest of the experiment (Table 9.4, Panel B). Thus, the statistical analyses of both the card

TABLE 9.4
Statistical Analysis of the Barlow et al. (1969) Sexual Urges Data.

Panel A: Model 9.13 Analysis

Variable	*DF*	*Parameter Estimate*	*Standard Error*	*T for H_0: Parameter = 0*	*Prob > |T|*
INTERCEPT	1	3.400	1.180	2.882	0.0121
X1	1	1.400	1.362	1.028	0.3215
X2	1	−15.237	3.021	−5.043	0.0002
X3	1	−19.200	5.834	−3.291	0.0054
T	1	1.000	0.356	2.811	0.0139
X1*(T-NA1)	1	−2.800	0.446	−6.279	0.0001
X2*(T-NB1)	1	−0.399	0.399	−1.001	0.3340
X3*(T-NA2)	1	−1.800	0.503	−3.578	0.0030

Panel B: Analysis of Sexual Urges Time-Series Using Rogosa's (1980) Method

Test	*Numerator*	*df*	*F-value*	*p-value*
Acquistion				
Observation 1	1.2070	1	0.9540	0.3453
Observation 2	8.4191	1	6.6542	0.0218
Observation 3	17.0083	1	13.4428	0.0025
Observation 4	24.1249	1	19.0675	0.0006
Observation 5	29.4259	1	23.2573	0.0003
Observation 6	33.2912	1	26.3122	0.0002
Extinction				
Observation 1	28.0217	1	22.1474	0.0003
Observation 2	24.5174	1	19.3777	0.0006
Observation 3	21.6040	1	17.0751	0.0010
Observation 4	19.1886	1	15.1661	0.0016
Observation 5	16.1355	1	13.5792	0.0024
Observation 6	15.5027	1	12.2528	0.0035
Observation 7	14.0904	1	11.1366	0.0049
Observation 8	12.8930	1	10.1902	0.0065
Observation 9	11.8701	1	9.3817	0.0084
Reacquisition				
Observation 1	14.8485	1	11.7357	0.0041
Observation 2	15.8006	1	12.4883	0.0033
Observation 3	16.5797	1	13.1041	0.0028
Observation 4	17.2089	1	13.6013	0.0024
Observation 5	17.7114	1	13.9985	0.0022
Error		14	1.2652	

sort and pedophilic urges data support the findings and interpretations reported by Barlow and his associates.

The appendix to this chapter shows the data set from Barlow et al. (1969) along with SAS (SAS Institute, 1993b) commands for the analyses completed. Having considered some the circumstances under which cyclicity may occur, we now turn to criteria of phase change and other methods to control for and assess cyclicity. Also, the extent to which each method protects against or is vulnerable to the threats to internal validity posed by cyclicity is discussed.

PROPOSED CRITERIA FOR CHANGING PHASES AND CONTROLLING CYCLICITY

According to Kazdin (1982), "Currently, no agreed-upon objective decision rules exist for altering phases in single-case experimental designs" (p. 272). A survey of the literature on experimental designs, single-case designs, and program evaluation, however, suggests four heuristics that may address cyclicity.

The Predetermined System

The first and simplest strategy might be called the *predetermined system*. In this system, one decides a priori how long some or all of the phases should be and the order in which they will occur. Although this strategy is rarely advocated explicitly, it is often advocated implicitly. For example, Barlow and Hersen (1973, 1984) stressed the advantages of having all phases of equivalent or nearly equivalent length. This implies that the length of at least all but the first phase must be predetermined to some extent.

The extent to which predetermining phase length increases or decreases the threat of cyclicity's confounding effects depends on exactly how phase lengths are "predetermined." One strategy is to ensure that every phase is as long as or longer than several full cycles. If each phase contains several full cycles, then phases cannot systematically sample different portions of one cycle, and, therefore, will not be confounded by cyclicity (Johnston & Pennypacker, 1980). Of course, if the cyclical nature of processes that confound the dependent variable are unknown, then the length of a cycle is unknown and determining the length of an experimental phase remains problematic. A related alternative strategy is to conduct a standard A-B-A-B design where the final B phase is extended for a period of time that is equal to or exceeds the period of the suspected cycle. If behavior is consistently maintained throughout the final B phase, then the threat of cyclicity is rendered less tenable.

As previously mentioned, the difficulty with these strategies is that they necessitate that one know in advance the approximate period of the cycle and/or one has the time available to run phases of such length. These conditions are sometimes met in basic laboratory research. For example, the length of the estrous cycle in most female rodents is known, and experiments can generally be conducted that far exceed this length. In contrast, these conditions are rarely met in applied and clinical research. Not only is it often unknown whether cyclicity exist in data a priori, but if periodicity is strongly suspected, the exact period of the cycle is often unknown. In addition, it may be ethically or practically unappealing to extend phases for several weeks, months, or years to rule out cyclicity. Months would be necessary if one needed to rule out seasonal cycles that are common (Aschoff, 1984). Years would be necessary only in the rare event that one suspected a cycle of greater duration, as Shirom and Mazeh (1988) found.

The second strategy is to predetermine relative phase lengths so as to minimize the threat of confounding. There seems to be some disagreement about how to do this. For example, Kazdin (1982) and Barlow and Hersen (1973) asserted that phases should be of equivalent lengths. Kazdin (1982) stated:

> The recommendation is based on the view that in a given period of time (e.g., a week or month), maturational or cyclical influences may lead to a certain pattern of performance that is mistaken for intervention effects. If phases are equal in duration, the effects of extraneous events maybe roughly constant or equal in each phase and will not be confused with intervention effects. (p. 271)

However, Edgington (1984) and Barrios and Hartmann (1988) contended just the opposite. Consider Barrios and Hartmann's (1988) statement:

> In order for the treatment to be the more credible of the two explanations [compared with cyclicity], the explanation of a recurrent, concomitant force must be rendered less plausible. This may be accomplished by varying the length of the treatment and nontreatment phases . . . as the length of phases becomes less systematic, a cyclic determinant that occurs independently of treatment becomes less likely. (p. 21)

It seems that the two strategies, equal versus unequal phase length, actually protect against two different confounding effects. When phase lengths are kept constant, one appears to be adhering to Barlow and Hersen's (1984) "one variable at a time" rule. That is, by not allowing phase length to vary systematically with experimental condition, the experiment cannot be confounded by any effects of phase length *qua* phase length. Although this strategy will control for the confounding effects of phase length, it is not clear how it will control for the confounding effects of sampling different portions of a cycle during different phases. With equal phase lengths, the estimation of this confound with equal phase lengths may occur only if cycle length is much different from phase length so that overlap will occur. Still, the interpretations of results would likely be confusing. Thus, although the experimenter does not induce another factor (i.e., phase length) to vary systematically with condition, another factor (i.e., position in the cycle) is allowed to vary with condition, and the potentially confounding effects of cyclicity remain.

In contrast, the different phase length strategy of Barrios and Hartmann (1988) seems to protect against the worst possibility that phase changes will occur regularly at the crests and troughs of cycles. However, it does not preclude the possibility of different phases sampling different portions of a cycle, and some potential for confounding remains.

Response-Guided Experimentation

The second strategy for deciding when to change phases has been called "response-guided experimentation because the experimental conditions are adjusted on the basis of responses the subject makes during the experiment" (Edgington, 1984, p. 88). In this system, very much in the tradition of Skinner (1966) and Sidman (1960), phases are changed when the experimenter has demonstrated behavioral stability. Stability has generally been taken to imply two things: minimal variability below some specified criterion, and no trend in the data (Johnston & Pennypacker, 1980; Sidman, 1960).

No universal criteria exist to determine when stability has occurred. Sidman (1960) stated that the specific criteria employed must depend on the phenomenon under study. He argued that "by following behavior over an extended period of time, with no change in experimental conditions, it is possible to make an estimate of the degree of stability that can eventually be maintained" (p. 258). This estimate allows the researcher to assume unit homogeneity and institute a scientific solution (i.e., Rubin, 1974), which can be used to guide the selection of a stability/phase change criterion. This strategy worked well for Snyder (1987) in treating the diabetic adolescent described earlier. Unfortunately, this approach may not be practical for many clinical or applied researchers who are often faced with solving pressing problems in a limited amount of time. Moreover, there is no objective means for determining what constitutes an "extended period of time."

An alternative approach is to define some statistical or visual criteria for judging stability so that the experimenter will recognize it when it occurs. Kelly, McNeil, and Newman (1973) indicated that stability in baseline behavior can be operationally defined as a within-baseline slope that does not significantly differ from zero. This can be tested statistically as long as nonlinear processes are not at work. Sidman (1960) offered two other examples of such criteria. In essence, each mathematically defines a minimum variance criterion. When variance is at or below the specified level for a predetermined number of data points, stability is said to have been reached and a phase change is implemented. Killeen (1978) provided a sophisticated treatment of the stability issue and evaluated various criteria, all of which have in common the search for the point at which the response rate approximates an asymptote. Graphically, trended range lines are useful in detecting the minimization of variance associated with behavioral stability.

Unfortunately, cyclical patterns make these approaches difficult to utilize. Furthermore, when cyclicity is present in the data but unknown to the experimenter, response-guided experimentation may maximize the possibility that the worst case scenario will occur, in that phase changes are more likely to coincide with crests and troughs of a cyclical pattern (Edgington, 1984). For example, Allison (1992) demonstrated that an experimenter searching for asymptotes as a sign to change phases could likely be "fooled" by the leveling off that occurs at the crest and troughs of sinusoidal and other cyclical patterns.

Randomization

Randomization is a common strategy in research with between-subject factors, and is often considered the *sine qua non* of the true experiment (Edgington, 1980). Although it is not commonly discussed, randomization has analogous applications in single-case designs. With between-group experiments, subjects are randomly assigned to conditions. Randomization guarantees that subjects in both experimental and control conditions can be expected to be equivalent on all relevant variables before the implementation of treatment. This is critical for the statistical solution to the Fundamental Problem of Causality (Holland, 1986). In many single-case or time-series designs, points in time can be randomly assigned to conditions (Edgington, 1980, 1987; Levin et al., 1978; Wampold & Worsham, 1986) that, under assumptions of behavioral stability and unit homogeneity, allow for the scientific approach to causal inference (Holland, 1986).

Randomization achieves its popularity because, in the long run, it controls for the potentially confounding effects of *both known and un-*

known variables (Edgington, 1984). Just as random assignment of subjects to treatments in a group design controls for the potentially confounding effects of subject characteristics, random assignment of times to treatment controls for the potentially confounding effects of time (including cyclicity) in single-case designs.

The general method of randomization is to divide the total time of the experiment into discrete units (e.g., days) and then randomly assign units or blocks of units to treatments. For example, if an experiment were to be conducted over the course of 100 days and a data point was to be collected every day, then there would be 100 days or time units. These days might be grouped into two blocks of 50 each and then one block randomly assigned to be a baseline (A) phase and the other a treatment (B) phase.

With only one A and one B phase, even with randomization, one cannot separate treatment for time effects, just as one could not separate treatment from subject effects with only two subjects in a between-groups design (Levin et al., 1978). The power of randomization to rule out cyclicity as a competing hypothesis for observed changes is directly related to the number of units or blocks of units that can be randomly assigned. Thus, a design in which two or more A phases and two or more B phases are randomly assigned to blocks of time is a true experiment. Analogous with the error term in a between-subjects design, time is the *random effect* in the single-case design. Thus, the more times that are randomly alternated, the less plausible cyclicity becomes as a confounding variable. With enough randomized pairings, timing effects will eventually cancel each other out (Levin et al., 1978).

However, it seems pertinent to discuss the practical nature of this phase-change criterion. First, it should be noted that randomization precludes the possibility of always having designs proceed in standard order. For example, A-B-A-B designs might sometimes turn out to be B-A-B-A designs. In clinical research, this would often be considered unacceptable for two reasons: it is unusual to begin a treatment without first collecting baseline data, and researchers wish to leave the intervention in place (assuming it is shown to be effective). Regarding the first concern, a researcher might collect a set of "natural observations" from a leading A phase that may be excluded from the analysis. Regarding the latter concern, the simple solution would be to end B-A-B-A designs with a final B phase, which would be considered "follow up" and not be used as a major piece of the experimental-interference process.

Second, phase changes might sometimes occur at inopportune times. For instance, in an experiment designed to reduce some response, a change from baseline to treatment might occur when data were already trending downward. Intervening when data are already trending in the desired direction is traditionally taboo, because it makes the interpretation of experimental effects ambiguous (Barlow & Hersen, 1984). However, Kazdin (1982) offered several means of handling this situation when one needs to intervene during a trend. These methods can be viewed as two categories: replication and statistical control. Replication consists of conducting more A-B (or B-A) pairings either across time (e.g., A-B-B-A-A-B-B-A-B-A) or across subjects, settings, or responses (i.e., multiple baselines). As stated previously, the power of randomization to rule out time factors (including trends, cyclicity, and history) as competing hypotheses is directly related to the number of blocks of units that can be randomly assigned. Alternatively, one can statistically control for the trend by partialing it out through regression-based methods (e.g., Allison & Gorman, 1993; Gorsuch, 1983; Green, 1978).

Finally, researchers employing group designs have traditionally controlled for unknown influences on dependent variables by ensuring that influences are uncorrelated with independent variables and then statistically treating the induced variability as random. Thus, there is the possibility of statistically partialing out cyclicity if an appropriate covariate (or control construct) is available with the *control construct design* to be discussed later. However, this goes against a strong tradition in single-case behavioral research. Sidman (1960) stated that variability in data is "a manifestation of an orderly process, we must not only identify the source of the variability but also control it" (p. 143). In Sidman's paradigm, cycles in data would be handled by identifying and controlling the cause(s) of the cyclicity before changing phases. The problem with this is that such identification and control are not always possible, particularly in applied settings. Human knowledge is limited, and human subjects cannot always wait for experimenters to identify all causes of all variation in their behavior. Moreover, even if all the causes of variability were known and could theoretically be controlled, it would often be impossible to actually control them for practical or ethical reasons.

Control Construct Designs

Because of the inference and logistic problems that between-group designs often present in applied research, the control construct design has been proposed in the area of program evaluation (McKillip, 1992; McKillip & Baldwin, 1990). This design combines characteristics of "interrupted time-series with non-equivalent dependent variables design" (Cook & Campbell, 1979) with those of single subjects designs (i.e., concurrent multiple baselines across behaviors). In the field of program evaluation, the rationale is that rather than estimating no-treatment baselines from subjects not exposed to an intervention, the control construct design uses measures of each experimental subject that are not necessarily the focus of the intervention. Thus, the design uses control constructs (measures) rather than control groups to estimate impact in a factorial ANOVA layout.

In the control construct design, measures of control constructs serve the same function as control groups in traditional between-group designs. Changes in levels of the control construct estimate the changes that would have occurred in the experimental construct without an intervention. Thus, in single-case designs where an intervention follows baseline observations, trends in the control construct estimate the changes that would have occurred in the target behavior without treatment (McKillip & Baldwin, 1990). To this extent, the control construct design can be used to estimate and control statistically the possibility of cyclicity. The important consideration when selecting control constructs is to choose issues/measures that could change as a result of an intervention similar to the one under investigation, but not as a result of the experimental programming. Such occurrences could be due to the constructs sharing measurement bias or because they are a function of the same underlying cyclical process. In either case, an experimental effect is most obviously indicated if the level of the experimental construct varies with the intervention program (e.g., A-B-A-B) while the levels of the control construct remain stable.

According to McKillip (1992), a good control construct is similar to the experimental construct in terms of historical interest, social desirability, and measurement reliability, but measures a different "true score." Error components that systematically bias experimental–control group comparisons, such as history, maturation, or testing, are controlled to the extent that they affect both experimental and control constructs equally. The inflation of error terms due to individual differences are controlled by the within-subject nature (i.e., multiple observations) of the control construct design. Thus, to the extent that experimental and control constructs are correlated at the level of the individual, the design has increased power from its ability to control for subject or response heterogeneity (Lipsey, 1990; McKillip & Baldwin, 1990). Therefore, the control construct is a covariate that is related to the experimental construct but is not affected by the intervention. McKillip's contention that experimental and control constructs should only share error variance may have been too constricting in single-subject experiments; however, the control construct design may provide a useful way to control cyclicity.

To employ a factorial ANOVA layout, a control construct design for a single-subject experiment includes two within subject factors: time of observation and constructs. The constructs factor has $(K - 1)$ *dfs*, where K is the number of measured constructs. Time of observation has $(T - 1)$

dfs, where T equals the total number of observed data points. The hypothesized effect of an intervention (i.e., changes in the experimental construct due to phase changes while the control construct remain stable) is revealed as part of an interaction between the time of observation and construct factors. Unfortunately, to assess this interaction there must be more than one observation per cell, which is impossible when applying the doubly repeated control construct design to a single-case experiment. Therefore, when using control construct designs for single-subject experiments three approaches are suggested.

First, the main effects and interaction may be based on constructs and *phase change* as factors; however, this is only appropriate when cyclicity is not suspected. That is, if observations are collapsed into treatment phases, the confounding effects of cyclicity could not be assessed. Thus, such an approach is relegated to assessing overall trends in treatment phase in the absence of cyclicity (preferably after cyclicity has been examined).

As a second alternative, within-phase observations may be grouped so that individual observation on each measured construct are nested within larger *observation blocks*. These blocks would be nested within treatment phases and crossed with constructs. Thus, a split-plot ANOVA could be performed. Constructs would still have $(K - 1)$ *dfs*. Phases would have *dfs* equal to the number of phases minus one $(J - 1)$. Observation blocks would have $(B - J)$ *dfs*, where B is the number of observation blocks. The interaction of constructs and observation blocks would estimate the differential trend in construct measures across the observations. Thus, the impact of the treatment while controlling the potential for cyclicity would be assessed. However, because it is necessary to collapse observations into blocks, this approach involves a considerable loss of precision and power.

A third alternative employs the previously elaborated regression-based methods of statistically controlling trends in data in order to assess treatment impact. These models (i.e., Equations 9.12 and 9.13) used time as a covariate; however, the control construct design allows the use of a covariate that is potentially more strongly correlated with the experimental dependent variable than is the time of observation. Thus, an ANCOVA approach with control constructs as covariates seems most appropriate because it allows for more flexible comparisons of experimental and control construct, whereas phase change hypotheses can still be modeled using standard ANOVA groupings, contrasts, or regression effect vectors. To elaborate, using the ANOVA solution assumes that the experimental and control constructs are measured on the same scale or are standardized, and because the main effect of constructs are not usually of interest this design is allowable. However, because AN-

COVA usually has more power, it may be preferred to ANOVA in the control construct design. It also seems appropriate because the control construct may provide a more useful covariate than time of observation as in Equations 9.12 and 9.13. For example, in the Barlow et al. experiment, if testosterone levels were available at each observation point, this measure is more likely to model the cyclical nature of sexual arousal and urges than time at which the data were gathered; however, the experimental interventions are not likely to affect hormonal levels. Thus, an ANCOVA type analysis (e.g., Equation 9.13) with testosterone levels as a covariate instead of time of observation would allow the researchers to estimate the impact of covert sensitization over and above the changes in hormonal levels.

CONCLUSIONS AND RECOMMENDATIONS

Based on the considerations presented, the following recommendations are made. First, before the start of the experiment researchers should determine if cyclicity is a reasonable possibility. As Hunter and Schmidt (1990) vigorously argued, the seminal list of threats to internal validity (Campbell & Stanley, 1966; Cook & Campbell, 1979) is a list of *potential* threats. Each researcher must decide if a particular potential threat is actually a plausible one. Of course, this decision is not easy. Seemingly cyclical patterns are ubiquitous in the behavior of organisms (Aschoff, 1984), which suggests that the threat of cyclicity is almost always plausible. Alternatively, one can clearly see gradations in the extent to which cyclicity is plausible. Cyclicity in the reading ability of third-grade children over the course of one month seems relatively less probable than cyclicity in the feeding, sleeping, and sexual behavior of bears across the seasons.

Ideally, practical considerations notwithstanding, one would like all experiments to employ the maximum protection against cyclicity. But practical considerations do stand. The welfare of subjects and limitations of time and other resources must be taken into consideration. Thus, as with many other issues of experimental control, prospective researchers must weigh the risks of threatening validity against the cost of controlling such risks.

In situations where the risk of cyclicity is high, preferable alternative strategies do exist. First, phases may be alternated randomly with as many alterations as possible. Carried to the extreme, this would turn A-B-A-B designs into alternating-treatments designs, where the order of treatments is determined randomly. If this is not feasible, an alternative is to ensure that all phases are at least as long as several full cycles. As was stated earlier, however, this requires that one know in advance the approximate period of the cycle. Predetermining phase lengths to have different durations provides only minimal protection against cyclicity, whereas predetermining phase lengths to be equal provides none. Last, when cyclicity is believed to be a plausible threat, response-guided treatment is not recommended because it maximizes the likelihood of confounding experimental effects. As Edgington eloquently stated:

> The very responses that guide the treatment manipulation may signal a change that would occur even without treatment manipulation; consequently, changes in behavior following treatment manipulation cannot justifiably be attributed to that manipulation. Prediction is not control, and response-guided experimentation allows the two to be confounded. (1984, p. 89)

An additional class of possibilities might also be considered. Researchers attempting to study the effects of treatment on behavior might select designs that are less susceptible to the effects of cyclicity. These include simultaneous treatment designs, changing criterion designs, and multiple baseline designs. In the event that the research question can be adequately addressed in the context of a between-groups design, the researcher may wish to consider this alternative as well.

Finally, statistical assessment and control of cyclicity may be an option. Interrupted time-series analysis may be used; however, without a comparison group or measure of trend, the effects of cyclicity may still be confounded with the onset of intervention. The control-construct design addresses this issue by combining facets of various research strategies. If the source of the cyclical pattern (or some valid correlate of it) can be measured, the researcher may logically compare the two patterns or statistically partial out the cyclical trend from the treatment effect without employing a comparison group. The adjusted scores across treatment phases would then model the effectiveness of the intervention.

In conclusion, it is suggested that researchers employing single-case designs should explicate the plausibility of cyclicity as threat to internal validity. As a rough guide for such a logical analysis, one should consider the previously elaborated categories related to cyclicity: biological rhythms, cyclically chained responses, and institutional schedules and/or schedules of reinforcement. If cyclicity is a strong possibility, then a researcher should specify the criteria used to determine phase changes and the rationale for their use. As an adjunct and a possible alternative to elaborate phase-change criteria, a researcher may consider statistical analyses. In this approach, control constructs and measures to be used as covariates to statistically partial out the effects of cyclicity should be obtained. If such control measures are not available, time of observation can be used as a covariate with one of various regression-based trend analysis approaches. It should be noted that cyclical processes may not have a linear function and, therefore, models should be based on a nonlinear analyses (i.e., curvilinear regression, differencing). From these considerations, it is believed that researchers and consumers alike can judge for themselves the plausibility of threat posed by cyclicity.

REFERENCES

Akyurek, A. (1985). Periodicity as a principle of organization in behavior. *Psychological Reports, 57,* 491–506.

Alarcon, R. D. (1985). Rapid cycling affective disorders: A clinical review. *Comprehensive Psychiatry, 26,* 522–540.

Allison, D. B. (1992). When cyclicity is a concern: A caveat regarding phase change criteria in single case designs. *Comprehensive Mental Health Care, 2*(2), 131–149.

Allison, D. B., & Gorman, B. S. (1993). Calculating an estimate of effect size for meta-analysis: The case of the single case. *Behavior Research and Therapy, 31,* 621–631.

Allison, D. B., Silverstein, J. M., & Galante, V. (1992). Relative effectiveness and cost-effectiveness of cooperative, competitive, and independent monetary incentive systems. *Journal of Organizational Behavioral Management, 13,* 85–112.

Almagor, M., & Ehrlich, S. (1990). Pesonality correlates and cyclicity in positive and negative affect. *Psychological Reports, 66,* 1159–1169.

Aschoff, J. (1984). A survey of biological rhythms. In J. Aschoff (Ed.), *Handbook of behavioral neurobiology, vol. 4, biological rhythms* (pp. 3–10). New York: Plenum.

Baer, D. (1977). "Perhaps it would be better not to know everything." *Journal of Applied Behavior Analysis, 10,* 167–172.

Barlow, D. H., & Hersen, M. (1973). Single-case experimental designs. *Archives of General Psychiatry, 26,* 522–540.

Barlow, D. H., & Hersen, M. (1984). *Single-case experimental designs: Strategies for studying behavior change.* New York: Pergamon.

Barlow, D. H., Leitenberg, H., & Agras, W. S. (1969). Experimental control of sexual deviation through manipulation of the noxious scene on covert sensitization. *Journal of Abnormal Psychology, 74,* 596–601.

Barrios, B. A., & Hartmann, D. P. (1988). Recent developments in single subject methodology: Methods for analyzing generalization, maintenance, and multicomponent treatments. *Progress in Behavior Modification, 22,* 11–47.

Biggers, J. (1980). Body rhythms, the school day, and academic achievement. *Journal of Experimental Education, 49,* 45–47.

Bloomfield, P. (1976). *Fourier analysis of time series: An introduction.* New York: Wiley.

Bohrer, R. E., & Porges, S. W. (1982). The application of time-series statistics to psychological research: An introduction. In G. Keren (Ed.), *Statistical and methodological issues in psychology and social science research* (pp. 309–345). Hillsdale, NJ: Lawrence Erlbaum Associates.

Box, G. E. P., & Jenkins, G. M. (1976). *Time series analysis: Forecasting and control.* San Francisco: Holden-Day.

Brillinger, D. R. (1975). *Time series data analysis and theory.* Chicago: Holt, Rinehart, & Winston.

Calpin, J. P., Edelstein, B., & Redmon, W. K. (1988). Performance feedback and goal setting to improve mental health center staff productivity. *Journal of Organizational Behavior Management, 9,* 35–58.

Campbell, D. T., & Stanley, J. C. (1966). *Experimental and quasi-experimental designs for research.* Chicago: Rand McNally.

Cataldo, M. F., & Fisher, W. W. (1991, April). *Limitations and extensions of current behavior analytic methods.* Paper presented at Destructive Behavior in Developmental Disabilities: A Conference of Destructive Behavior, Minneapolis, MN.

Center, B. A., Skiba, R. J., & Casey, A. (1985–1986). A methodology for the quantitative synthesis of intra-subject design research. *Journal of Special Education, 19,* 387–400.

Chapple, E. D. (1970). *Culture and biological man: Explorations in behavioral anthropology.* New York: Holt, Rinehart, & Winston.

Colquhoun, W. P. (1971). Circadian variations in mental efficiency. In W. P. Colquhoun (Ed.), *Biological rhytms and human preference.* London: Academic Press.

Cook, T. D., & Campbell, D. T. (1979). *Quasi-experimentation: Design and analysis issues for field settings.* Chicago: Rand McNally.

Crosbie, J. (1989). The inappropriateness of the C statistic for assessing stability or treatment effects with single-subject data. *Behavioral Assessment, 11,* 315–325.

DeProspero, A., & Cohen, S. (1979). Inconsistent visual analysis of intrasubject data. *Journal of Applied Behavior Analysis, 12,* 513–519.

Earls, C. M., & Castonguay, L. G. (1989). The evaluation of olfactory aversion for a bisexual pedophile with a single case multiple baseline design. *Behavior Therapy, 20,* 137–146.

Edgington, E. S. (1980). Random assignment and statistical tests for one-subject experiments. *Behavioral Assessment, 2,* 19–28.

Edgington, E. S. (1982). Nonparametric tests for single-subject multiple schedule experiments. *Behavioral Assessment, 4,* 83–91.

Edgington, E. S. (1984). Statistics and single case analysis. In M. Hersen, R. M. Eisler, & P. M. Miller (Eds.), *Progress in behavior modification* (Vol. 16, pp. 83–119). New York: Academic Press.

Edgington, E. S. (1987). Randomizing single subject experiments and statistical tests. *Journal of Counseling Psychology, 34,* 437–442.

Edgington, E. S. (1992). Nonparametric tests for single-case experiments. In T. R. Kratochwill & J. R. Levin (Eds.), *Single case research design and analysis: New Directions for psychology and education* (pp. 133–158). New York: Academic Press.

Ezekiel, M., & Fox, K. A. (1959). *Methods of correlation and regression analysis: Linear and curvilinear.* New York: Wiley.

Ferster, C. B., & Skinner, B. F. (1957). *Schedules of reinforcement.* New York: Appleton-Century-Crofts.

Fisher, W. W., Piazza, C. C., Harrell, R., & Chinn, S. (1990, May). *Applied behavior analysis for clients with dual diagnoses: Cyclical disorders in nonverbal, retarded adolescents.* Paper presented at the annual convention of the Association for Behavior Analysis, Nashville, TN.

Freeman, G., & Hovland, C. (1934). Diurnal variations in performance and related physiological processes. *Psychological Bulletin, 31,* 777–799.

Furlong, M. J., & Wampold, B. E. (1982). Intervention effects and relative variation as dimensions in experts' use of visual inference. *Journal of Applied Sciences, 15,* 415–421.

Gentile, J. R., Roden, A. H., & Klein, R. D. (1972). An analysis-of-variance model for the intrasubject replication design. *Journal of Applied Behavior Analysis, 5,* 193–198.

Gerada, C., & Reveley, A. (1988). Schizophreniform psychosis associated with the menstrual cycle. *British Journal of Psychiatry, 152,* 703–704.

Glass, G. V., Wilson, V. L., & Gottman, J. M. (1975). *Design and analysis of time series experiments*. Boulder: University of Colorado Press.

Glue, P. (1989). Rapid cycling affective disorders in the mentally retarded. *Biological Psychiatry, 26*, 250–256.

Gorsuch, R. L. (1983). Three methods for analyzing limited time-series ($N = 1$) data. *Behavioral Assessment, 5*, 141–154.

Gottman, J. M., & Glass, G. V. (1978). Analysis of interrupted time-series experiments. In T. R. Kratochwill (Ed.), *Single subject research: Strategies for evaluating change* (pp. 287–312). New York: Academic Press.

Gouse, A. S. (1984). The effects of organizational stress on inpatient psychiatric medication patterns. *American Journal of Psychiatry, 141*, 878–881.

Green, P. E. (1978). *Analyzing multivariate data*. Hinsdale, IL: Dryden.

Hall, R. V., & Fox, R. G. (1977). Changing-criterion designs: An alternate applied behavior analysis procedure. In B. C. Etzel, J. M. Le Blanc, & D. M. Baer (Eds.), *New developments in behavioral research: Theory, method and application: In honor of Sidney W. Bijon*. (pp. 151–161). Hillside, NJ: Lawrence Erlbaum Associates.

Hardin, T. A., Wehr, T. A., Brewerton, T., Kasper, S., Berrettini, W., Rabkin, J., & Rosenthal, N. E. (1991). Evaluation of seasonality in six clinical populations and two normal populations. *Journal of Psychiatric Research, 25*(3), 75–87.

Harrop, J. W., & Velicer, W. F. (1990). Computer programs for interrupted time series analysis: II. A quantitative evaluation. *Multivariate Behavioral Research, 25*, 233–249.

Hartmann, D. P. (1974). Forcing square pegs into round holes: Some comments on "An analysis-of-variance model for the intrasubject replication design." *Journal of Applied Behavior Analysis, 10*, 113–116.

Hartmann, D. P., & Hall, R. V. (1976). The changing criterion design. *Journal of Applied Behavior Analysis, 9*, 527–532.

Hoagland, H. (1933). The physiological control of judgments of duration: Evidence for a chemical clock. *Journal of General Psychology, 9*, 267–287.

Holland, P. W. (1986). Statistics and causal inference. *Journal of the American Statistical Association, 81*, 945–960.

Horn, W. F., & Heerboth, J. (1982). Single case experimental designs and program evaluation. *Evaluation Review, 6*, 403–424

Horne, G. P., Yang, M. C. K., & Ware, W. B. (1982). Time series analysis for single-subject designs. *Psychological Bulletin, 91*, 178–189.

Huitema, B. E. (1985). Autocorrelation in applied behavior analysis: A myth. *Behavioral Assessment, 7*, 107–118.

Huitema, B. E. (1986). Autocorrelation in behavior modification data: Wherefore art thou? In A. Poling, R. W. Fuqua, & R. Ulrich (Eds.), *Research methodology in applied behavior analysis: Issues and advances* (pp. 187–208). New York: Plenum.

Huitema, B. E., & McKean, J. W. (1991). Autocorrelation estimation and inference with small samples. *Psychological Bulletin, 110*, 291–304.

Hunter, J. E., & Schmidt, F. L. (1990). *Methods for meta-analysis*. Newbury Park, CA: Sage.

Iwata, B. A., Dorsey, M. F., Slifer, K. J., Bauman, K. E., & Richman, G. S. (1982). Toward a functional analysis of self-injury. *Analysis and Intervention in Developmental Disabilities, 2*, 3–21.

Jennings, E. (1988). Analysis of covariance with nonparallel regression lines. *Journal of Experimental Education, 56*, 129–134.

Johnson, P. O., & Neyman, J. (1936). Tests of certain linear hypotheses and their application to some educational problems. *Statistical Research Memoirs, 1*, 57–93.

Johnston, J. M., & Pennypacker, H. S. (1980). *Strategies and tactics of human behavioral research*. Hillsdale, NJ: Lawrence Erlbaum Associates.

Jones, R. R., Vaught, R. S., & Weinrott, M. (1977). Time-series analysis in operant research. *Journal of Applied Behavior Analysis, 10,* 151–166.

Kanji, G. K. (1993). *100 statistical tests.* Thousand Oaks, CA: Sage.

Kazdin, A. E. (1982). *Single-case research designs: Methods for clinical and applied settings.* New York: Oxford University Press.

Kazdin, A. E. (1984). *Single-case research designs: Methods for clinical and applied settings* (2nd ed.). New York: Oxford University Press.

Kelly, F. J., McNeil, K., & Newman, I. (1973). Suggested inferential statistical models for research in behavior modification. *Journal of Experimental Education, 41*(4), 54–63.

Killeen, P. R. (1978). Stability criteria. *Journal of the Experimental Analysis of Behavior, 29,* 17–25.

Kleitman, N. (1982). Basic rest-activity cycle—22 years later. *Sleep, 5,* 311–317.

Kleitman, N., Titelbaum, S., & Feiveson, P. (1938). The effect of body temperature on reaction time. *American Journal of Physiology, 121,* 495–501.

Kruse, J. A., & Gottman, J. M. (1982). Time series methodology in the study of sexual hormonal and behavioral cycles. *Archives of Sexual Behavior, 11,* 405–415.

Lavender, A. (1981). A behavioral approach to the treatment of epilepsy. *Behavioral Psychotherapy, 9,* 231–243.

Leaventhal, H., & Cleary, P. D. (1980). The smoking problem: A review of the research and theory in behavioral risk modification. *Psychological Bulletin, 88,* 370–405.

Levin, J. R., Marascuilo, L. A., & Hubert, L. J. (1978). *N* = nonparametric randomization tests. In T. R. Kratochwill (Ed.), *Single subject research: Strategies for evaluating change* (pp. 167–197). New York: Academic Press.

Lipsey, M. (1990). *Design sensitivity: Statistical power for experimental research.* Newbury Park, CA: Sage.

Ljung, G. M., & Box, G. E. P. (1978). On a measure of lack of fit in time series models. *Biometrika, 65,* 297–303.

McDowall, D., McCleary, R., Meidinger, E. E., & Hay, Jr., R. A. (1980). *Interrupted time series analysis.* Newbury Park, CA: Sage.

McKillip, J. (1992). Research without control groups: A control construct design. In F. B. Bryant et al. (Eds.), *Methodological issues in applied social psychology* (pp. 159–175). New York: SPSSI/Plenum.

McKillip, J., & Baldwin, K. (1990). Evaluation of an STD education media campaign: A control construct design. *Evaluation Review, 14,* 331–346.

Meier-Koll, A., Fels, T., Kofler, B., Schulz-Weber, U., & Thiesses, M. (1977). Basic rest activity cycle and stereotyped behavior of a mentally defective child. *Neuropaediatrica, 8,* 172–180.

Morley, S., & Adams, M. (1991). Graphical analysis of single case time series data. *British Journal of Clinical Psychology, 30,* 97–115.

Neter, J., & Wasserman, W. (1974). *Applied linear statistical models.* Homewood, IL: Irwin.

Onghena, P. (1992). Randomization tests for extensions and variations of ABAB single-case experimental designs: A rejoinder. *Behavioral Assessment, 14,* 153–171.

Park, H. S., Marascuilo, L. A., & Gaylord-Ross, R. (1990). Visual inspection and statistical analysis in single case designs. *Journal of Experimental Education, 58,* 311–320.

Parsonson, B. S., & Baer, D. M. (1978). The analysis and presentation of graphic data. In T. R. Kratochwill (Ed.), *Single subject research: Strategies for evaluating change* (pp. 101–167). New York: Academic Press.

Rico, H., Revilla, M., Cardenas, J. L., Villa, L. F., Fraile, E., Martin, F. J., & Arribas, I. (1994). Influence of weight and seasonal changes on radiogrammetry and bone densitometry. *Calcified Tissue International, 54,* 385–388.

Roberts, D. C. S., Bennett, S. A. L., & Vickers, G. J. (1989). The estrous cycle affects cocaine self-administration on a progressive ratio schedule in rats. *Psychopharmacology, 98*, 408–411.

Rogosa, D. (1980). Comparing nonparallel regression lines. *Psychological Bulletin, 88*, 307–321.

Rubin, D. B. (1974). Estimating causal effects of treatments in randomized and nonrandomized studies. *Journal of Educational Psychology, 66*, 688–701.

SAS Institute Inc. (1993a). *SAS/ETS (Version 7): Users' guide.* Cary, NC: Author.

SAS Institute Inc. (1993b). *SAS/STAT (Version 7): Users' guide.* Cary, NC: Author.

Shine, L. C., & Bower, S. M. (1971). A one-way analysis of variance for single- subject designs. *Educational and Psychological Measurement, 31*, 105–113.

Shirom, A., & Mazeh, T. (1988). Periodicity in seniority–job satisfaction relationship. *Journal of Vocational Rehabilitation, 33*, 38–49.

Sidman, M. (1960). *Tactics of scientific research: Evaluation of experimental data in psychology.* New York: Basic Books.

Siegel, S., & Castellan, N. J., Jr. (1988). *Nonparametric statistics for the behavioral sciences* (2nd ed.). New York: McGraw-Hill.

Skinner, B. F. (1953). *Science and human behavior.* New York: The Free Press.

Skinner, B. F. (1963). Operant behavior. *American Psychologist, 18*, 503–515.

Skinner, B. F. (1966). Operant behavior. In W. K. Honig (Ed.), *Operant behavior: Areas of research and applications* (pp. 12–32). New York: Appleton-Century-Crofts.

Smith, K. W., & Sasaki, M. S. (1979). Decreasing multicollinearity: A method for models with multiplicative functions. *Sociological Methods & Research, 8*, 35–56.

Snyder, J. (1987). Behavioral analysis and treatment of poor diabetic self-care and antisocial behavior: A single subject experimental study. *Behavior Therapy, 18*, 251–263.

Solomon, R. L., & Corbit, J. D. (1973). An opponent-process theory of motivation: II. Cigarette addiction. *Journal of Abnormal Psychology, 81*, 158–171.

Sorosky, A., Ornitz, E., Brown, R., & Ritvo, T. (1968). Systematic observations of autistic behavior. *Archives of General Psychiatry, 18*, 439–449.

Suen, H. K., & Ary, D. (1989). *Analyzing quantitative behavioral observation data.* Hillsdale, NJ: Lawrence Erlbaum Associates.

Tate, R. L. (1984). Limitations of centering for interactive models. *Sociological Methods & Research, 13*, 251–271.

Taylor, C. B., & Stunkard, A. J. (1993). Public health approaches to weight control. In A. J. Stunkard & T. A. Wadden (Eds.), *Obesity: Theory and therapy* (2nd ed., pp. 335–353). New York: Raven.

Trochim, W. M. K. (1984). *Research design for program evaluation: The regression discontinuity approach.* Newbury Park, CA: Sage.

Tryon, W. W. (1982). A simplified time-series analysis for evaluating treatment interventions. *Journal of Applied Behavior Analysis, 15*, 423–429.

vonNeumann, J. (1941). Distribution of the ratio of the mean square successive difference to the variance. *Annals of Mathematical Statistics, 12*, 367–395.

vonNeumann, J., Kent, R. H., Bellinson, H. R., & Hart, B. I. (1941). The mean successive difference. *Annals of Mathematical Statistics, 12*, 153–162.

Wacker, D. P., Steege, M., & Berg, W. K. (1988). Use of single-case designs to evaluate manipulable influences on school performance. *School Psychology Review, 17*, 651–657.

Wampold, B. E., & Furlong, M. J. (1981). The heuristics of visual inference. *Behavioral Assessment, 3*, 79–92.

Wampold, B. E., & Worsham, N. L. (1986). Randomization tests for multiple-baseline designs. *Behavioral Assessment, 8*, 135–143.

Warner, R. M. (1979). Periodic rhythms in converational speech. *Language and Speech, 22*, 381–396.

Warner, R. M., Malloy, D., Schneinder, K., Knoth, R., & Wilder, B. (1987). Rhythmic organization of social interaction and observaer ratings of positive affect and involvement. *Journal of Nonverbal Behavior, 11,* 57–74.

Warner, R. M., & Mooney, K. (1988). Individual differences in vocal activity rhythm: Fourier analysis of cyclicity in amount of talk. *Journal of Psycholinguistic Research, 17,* 99–111.

Watson, P. J., & Workman, E. A. (1981). The non-concurrent multiple baseline across-individuals design: An extension of the traditional multiple baseline design. *Journal of Behavior Therapy and Experimental Psychiatry, 12,* 257–259.

Weidlich, W. (1988). Stability and cyclicity in social systems. *Behavioral Science, 33,* 241–256.

Yi, Y. (1989). On the evaluation of main effects in multplicative regression models. *Journal of the Market Research Society, 31,* 133–138.

APPENDIX

SAS commands for Model 9.13 Rogosa (1980) analyses of the Barlow et al. (1969) data

```
data barlow;
input time csort urge x1 x2 x3 phase;
na1 = 5; nb1 = 11; na2 = 18;
if phase = 1 then tt = time - na1;
if phase = 2 then tt = time - nb1;
if phase = 3 then tt = time - na2;
xlm=x1*tt; x2m=x2*tt; x3m=x3*tt;
cards;
 1   17   4   0   0   0   1
 2   13   6   0   0   0   1
 3   19   6   0   0   0   1
 4   17   8   0   0   0   1
 5   18   8   0   0   0   1
 6   12   8   1   0   0   2
 7   12   6   1   0   0   2
 8   15   6   1   0   0   2
 9    8   1   1   0   0   2
10    7   0   1   0   0   2
11    6   0   1   0   0   2
12    5   1   0   1   0   3
13    3   0   0   1   0   3
14    2   0   0   1   0   3
15    6   1   0   1   0   3
16    8   .   0   1   0   3
17    6   .   0   1   0   3
18    .   4   0   1   0   3
19   16   4   0   1   0   3
20   18   7   0   1   0   3
21    5   4   0   0   1   4
22    3   0   0   0   1   4
23    2   0   0   0   1   4
24    2   0   0   0   1   4
25    0   0   0   0   1   4
proc reg;model csort=x1 x2 x3 tt x1m x2m x3m;
    test x1 + 1*x1m = 0; test x1 + 2*x1m = 0; test x1 + 3*x1m = 0; test x1 + 4*xlm = 0;
        test x1 + 5*x1m = 0; test x1 + 6*x1m = 0;
    test x2 + 1*x2m = 0; test x2 + 2*x2m = 0; test x2 + 3*x2m = 0; test x2 + 4*x2m = 0;
        test x2 + 5*x2m = 0; test x2 + 6*x2m = 0; test x2 + 7*x2m = 0;
        test x2 + 8*x2m = 0; test x2 + 9*x2m = 0;
test x3 + 1*x3m = 0; test x3 + 2*x3m = 0; test x3 + 3*x3m = 0; test x3 + 4*x3m = 0;
        test x3 + 5*x3m = 0;
model urge = x1 x2 x3 tt x1m x2m x3m;
test x1 + 1*x1m = 0; test x1 + 2*x1m = 0; test x1 + 3*x1m = 0; test x1 + 4*x1m = 0;
        test x1 + 5*x1m = 0; test x1 + 6*x1m = 0;
    test x2 + 1*x2m = 0; test x2 + 2*x2m = 0; test x2 + 3*x2m = 0; test x2 + 4*x2m = 0;
        test x2 + 5*x2m = 0; test 2 + 6*x2m = 0; test x2 + 7*x2m = 0;
        test x2 + 8*x2m = 0; test x2 + 9*x2m = 0;
test x3 + 1*x3m = 0; test x3 + 2*x3m = 0; test x3 + 3*x3m = 0; test x3 + 4*x3m = 0;
        test x3 + 5*x3m = 0;
```

10

Power, Sample Size Estimation, and Early Stopping Rules

David B. Allison
Obesity Research Center
St. Luke's/Roosevelt Hospital Center
Columbia University College of Physicians and Surgeons

Jay M. Silverstein
Milestone School For Child Development
Crossroads School For Child Development

Bernard S. Gorman
Hofstra University

INTRODUCTION

In 1962, Cohen published a seminal article pointing out that the majority of psychological studies were conducted with inadequate power. Subsequently, several other surveys of research literature in both psychology (Rossi, 1990; Sedlmeir & Girgenzer, 1989) and related fields (Daniel, 1993; Kawano, 1993; Kosciulek & Szymanski, 1993) reaffirmed the existence of this problem. Consequently, there is now increasing recognition of the need to design studies with adequate power. One indicator of this is the requirement of power analyses in any application for federal research support, and a second indicator is the steady increase in the practice of reporting measures of effect in psychological research (Dar, Serlin, & Omer, 1994). It is ironic that during this time of increased (and appropriate) emphasis on statistical power, researchers, clinicians, social service agencies, and funding agencies are simultaneously under ever-tightening budgetary constraints. This means that it is essential to design studies with maximal efficiency; that is, studies that are both powerful and minimize the consumption of resources (Allison, Allison,

Faith, Paultre, & Pi-Sunyer, submitted). In this chapter we consider power in the context of single-subject research design. To our knowledge, only one other discussion of power in single-case research has appeared in the literature (Johannessen & Fosstvedt, 1991).

Our discussion contains four sections. First, we introduce the basic statistical terms and concepts surrounding power analysis and sample size estimation. Second, we discuss computational strategies for conducting power analysis emphasizing practical issues, including the use of tables and software and the estimation of effect sizes. Third, we discuss some "advanced" topics in estimating effect sizes and methods for including cost considerations into study designs. Fourth, we offer a brief introduction to early stopping rules and their potential uses in single-case research.

Before proceeding further, two terminological points warrant discussion. We have chosen to present our discussion of power analysis and study design within the framework of treatment-based research. However, the mathematical and statistical issues are the same for both treatment- and nontreatment-based research. That is, all of the tables, software, and formulae we present are applicable to both treatment and nontreatment studies. Moreover, when we describe the magnitude of the association between the independent and dependent variable(s), we have chosen to utilize the term *effect size* because we have chosen to present single-case research with designed experiments (i.e., those studies in which the investigator manipulates levels of the independent variable). However, we recognize that some investigators may conduct single-case research using observational data. In this instance one should read "association" or "relationship" where we write "effect size."

Additionally, it is important to clarify an aspect of our statistical approach. It is our belief that in conducting power analyses one makes many guesses about the population from which the data will be sampled. Because these guesses are just that, guesses, power analyses are best considered methods to provide ballpark estimates of necessary sample sizes. Given this background, we suggest three things. First, good approximations for power that are computationally tractable are often preferable to exact but computationally unwieldy formulae. As a corollary to this, we present power for parametric statistics even though single-case researchers often use nonparametric statistical tests such as randomization tests (see Gorman & Allison, chap. 6, this volume, for details). This is because randomization tests have generally been shown to be as powerful as their parametric counterparts (Donegani, 1991; White & Still, 1987). Finally, because our estimates of power (if not all estimates of power) are only approximations, we recommend that researchers be liberal in planning designs; that is, that they err on the side of collecting a few more observations than necessary rather than the converse.

A PRIMER OF BASIC TERMS AND CONCEPTS

Before proceeding further, we define the basic terms and concepts involved in power analysis and sample size estimation. The philosopher of science Karl Popper (1959) theorized that we can never "prove" anything, but rather our strongest support for an idea comes from our repeated unsuccessful attempts to disprove that idea. Popper's thinking establishes the cognitive set that is the foundation of power analysis. Traditionally, hypothesis testing begins with the specification of a "null hypothesis."

The Null Hypothesis

The null hypothesis (H_o) typically states that no relationship exists between the independent variable and the dependent variable. For example, in a study comparing a treatment condition to a no-treatment control condition, the null hypothesis is that the treatment has no effect. An operational definition of H_o using statistical modeling might say that the population mean under treatment conditions is equal to the population mean under no treatment conditions.

Type-I Error

Two possibilities exist with respect to the null hypothesis: It is either true or it is not true. Similarly, in analyzing experimental evidence, two conclusions are possible: We can conclude that the null hypothesis is true, or we can conclude that the null hypothesis is not true. Many scientists prefer the phrases "fail to reject the null hypothesis" and "reject the null hypothesis," respectively. These two possibilities in nature and two possible conclusions yield the two-by-two table in Fig. 10.1. When researchers reject the null hypothesis when the null hypothesis is, in fact, true, they commit a Type-I error. The probability of making a Type-I error is usually fixed in advance by the experimenter (typically as .01 or .05 by convention). This probability is generally denoted α. In other words, if one conducted a particular experiment an infinite number of times, the null hypothesis would be rejected $\alpha(100)\%$ of the time, if, in fact, the null hypothesis were true. One minus α is conceptually akin to

		Reality	
		Null is True	Null is False
	Null True	Correct Decision Specificity 1-α	Type II error β
Conclusion			
	Null False	α Type I error	Correct Decision 1- β Power Sensitivity

FIG. 10.1. Graphical presentation of the inferential process.

the definition of specificity in diagnostic testing (see Primavera, Allison, & Alfonso, chap. 3, this volume). In diagnostic testing, specificity is the probability that an individual who does *not* have the disease in question will test negative for the disease (i.e., the probability of true negative).

Type-II Error

A Type-II error is defined as a failure to reject the null hypothesis when the null hypothesis is, in fact, false. The probability of making a Type-II error is typically denoted β [note that on the other side of the Atlantic the probability of making a Type-II error is typically denoted $(1 - \beta)$]. Whereas α can be fixed in advance by the experimenter under the assumption of the null hypothesis, β can only be fixed in advance given the assumption of a specific alternative hypothesis. Traditionally, many psychologists have ignored β, but there is now increased recognition of the importance of minimizing β.

Power

Power is the probability of finding an effect when an effect actually exists. Power is one minus β. When we say that investigators are increasingly concerned with minimizing β, this is equivalent to saying that they are increasingly concerned with maximizing power. Although there is no fixed level of power that is universally considered "acceptable and desirable," consensus is beginning to coalesce. Many investigators consider .80 an "acceptable" level of power and .90 a "desirable" level, as suggested by Cohen (1988, 1992b). In other words, we're allowing ourselves an 80% to 90% chance of finding an effect. Our preference for Type-II errors over Type-I errors is not completely arbitrary. It reflects the consideration of many investigators that the alternative of erroneously hailing an ineffective treatment is far more problematic than failing to detect an effective treatment.

When determining acceptable levels of α and β, each individual researcher, based on his or her values and the nature of the phenomenon being investigated, may place α and β at different levels. The following factors will inevitably be considered in any such determination: financial burden associated with treatment, availability of alternative treatments, seriousness of disorder, and side effects of potential treatment. Two examples provide perspective on this discussion. A researcher looking at a potential cure for the AIDS virus might consider the four variables previously mentioned. Given the lack of effective treatment alternatives currently existing for AIDS, and the rates of fatality associated with the disorder, the researcher might risk an erroneous claim of treatment efficacy as a small price to pay for increasing the possibility of detecting an effect. Hence, the researcher might set power at a higher level, accepting the increased risk of a Type-I error.

In a second example, a researcher is asked to assess the efficacy of a new pharmacological treatment for hyperactivity in children. The researcher considers that there are other available treatments, financial burden, seriousness of disorder, and side effects, and concludes that he or she wants to be as confident as possible in treatment efficacy before advocating clinical use of the drug. To this end, the researcher strives to avoid a false claim of efficacy and will set the Type-I error rate quite low. The researcher can further address the concern with side effects by performing a separate power analysis in the test of significance for side effects. In this case, the researcher might tolerate a greater probability of a Type-I error, or saying that a side effect exists when it does not, in an effort to increase the power of detecting potentially detrimental side effects.

Effect Size

As implied earlier, the probabilities denoted by $1 - \beta$ (i.e., power) are conditional probabilities. That is, $1 - \beta$ is the probability of rejecting the null hypothesis given a particular relationship between the independent variable and the dependent variable. With sample size and α held constant, power increases and β decreases as the strength of the relationship between the independent variable (IV) and dependent variable (DV) increases. There are many ways to express the relationship between the IV and DV, which we detail more fully later in the chapter. However, a generic term to describe the magnitude of the relationship between an independent variable and dependent variable is "effect size." In other words, effect size is a measure of the size of the effect produced by the independent variable (e.g., a treatment). Presently, we use the symbol δ to refer to effect size in general without meaning to refer to any specific statistic.

The rapid growth of meta-analysis has played a large role in the upsurge of interest in δ, and researchers, clinicians, and policymakers increasingly recognize that a statistically significant finding is only important when accompanied by δ of practical value. Specifically, statistical significance demonstrates that the observed effect is unlikely to have occurred by chance, whereas δ addresses the magnitude of the effect.

Sample Size

In group designs, sample size is defined by the number of individual subjects included in a study. However, in single-case designs, the unit of measure is the number of separate observations. An important goal for the single-case researcher is to determine the number of observations necessary to make the study worthwhile, both statistically and clinically.

When defining sample size in single-case designs, factors not typically considered in group designs must be addressed. Simple numerical quantity will not suffice, because observations must be spread over a time period large enough to control for trends, cyclicity, and autocorrelation (Beasley, Allison, & Gorman, chap. 9, this volume). As is discussed later, the costs, both ethically and financially, of gathering data over a prolonged time period must be considered.

IMPLEMENTATION OF A POWER ANALYSIS

The four quantities—sample size, effect size, significance level, and power—defined in the first section are connected in a deterministic system. In other words, if one knows any three values, the fourth is fixed. Thus, the general approach to power analysis is to fix three of the values and solve for the fourth. Although some people fix α, n, and δ and solve for β, the more common approach is to set α and β, estimate δ, and solve for the necessary sample size. We take this latter approach for the remainder of the chapter.

Step I—Setting Alpha

Theoretically, a researcher could directly alter the power of the design with a simple manipulation of α (Bird & Hall, 1986). This option is rarely exercised as a strong tradition in scientific research exists not to allow α to exceed the .05 level. However, in certain cases, such as research that is exploratory in nature, a larger Type-I error rate may be acceptable (Cohen, 1992a). Another option that will increase power is the use of one-tailed rather than two-tailed significance tests. The use of a one-sided test can achieve higher power without altering the conventional .05 significance level. The problem, however, will arise in the case that the relationship between variables exists in the alternate direction, in which case the one-sided test will fail to detect any effect (Cohen, 1992b). In other words, there is no power to detect an effect in the unexpected direction. In general, we strongly advocate against the use of one-tailed significance testing (see Allison, Gorman, & Primavera, 1993; Cohen, 1965).

The choice of α level represents an area that will potentially alter power, and the decision as to which level will be utilized remains largely at the discretion of the researcher. The optimal level of significance should be determined with an analysis of the trade-offs inherent in each option (Muenz, 1989). A power curve can assist the researcher in analyzing the ramifications of each decision (e.g. power, sample size, δ). Additionally, the specific research question posed by each design must be considered on an individual basis. A Type-I error rate of .01 will reduce the probability of falsely claiming a treatment has a significant effect. However, it will also serve to reduce the probability that an effect will be detected.

Step 2—Setting Beta

The probability of committing a Type-II error (β) is equal to one minus power. Cohen (1992b) proposed an admittedly arbitrary value of .80 as the desired power for scientific research, thus tolerating a 20% chance of committing a Type-II error. This contrasts with the conventionally accepted .05 probability of making a Type-I error and reflects the higher priority given to avoid a Type-I versus a Type-II error. Many researchers are far more comfortable (perhaps four times) with failing to detect a true effect than with stating incorrectly that an effect exists.

Others (Bird & Hall, 1986) maintain that the greater import given to the avoidance of Type-I versus Type-II error, although arguably accepted as convention in the social sciences, may not be universally acknowledged. These authors concurred with Cohen's suggestion to use .80 as a starting point for desired power. However, they assert, that, if greater power can be achieved with little cost, it should be pursued.

Step 3—Determining an Effect Size

Estimating δ is undoubtedly the most challenging aspect of conducting any power analysis. The problem is that there is a Catch-22 involved. Specifically, one is conducting the proposed research because one believes that knowledge regarding the phenomena under study is incomplete. Were knowledge complete, there would be no need to conduct further research. Thus one must make inferences and guesses about the δ for the proposed research based on knowledge that is, by necessity, incomplete. In other words, when the investigator questions the statistical consultant as to how many subjects are needed, the cautious consultant replies that in order to do this, one needs the results from a study that is well designed, has ample power, and tests the same hypothesis. The investigator, however, replies that if such a study were available, there would be no need to do the proposed study. In practice, there are several different approaches to picking an δ based on incomplete knowledge.

Past Research

As previously stated, it is unlikely that the exact study under consideration already been done. However, previous research can frequently shed some light on the expected δ.

First, a similar study may have been done and the results from that study can be used to define the expected effect. This is a particularly useful strategy when one is preparing to replicate an earlier study. However, as stated earlier, no two studies are identical and it may be necessary to adjust a δ estimated from a prior study for expected differences in such factors as dependent variable reliability and others (see the next section). A final potential problem with this approach is that occasionally the statistical reporting is so poor that it is impossible to extract an estimate of δ (Green & Hall, 1984).

Second, a pilot study can be done to provide an initial estimate of the δ. This approach has the advantage of basing the δ estimate on a study that is usually extremely similar to the planned study. However, the disadvantage is that pilot studies are typically quite small. Therefore, the estimate of δ derived from them will be quite imprecise; that is, it may vary substantially from the population δ and therefore provide a poor basis for sample size calculations.

Finally, meta-analyses of prior research can be used to provide estimates of δ (Davis, Janicak, Wang, Gibbons, & Sharma, 1992). Assuming a relevant meta-analysis has been conducted, this approach has several advantages. First, one of the primary objectives of meta-analysis is to provide an estimate of δ. Therefore, δ estimates are usually prominently displayed in meta-analyses. Second, meta-analyses are often based on very large sample sizes (once the data are pooled) and, therefore, often provide very precise estimates of δ. Third, meta-analysts typically attempt to include *all* relevant studies in their analyses. Thus, a δ estimated from a meta-analysis is less likely to be biased than an estimate of δ obtained from an investigator's "hand-picked" study. Finally, some meta-analysts evaluate the extent to which δ appears to be a function of various study features (Faith, Allison, & Gorman, chap. 8, this volume; Hedges & Olkin, 1985). These estimated functions can then be used to help tailor the δ estimate for the planned study.

Specifying the Minimum Effect of Interest

A second major approach to estimating δ is simply to specify the minimum effect of interest. Consider the following hypothetical example. A child, Beth, exhibits a degree of hyperactive behavior that is distressing to her teacher and the other students in her class. Her teacher completes a standardized rating scale of hyperactivity for Beth on a daily basis. Beth's average is 80, with a standard deviation of 10. Assume that the population mean on this scale is 50, with a standard deviation of 10. It might be reasonable to argue that in order for any cumbersome or expensive treatment to be considered "clinically significant," it must bring Beth's behavior into the normal range. The "normal" range is often defined as within two standard deviations of the population mean. In this case, it means that Beth's daily average must be reduced to or below 70 in order for the treatment to be declared a success. Thus, the minimum δ of interest is a 10-point reduction in average daily hyperactivity score. As we see shortly, it is often useful to reexpress the δ in standard deviation units. This entails dividing the desired difference by the appropriate standard deviation (SD). The resulting statistic is generally referred to as *d* (Cohen, 1988). In single-case research the appropriate SD is the *within-person* SD. In this hypothetical case, the within-person SD happens to be the same as the between-person SD (i.e., 10). Thus, we divide 10 by 10, yielding a minimum desired effect size of $d = 1.00$.

Finally, some investigators find it difficult to express their minimum desired δ in raw units but are comfortable expressing it in terms of a percent of variance (e.g., "I'm only interested in a treatment that accounts for X% of the variance in the dependent variable"). This statement essentially casts the δ into r^2 or ω^2 terms which, as we will see in the following section, are well suited for subsequent sample size estimation.

Quantifying Effect Size

As we have indicated, δ expresses the general concept of magnitude of effect or, alternatively, magnitude of association. In terms of statistical expression, there are many ways to quantify δ. For the moment, let us assume that we wish to quantify δ from a study that compared two conditions, treatment and control. One measure might be the simple difference between the two means (or medians, or modes, or any other measure of central tendency). If the measurement scale of the dependent variable had some intrinsic meaning (e.g., weight in pounds), such a raw difference alone might suffice and, in fact, might be preferred in certain contexts. However, as measures of δ, they are less easily used in power analyses than "standardized" measures. By standardized δ measures, we mean those that incorporate a measure of variance. The two most widely used of these measures are *r* and *d*. The first, *r*, is the Pearson product-moment correlation coefficient. In the case of a dichotomous independent variable (e.g., treatment vs. control), *r* is a point-biserial correlation coefficient but has the same general interpretation. More generally, measures of effect from virtually any design or analysis can be converted to a correlation-type metric, which Friedman (1982) refers to as r_m. For example, eta from an anova is equivalent to r_m and omega, also from an anova, and is simply an adjusted or unbiased estimator of r_m. The second effect metric that is quite useful and common is *d*. One can define *d* as the mean difference between conditions divided by the pooled within condition standard deviation. The choice between *d* and r_m is relatively arbitrary, because one can be converted to the other. Table 10.1 provides formulae to convert many statistics and effect size metrics to *d* or r_m.

Step 4—Solving for n

Having determined Type-I error (α), Type II error (β), and estimated effect size (δ), one is now in a position to solve for sample size (*n*). Basically, there are four ways to solve for n: analytically, via published power tables, via specialized software, and via Monte Carlo simulation. We discuss the first three here. The fourth, simulation, is undoubtedly the most precise and flexible way to obtain power estimates and sample size requirements because no particular distributional assumptions are necessary. Users can model any distributions they like. Unfortunately,

TABLE 10.1
Conversion of Some Common Test Statistics to r_m and d Values

Statistic	*r_m-value*	*d-value*
t	$r_m = \frac{t}{\sqrt{t^2 + df}}$	$d = 2\frac{t}{\sqrt{df}}$
Z	$r_m = \frac{Z}{\sqrt{Z^2 + df}}$	$d = 2\frac{Z}{\sqrt{N}}$
$F(df_n = 1)$	$r_m = \sqrt{\frac{F}{F = df_d}}$	$d = 2\sqrt{\frac{F}{df_d}}$
$F(df_n > 1)$	$r_m = \sqrt{\frac{Fdf_n}{Fdf_n + df_d}}$	$d = 2\sqrt{\frac{df_n F}{df_d}}$
$\chi^2(df = 1)$	$r_m = \sqrt{\frac{\chi^2}{N}}$	$d = \sqrt{\frac{4\chi^2}{N - \chi^2}}$
$\chi^2(df > 2)$	$r_m = \sqrt{\frac{\chi^2}{N + \chi^2}}$	$d = 2\sqrt{\frac{\chi^2}{N}}$
r	$r_m = r$	$d = \sqrt{\frac{4r_m^2}{(1 - r_m^2)}}$
d	$r_m = \sqrt{\frac{d^2}{d^2 + 4}}$	$d = d$

Note. df_n = numerator df; df_d = denominator df. From: Friedman, H. (1982). *Educational and Psychological Measurement, 42,* 521–526.

explicating the use of this technique is beyond the scope of the chapter. Fortunately, the other three methods are quite adequate for most situations we encounter, even when certain assumptions (i.e., normality) do not hold (Sawilowsky & Hillman, 1991).

Analytic Formulae. Analytic formulae for power and sample size requirements are of two varieties: exact formulae and approximations. Exact formulae typically require integration of noncentral statistical distributions such as the noncentral t, F, and χ^2 distributions. This is a difficult problem and is often addressed through various approximations and numerical methods. We do not discuss these further in this chapter; however, the interested reader is referred to other sources (Odeh & Fox, 1975; Winer, Brown, & Michels, 1991).

Within the realm of approximations, there are two varieties. The first are very rough-and-ready approximations. These are often useful as first approximations when applied data analysts are called on to provide crude estimates at planning meetings while "standing on their feet." The second type consists of more precise approximations that we advocate for general use.

Lehr (1992) provided an easy-to-remember, rough-and-ready formula for estimating the sample size necessary to detect a difference between two treatment conditions with 80% power at a two-tailed α of .05: "Sixteen *s*-squared over *d*-squared." Specifically, $N = 16\ s^2/d^2$. Here, N is the number of observations necessary in each experimental condition (e.g., treatment or baseline), s is an estimate of the within-group standard deviation, and d is the difference between-group means. (Note that in Lehr's notation, d is simply a raw difference. No division by s has occurred.) Dallal (1992) independently derived a similar approximation where the constant 16 is replaced by 17 for an independent samples test and 10 for a dependent (paired) samples test. In the dependent samples test, s is the estimated standard deviation of the paired differences.

Here we present two other, more precise approximations that were offered by Hays (1988) and Darlington (1990).

Hays' (1988) Approximation

Hays (1988) provided the following approximation. With equal *N*s per condition, the total N needed is:

$$N = \frac{(Z_{(1-B)} - Z_{(\alpha/2)})^2(1 - \omega^2)}{\omega^2} \qquad (10.1)$$

where $Z_{(1-\beta)}$ is the standard normal deviate that cuts off the *upper* $(\beta 100)\%$ of the normal distribution, and $Z_{(\alpha/2)}$ is the standard normal deviate that cuts off the *lower* $(\alpha 100)/2\%$ of the normal distribution, using a two-tailed test. Note that ω^2 is an effect size indicator, the proportion of variance in the dependent variable explained by the independent variable, and is defined more explicitly later.

Equation 10.1 is for a two-condition design. For an m condition design, the right side of Equation 10.1 needs to be multiplied by $m/2$. However, because most investigators are interested in testing all pairwise comparisons, it is probably best to conduct one's power analysis such that there is sufficient power to test all pairwise comparisons.

Researchers considering costs may at times wish to assign different numbers of observations to conditions if the cost of the protocol for some conditions is greater than the cost in others (Allison et al., submitted). In the case of unequal *N*s, the effective *N* equals *m* times the harmonic mean of the N_i. N_i is the *N* for condition *i* where *i* is 1 to *m* and there are *m* conditions.[1] Allowing for *m* conditions and unequal *N*s, Equation 10.1 generalizes to:

$$N = \left[\frac{(Z_{(1-B)} - Z_{(\alpha/2)})^2(1 - \omega^2)}{2\omega^2 m} \right] \Sigma P_i^{-1} \tag{10.2}$$

condition.

Note that ω^2 is an effect size indicator, the proportion of variance in the dependent variable explained by the independent variable. In the two-condition case it is:

$$\omega^2 = \frac{(\mu_1 - \mu_2)^2}{4\sigma_e^2} \tag{10.3}$$

where μ_1 is the mean of condition 1, μ_2 is the mean of condition 2, and σ_e^2 is the within condition variance of the dependent variable. Many investigators find it difficult to specify μ_1, μ_2, and σ_e^2, but they often find it easy to specify the minimum proportion of explained variance they expect or are interested in (i.e., ω^2; Allison et al., 1993; Friedman, 1982; Harris & Quade, 1992).

In the case of *m* conditions, ω^2 can be expressed as:

$$\omega^2 = \frac{\frac{1}{m}\Sigma(\mu_i - \mu)^2}{\sigma_e^2 + \frac{1}{m}\Sigma(\mu_i - \mu)^2} \tag{10.4}$$

where μ_i is the mean for the *i*th condition and μ is the grand mean (Winer et al., 1991).

Darlington (1990)

Darlington's approximation is based on the correlation coefficient, so that it is necessary to express one's expected effect size as *r*. Let:

r = The expected effect size or the minimum effect size of interest expressed as a correlation coefficient.

Z_α = The standard normal deviate (i.e., *z*-score) that cuts off the *upper* $\alpha/2\%$ of the normal distribution. In the case of a two-

[1]*Effective N* is not the actual number of subjects in the trial but, rather, the number that would yield equivalent power if the allocation of subjects to each group were equal. This concept is explained in more detail elsewhere in the chapter.

tailed test at the .05 level, Z_α is 1.96. This can be obtained from a table of normal probabilities in the back of virtually every statistics text.

Z_β = The standard normal deviate (i.e., z-score) that cuts off the *upper* β% of the normal distribution. If 80% power is desired, Z_β is .84. Again, this can be obtained from a table of normal probabilities.

Given these delineations, Darlington's (1990, pp. 385–386) formulae can be rearranged to yield the following simple result:

$$N = \left[\frac{2(Z_\beta - Z_\alpha)}{\ln\left(\frac{1 + r}{1 - r}\right)} \right]^2 + 3 \qquad (10.5)$$

Given Equation 10.5, investigators can easily solve for their required sample size. Equation 10.5 is the basis of the program POWPAL (Gorman, Primavera, & Allison, 1995) and is generally quite accurate.

Tables. Numerous tables have been published to help one determine the sample sizes necessary to achieve a given level of power. In fact, some books on power are almost entirely compendiums of power tables and charts (e.g., Cohen, 1988; Odeh & Fox, 1975). Because it is impossible to reproduce all or even a large sample of the available tables here, we include only two tables. Table 10.2 is a "table of tables." In it we list some of the tables for estimating power and sample size that readers may wish to pursue. Although it is by no means exhaustive, we have attempted to be thorough. It is often useful to have several tables at one's disposal because each has different advantages and applications. Table 10.3 is an adaptation of our favorite table. This is adapted from Friedman (1982).

Table 10.3 can be used to estimate sample size, given power, effect size, and significance level. Alternatively, it could be used to evaluate post-hoc power, given sample size, significance levels, and effect size. The columns of the table represent r_m effect sizes ranging from .05 to .95. Values of alternative effect size measures are presented beneath the r_m values for those who wish to use proportions of variance (r^2), Cohen's (1992b) d or f^2 or f ($f^2 = r^2/(1 - r^2)$) as effect size measures. The table has rows for power levels ranging from .10 to .90 in increments of .10. The cells of the table are degrees of freedom. For correlation coefficients and two-condition experiments, $N = df + 2$. However, df may vary for other statistical analyses.

As an example of sample size estimation, suppose that a researcher

TABLE 10.2

Source	*Application*	*Comments*
Bartko, Pulver, & Carpenter (1988)	Provides two extremely simple-to-use nomograms for calculating sample size for t-tests.	Nomograms available for both dependent and independent t-tests.
Bird & Hall (1986)	Provide tables that are especially useful with multiple comparison procedures, such as the Bonferroni and Scheffé.	
Freedman (1982)	Presents tables of necessary sample size for use of the log-rank test in survival analysis.	Probably not applicable to most single-case research.
Friedman (1982)	Any analysis within the "general linear model."	The basis of Table 10.3 printed herein.
Gatsonis & Sampson (1989)	Multiple regression and correlation.	Exact sample size requirements meant to be an improvement over Cohen's (1988) approximations.
Hinkle & Oliver (1983)	Provides a table for the one-factor ANOVA design with 2 to 8 levels.	A fairly limited range and number of effect sizes are incorporated.
Kraemer & Thiemann (1987)	Presents a large "master table" covering various levels of α, β, and δ, where δ is a measure of effect size (the intraclass correlation coefficient).	No estimates are provided for sample sizes less than 10.
Lipsey (1990)	Provides power charts (curves) for one- and two-tailed tests for α = .01, .05, .10, .15, and .20.	May require some difficult "eyeball" interpolation.
Lui (1991)	Presents very useful tables for determining necessary sample sizes for studies involving a dichotomous outcome.	Incorporates repeated measures designs and cost considerations.
Schoenfeld & Richter (1982)	Provide easy-to-use nomograms when the dependent variable is time to an event (i.e., survival analysis).	May not be applicable to most single-case research.
Shuster (1990)	Used primarily for planning large clinical trials where outcome is time to an event (i.e., survival analyses).	Very extensive tables. Software is available to accompany the book and tables.

TABLE 10.3
Power, Degrees of Freedom, and Effect Sizes for Selected Two-Tailed Significance Levels

Effect Measure							*Effect Sizes*	***Alpha* = *.05***											
rm	0.05	0.10	0.15	0.20	0.25	0.30	0.35	0.40	0.45	0.50	0.55	0.60	0.65	0.70	0.75	0.80	0.85	0.90	0.95
r^2	0.00	0.01	0.02	0.04	0.06	0.09	0.12	0.16	0.20	0.25	0.30	0.36	0.42	0.49	0.56	0.64	0.72	0.81	0.90
d	0.10	0.20	0.30	0.41	0.52	0.63	0.75	0.87	1.01	1.15	1.32	1.50	1.71	1.96	2.27	2.67	3.23	4.13	6.08
f	0.05	0.10	0.15	0.20	0.26	0.31	0.37	0.44	0.50	0.58	0.66	0.75	0.86	0.98	1.13	1.33	1.61	2.06	3.04
f^2	0.00	0.01	0.02	0.04	0.07	0.10	0.14	0.19	0.25	0.33	0.43	0.56	0.73	0.96	1.29	1.78	2.60	4.26	9.26
Power																			
0.1	185	47	21	12	8	6	4	4	3	3	2	2	2	2	1	1	1	1	1
0.2	501	125	56	31	20	14	10	8	6	5	4	4	3	3	2	2	2	2	1
0.3	825	206	91	51	33	23	16	12	10	8	6	5	4	4	3	3	2	2	2
0.4	1165	291	129	72	46	31	23	17	13	11	9	7	6	5	4	3	3	2	2
0.5	1536	383	169	94	60	41	30	22	17	14	11	9	7	6	5	4	3	3	2
0.6	1957	488	215	120	76	52	38	28	22	17	14	11	9	8	6	5	4	3	2
0.7	2466	614	271	151	96	65	47	35	27	21	17	14	11	9	8	6	5	4	3
0.8	3136	781	345	192	121	83	60	45	34	27	22	17	14	11	9	8	6	5	3
0.9	4198	1045	461	257	162	111	80	60	46	36	28	23	18	15	12	10	8	6	4

Effect Measure									*Effect Sizes*	***Alpha* = *.01***									
rm	0.05	0.10	0.15	0.20	0.25	0.30	0.35	0.40	0.45	0.50	0.55	0.60	0.65	0.70	0.75	0.80	0.85	0.90	0.95
r^2	0.00	0.01	0.02	0.04	0.06	0.09	0.12	0.16	0.20	0.25	0.30	0.36	0.42	0.49	0.56	0.64	0.72	0.81	0.90
d	0.10	0.20	0.30	0.41	0.52	0.63	0.75	0.87	1.01	1.15	1.32	1.50	1.71	1.96	2.27	2.67	3.23	4.13	6.08
f	0.05	0.10	0.15	0.20	0.26	0.31	0.37	0.44	0.50	0.58	0.66	0.75	0.86	0.98	1.13	1.33	1.61	2.06	3.04
f^2	0.00	0.01	0.02	0.04	0.07	0.10	0.14	0.19	0.25	0.33	0.43	0.56	0.73	0.96	1.29	1.78	2.60	4.26	9.26
Power																			
0.1	670	167	74	42	27	18	14	10	8	7	5	4	4	3	3	2	2	2	1
0.2	1203	300	133	74	47	32	24	18	14	11	9	7	6	5	4	3	3	2	2
0.3	1683	419	185	103	66	45	33	24	19	15	12	10	8	7	5	4	4	3	2
0.4	2156	537	237	132	84	57	41	31	24	19	15	12	10	8	7	5	4	3	3
0.5	2651	660	292	162	103	70	51	38	29	23	18	15	12	10	8	6	5	4	3
0.6	3197	796	351	196	124	85	61	46	35	28	22	18	14	12	9	8	6	5	3
0.7	3839	956	422	235	148	101	73	55	42	33	26	21	17	14	11	9	7	5	4
0.8	4665	1161	512	285	180	123	88	66	51	40	32	25	20	17	13	11	8	6	4
0.9	5944	1479	653	363	229	156	112	84	64	50	40	32	26	21	17	13	10	8	5

Note. From Friedman (1982). Simplified determinations of statistical power, magnitude of effect, and research sample sizes. *Educational and Psychological Measurement*, 521–526. Reprinted by permission of Sage Publications, Inc.

wishes to estimate the sample size for a "large" effect at .80 power and the .05 two-tailed significance level. By defining "large" as an r_m of .50, we look at the block in the table for α =.05. We then look at the intersection of the row for power = .80 and the column for effect size of r_m = .50 and obtain the cell value of 27 degrees of freedom. Given that the sample size for a two-condition experiment is $N = df + 2$, at least 29 observations will be needed. It should be noted that the value 29 represents N_e, the "effective sample size" that was defined earlier.

As an example of a post-hoc power analysis, suppose that a researcher conducted a study in which the effect size was an r_m of .4, the significance level was .05, and the sample size was 60. We first look at the block in the table for α = .05. We then look down the column for an r_m of .40 and find the cell entry for degrees of freedom closest to the sample size used in the study. We then find the power value for the row in which the cell value closest to our sample size (60) was found. In the present case, the researcher would notice that the value of 60 degrees of freedom lies in the row for power = .90. Therefore, the researcher could conclude that the sample size provided a 90% chance of obtaining a statistically significant result at the .05 two-tailed level. Had the researcher wished to work at a lower power level, then a smaller sample size would have been adequate.

Software. As with most other computer applications, the availablity of software for power analysis has expanded rapidly in recent years. A thorough review of software available through 1989 was provided by Goldstein (1989). Since then, many other programs have become available (e.g., Allison & Gorman, 1993; Borenstein & Cohen, 1988; Borenstein, Cohen, Rothstein, Pollack, & Kane, 1990; Brecht, Woodward, & Bonett, 1990; Brown et al., 1990; Dallal, 1985; 1993; Dupont & Plummer, 1990; Gorman et al., 1995; Gorsuch, 1990; Ness, 1994; Neale, 1993; Rothstein, Borenstein, Cohen, & Pollack, 1990; Schwarzer, 1990; SERC, 1993; SPSS, 1990; Von Tress, 1994). Each program has its advantages and unique features, and no one program will do all of the things an investigator is likely to require at different points. Thus, we recommend that investigators build personal "libraries" of these programs. An overview of these programs is provided in Table 10.4.

ADVANCED TOPICS

Special Issues in Estimating δ

There are several nuances regarding the estimation of δ that are worth brief consideration. In general, these nuances boil down to the recognition that the planned study probably has some important, and perhaps

TABLE 10.4
Power Analysis Software

Test or Parameter	*PASS* *Enas (1988)*	*STATISTICAL POWER ANALYSIS* *Borenstein & Cohen (1988)*	*PC-SIZE* *Dallal (1986)*	*POWER* *Dupont & Plummer (1990)*	*EGRET SIZ* *SERC, Inc.* *(1993)*
Poisson					
Normal distribution	X				
Exponential					
Binomial					
1-sample median					
1-sample t-test	X			X	
2-sample t-test	X	X	X	X	
Paired t-test	X		X	X	
One-way ANOVA	X	X	X		
N-way ANOVA	X	X	X		
Generic F			X		
Randomized blocks ANOVA			X		
MANOVA					
Single correlation	X	X	X		
Two independent rs					
Two or more dependent rs					
Intraclass correlation					
Logistic regression					X
Poisson regression					
Multiple regression	X	X	X		
Chi-square	X	X	X	X	
Fisher's exact test				X	
Proportions		X			

(**Continued**)

TABLE 10.4 (*Continued*)

Test or Parameter	*PASS* *Enas (1988)*	*STATISTICAL POWER ANALYSIS* *Borenstein & Cohen (1988)*	*PC-SIZE* *Dallal (1986)*	*POWER* *Dupont & Plummer (1990)*	*EGRET SIZ* *SERC, Inc.* *(1993)*
Survival curves	X			X	X
Case control				X	
Hazard rates					
Somer's *D*					
Wilcoxon's *W*					
Sign test					
Kruskal-Wallis					
Median test					
Mann-Whitney *U*					
Kendall's tau					
Goodman-Kruskal gamma					
Structural equation models					

Test or Parameter	*MX* *Neale (1993)*	*POWCOR* *Allison & Gorman (1993)*	*GANOVA* *Brecht, Woodward, & Bonett (1989)*	*POWFIX* *Darlington (1990)*	*ICC* *Dallal (1993)*
Poisson					
Normal distribution					
Exponential					
Binomial					
1-sample median					
1-sample *t*-test			X		
2-sample *t*-test			X		
Paired *t*-test			X		

One-way ANOVA			X		
N-way ANOVA			X		
Generic F				X	
Randomized blocks ANOVA					
MANOVA			X		
Single correlation	X				
Two independent rs		X			
Two or more dependent rs		X			
Intraclass correlation					X
Logistic regression					
Poisson regression					
Multiple regression	X				
Chi-square			X		
Fisher's exact test					
Proportions					
Survival curves					
Case control					
Hazard rates					
Somer's D					
Wilcoxon's W					
Sign test					
Kruskal-Wallis					
Median test					
Mann-Whitney U					
Kendall's tau					
Goodman-Kruskal gamma					
Structural equation models	X				

(*Continued*)

TABLE 10.4 (*Continued*)

Test or Parameter	*ECHIP (1995)*	*EX-SAMPLE Brent, Mirielli, & Thompson (1993)*
Poisson	X	
Normal distribution	X	X
Exponential		
Binomial	X	
1-sample median		X
1-sample t-test	X	X
2-sample t-test	X	X
Paired t-test		X
One-way ANOVA		X
N-way ANOVA		X
Generic F		
Randomized blocks ANOVA		
MANOVA		
Single correlation	X	X
Two independent rs		X
Two or more dependent rs		
Intraclass correlation		X
Logistic regression		X
Poisson regression		
Multiple regression		X
Chi-square		X
Fisher's exact test	X	
Proportions	X	X
Survival curves	X	X
Case control	X	
Hazard rates	X	X

Somer's *D*					
Wilcoxon's *W*					
Sign test		X			
Kruskal-Wallis		X			
Median test					
Mann-Whitney *U*					
Kendall's tau		X			
Goodman-Kruskal gamma					
Structural equation models		X			

Test or Parameter	*STATPLAN* *Brown et al.* *(1990)*	*SIMSTAT* *BOOTSTRAP* *Peladeau (1994)*	*POWPAL* *Gorman, Primavera, & Allison (1995)*	*2N* *Hauer-Jenson* *(1993)*	*WDIST* *Von Tress* *(1994)*
Poisson	X				
Normal distribution	X	X	X	X	X
Exponential	X				
Binomial	X				
1-sample median		X			
1-sample *t*-test	X	X	X	X	X
2-sample *t*-test	X	X	X	X	X
Paired *t*-test		X	X		X
One-way ANOVA		X	X	X	X
N-way ANOVA			X		
Generic *F*			X	X	
Randomized blocks ANOVA			X		
MANOVA			X		
Single correlation	X		X	X	
Two independent *r*s					
Two or more dependent *r*s					
Intraclass correlation					

(**Continued**)

TABLE 10.4 (*Continued*)

Test or Parameter	*STATPLAN Brown et al. (1990)*	*SIMSTAT BOOTSTRAP Peladeau (1994)*	*POWPAL Gorman, Primavera, & Allison (1995)*	*2N Hauer-Jenson (1993)*	*WDIST Von Tress (1994)*
Logistic regression					
Poisson regression		X			
Multiple regression		X	X		
Chi-square			X		
Fisher's exact test	X				X
Proportions	X			X	X
Survival curves	X			X	
Case control	X				
Hazard rates	X	X			
Somer's *D*		X			
Wilcoxon's *W*		X			
Sign test		X			X
Kruskal-Wallis		X			
Median test		X			
Mann-Whitney *U*		X		X	
Kendall's tau		X			
Goodman-Kruskal gamma		X			
Structural equation models					

quantifiable, differences from the study on which an estimate of δ may be based.

One of the most common situations we encounter in this context is the expected differential reliability of measurements. Suppose that a study reports an observed effect size expressed as an r of .4 and that the reliability of the dependent measure was .60. It is well known that unreliability attenuates effect sizes. Specifically (assuming the independent variable is perfectly reliable):

$$r = r_t\sqrt{r_{yy}} \tag{10.6}$$

where r_{yy} is the reliability of the dependent variable and r_t is the "true" unattenuated effect size. Consequently, in our example, r_t is .52. If in our planned study r_{yy} is expected to be .90 instead of .60, then we can actually expect to observe an effect size of r = .49 (i.e., $.52(.90)^2$). Thus, we see that planning for and taking into account greater reliability in the dependent variable allows us to adjust our estimate of δ upward.

There are numerous other ways in which expected δs may differ between studies, including, but not limited to, restriction of range (Hunter & Schmidt, 1990), enhancement of range (Abrahams & Alf, 1978; Alf & Abrahams, 1975), and polychotomization of dependent variables (Peters & Van Voorhis, 1940). It is impossible to enumerate all the factors that may play such a role and provide a cookbook of responses to them. Rather, the astute investigator must simply be on the lookout for such factors and creatively manage them by drawing on statistical and psychometric theory.

Power, Cost, and Design Efficiency

Although most investigators would ideally like to have well-powered studies, "well powered" often translates to "more observations." This can be onerous from a financial and clinical point of view, because increasing the number of observations typically entails increasing the cost of the study and the length of time the subject is under study. In response to this quandary, several investigators have begun exploring design strategies that maximize power while minimizing costs or the required number of observations (e.g., Allison et al., submitted; Overall, 1991; Overall & Dallal, 1965; Thornquist et al., 1993; Urban et al., 1990).

Hansen and Collins (1994) described seven methods for increasing power without increasing the number of observations. Although not all are applicable to the single-case context, several are and we briefly describe those here (see Hansen & Collins, 1994, for more details).

Missing Data Analysis. Almost all studies fail to collect some of the data originally intended. For example, a researcher may plan to measure afternoon behavior every day following a noontime administration of a drug or placebo, and to use morning behavior as a covariate (see discussion, later in this chapter, of the advantages of using such a covariate). Now on some days, due to the usual vagaries of research in the real world, morning behavior will be measured but afternoon behavior will not and, on some others, afternoon behavior will be measured but morning behavior will not. Perhaps the most commonly used approach to managing missing data is listwise deletion, which entails dropping any observation that does not have complete data available for all the variables used in the analysis (Allison et al., 1993). Unfortunately, in the situation described, this would be tantamount to discarding information that will lower the overall power of the study. In contrast, several more modern and powerful methods for handling missing data have been developed that take full advantage of the available data (Little & Rubin, 1987; McArdle, 1994). Although an explanation of these techniques is beyond the scope of this chapter, use of these methods serves to increase power without increasing trial length.

Targeting Appropriate Mediators. Hansen and Collins (1994) pointed out that targeting known or hypothesized mediators of behavior change should increase treatment efficacy, which will increase δ and therefore power. This is equivalent to saying "Design a good treatment."

Maintain Treatment Integrity. Just as it is important to design a good treatment, it is also important to ensure that the treatment is implemented as designed. Gresham (chap. 4, this volume) discussed this in depth. It has been shown that treatment integrity does indeed moderate δ and therefore power (Allison & Engel, 1996).

Use Reliable and Valid Measures. Although there are special exceptions (Humphreys & Drasgow, 1989a, 1989b; Kopriva & Shaw, 1991; Overall, 1989a; Zimmerman & Williams, 1986), in general, more reliable measures produce greater effects. Thus, it is essential to use reliable measurement to maintain adequate power (Hansen & Collins, 1994).

Allison et al. (submitted) focused on the minimization of financial costs while maintaining adequate power. They discussed five methods in detail and provided references to several other methods. We consider three of those situations here: The optimal allocation of observations (time points) to different treatment conditions; the use of covariates and ANCOVA; and choosing between obtaining more observations or taking more replicate measurements on each observation. In addition, we show next how the use of early stopping rules can decrease the *expected* sample size while maintaining adequate power.

Unequal Treatment Allocation

Consider a simple example. A study is planned in which observations are randomly assigned to one of two conditions (*treatment* and *control*). At this point it is important to reiterate the concept of the *effective* N (N_e). N_e is equivalent to two times the harmonic mean of the N for the treatment condition (N_t) and the N for the control condition (N_c).

$$N_e = 2\left[\frac{1}{\left(\frac{1}{N_t} + \frac{1}{N_c}\right)/2}\right] \tag{10.7}$$

In a K condition design, N_e is K times the harmonic mean of the K treatment conditions. N_e refers not to the total number of observations, but instead to the number that would yield equivalent power *if* the allocation to conditions were equal. For example, if one has 60 observations in the treatment condition and 40 observations in the control condition, N_e is 96. In other words, one has as much power as if 96 observations were assigned at an equal allocation rate (i.e., 48 per condition). Equation 10.7 reveals that if N_e (and therefore power) is held constant, as the number of observations in the less expensive condition approaches $+\infty$, the lower limit of the sample size in the more expensive group is $N_e/4$. This implies that regardless of how many observations can be collected in one condition, the number of observations in the other condition must be at least half of what it would be under equal allocation to maintain power.

Equation 10.7 also allows for cost minimization when the costs of treatment and control observations are different. Let the cost of obtaining one treatment observation be C_t and the cost of obtaining one control observation be C_c. Total cost, C, is, therefore, $(C_tN_t + C_cN_c)$. Allison et al. (submitted) show that the total trial cost is minimized when:

$$N_t = \frac{N_e + N_e\sqrt{C_c/C_t}}{4} \tag{10.8}$$

After N_t is obtained from Equation 10.8, it can be substituted into Equation 10.7 and one can solve for N_c. Using these results, Allison et al. (submitted) showed: (a) For any desired level of power, the total study cost is minimized when the ratio $N_t/N_c = (C_c/C_t)^{.5}$; and, conversely, (b) for any fixed cost, power is maximized when the ratio $N_t/N_c = (C_c/C_t)^{.5}$.

Consider the following example. A clinician has determined that ingesting garlic reduces a particular patient's blood pressure (Estrada & Young, 1993). The clinician wishes to test a commercial garlic preparation that is claimed to be superior to raw garlic. Assume that doses of raw garlic cost \$0.10 per day. In contrast, the commercial preparation costs \$5.00 per day. Then, if simply administering the study (taking blood pressure measurements, etc.) costs \$2.00 per day regardless of condition, C_c = \$2.00 + \$0.10= \$2.10 and C_T = \$2.00 + \$5.00 = \$7.00. Assume further that a power analysis was done assuming equal numbers of observation assigned to the raw and commercial garlic preparations and indicated a need for 50 observations per condition. Thus, N_e = 100. Substituting these figures into Equation 10.8 gives,

$$N_t = \frac{100 + 100\sqrt{2.10/7.00}}{4} = 39 \qquad (10.9)$$

and, therefore, N_C must be 71. Thus, the total number of observations increases from 100 to 110. However, the total study cost decreases from \$455 [i.e., (50)(2.1) + (50)(7.00)] to \$422.10 [i.e., (71)(2.1) + (39)(7.00)], a savings of about 7% in total trial costs.

These equations apply only to situations in which the dependent variable is continuously and approximately normally distributed. Furthermore, these expressions assume homogeneity of variance, as does the use of most statistical tests. Statistical tests and ANOVA become especially sensitive to violations of the homogeneity assumption when *N*s are unequal (Winer et al., 1991). Thus, when using unequal *N*s, it is especially important to test for homogeneity of variance and apply corrective measures (e.g., variance-stabilizing transformations) when heterogeneity is found.

Use of a Covariate and ANCOVA

One of the best methods of increasing power in a randomized experiment without increasing sample size is the use of a covariate (Maxwell & Delaney, 1990). Using a covariate can markedly increase power in randomized studies because, to the degree that the covariate and the dependent variable (DV) are correlated, use of the covariate reduces the within-group variance and consequently increases δ and the power of the test. Moreover, random assignment ensures that the *expected* distribution of the covariate is the same in each condition. Therefore, the expected differences between condition means on the DV remain unchanged. Thus, using well-chosen covariates increases δ and power without increasing N. Finally, Allison (in press) derived expressions that allow one to decide when it is better to collect fewer observations but incur the cost of measuring the covariate versus collect more observations but avoid the cost of the covariate.

Consider the following examples. Gorman and Allison (chap. 6, this volume) presented several reanalyses of a case first described by Silverstein and Allison (1994). This was a single-case alternating treatments design comparing Ritalin (Methlyplenidate), antecedent exercise, and placebo with a hyperactive preschool boy, Max. One of the interesting aspects of this case is that Max's behavior worsened over time, independent of the treatment. This time trend added variance to the data but was largely uncorrelated with the treatment because the study was randomized. Thus, analyzing the data as an ANCOVA with time as a covariate rather than as an ANOVA should yield a more powerful test of treatment effects. Indeed, this is exactly what Gorman and Allison (chap. 6, this volume) showed.

As a second example, consider that a researcher will compare a treatment with a control condition and believes the effect size to be an ω^2 of .25. Alpha is set at .05 and β at .80. Substituting these numbers into Equation 10.1, yields a required N of 24 (i.e., 12 per condition). The dependent variable in this study will be the subject's behavior in the afternoon after having been given a drug or placebo at noontime. An obvious potential covariate is the subject's behavior in the morning. The rationale is that, independent of the drug, the subject has some "good days" and some "bad days." This adds extraneous variance or "noise" to the data. If "good versus bad days" affect both morning and afternoon behavior, then morning and afternoon behavior will be correlated. Call this correlation ρ. Allison (1995) showed that in a two-condition design with equal Ns and one covariate, Equation 10.1 becomes,

$$N = \frac{(Z_{(1-\beta)} - Z_{\alpha/2})^2\left(1 - \dfrac{\omega^2}{1-\rho^2}\right)}{(\omega^2)/(1 - R^2)} + 1 \qquad (10.10)$$

In our example, let $p = .55$. Then substituting these values in Equation 10.10, the necessary N is 14 (i.e., 7 per condition). Thus, in this hypothetical example, taking the extra time and trouble to measure morning behavior as a covariate cuts the study nearly in half while maintaining power. Related discussion of this issue can be found in Johannessen and Fosstvedt (1991).

Selecting the Optimal Number of Replicate Measures

As intimated earlier when discussing the need for reliable measurements, conceptually power depends not so much on the number of data points as on the amount of *information* in a study. "Information" can be conceptualized as "reliability" or the complement of error. No measurement is perfectly reliable. More reliable measurements contain more information and therefore produce more powerful statistical tests (Hansen & Collins, 1994; Kraemer, 1981). Although this is not strictly true in all cases, in most applications this will hold. More complete discussions regarding the relationship between power and reliability can be found in Humphreys and Drasgow (1989a, 1989b), Maxwell (1980), Overall (1989a, 1989b), and Zimmerman and Williams (1986).

Taking replicate measurements is one way to increase the amount of information in a study because the reliability of the average of k replicate measurements increases monotonically as k increases (this is the essence of the Spearman-Brown prophesy formula from classic psychometrics). A question one might ask is "What is the optimal number of replicate measurements per observation?"

In answer, two levels of costs must be considered. At the first level, there are the costs associated with obtaining one observation. Call this cost C_e. C_e might include the cost of providing the treatment to the subject for one day and any administrative costs associated with running the study for one day. Call the cost of obtaining one measurement on one day C_m. This might include the cost of having one rater fill out one rating scale.

Several authors have considered the minimization of costs in this situation. A very readable account was provided by Hujoel and DeRouen (1992), who showed that the optimal number of replicate measurements is equal to:

$$m = \sqrt{\frac{C_e(1 - \rho)}{C_m\rho}} \tag{10.11}$$

where ρ is the average pairwise correlation among replicate measurements. An estimate of ρ can often be derived from past research, pilot data, or general knowledge of the field.

Consider the following hypothetical example adapted from an actual study by Allison, Silverstein, and Galante (1992). Three monetary incentive systems designed to improve staff performance among five teacher's assistants at a small child care center are compared. The dependent variable is staff performance rated by an unobtrusive observer. The analysis is conducted separately for each subject to determine whether subjects respond differently to the different incentive conditions. The expected true effect size is an r_m of .30. The reliability of observational measurement is .70 expressed in a correlation metric. Finally, each observation is videotaped for later coding by one or more undergraduate research assistants. This coding takes approximately 10 minutes and therefore costs $1 (assuming undergraduate assistants are paid $6/hour). Moreover, the daily cost of implementing and administering the incentives is $10 (including the incentives). Thus, $C_e = 10$, $C_m = 1$, and $\rho = .70$. Substituting these values into Equation 10.11 shows that m, the optimal number of replicates, is approximately 2. In other words, for any fixed level of power, study costs are minimized when two separate students code each tape and their scores are averaged.

To see the effect of the decision to use two raters instead of one, we computed the necessary number of observations and corresponding study cost for both situations. With one rater, the expected observed effect size is not an r_m of .30 but, rather, using Equation 10.11, $.30(.70)^{.5}$, or .25. If the two-tailed .05 level is used and 80% power is desired, Table 10.3 indicates that 120 observations are required with $r_m = .25$. The corresponding cost is $N(10 + 1)$, or $1,375. In contrast, if two raters are used, the reliability of their *average* score is not .70 but rather .82. This can be obtained from the Spearman-Brown Prophecy formula (see any psychometrics text or, e.g. Rosenthal & Rosnow, 1991, p. 51). Then, the expected observed effect size is an r_m $.30^*(82.)^{.5}$, or .27, which, according to Powpal (Gorman et al., 1995) necessitates 105 observations. The corresponding cost of this study is $N[10 + (1)(2)]$, or $1,260, a savings of 8.5%.

Summary

The preceding is by no means an exhaustive presentation of all methods whereby one could maximize power while minimizing costs or maximize power without increasing N. Although the techniques presented should prove useful, the greater point is the demonstration that judicious designs can often yield adequate power while maintaining costs at a level that is markedly reduced compared to apparently reasonable alternatives. We encourage researchers to consider this when designing their investigations.

EARLY STOPPING RULES

Early stopping rules (also referred to as *interim analysis, group sequential methods*, etc.) were developed to allow investigators conducting clinical trials to test their hypotheses as the data accumulated so that trials could be ended as quickly as possible. There is an inherent relationship between early stopping rules and response-guided experimentation. The latter can be conceptualized as a more informal approach to monitoring clinical trials than the monitoring and early stopping procedures discussed presently. Researchers who have traditionally employed response-guided experimentation allow the accumulated data to assist in guiding experimental decisions as the study progresses. Because multiple testing can inflate the Type-I error rate (Armitage, McPherson, & Rowe, 1969), special "rules" have been developed to allow this multiple testing while maintaining the Type-I error rate at some reasonable level (see Demets, 1987; Gail, 1982, for reviews).

The primary motivation for the development of clinical monitoring and early stopping rules was ethical, not statistical; that is, investigators sought to minimize the number of patients that might be exposed to an inferior treatment. Early stopping rules, grounded in strong statistical theory, allow the researcher to safeguard individuals while maintaining the integrity of research conclusions.

Despite their origin, there is no reason why early stopping rules must be confined to clinical trials or cannot be used for economic reasons as well. With an appropriate early stopping rule, the Type-I error rate will be held at a reasonable level under the null hypothesis. When the null hypothesis is *not* true, some early stopping rules will increase power slightly, whereas others will decrease power slightly. More important, the early stopping rule can substantially reduce the number of necessary subjects (Berntsen, Rasmussen, & Bjornstad, 1991).

An early stopping rule that we sometimes favor is adapted from a procedure developed by Haybittle (1971). It entails analyzing the data at a very stringent level of α for all interim analyses. We suggest a maximum of four evenly spaced interim analyses. At the final point, the α level is set at the ordinary desired level (e.g., .05). Thus, data are analyzed after the collection of each fifth of the maximum amount of data to be collected. The trial is stopped when a significant result is obtained or when the maximum amount of data is collected—whichever comes first. This method has three distinct advantages. First, the interim analysis will only result in significance and termination of the study if the effect is exceptionally clear and convincing. Second, the final test is conducted at the desired α level; therefore, one is not left in the difficult predicament of having a final result that would ordinarily be significant but cannot be called significant because of the statistical correction employed. Third, because the interim analyses are conducted at a relatively stringent level, the overall α for the entire trial will not be markedly greater than the desired level of α.

We recommend that for the interim analyses, the α level (Type-I error probability) be set equivalent to a standard normal deviate (*z*-score) of

TABLE 10.5

Effect Size (d)	*Total N*	*Analytic Power*	*Early N*	*Actual Power*
.20	790	.799	682	.827
.30	350	.794	301	.829
.50	130	.793	112	.799
.80	50	.753	44	.825
1.00	40	.823	35	.863

3.00; in other words, at .0027. The study is stopped when the null hypothesis of no difference between conditions can be rejected or when the maximum duration is reached, whichever occurs first. Via Monte Carlo simulation, we computed the total Type-I error probability for this procedure. Using a nominal α of .05, the total α was only .0599. Table 10.5 shows some representative results from simulations we conducted under various alternative hypotheses. Effect size is expressed as the standardized mean difference (d); total N is the total number of observations required to achieve the level of power labeled "analytic power," calculated with standard power analysis software (Gorman, Primavera, & Allison, 1995); early N is the average number of observations that actually needed to be collected over 1,000 simulated experiments; and actual power is the proportion of times a significant result occurred over the 1,000 simulations.

What is apparent is that the power is slightly greater with the early stopping rule and, more important, there is an average saving of approximately 12% on trial costs. Berntsen et al. (1991) discussed the possibility of further reducing average trial costs by incorporating "futility tests" in which one can abandon a trial midway through when interim analyses suggest that there is virtually no chance of obtaining a significant result, even if the trial was extended to its maximum.

Of course, it should be noted that the exact results reported here apply only to the particular early stopping rule described. But the point is that judicious use of an appropriate stopping rule often will reduce the total number of required observations.

SUMMARY

In conclusion, it can be seen that there is no substitute for a well-designed, well-powered study. The prudent investigator will devote as much time to statistically planning his or her study as to analyzing the study. We hope that this chapter makes the task a bit more tractable.

REFERENCES

Abrahams, N. M., & Alf, E. F. (1978). Relative costs and statistical power in the extreme groups approach. *Psychometrika, 43,* 11–17.

Alf, E. F., & Abrahams, N. M. (1975). The use of extreme groups in assessing relationships. *Psychometrika, 40,* 563–572.

Allison, D. B. (1995). When is it worth measuring a covariate in a randomized clinical trial. *Journal of Consulting and Clinical Psychology, 63,* 339–343.

Allison, D. B., Allison, R. L., Faith, M., Paultre, F., & Pi-Sunyer, F. X. *Power & money.* Manuscript submitted for publication.

Allison, D. B., & Engel, C. (1996). Obesity prevention: Theoretical and methodological issues. In A. Angel, H. Anderson, C. Bouchard, D. Lau, L. Leiter, & R. Mendelson (Eds.), *Progress in obesity research* (pp. 607–612). London, England: John Libbey & Co., Ltd.

Allison, D. B., & Gorman, B. S. (1993). POWCOR: A power analysis and sample size program for testing differences between dependent and independent correlations. *Educational & Psychological Measurement, 53,* 133–137.

Allison, D. B., Gorman, B. S., & Primavera, L. H. (1993). Some of the most common questions asked of statistical consultants: Our favorite responses and recommended readings. *Genetic, Social, and General Psychology Monographs, 119,* 155–185.

Allison, D. B., Silverstein, J. M., & Galante, V. (1992). Relative effectiveness and cost-effectiveness of cooperative, competitive, and independent monetary incentive systems for improving staff performance. *Journal of Organizational Behavior Management, 13,* 85–112.

Armitage, P., McPherson, C. K., & Rowe, B. C. (1969). Repeated significance tests on accumulating data. *Journal of the Royal Statistical Society, Series A, 132,* 235–244.

Bartko, J. J., Pulver, A. E., & Carpenter, W. T. (1988). The power of analysis: Statistical perspectives. Part II. *Psychiatry Research, 23,* 301–309.

Berntsen, R. F., Rasmussen, K., & Bjornstad, J. F. (1991). Monitoring a randomized clinical trial for futility: The North-Norwegian lidocaine intervention trial. *Statistics in Medicine, 10,* 405–412.

Bird, K. D., & Hall, W. (1986). Statistical power in psychiatric research. *Australian and New Zealand Journal of Psychiatry, 20,* 189–200.

Borenstein, M., & Cohen, J. (1988). *Statistical power analysis: A computer program.* Hillsdale, NJ: Lawrence Erlbaum Associates.

Borenstein, M., Cohen, J., Rothstein, H. R., Pollack, S., & Kane, J. (1990). Statistical power analysis for one-way analysis of variance [Computer software]. *Behavior Research Methods, Instruments, & Computers, 22,* 271–281.

Brecht, M. L., Woodward, J. A., & Bonett, D. G. (1990). GANOVA 4. In J. A. Woodward, D. G. Bonnet, & M. L. Brecht. (Eds.), *Introduction to linear models and experimental design* (pp. 556–595). San Diego, CA: Harcourt Brace Jovanovich.

Brent, E. E., Mirielli, E. J., & Thompson, A. (1993). *Ex-Sample™: An expert system to assist in determining sample size* (Version 3.0). [Computer software]. Columbia, MO: The Idea Works, Inc.

Brown, B. W., Chan, A., Gutierrez, D., Herson, J., Lovato, J., & Polsley, J. (1990). *STPLAN 1993: Calculations for sample sizes and related problems* (Version 4.0) [Computer software]. The University of Texas M.D. Anderson Cancer Center Department of Biomathematics, Box 237, 1515 Holcombe Boulevard, Houston, TX 77030.

Cohen, J. (1962). The statistical power of abnormal-social psychological research: A review. *Journal of Abnormal and Social Psychology, 65,* 145–153.

Cohen, J. (1965). Some statistical issues in psychological research. In B. B. Wolman (Ed.), *Handbook of clinical psychology* (pp. 120–142). New York: McGraw-Hill.

Cohen J. (1988). *Statistical power analysis for the behavioral sciences* (2nd ed.). Hillsdale, NJ: Lawrence Erlbaum Associates.

Cohen, J. (1992a). Statistical power analysis. *Current Directions in Psychological Science, 1,* 98–101.

Cohen, J. (1992b). A power primer. *Psychological Bulletin, 112,* 155–159.

Dallal, G. E. (1985). *PC-SIZE: A program for sample size determinations (Version 2.13)* [Computer software]. Andover, MA: Author.

Dallal G. E. (1986). PC-SIZE: A program for sample-size determinations. *The American Statistician, 40,* 52.

Dallal, G. E. (1992). The 17/10 rule for sample size determinations. *American Statistician, 46,* 70.

Dallal, G. E. (1993). *ICC: A program for sample size determinations for the intra-class correlation coefficient* (Version 0.1). Andover, MA: Author.

Daniel, T. D. (1993, November). *A statistical power analysis of the quantitative techniques used in the* Journal of Research in Music Education, 1987 through 1991. Paper presented at the annual meeting of the Mid-South Educational Research Association, New Orleans, LA.

Dar, R., Serlin, R. C., & Omer, H. (1994). Misuse of statistical tests in three decades of psychotherapy research. *Journal of Consulting and Clinical Psychology, 62,* 75–82.

Darlington, R. B. (1990). *Regression and linear models.* New York: McGraw-Hill.

Davis, J. M., Janicak, P. G., Wang, Z., Gibbons, R. D., & Sharma, R. P. (1992). The efficacy of psychotropic drugs: Implications for power analysis. *Psychopharmacology Bulletin, 28,* 151–155.

Demets, D. L. (1987). Practical aspects of data monitoring: A brief review. *Statistics in Medicine, 6,* 753–760.

Donegani, M. (1991). An adaptive and powerful randomization test. *Biometrika, 78,* 930–933.

Dupont, W. D., & Plummer W. D., Jr. (1990). Power and sample size calculations: A review and computer program. *Controlled Clinical Trials, 11,* 116–28.

ECHIP, Inc. 724 Yorklyn Road, Hockessin, Delaware 19707.

EGRET SIZ: Sample size and power for nonlinear regression models (Reference manual). Seattle: Statistics and Epidemiological Research Corporation.

Enas, N. (1988). PASS: A quick and easy power and sample-size calculation program. *The American Statistician, 42*(3), 229.

Estrada, C. A., & Young, M. J. (1993). Patient preferences for novel therapy: An N-of-1 trial of garlic in the treatment of hypertension. *Journal of General Internal Medicine, 8,* 619–621.

Freedman, L. S. (1982). Tables of the number of patients required in clinical trials using the logrank test. *Statistics in Medicine, 1,* 121–129.

Friedman, H. (1982). Simplified determinations of statistical power, magnitude of effect and research sample sizes. *Educational and Psychological Measurement, 42,* 521–526.

Gail, M. H. (1982). Monitoring and stopping clinical trials. In V. Miké & K. E. Stanley (Eds.), *Statistics in medical research* (pp. 455–484). New York: Wiley.

Gatsonis, C., & Sampson, A. R. (1989). Multiple correlation: Exact power and sample size calculation. *Psychological Bulletin, 106,* 516–524.

Goldstein, R. (1989). Power analysis and sample size via MS/PC-DOS computer. *American Statistician, 41,* 253–260.

Gorman, B. S., Primavera, L. H., & Allison, D. B. (1995). PowPal: Software for generalized power analysis. *Educational and Psychological Measurement, 55,* 773–776.

Gorsuch, R. L. (1990). *Unimult guide.* Attadena, CA: Unimult.

Green, B. F., & Hall, J. A. (1984). Quantitative methods for literature reviews. *Annual Review of Psychology, 35*, 37–53.

Hansen, W. B., & Collins, L. M. (1994). Seven ways to increase power without increasing N. *NIDA Research Monographs, 141*, 184–195.

Harris, R. J., & Quade, D. (1992). The minimally important difference significant criterion of sample size. *Journal of Educational Statistics, 17*, 27–49.

Hauer-Jensen, M. (1993). Sample size calculation, power analysis and randomization: Research project design in Windows. *Computer Applications in the Biosciences, 9*(1), 45–47.

Haybittle, J. L. (1971). Repeated assessment of results in clinical trials of cancer treatment. *British Journal of Radiology, 44*, 793–797.

Hays, W. L. (1988). *Statistics* (4th ed.). Philadelphia: Holt, Rinehart, & Winston.

Hedges, L. V., & Olkin, I. (1985). *Statistical methods for meta-analysis.* Orlando, FL: Academic Press.

Hinkle, D. E., & Oliver, J. D. (1983). How large should the sample be? A question with no simple answer? Or . . . *Educational and Psychological Measurement, 43*, 1051–1060.

Hujoel, P. P., & DeRouen, T. A. (1992). Determination and selection of the optimal number of sites and patients for clinical studies. *Journal of Dental Research, 71*, 1516–1521.

Humphreys, L. G., & Drasgow, F. (1989a). Some comments on the relation between reliability and statistical power. *Applied Psychological Measurement, 13*, 419–425.

Humphreys, L. G., & Drasgow, F. (1989b). Paradoxes, contradictions, and illusions. *Applied Psychological Measurement, 13*, 429–431.

Hunter, J. E., & Schmidt, F. L. (1990). *Methods of meta-analysis.* Newbury Park, CA: Sage.

Johannessen, T., & Fosstvedt, D. (1991). Statistical power in single subject trials. *Family Practice, 8*, 384–387.

Kawano, T. (1993). School psychology journals: Relationships with related journal and external and internal quality indices. *Journal of School Psychology, 31*, 407–424.

Kopriva, R. J., & Shaw, D. G. (1991). Power estimates: The effect of dependent variable reliability on the power of one-factor ANOVAs. *Educational and Psychological Measurement, 51*, 585–595.

Kosciulek, J. F., & Szymanski, E. M. (1993). Statistical power analysis of rehabilitation counseling research. *Rehabilitation Counseling Bulletin, 36*, 212–219.

Kraemer, H. C. (1981). Coping strategies in psychiatric clinical research. *Journal of Consulting and Clinical Psychology, 49*, 303–319.

Kraemer, H. C., & Thiemann, S. (1987). *How many subjects? Statistical power analysis in research.* Newbury Park, CA: Sage.

Lehr, R. (1992). Sixteen *S*-squared over *D*-squared: A relation for crude sample estimates. *Statistics in Medicine, 11*, 1099–1102.

Lipsey, M. W. (1990). *Design sensitivity: Statistical power for experimental research.* Newbury Park, CA: Sage.

Little, R. J. A., & Rubin, D. B. (1987). *Statistical analysis with missing data.* New York: Wiley.

Lui, K. (1991). Sample sizes for repeated measurements in dichotomous data. *Statistics in Medicine, 10*, 463–472.

Maxwell, S. E. (1980). Dependent variable reliability and determination of sample size. *Applied Psychological Measurement, 4*, 253–260.

Maxwell, S. E., & Delaney, H. D. (1990). *Designing experiments and analyzing data.* Belmont, CA: Wadsworth.

McArdle, J. J. (1994). Structural factor analysis experiments with incomplete data. *Multivariate Behavioral Research, 29*, 409–454.

Muenz, L. R. (1989). Power calculations for statistical design. In J. Schneiderman, S. M. Weiss, & P. Kaufmann (Eds.), *Handbook of research methods in cardiovascular behavioral medicine* (pp. 615–633). New York: Plenum.

NCSS, Inc. (1994). *PASS: Power analysis and sample size.* Kaysville, UT: NCSS.

Neale, M. C. (1993). *MX: Statistical modelling*. Richmond, VA: Medical College of Virginia.
Odeh, R. E., & Fox, M. (1975). *Sample size choice: Charts for experiments with linear models*. New York: Dekker.
Overall, J. E. (1989a). Contradictions can never resolve a paradox. *Applied Psychological Measurement, 13*, 426–428.
Overall, J. E. (1989b). Distinguishing between measurements and dependent variables. *Applied Psychological Measurement, 13*, 432–33.
Overall, J. E. (1991). Statistical efficiencies that the FDA should encourage. *Psychopharmacology Bulletin, 27*, 211–216.
Overall, J. E., & Dallal, S. N. (1965). Design of experiments to maximize power relative to cost. *Psychological Bulletin, 64*, 339–350.
Peladeau, N. (1994). *SIMSTAT 2.1*. Montreal: Provalis Research.
Peters, C. C., & Van Voorhis, W. R. (1940). *Statistical procedures and their mathematical bases*. New York: McGraw-Hill.
Popper, K. R. (1959). *The logic of scientific discovery*. London: Hutchinson and Company.
Rosenthal, R., & Rosnow, R. I. (1991). *Essentials of behavioral research: Methods and data analysis* (2nd ed.). New York: McGraw-Hill.
Rossi, J. S. (1990). Statistical power of psychological research: What have we gained in 20 years? *Journal of Consulting and Clinical Psychology, 58*, 646–656.
Rothstein, H. R., Borenstein, M., Cohen, J., & Pollack, S. (1990). Statistical power analysis for multiple regression/correlation: [Computer software]. *Educational and Psychological Measurement, 50*, 819–831.
Sawilowsky, S. S., & Hillman, S. B. (1991, August). *Sample size tables, t-test, and a prevalent psychometric distribution*. Paper presented at the 99th annual meeting of the American Psychological Association, San Francisco.
Schoenfeld, D. A., & Richter, J. R. (1982). Nomograms for calculating the number of patients needed for a clinical trial with survival as an endpoint. *Biometrics, 38*, 163–170.
Schwarzer, R. (1990). *Metanalysis programs (Version 5.1)*. Berlin: Author.
Sedlmeier, P., & Girgenzer, G. (1989). Do studies of statistical power have an effect on the power of studies? *Psychological Bulletin, 105*, 309–316.
SERC, Inc. (1993). *EGRET SIZE: Sample size and power for nonlinear regression models* (Reference manual). Seattle, WA: Statistics and Epidemiology Research Corporation.
Shuster, J. J. (1990). *Practical handbook of sample size guidelines for clinical trials*. Boca Raton, FL: CRC.
Silverstein, J. M., & Allison, D. B. (1994). The comparative efficacy of antecedent exercise and Methylphenidate: A single-case randomized trial. *Child: Care, Health and Development, 20*, 47–60.
SPSS, Inc. (1990). *SPSS reference guide*. Chicago: Author.
Thornquist, M. D., Urban, N., Tseng, A., Edelstein, C., Lund, B., & Omenn, G. S. (1993). Research cost analyses to aid in decision making in the conduct of a large prevention trial, CARET. *Controlled Clinical Trials, 14*, 325–339.
Urban, N., Self, S., Kessler, L., Prentice, R., Henderson, M., Iverson, D., Thompson, D., Byar, D., Insull, W., & Gorbach, S. L. (1990). Analysis of the costs of a large prevention trial. *Controlled Clinical Trials, 11*, 129–146.
Von Tress, M. (1994). *Distribution functions*. A freeware program [computer software]. Arlington, TX: Author.
White, A. P., & Still, A. W. (1987). Analysis of variance versus randomization tests—a comparison. *British Journal of Mathematical and Statistical Psychology, 40*, 177–195.
Winer, B. J., Brown, D. R., & Michels, K. M. (1991). *Statistical principles in experimental design* (3rd ed.). New York: McGraw-Hill.
Zimmerman, D. W., & Williams, R. H. (1986). Note on the reliability of experimental measures and the power of significance tests. *Psychological Bulletin, 100*, 123–124.

Author Index

C

I

J

K

L

M

N

O

P

T

Subject Index

A

B

C

D

E

F

K

L

M

N

O

S

T